SHERMAN'S LAGOON

ATE THAT, WHAT'S NEXT?

BY JIM TOOMEY

Andrews McMeel Publishing

Kansas City

Sherman's Lagoon is distributed internationally by Creator's Syndicate.

Sherman's Lagoon: Ate That, What's Next? copyright © 1997 by J.P. Toomey. All rights reserved. Printed in the United States of America. No part of this book may be used or reproduced in any manner whatsoever without written permission except in the case of reprints in the context of reviews. For information write Andrews McMeel Publishing, an Andrews McMeel Universal company, 4520 Main Street, Kansas City, Missouri 64111.

www.andrewsmcmeel.com

ISBN: 0-8362-3660-2

Library of Congress Catalog Card Number: 97-71636

Sherman's Lagoon may be viewed on the world wide web at:
http://www.slagoon.com

98 99 00 01 BAH 10 9 8 7 6 5 4 3

To Mary and John

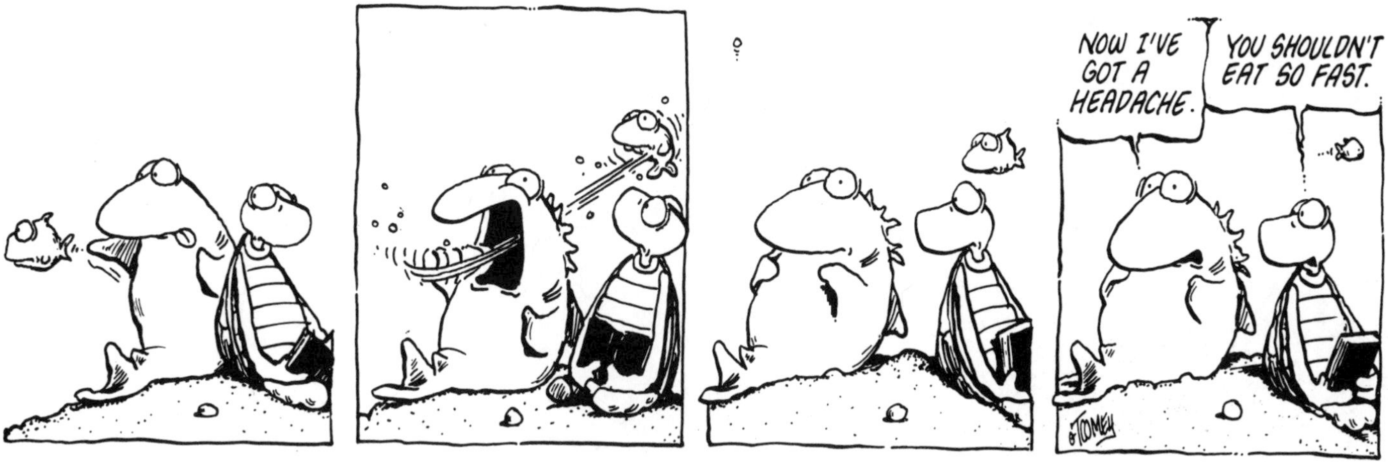
NOW I'VE GOT A HEADACHE.
YOU SHOULDN'T EAT SO FAST.

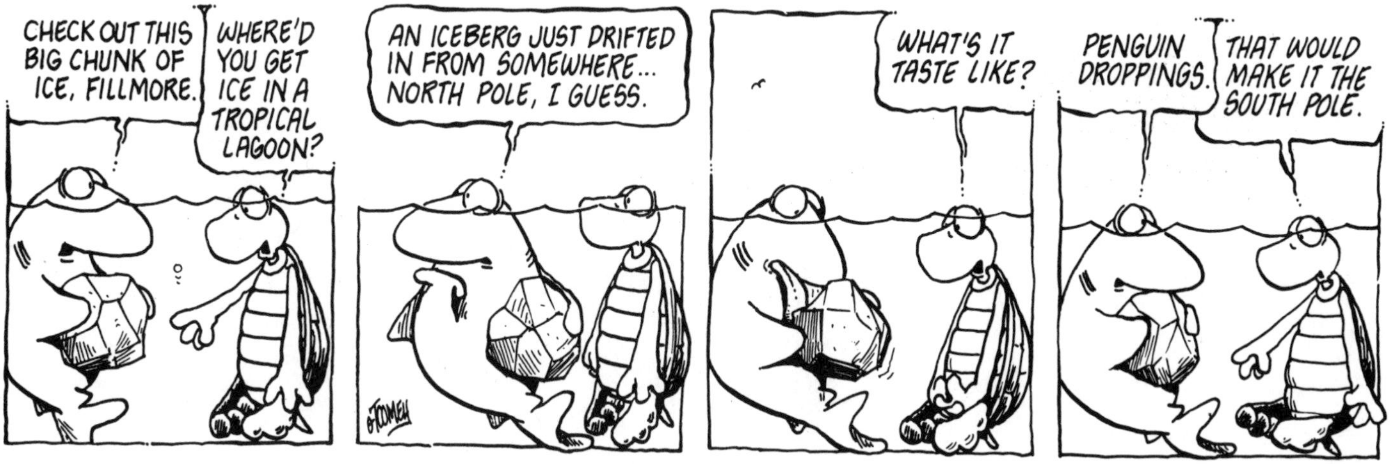
CHECK OUT THIS BIG CHUNK OF ICE, FILLMORE.
WHERE'D YOU GET ICE IN A TROPICAL LAGOON?
AN ICEBERG JUST DRIFTED IN FROM SOMEWHERE... NORTH POLE, I GUESS.
WHAT'S IT TASTE LIKE?
PENGUIN DROPPINGS.
THAT WOULD MAKE IT THE SOUTH POLE.

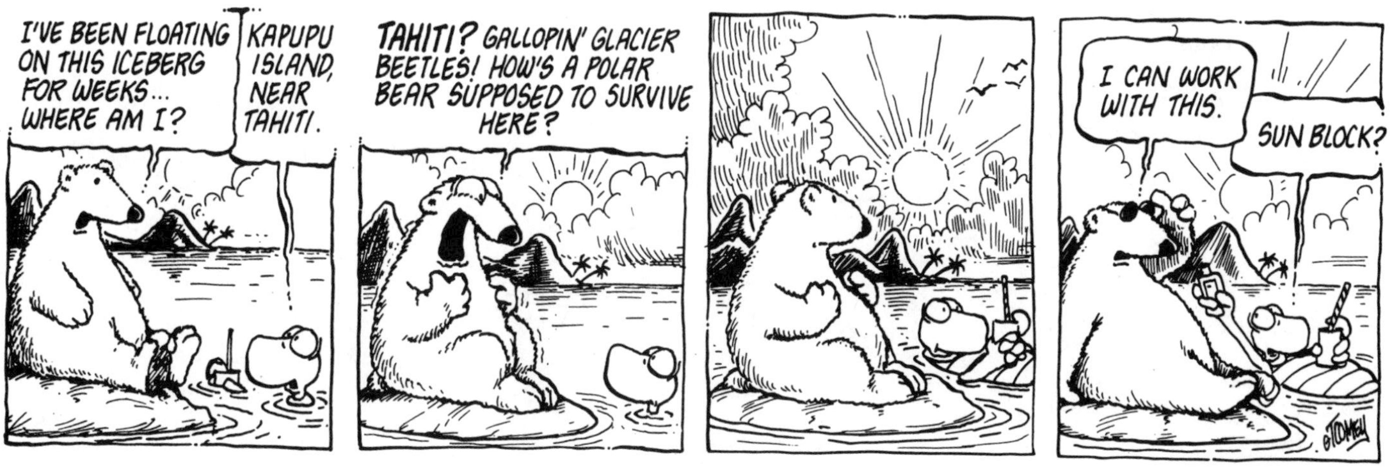
I'VE BEEN FLOATING ON THIS ICEBERG FOR WEEKS... WHERE AM I?
KAPUPU ISLAND, NEAR TAHITI.
TAHITI? GALLOPIN' GLACIER BEETLES! HOW'S A POLAR BEAR SUPPOSED TO SURVIVE HERE?
I CAN WORK WITH THIS.
SUN BLOCK?

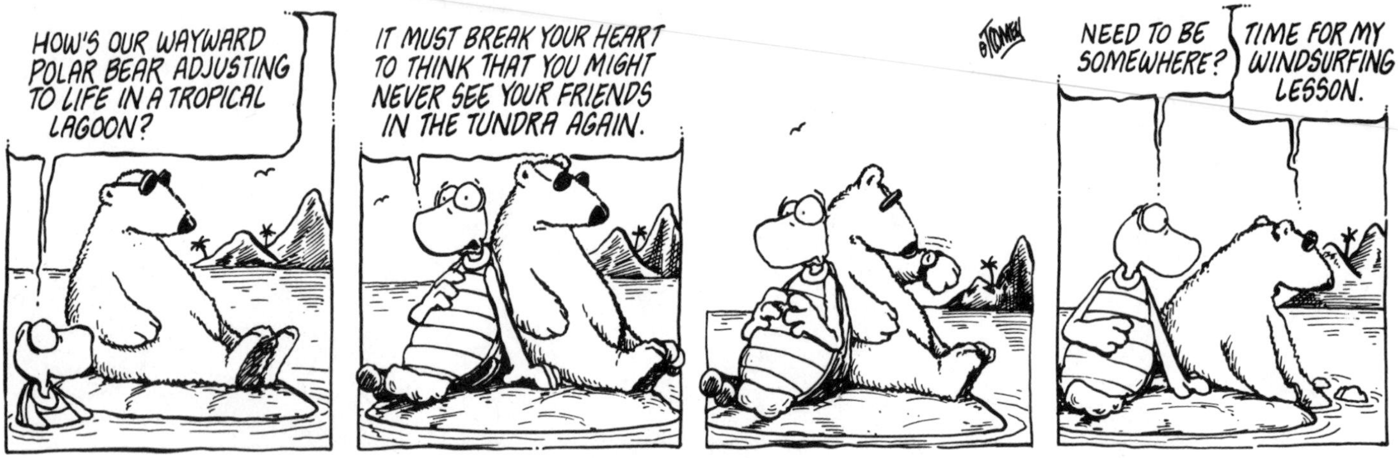
HOW'S OUR WAYWARD POLAR BEAR ADJUSTING TO LIFE IN A TROPICAL LAGOON?
IT MUST BREAK YOUR HEART TO THINK THAT YOU MIGHT NEVER SEE YOUR FRIENDS IN THE TUNDRA AGAIN.
NEED TO BE SOMEWHERE?
TIME FOR MY WINDSURFING LESSON.

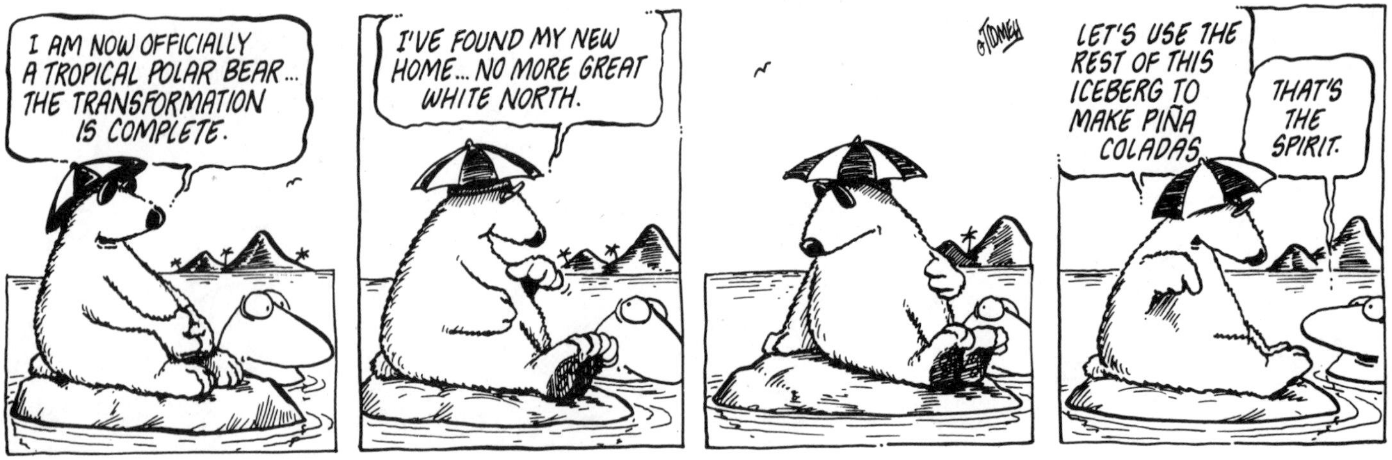
I AM NOW OFFICIALLY A TROPICAL POLAR BEAR... THE TRANSFORMATION IS COMPLETE.
I'VE FOUND MY NEW HOME... NO MORE GREAT WHITE NORTH.
LET'S USE THE REST OF THIS ICEBERG TO MAKE PIÑA COLADAS
THAT'S THE SPIRIT.

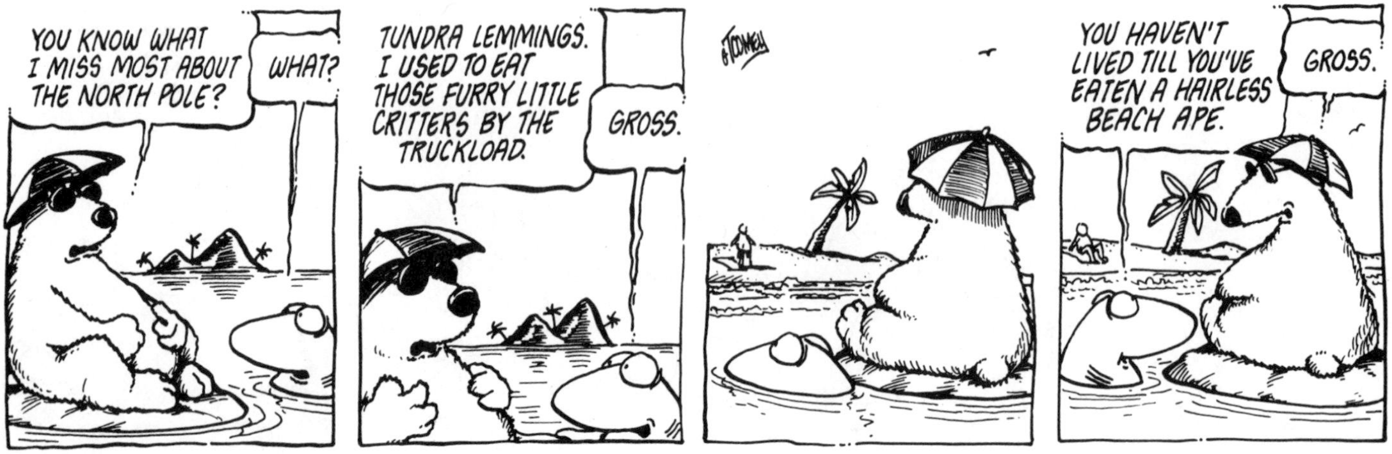
YOU KNOW WHAT I MISS MOST ABOUT THE NORTH POLE?
WHAT?
TUNDRA LEMMINGS. I USED TO EAT THOSE FURRY LITTLE CRITTERS BY THE TRUCKLOAD.
GROSS.
YOU HAVEN'T LIVED TILL YOU'VE EATEN A HAIRLESS BEACH APE.
GROSS.

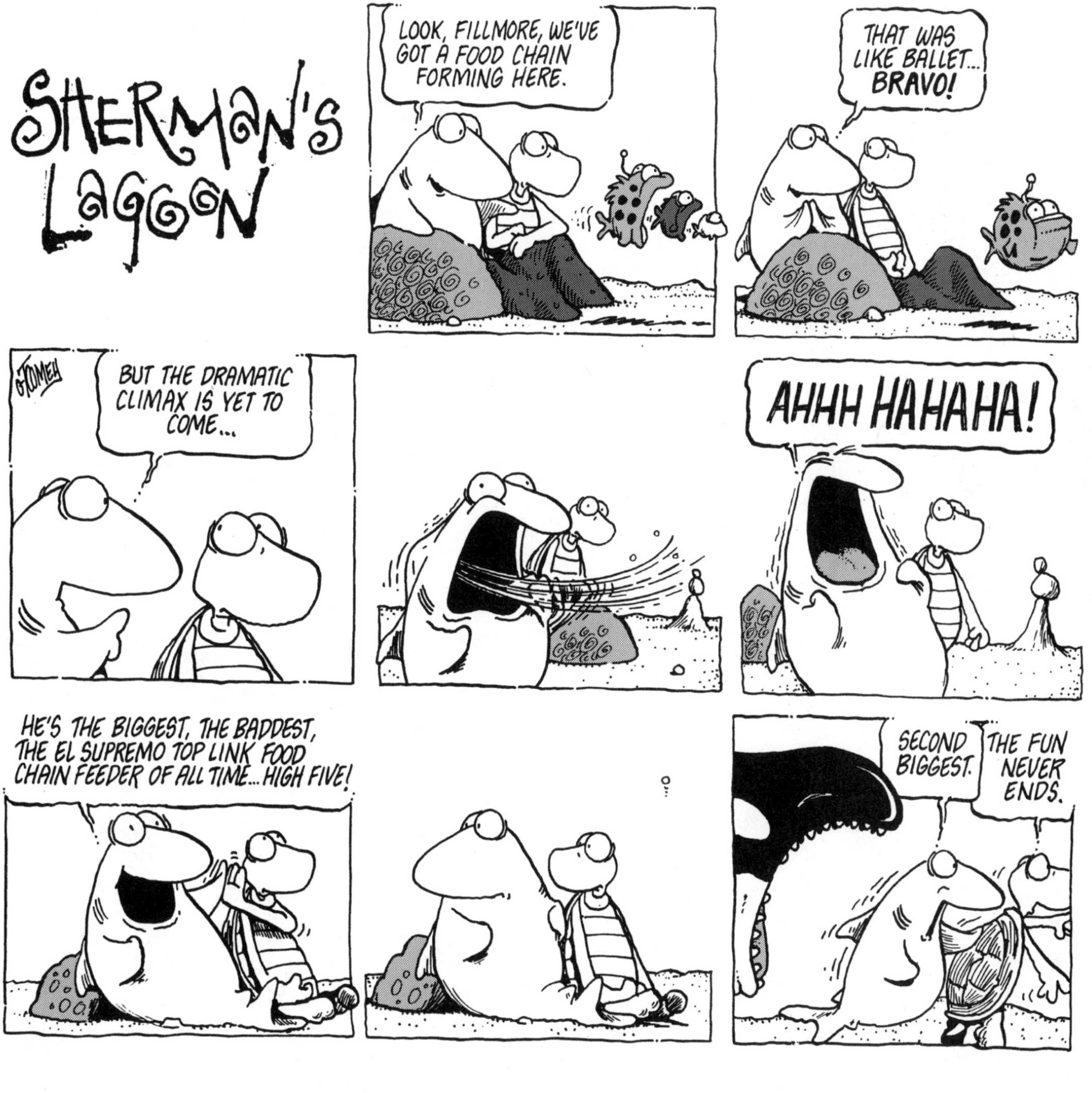
SHERMAN'S LAGOON
LOOK, FILLMORE, WE'VE GOT A FOOD CHAIN FORMING HERE.
THAT WAS LIKE BALLET... BRAVO!
BUT THE DRAMATIC CLIMAX IS YET TO COME...
AHHH HAHAHA!
HE'S THE BIGGEST, THE BADDEST, THE EL SUPREMO TOP LINK FOOD CHAIN FEEDER OF ALL TIME... HIGH FIVE!
SECOND BIGGEST.
THE FUN NEVER ENDS.

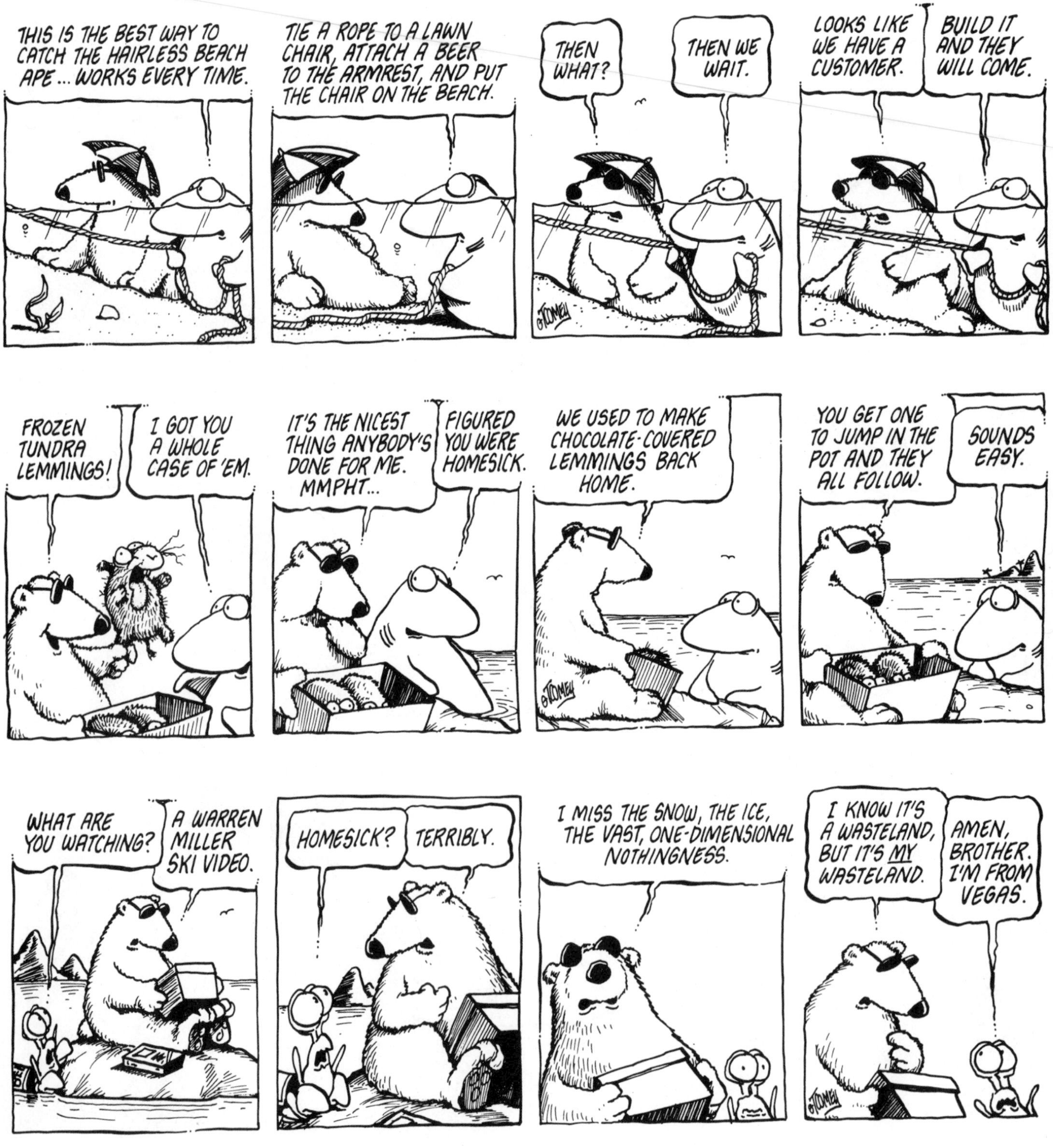
THIS IS THE BEST WAY TO CATCH THE HAIRLESS BEACH APE ... WORKS EVERY TIME.
TIE A ROPE TO A LAWN CHAIR, ATTACH A BEER TO THE ARMREST, AND PUT THE CHAIR ON THE BEACH.
THEN WHAT?
THEN WE WAIT.
LOOKS LIKE WE HAVE A CUSTOMER.
BUILD IT AND THEY WILL COME.
FROZEN TUNDRA LEMMINGS!
I GOT YOU A WHOLE CASE OF 'EM.
IT'S THE NICEST THING ANYBODY'S DONE FOR ME. MMPHT...
FIGURED YOU WERE HOMESICK.
WE USED TO MAKE CHOCOLATE-COVERED LEMMINGS BACK HOME.
YOU GET ONE TO JUMP IN THE POT AND THEY ALL FOLLOW.
SOUNDS EASY.
WHAT ARE YOU WATCHING?
A WARREN MILLER SKI VIDEO.
HOMESICK?
TERRIBLY.
I MISS THE SNOW, THE ICE, THE VAST, ONE-DIMENSIONAL NOTHINGNESS.
I KNOW IT'S A WASTELAND, BUT IT'S MY WASTELAND.
AMEN, BROTHER. I'M FROM VEGAS.

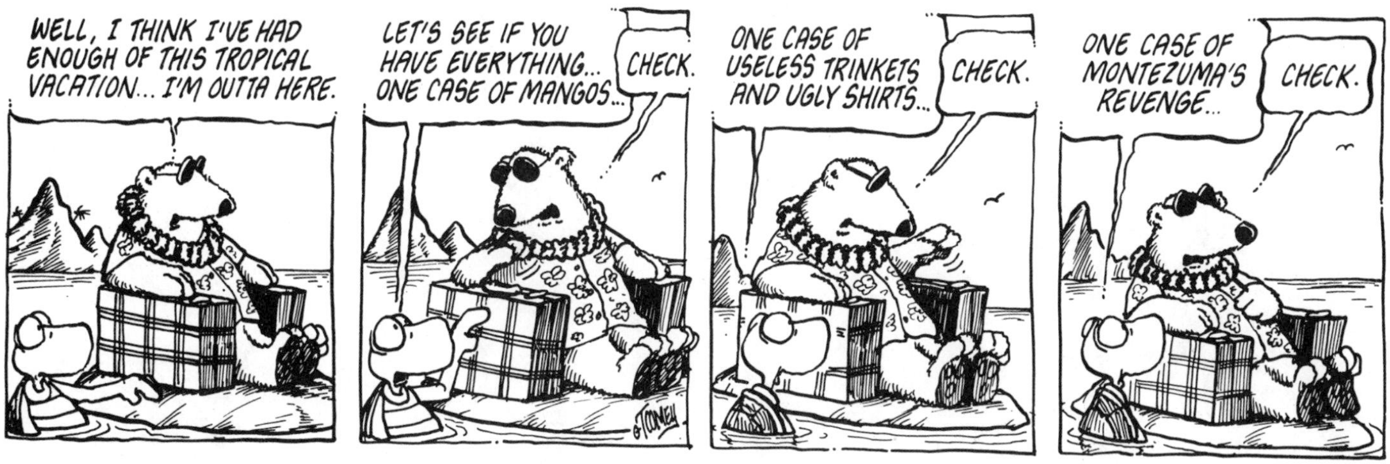
WELL, I THINK I'VE HAD ENOUGH OF THIS TROPICAL VACATION... I'M OUTTA HERE.
LET'S SEE IF YOU HAVE EVERYTHING... ONE CASE OF MANGOS...
CHECK.
ONE CASE OF USELESS TRINKETS AND UGLY SHIRTS...
CHECK.
ONE CASE OF MONTEZUMA'S REVENGE...
CHECK.

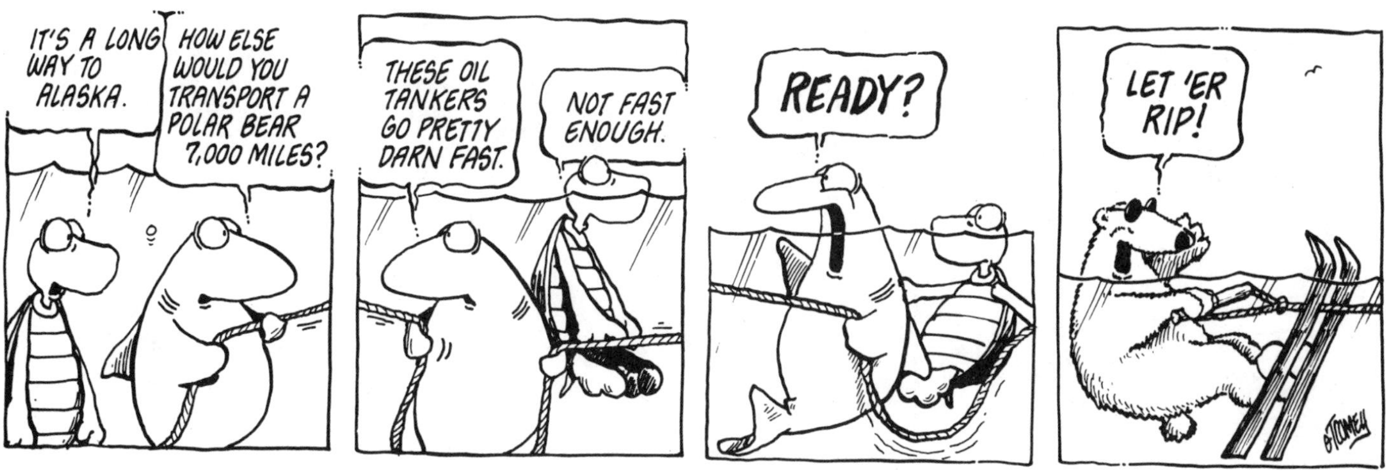
IT'S A LONG WAY TO ALASKA.
HOW ELSE WOULD YOU TRANSPORT A POLAR BEAR 7,000 MILES?
THESE OIL TANKERS GO PRETTY DARN FAST.
NOT FAST ENOUGH.
READY?
LET 'ER RIP!

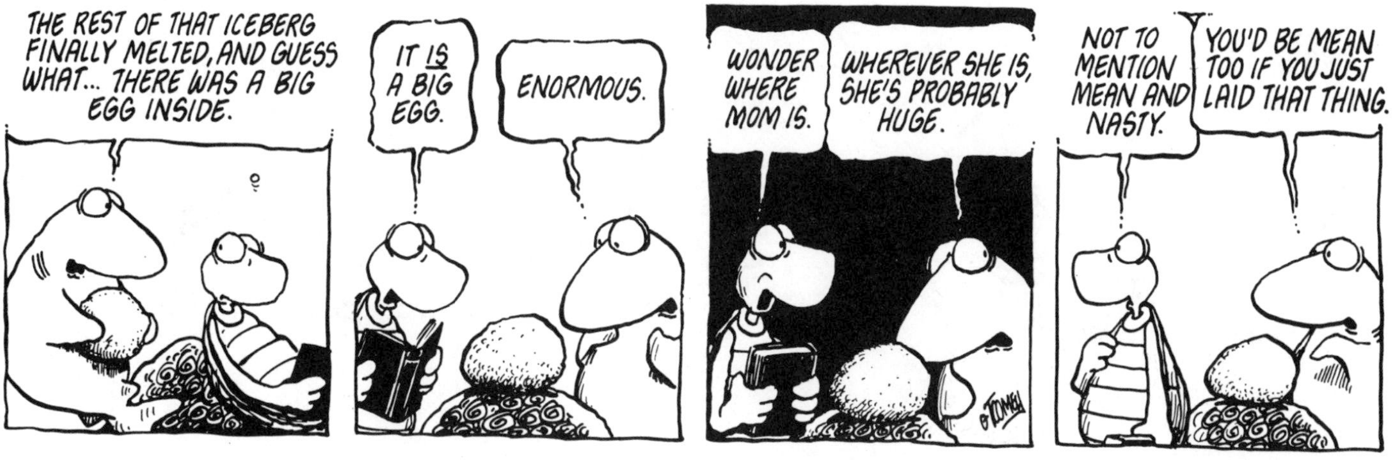
THE REST OF THAT ICEBERG FINALLY MELTED, AND GUESS WHAT... THERE WAS A BIG EGG INSIDE.
IT IS A BIG EGG.
ENORMOUS.
WONDER WHERE MOM IS.
WHEREVER SHE IS, SHE'S PROBABLY HUGE.
NOT TO MENTION MEAN AND NASTY.
YOU'D BE MEAN TOO IF YOU JUST LAID THAT THING.

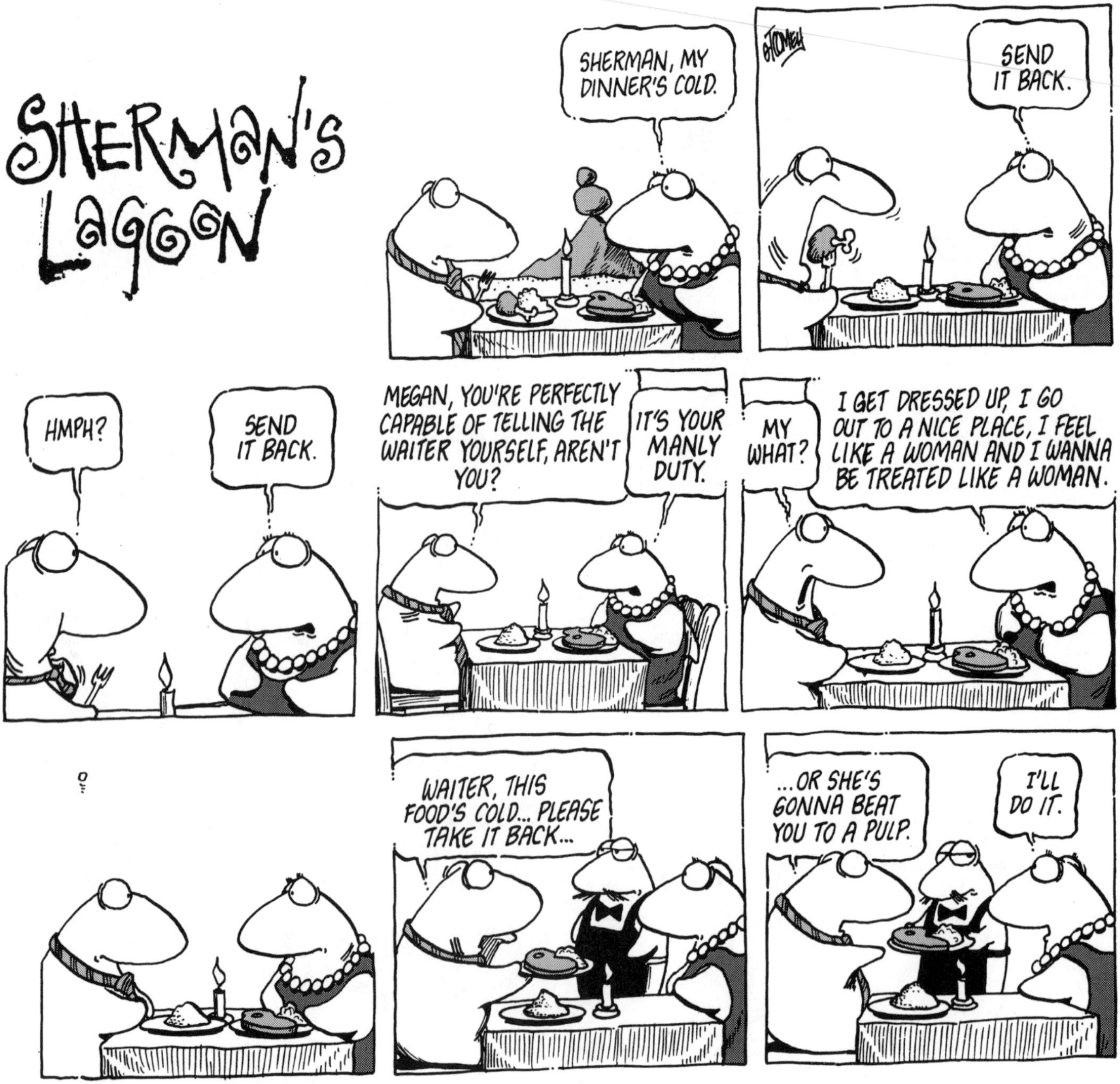
SHERMAN'S LAGOON
SHERMAN, MY DINNER'S COLD.
SEND IT BACK.
HMPH?
SEND IT BACK.
MEGAN, YOU'RE PERFECTLY CAPABLE OF TELLING THE WAITER YOURSELF, AREN'T YOU?
IT'S YOUR MANLY DUTY.
MY WHAT?
I GET DRESSED UP, I GO OUT TO A NICE PLACE, I FEEL LIKE A WOMAN AND I WANNA BE TREATED LIKE A WOMAN.
WAITER, THIS FOOD'S COLD... PLEASE TAKE IT BACK...
...OR SHE'S GONNA BEAT YOU TO A PULP.
I'LL DO IT.

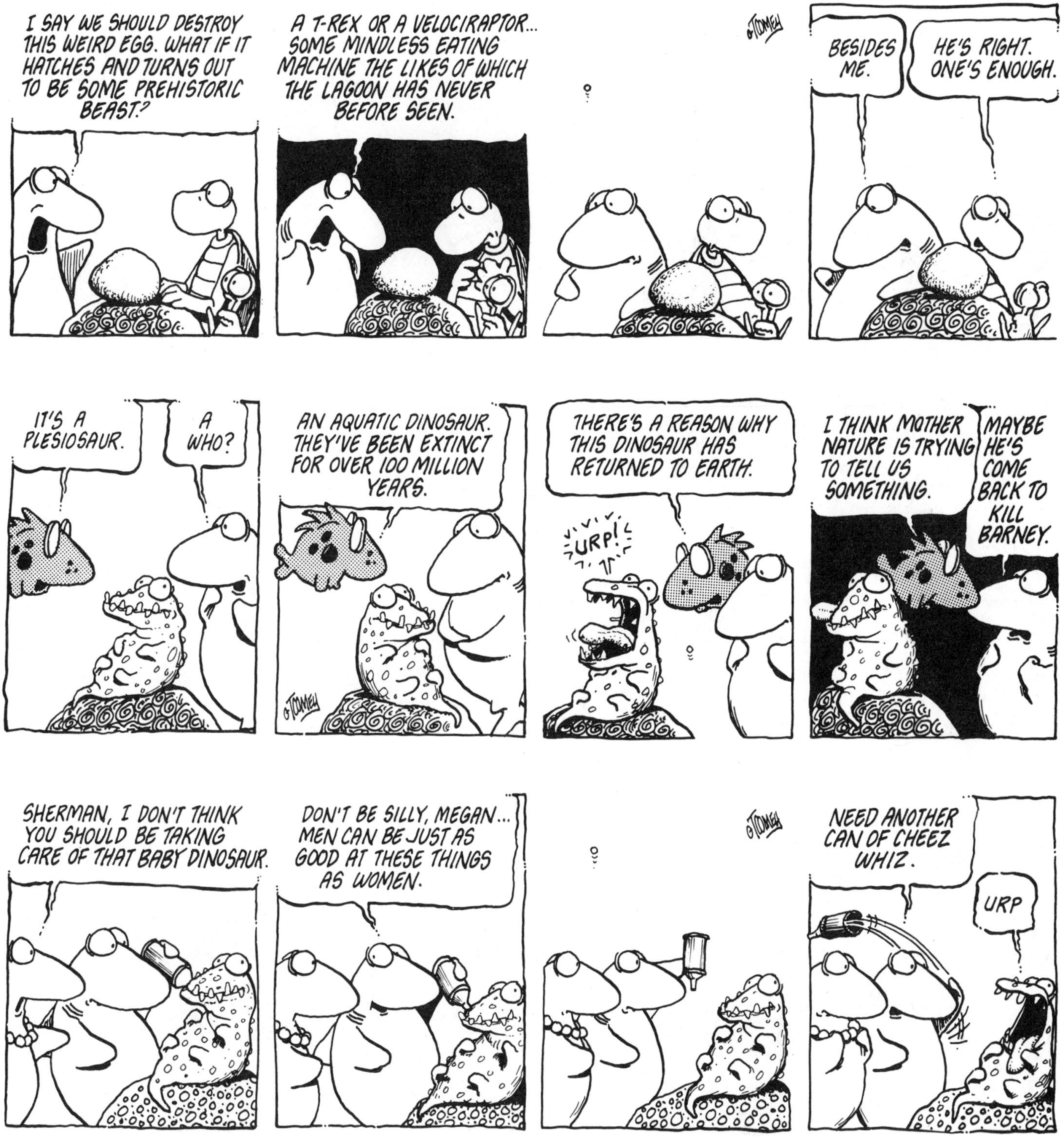

I SAY WE SHOULD DESTROY THIS WEIRD EGG. WHAT IF IT HATCHES AND TURNS OUT TO BE SOME PREHISTORIC BEAST?
A T-REX OR A VELOCIRAPTOR... SOME MINDLESS EATING MACHINE THE LIKES OF WHICH THE LAGOON HAS NEVER BEFORE SEEN.
BESIDES ME.
HE'S RIGHT. ONE'S ENOUGH.
IT'S A PLESIOSAUR.
A WHO?
AN AQUATIC DINOSAUR. THEY'VE BEEN EXTINCT FOR OVER 100 MILLION YEARS.
URP!
THERE'S A REASON WHY THIS DINOSAUR HAS RETURNED TO EARTH.
I THINK MOTHER NATURE IS TRYING TO TELL US SOMETHING.
MAYBE HE'S COME BACK TO KILL BARNEY.
SHERMAN, I DON'T THINK YOU SHOULD BE TAKING CARE OF THAT BABY DINOSAUR.
DON'T BE SILLY, MEGAN... MEN CAN BE JUST AS GOOD AT THESE THINGS AS WOMEN.
NEED ANOTHER CAN OF CHEEZ WHIZ.
URP

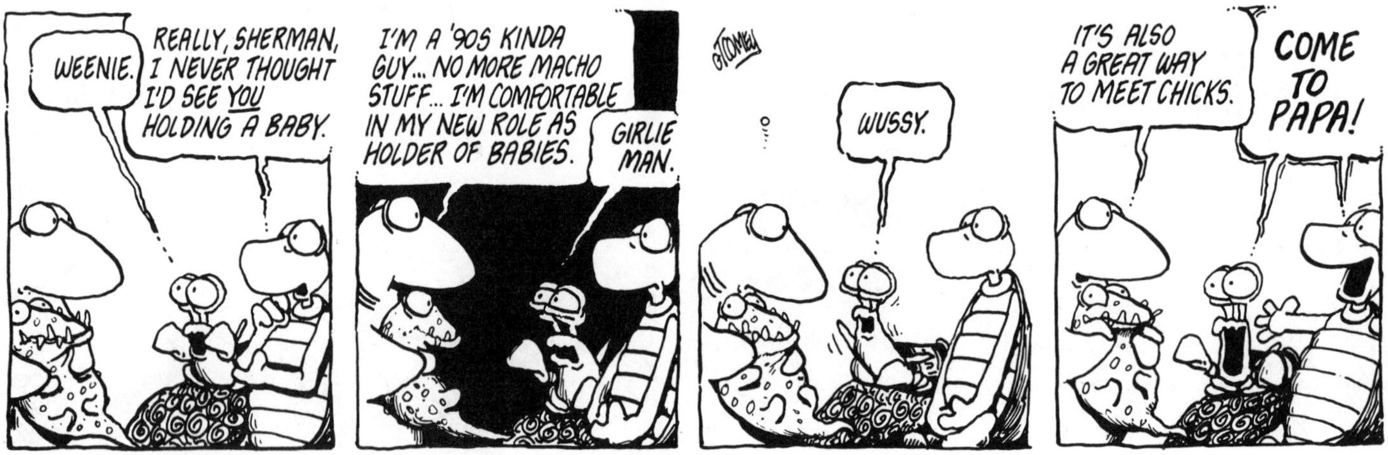

WEENIE.
REALLY, SHERMAN, I NEVER THOUGHT I'D SEE YOU HOLDING A BABY.
I'M A '90S KINDA GUY... NO MORE MACHO STUFF... I'M COMFORTABLE IN MY NEW ROLE AS HOLDER OF BABIES.
GIRLIE MAN.
WUSSY.
IT'S ALSO A GREAT WAY TO MEET CHICKS.
COME TO PAPA!

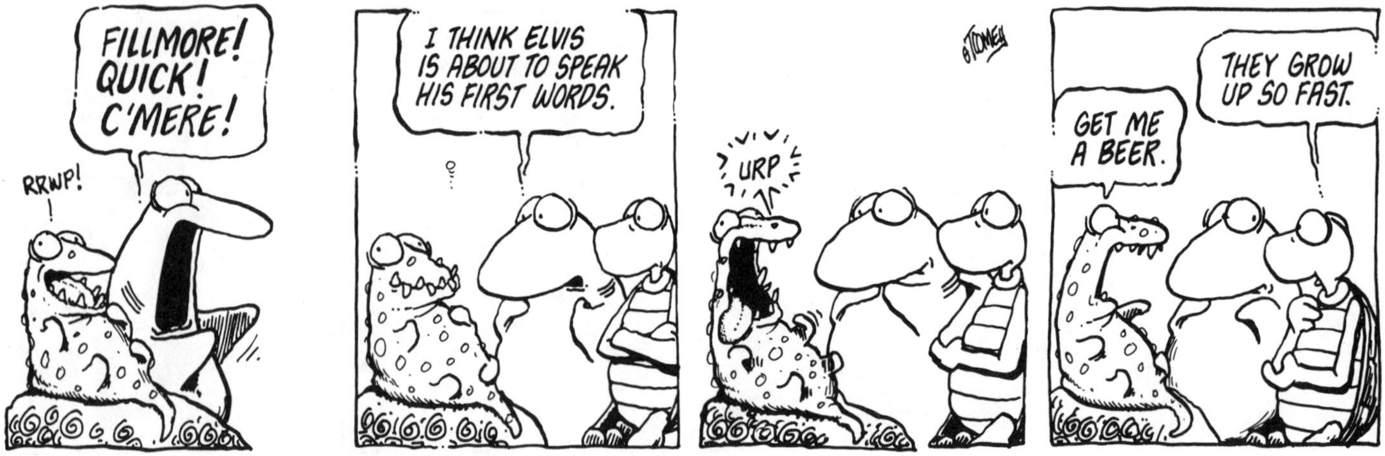

FILLMORE! QUICK! C'MERE!
RRWP!
I THINK ELVIS IS ABOUT TO SPEAK HIS FIRST WORDS.
URP
GET ME A BEER.
THEY GROW UP SO FAST.

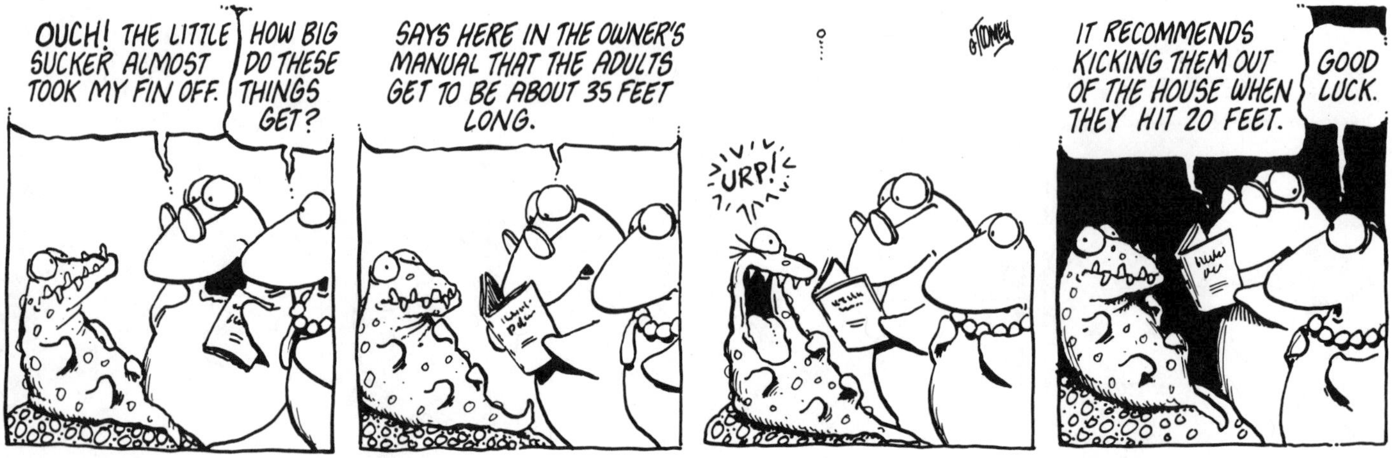

OUCH! THE LITTLE SUCKER ALMOST TOOK MY FIN OFF.
HOW BIG DO THESE THINGS GET?
SAYS HERE IN THE OWNER'S MANUAL THAT THE ADULTS GET TO BE ABOUT 35 FEET LONG.
URP!
IT RECOMMENDS KICKING THEM OUT OF THE HOUSE WHEN THEY HIT 20 FEET.
GOOD LUCK.

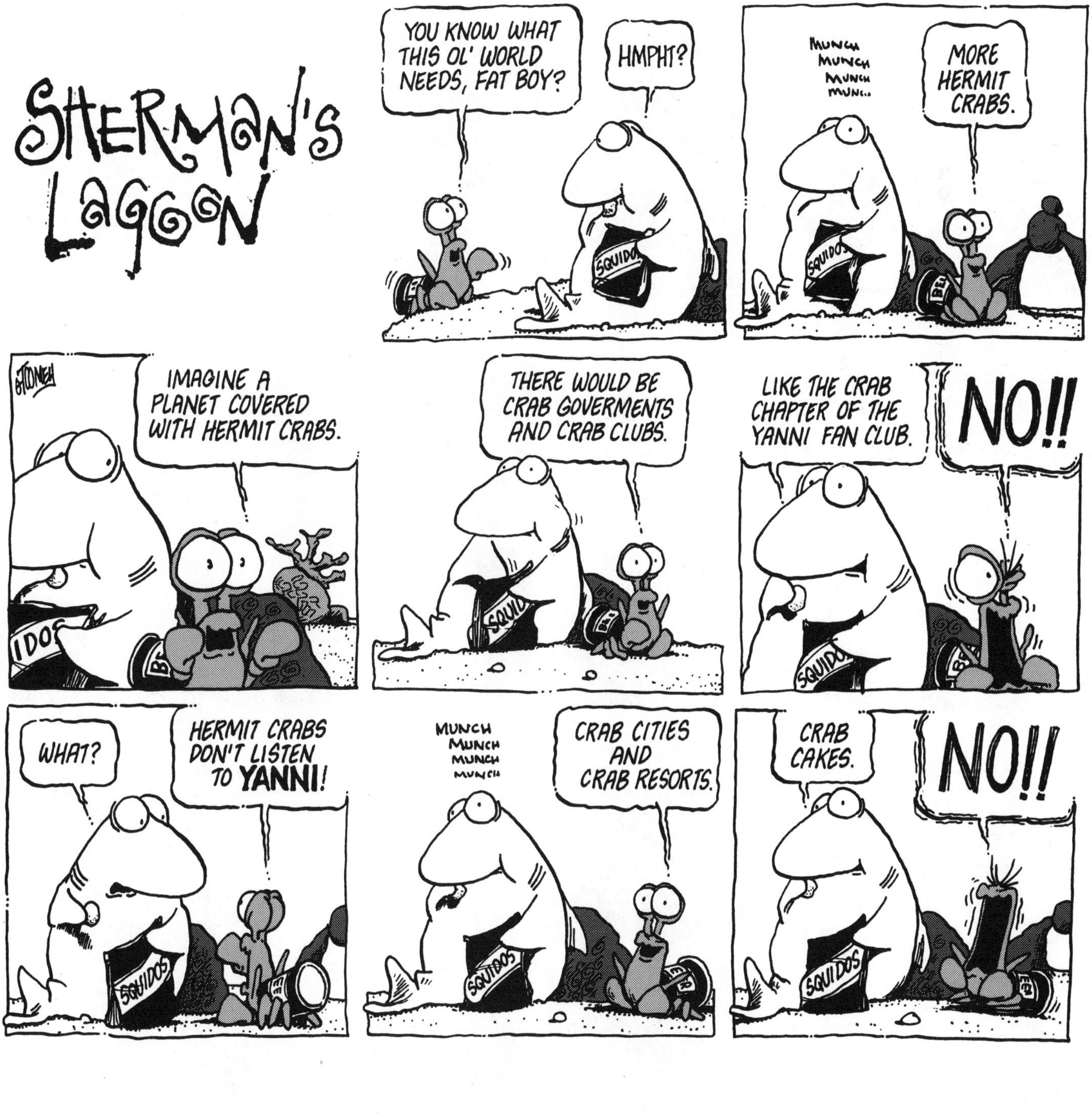
SHERMAN'S LAGOON
YOU KNOW WHAT THIS OL' WORLD NEEDS, FAT BOY?
HMPH?
MUNCH MUNCH MUNCH MUNCH
MORE HERMIT CRABS.
IMAGINE A PLANET COVERED WITH HERMIT CRABS.
THERE WOULD BE CRAB GOVERMENTS AND CRAB CLUBS.
LIKE THE CRAB CHAPTER OF THE YANNI FAN CLUB.
NO!!
WHAT?
HERMIT CRABS DON'T LISTEN TO YANNI!
MUNCH MUNCH MUNCH MUNCH
CRAB CITIES AND CRAB RESORTS.
CRAB CAKES.
NO!!
SQUIDOS

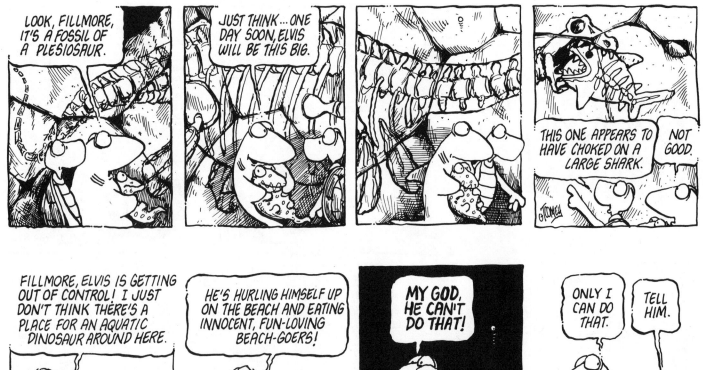

LOOK, FILLMORE, IT'S A FOSSIL OF A PLESIOSAUR.

JUST THINK... ONE DAY SOON, ELVIS WILL BE THIS BIG.

THIS ONE APPEARS TO HAVE CHOKED ON A LARGE SHARK.

NOT GOOD.

FILLMORE, ELVIS IS GETTING OUT OF CONTROL! I JUST DON'T THINK THERE'S A PLACE FOR AN AQUATIC DINOSAUR AROUND HERE.

HE'S HURLING HIMSELF UP ON THE BEACH AND EATING INNOCENT, FUN-LOVING BEACH-GOERS!

MY GOD, HE CAN'T DO THAT!

ONLY I CAN DO THAT.

TELL HIM.

HOW'RE YOU GOING TO GET RID OF ELVIS?

I'M GOING TO BE BRUTALLY HONEST WITH HIM.

ELVIS, YOU'RE NOTHING BUT A BIG, BUMPY, HAIRY, GROSS, SMELLY LIZARD, AND I WANT YOU OUT OF MY LIFE, NOW!

WELL PUT.

THAT'S HOW CINDY CRAWFORD DUMPED RICHARD GERE.

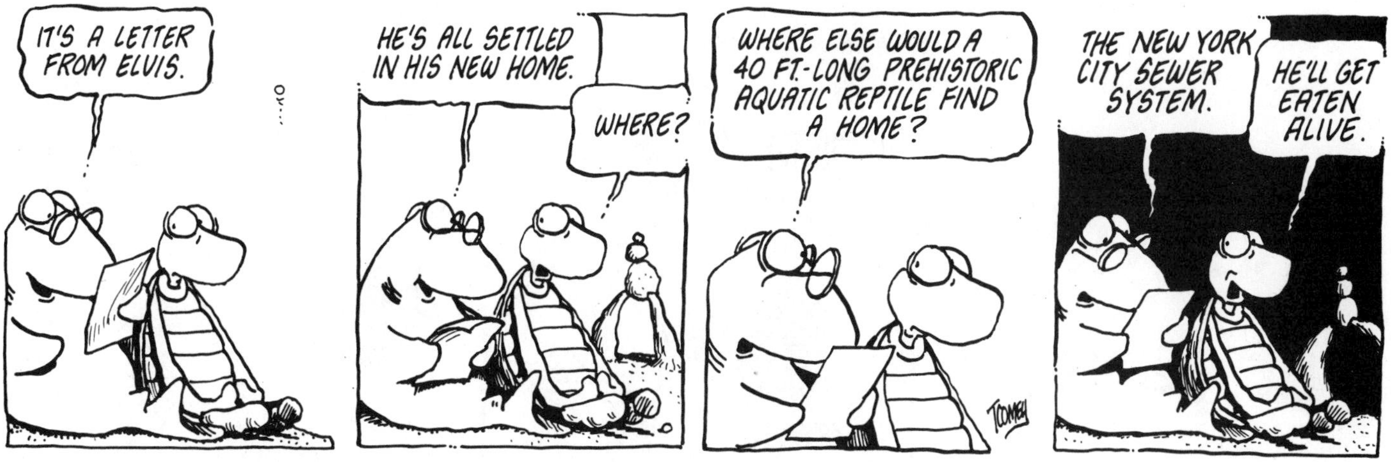
IT'S A LETTER FROM ELVIS.
HE'S ALL SETTLED IN HIS NEW HOME.
WHERE?
WHERE ELSE WOULD A 40 FT.-LONG PREHISTORIC AQUATIC REPTILE FIND A HOME?
THE NEW YORK CITY SEWER SYSTEM.
HE'LL GET EATEN ALIVE.
TOOMEY

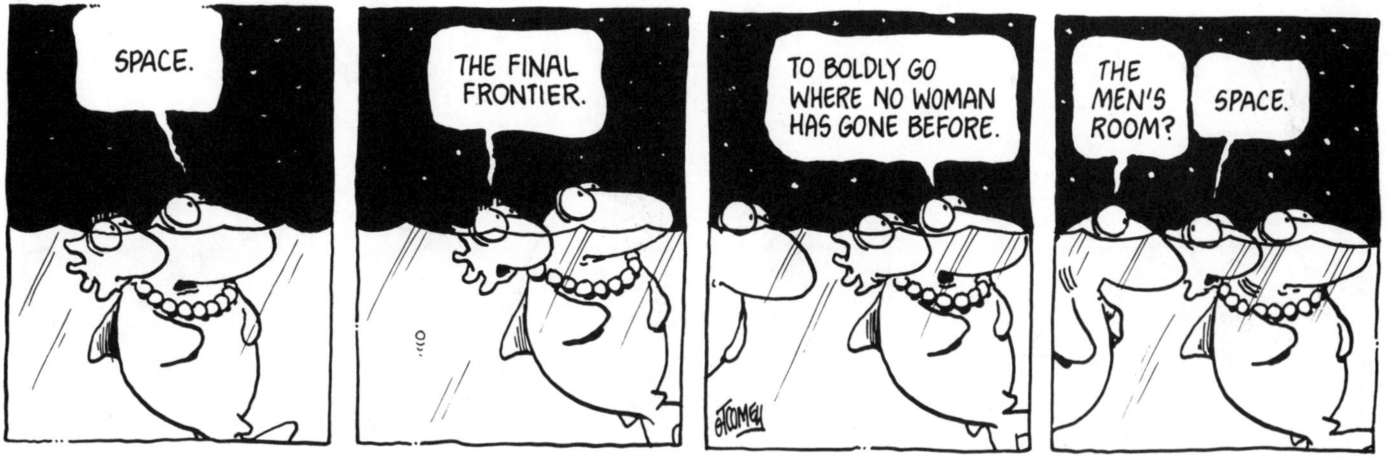
SPACE.
THE FINAL FRONTIER.
TO BOLDLY GO WHERE NO WOMAN HAS GONE BEFORE.
THE MEN'S ROOM?
SPACE.

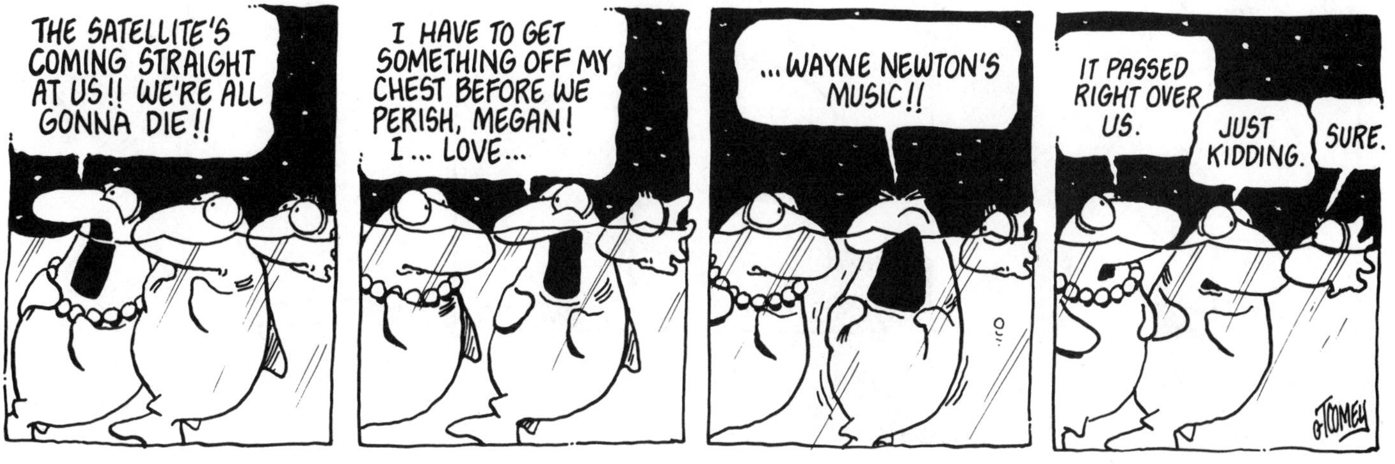
THE SATELLITE'S COMING STRAIGHT AT US!! WE'RE ALL GONNA DIE!!
I HAVE TO GET SOMETHING OFF MY CHEST BEFORE WE PERISH, MEGAN! I ... LOVE...
... WAYNE NEWTON'S MUSIC!!
IT PASSED RIGHT OVER US.
JUST KIDDING.
SURE.

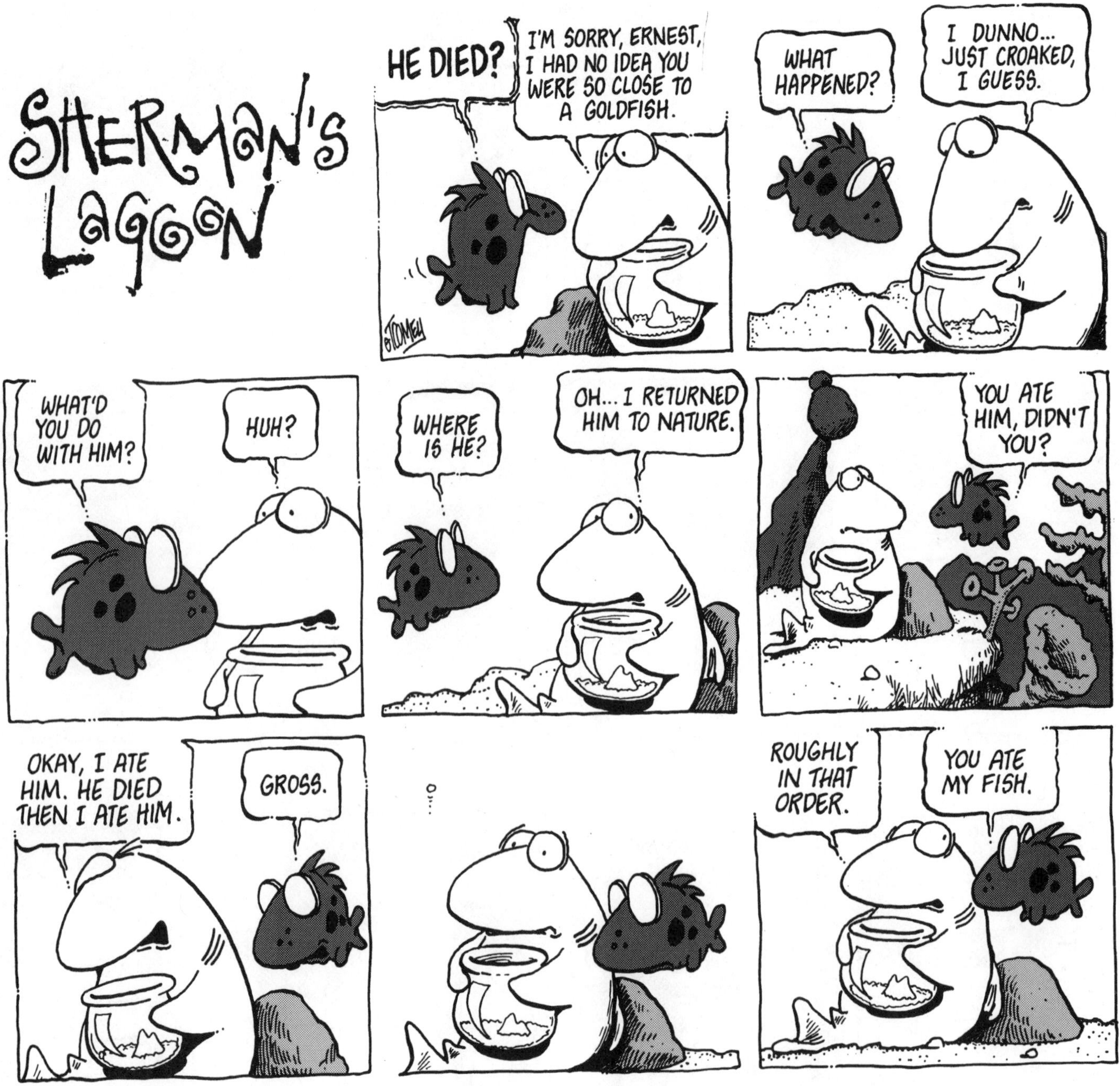
SHERMAN'S LAGOON
HE DIED?
I'M SORRY, ERNEST, I HAD NO IDEA YOU WERE SO CLOSE TO A GOLDFISH.
WHAT HAPPENED?
I DUNNO... JUST CROAKED, I GUESS.
WHAT'D YOU DO WITH HIM?
HUH?
WHERE IS HE?
OH... I RETURNED HIM TO NATURE.
YOU ATE HIM, DIDN'T YOU?
OKAY, I ATE HIM. HE DIED THEN I ATE HIM.
GROSS.
ROUGHLY IN THAT ORDER.
YOU ATE MY FISH.

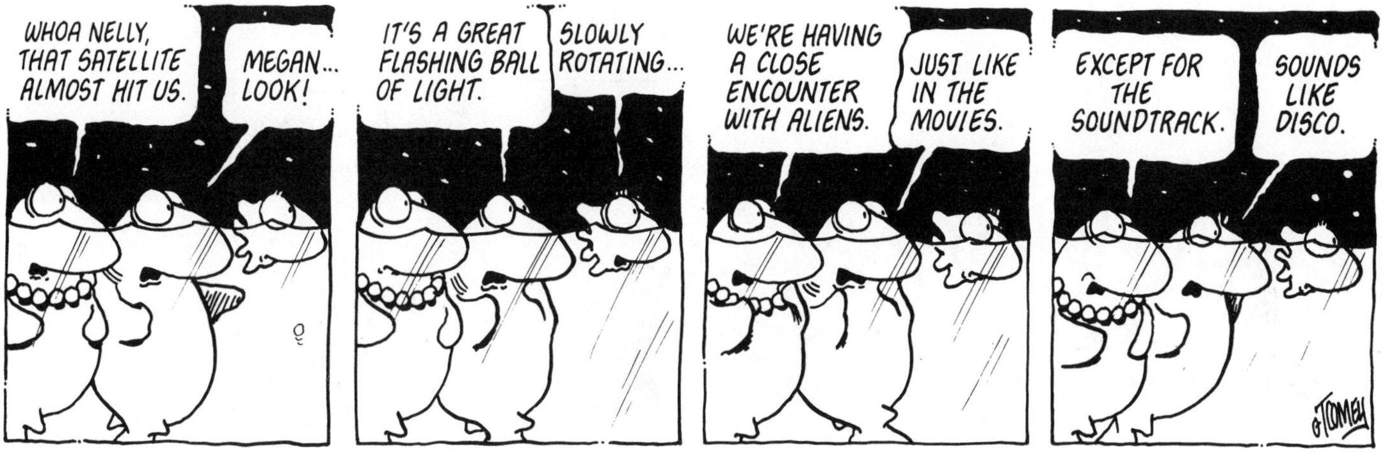
WHOA NELLY, THAT SATELLITE ALMOST HIT US.
MEGAN... LOOK!
IT'S A GREAT FLASHING BALL OF LIGHT.
SLOWLY ROTATING...
WE'RE HAVING A CLOSE ENCOUNTER WITH ALIENS.
JUST LIKE IN THE MOVIES.
EXCEPT FOR THE SOUNDTRACK.
SOUNDS LIKE DISCO.

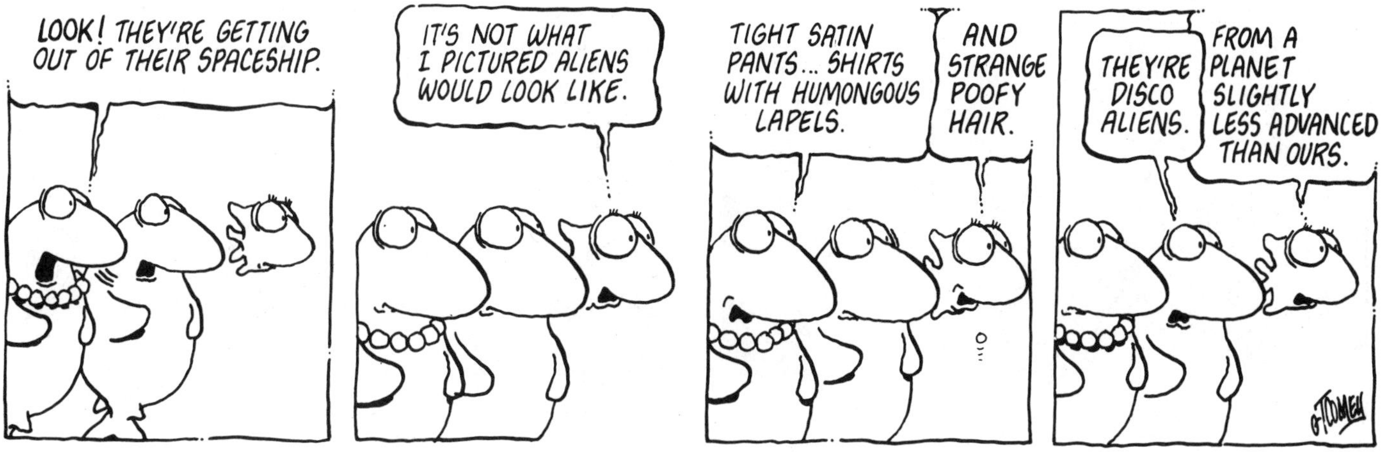
LOOK! THEY'RE GETTING OUT OF THEIR SPACESHIP.
IT'S NOT WHAT I PICTURED ALIENS WOULD LOOK LIKE.
TIGHT SATIN PANTS... SHIRTS WITH HUMONGOUS LAPELS.
AND STRANGE POOFY HAIR.
THEY'RE DISCO ALIENS.
FROM A PLANET SLIGHTLY LESS ADVANCED THAN OURS.

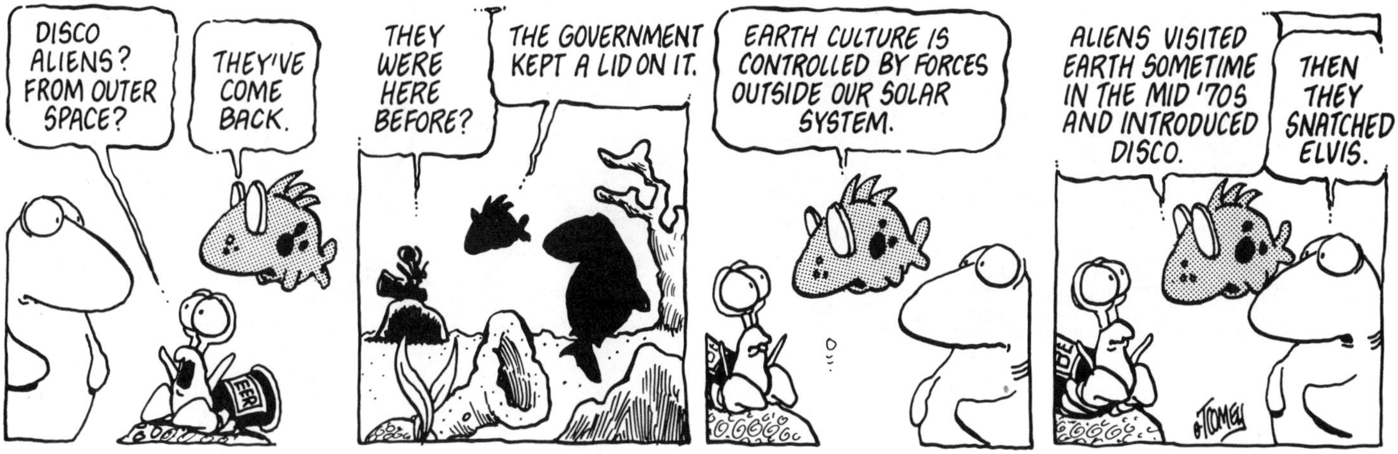
DISCO ALIENS? FROM OUTER SPACE?
THEY'VE COME BACK.
THEY WERE HERE BEFORE?
THE GOVERNMENT KEPT A LID ON IT.
EARTH CULTURE IS CONTROLLED BY FORCES OUTSIDE OUR SOLAR SYSTEM.
ALIENS VISITED EARTH SOMETIME IN THE MID '70S AND INTRODUCED DISCO.
THEN THEY SNATCHED ELVIS.

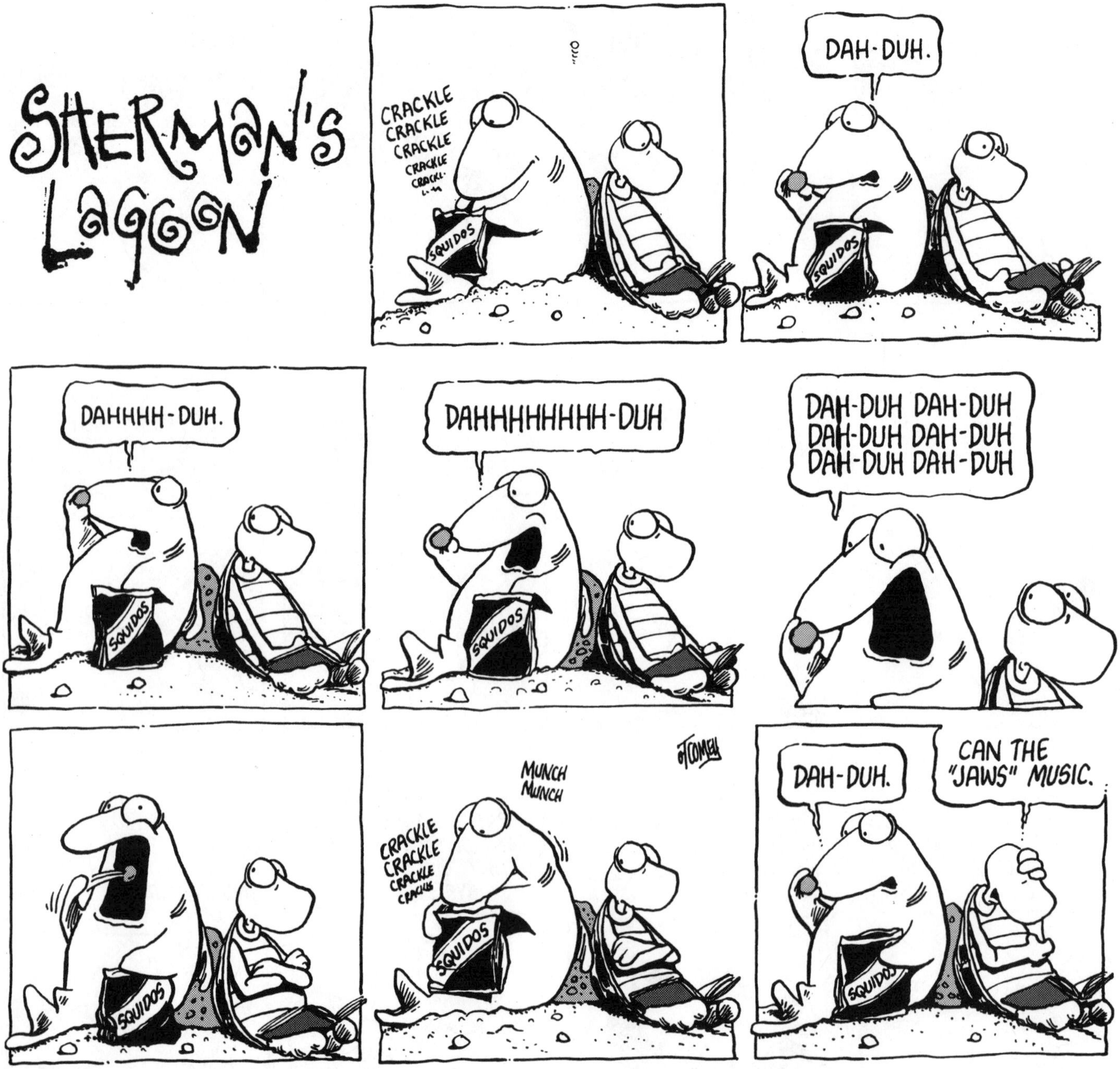
SHERMAN'S LAGOON
CRACKLE CRACKLE CRACKLE CRACKLE CRACKLE
SQUIDOS
DAH-DUH.
DAHHHH-DUH.
DAHHHHHHHH-DUH
DAH-DUH DAH-DUH DAH-DUH DAH-DUH DAH-DUH DAH-DUH
MUNCH MUNCH
CRACKLE CRACKLE CRACKLE
DAH-DUH.
CAN THE "JAWS" MUSIC.

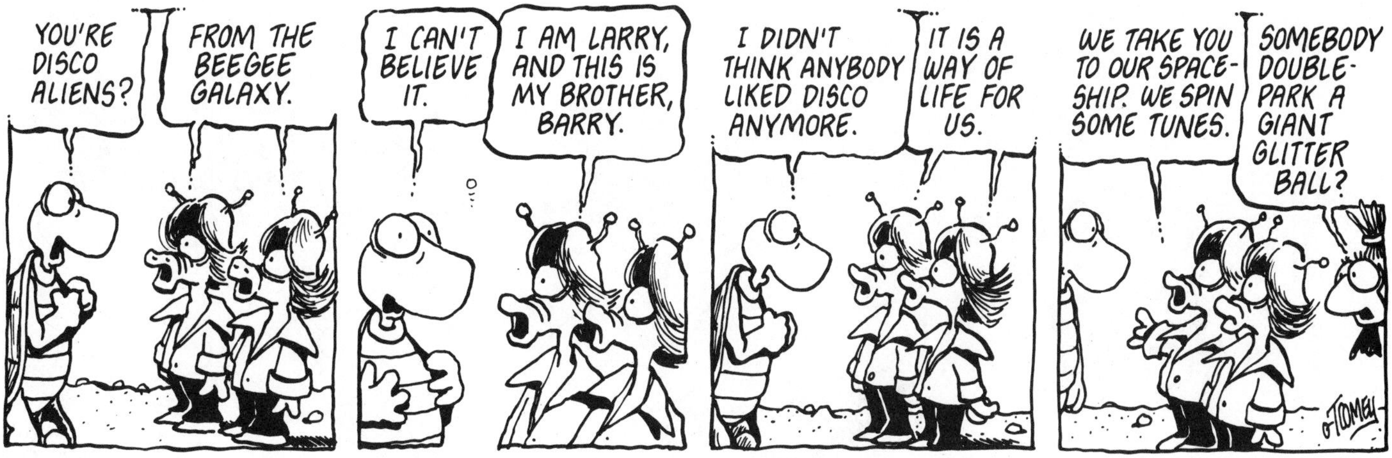
YOU'RE DISCO ALIENS?
FROM THE BEEGEE GALAXY.
I CAN'T BELIEVE IT.
I AM LARRY, AND THIS IS MY BROTHER, BARRY.
I DIDN'T THINK ANYBODY LIKED DISCO ANYMORE.
IT IS A WAY OF LIFE FOR US.
WE TAKE YOU TO OUR SPACESHIP. WE SPIN SOME TUNES.
SOMEBODY DOUBLE-PARK A GIANT GLITTER BALL?
TOOMEY

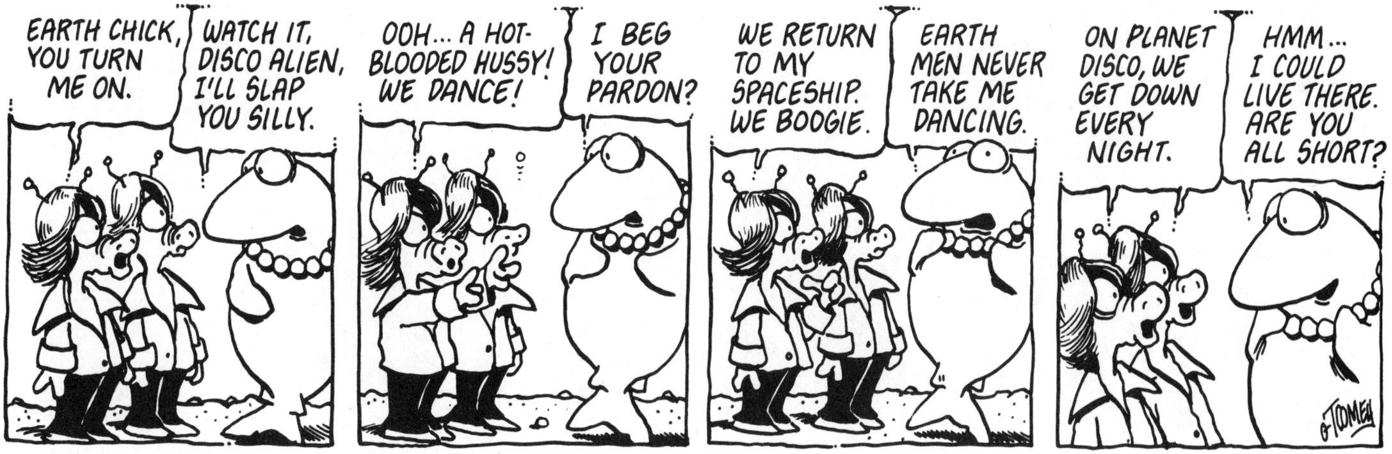
EARTH CHICK, YOU TURN ME ON.
WATCH IT, DISCO ALIEN, I'LL SLAP YOU SILLY.
OOH... A HOT-BLOODED HUSSY! WE DANCE!
I BEG YOUR PARDON?
WE RETURN TO MY SPACESHIP. WE BOOGIE.
EARTH MEN NEVER TAKE ME DANCING.
ON PLANET DISCO, WE GET DOWN EVERY NIGHT.
HMM... I COULD LIVE THERE. ARE YOU ALL SHORT?
TOOMEY

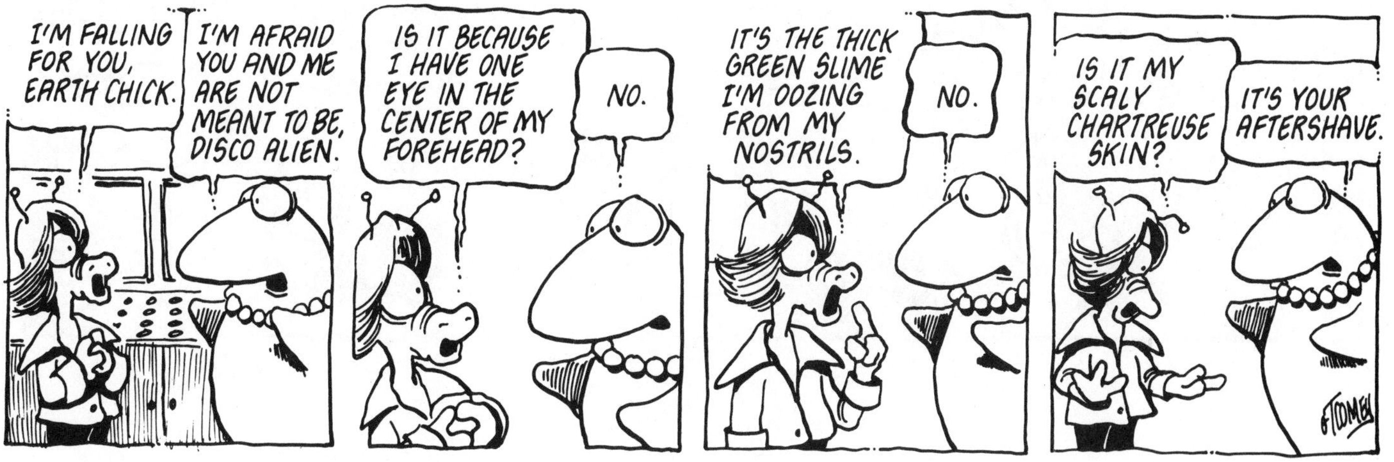
I'M FALLING FOR YOU, EARTH CHICK.
I'M AFRAID YOU AND ME ARE NOT MEANT TO BE, DISCO ALIEN.
IS IT BECAUSE I HAVE ONE EYE IN THE CENTER OF MY FOREHEAD?
NO.
IT'S THE THICK GREEN SLIME I'M OOZING FROM MY NOSTRILS.
NO.
IS IT MY SCALY CHARTREUSE SKIN?
IT'S YOUR AFTERSHAVE.
TOOMEY

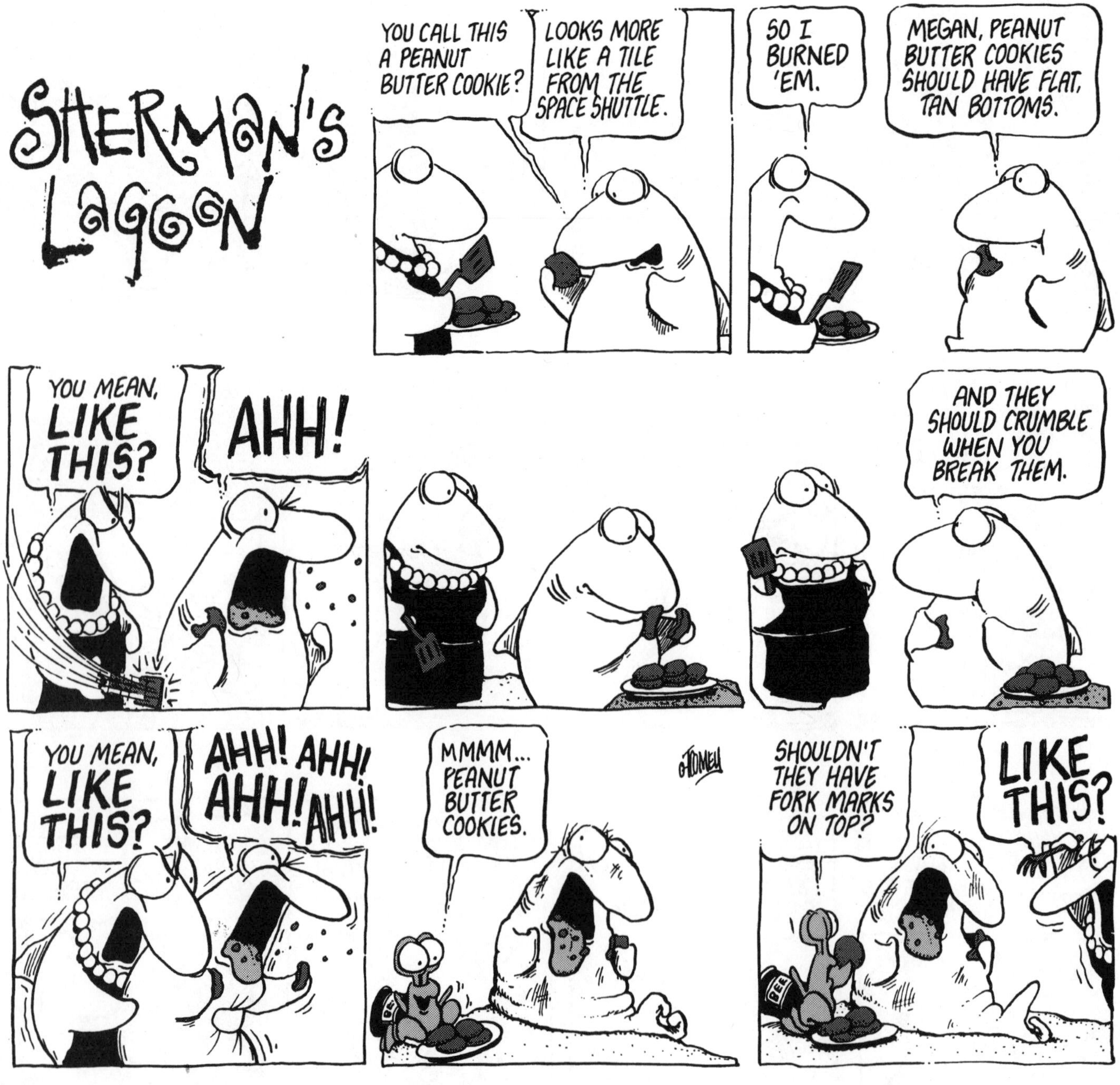
SHERMAN'S LAGOON
YOU CALL THIS A PEANUT BUTTER COOKIE?
LOOKS MORE LIKE A TILE FROM THE SPACE SHUTTLE.
SO I BURNED 'EM.
MEGAN, PEANUT BUTTER COOKIES SHOULD HAVE FLAT, TAN BOTTOMS.
YOU MEAN, LIKE THIS?
AHH!
AND THEY SHOULD CRUMBLE WHEN YOU BREAK THEM.
YOU MEAN, LIKE THIS?
AHH! AHH! AHH! AHH!
MMMM... PEANUT BUTTER COOKIES.
SHOULDN'T THEY HAVE FORK MARKS ON TOP?
LIKE THIS?

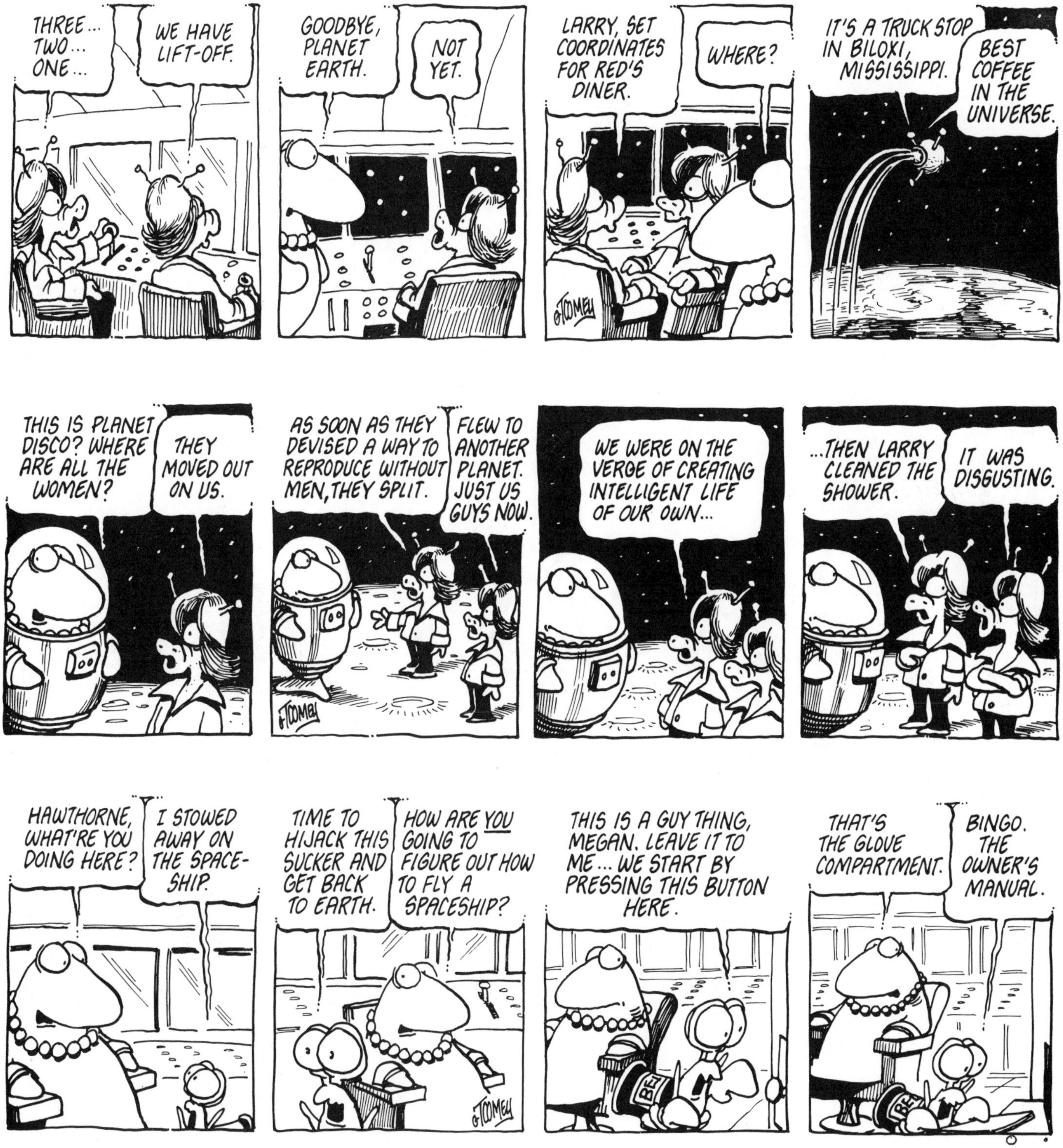
THREE... TWO... ONE...
WE HAVE LIFT-OFF.
GOODBYE, PLANET EARTH.
NOT YET.
LARRY, SET COORDINATES FOR RED'S DINER.
WHERE?
IT'S A TRUCK STOP IN BILOXI, MISSISSIPPI.
BEST COFFEE IN THE UNIVERSE.
TOOMEY
THIS IS PLANET DISCO? WHERE ARE ALL THE WOMEN?
THEY MOVED OUT ON US.
AS SOON AS THEY DEVISED A WAY TO REPRODUCE WITHOUT MEN, THEY SPLIT.
FLEW TO ANOTHER PLANET. JUST US GUYS NOW.
TOOMEY
WE WERE ON THE VERGE OF CREATING INTELLIGENT LIFE OF OUR OWN...
...THEN LARRY CLEANED THE SHOWER.
IT WAS DISGUSTING.
HAWTHORNE, WHAT'RE YOU DOING HERE?
I STOWED AWAY ON THE SPACE-SHIP.
TIME TO HIJACK THIS SUCKER AND GET BACK TO EARTH.
HOW ARE YOU GOING TO FIGURE OUT HOW TO FLY A SPACESHIP?
TOOMEY
THIS IS A GUY THING, MEGAN. LEAVE IT TO ME... WE START BY PRESSING THIS BUTTON HERE.
THAT'S THE GLOVE COMPARTMENT.
BINGO. THE OWNER'S MANUAL.

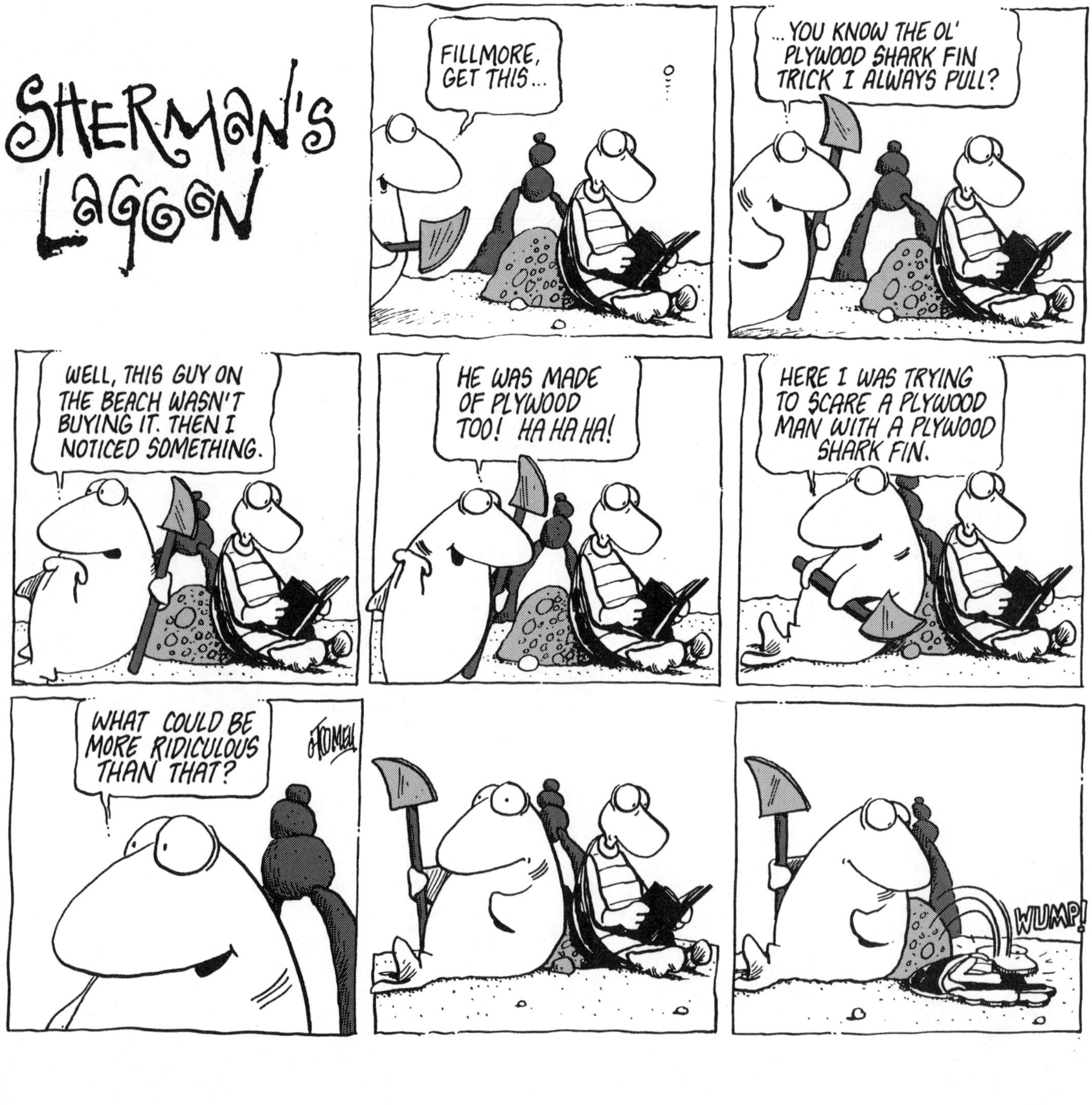
SHERMAN'S LAGOON
FILLMORE, GET THIS...
...YOU KNOW THE OL' PLYWOOD SHARK FIN TRICK I ALWAYS PULL?
WELL, THIS GUY ON THE BEACH WASN'T BUYING IT. THEN I NOTICED SOMETHING.
HE WAS MADE OF PLYWOOD TOO! HA HA HA!
HERE I WAS TRYING TO SCARE A PLYWOOD MAN WITH A PLYWOOD SHARK FIN.
WHAT COULD BE MORE RIDICULOUS THAN THAT?
WUMP!

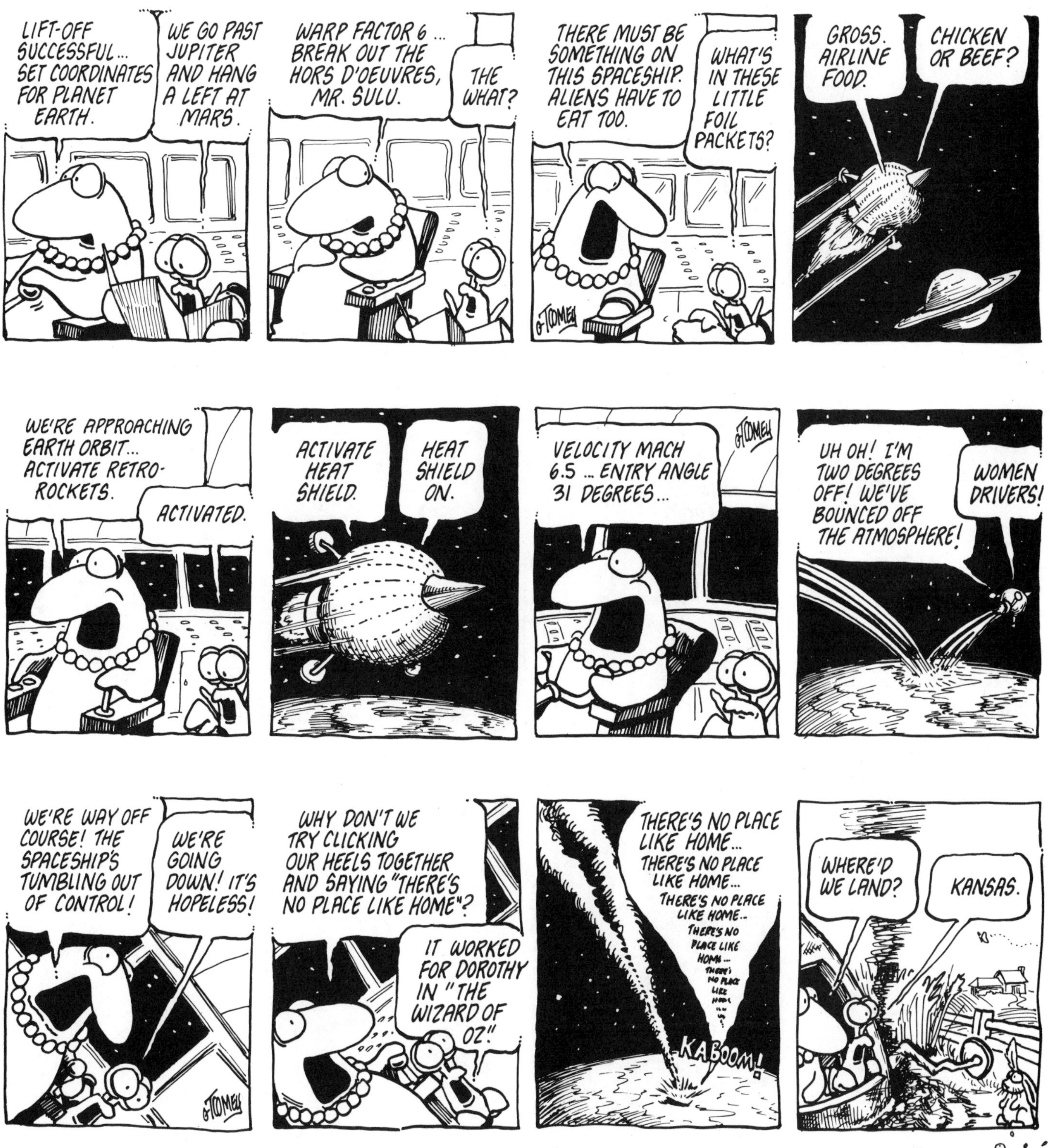
LIFT-OFF SUCCESSFUL... SET COORDINATES FOR PLANET EARTH.
WE GO PAST JUPITER AND HANG A LEFT AT MARS.
WARP FACTOR 6 ... BREAK OUT THE HORS D'OEUVRES, MR. SULU.
THE WHAT?
THERE MUST BE SOMETHING ON THIS SPACESHIP. ALIENS HAVE TO EAT TOO.
WHAT'S IN THESE LITTLE FOIL PACKETS?
GROSS. AIRLINE FOOD.
CHICKEN OR BEEF?
WE'RE APPROACHING EARTH ORBIT... ACTIVATE RETRO-ROCKETS.
ACTIVATED.
ACTIVATE HEAT SHIELD.
HEAT SHIELD ON.
VELOCITY MACH 6.5 ... ENTRY ANGLE 31 DEGREES...
UH OH! I'M TWO DEGREES OFF! WE'VE BOUNCED OFF THE ATMOSPHERE!
WOMEN DRIVERS!
WE'RE WAY OFF COURSE! THE SPACESHIP'S TUMBLING OUT OF CONTROL!
WE'RE GOING DOWN! IT'S HOPELESS!
WHY DON'T WE TRY CLICKING OUR HEELS TOGETHER AND SAYING "THERE'S NO PLACE LIKE HOME"?
IT WORKED FOR DOROTHY IN "THE WIZARD OF OZ."
THERE'S NO PLACE LIKE HOME... THERE'S NO PLACE LIKE HOME... THERE'S NO PLACE LIKE HOME... THERE'S NO PLACE LIKE HOME...
KABOOM!
WHERE'D WE LAND?
KANSAS.

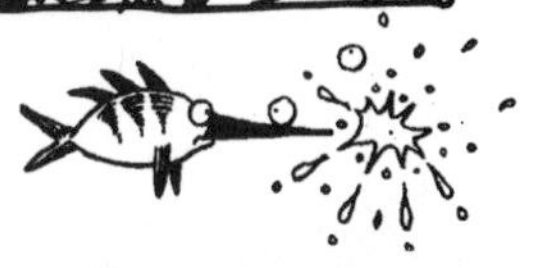

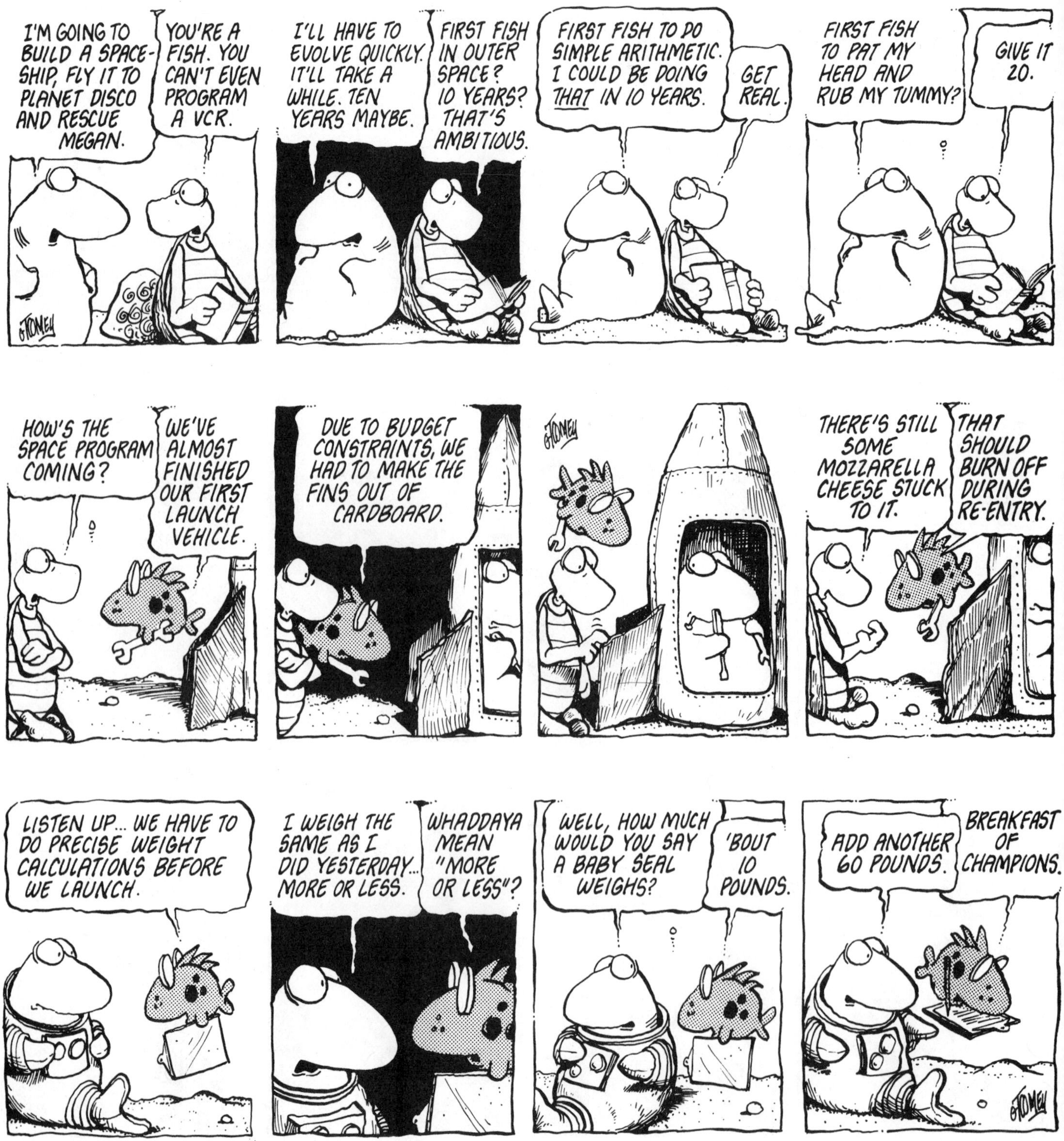
I'M GOING TO BUILD A SPACE-SHIP, FLY IT TO PLANET DISCO AND RESCUE MEGAN.
YOU'RE A FISH. YOU CAN'T EVEN PROGRAM A VCR.
I'LL HAVE TO EVOLVE QUICKLY. IT'LL TAKE A WHILE. TEN YEARS MAYBE.
FIRST FISH IN OUTER SPACE? 10 YEARS? THAT'S AMBITIOUS.
FIRST FISH TO DO SIMPLE ARITHMETIC. I COULD BE DOING THAT IN 10 YEARS.
GET REAL.
FIRST FISH TO PAT MY HEAD AND RUB MY TUMMY?
GIVE IT 20.
HOW'S THE SPACE PROGRAM COMING?
WE'VE ALMOST FINISHED OUR FIRST LAUNCH VEHICLE.
DUE TO BUDGET CONSTRAINTS, WE HAD TO MAKE THE FINS OUT OF CARDBOARD.
THERE'S STILL SOME MOZZARELLA CHEESE STUCK TO IT.
THAT SHOULD BURN OFF DURING RE-ENTRY.
LISTEN UP... WE HAVE TO DO PRECISE WEIGHT CALCULATIONS BEFORE WE LAUNCH.
I WEIGH THE SAME AS I DID YESTERDAY... MORE OR LESS.
WHADDAYA MEAN "MORE OR LESS"?
WELL, HOW MUCH WOULD YOU SAY A BABY SEAL WEIGHS?
'BOUT 10 POUNDS.
ADD ANOTHER 60 POUNDS.
BREAKFAST OF CHAMPIONS.

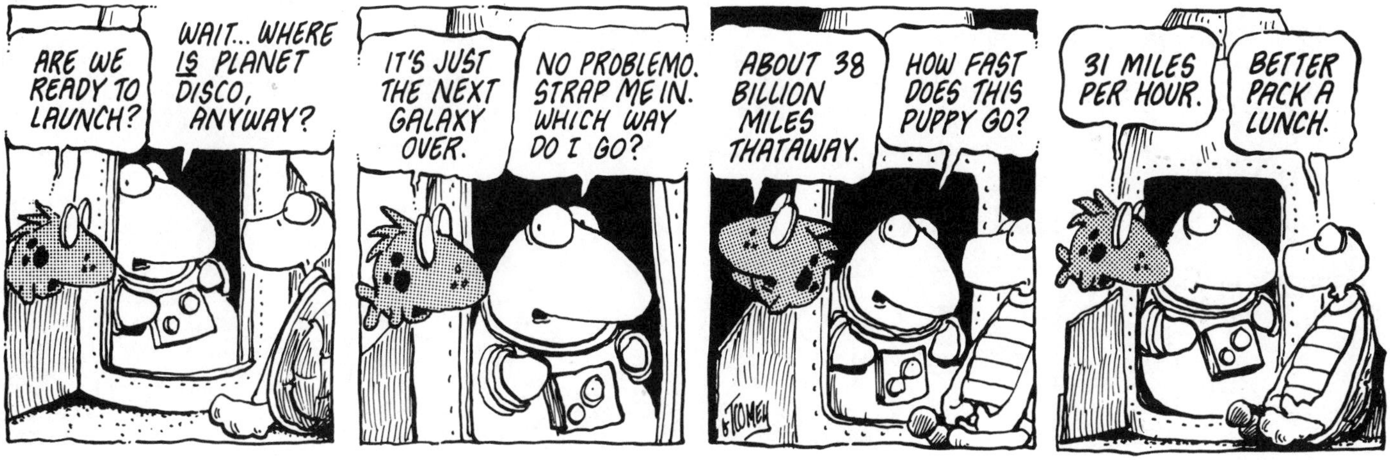
ARE WE READY TO LAUNCH?
WAIT... WHERE IS PLANET DISCO, ANYWAY?
IT'S JUST THE NEXT GALAXY OVER.
NO PROBLEMO. STRAP ME IN. WHICH WAY DO I GO?
ABOUT 38 BILLION MILES THATAWAY.
HOW FAST DOES THIS PUPPY GO?
31 MILES PER HOUR.
BETTER PACK A LUNCH.

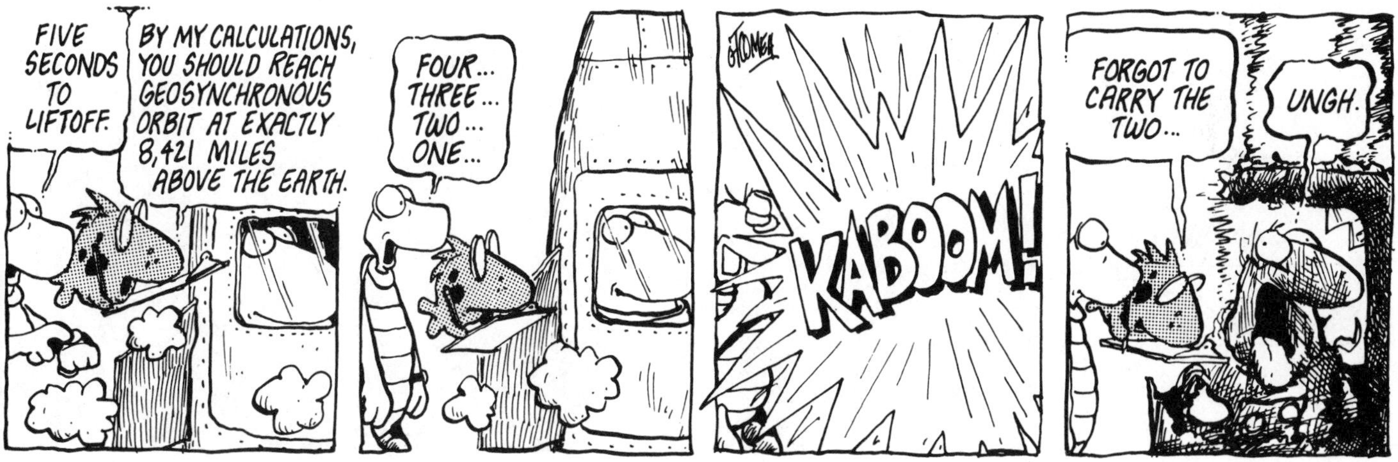
FIVE SECONDS TO LIFTOFF.
BY MY CALCULATIONS, YOU SHOULD REACH GEOSYNCHRONOUS ORBIT AT EXACTLY 8,421 MILES ABOVE THE EARTH.
FOUR... THREE... TWO... ONE...
KABOOM!
FORGOT TO CARRY THE TWO...
UNGH.

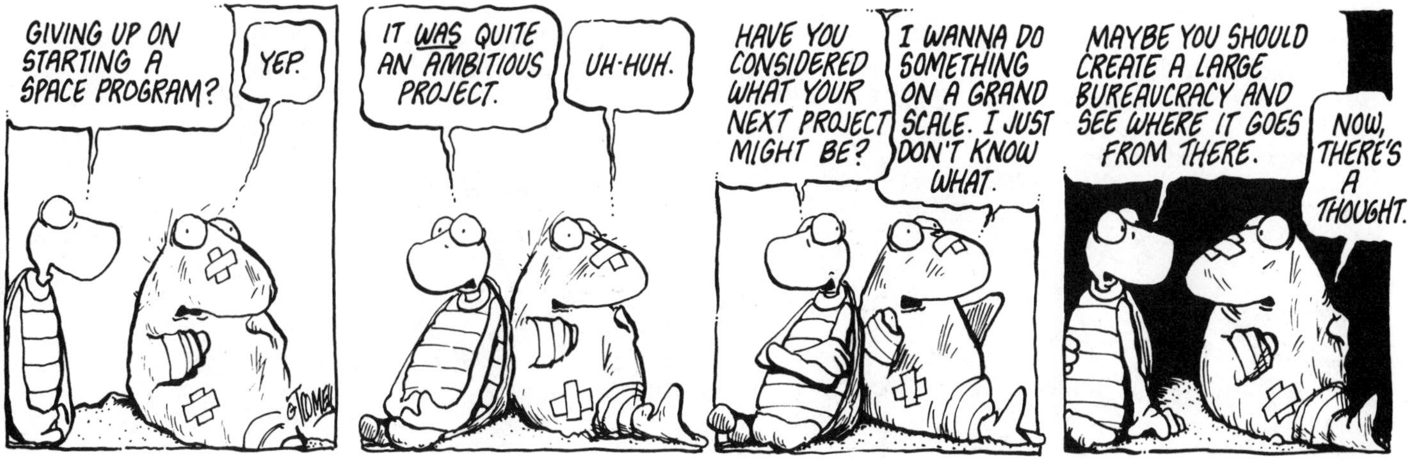
GIVING UP ON STARTING A SPACE PROGRAM?
YEP.
IT WAS QUITE AN AMBITIOUS PROJECT.
UH-HUH.
HAVE YOU CONSIDERED WHAT YOUR NEXT PROJECT MIGHT BE?
I WANNA DO SOMETHING ON A GRAND SCALE. I JUST DON'T KNOW WHAT.
MAYBE YOU SHOULD CREATE A LARGE BUREAUCRACY AND SEE WHERE IT GOES FROM THERE.
NOW, THERE'S A THOUGHT.

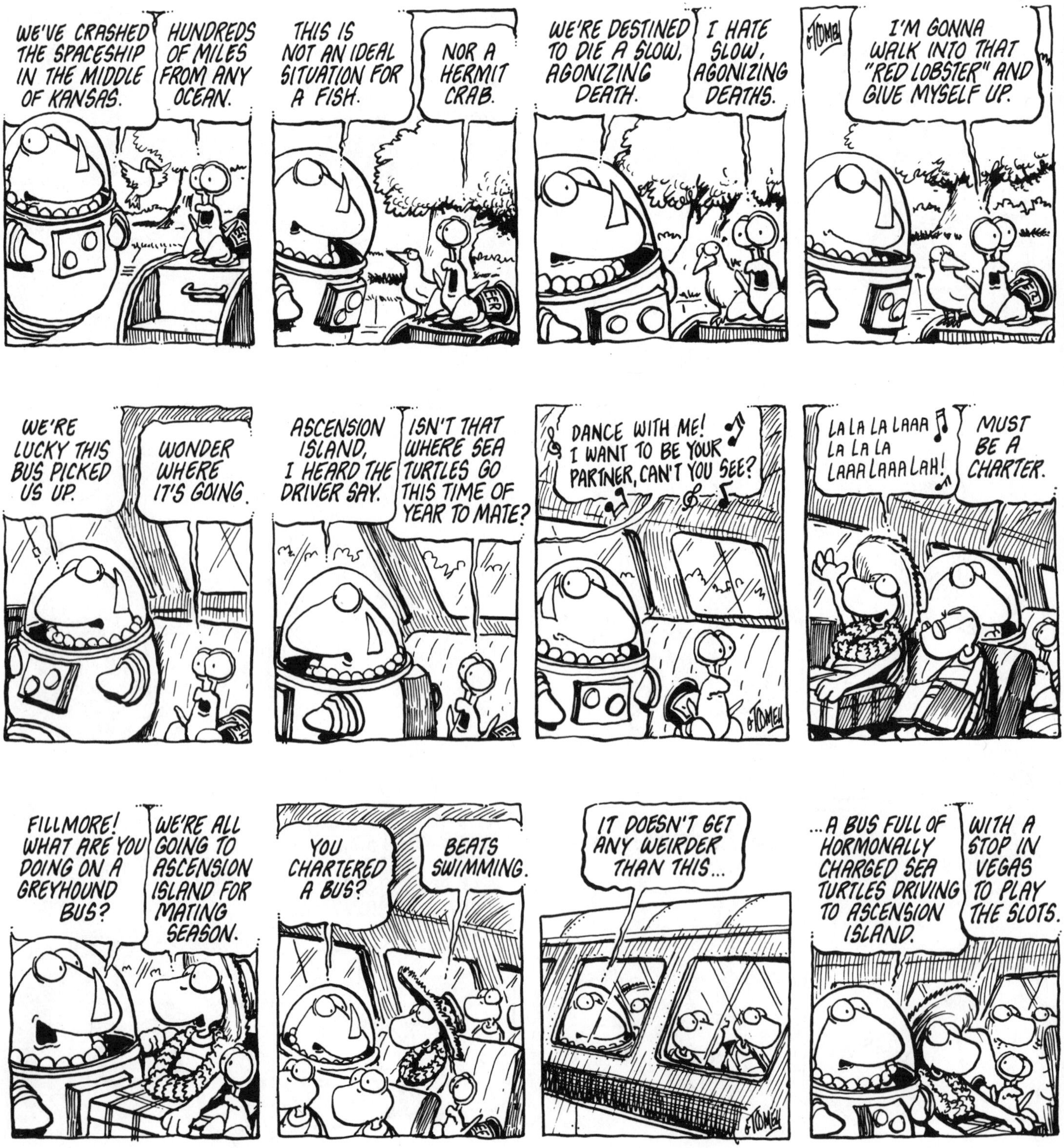
WE'VE CRASHED THE SPACESHIP IN THE MIDDLE OF KANSAS.
HUNDREDS OF MILES FROM ANY OCEAN.
THIS IS NOT AN IDEAL SITUATION FOR A FISH.
NOR A HERMIT CRAB.
WE'RE DESTINED TO DIE A SLOW, AGONIZING DEATH.
I HATE SLOW, AGONIZING DEATHS.
I'M GONNA WALK INTO THAT "RED LOBSTER" AND GIVE MYSELF UP.
WE'RE LUCKY THIS BUS PICKED US UP.
WONDER WHERE IT'S GOING.
ASCENSION ISLAND, I HEARD THE DRIVER SAY.
ISN'T THAT WHERE SEA TURTLES GO THIS TIME OF YEAR TO MATE?
DANCE WITH ME! I WANT TO BE YOUR PARTNER, CAN'T YOU SEE?
LA LA LA LAAA LA LA LA LAAA LAAA LAH!
MUST BE A CHARTER.
FILLMORE! WHAT ARE YOU DOING ON A GREYHOUND BUS?
WE'RE ALL GOING TO ASCENSION ISLAND FOR MATING SEASON.
YOU CHARTERED A BUS?
BEATS SWIMMING.
IT DOESN'T GET ANY WEIRDER THAN THIS...
...A BUS FULL OF HORMONALLY CHARGED SEA TURTLES DRIVING TO ASCENSION ISLAND.
WITH A STOP IN VEGAS TO PLAY THE SLOTS.

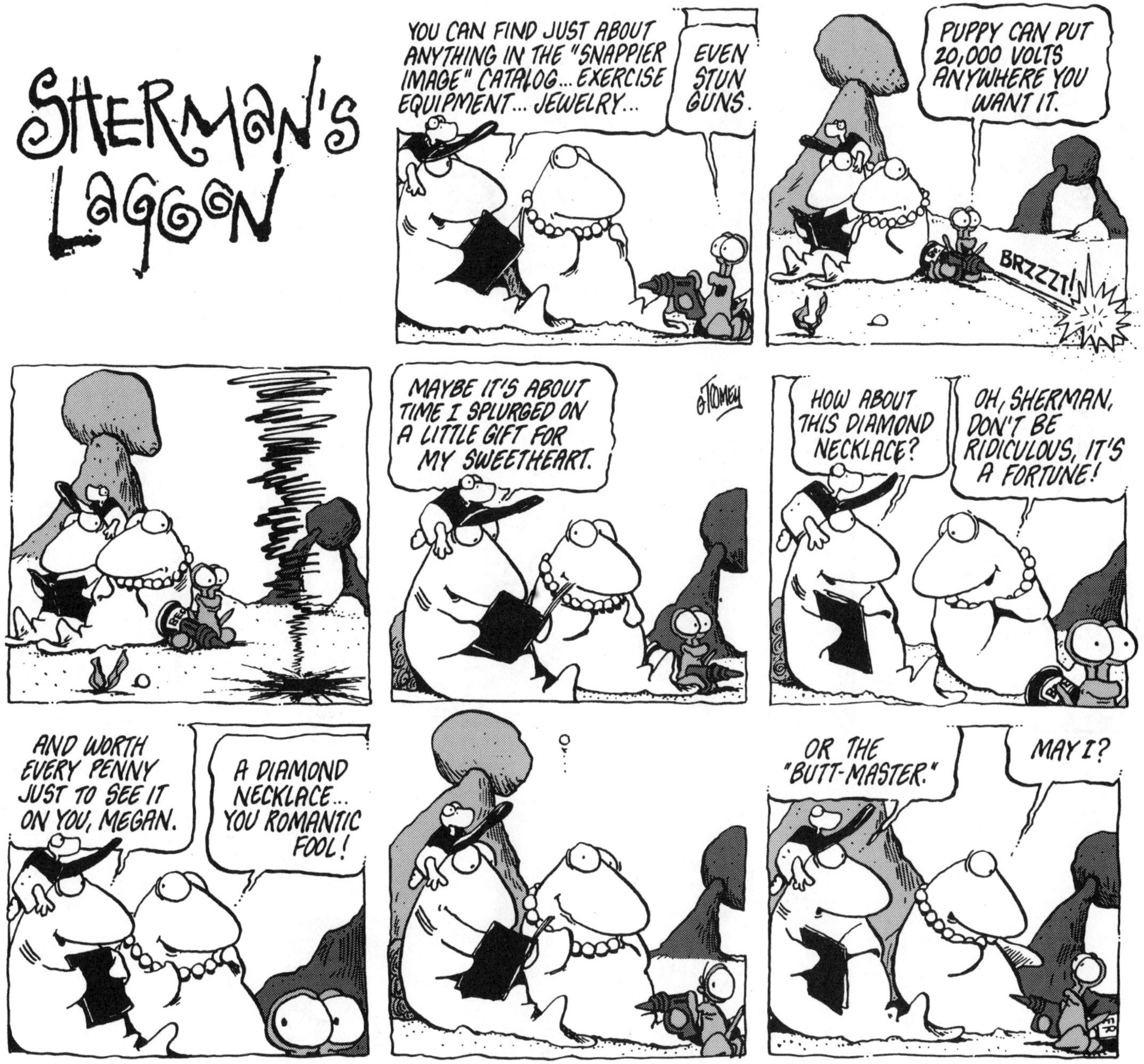
SHERMAN'S LAGOON
YOU CAN FIND JUST ABOUT ANYTHING IN THE "SNAPPIER IMAGE" CATALOG... EXERCISE EQUIPMENT... JEWELRY...
EVEN STUN GUNS.
PUPPY CAN PUT 20,000 VOLTS ANYWHERE YOU WANT IT.
BRZZZT!
MAYBE IT'S ABOUT TIME I SPLURGED ON A LITTLE GIFT FOR MY SWEETHEART.
HOW ABOUT THIS DIAMOND NECKLACE?
OH, SHERMAN, DON'T BE RIDICULOUS, IT'S A FORTUNE!
AND WORTH EVERY PENNY JUST TO SEE IT ON YOU, MEGAN.
A DIAMOND NECKLACE... YOU ROMANTIC FOOL!
OR THE "BUTT-MASTER."
MAY I?

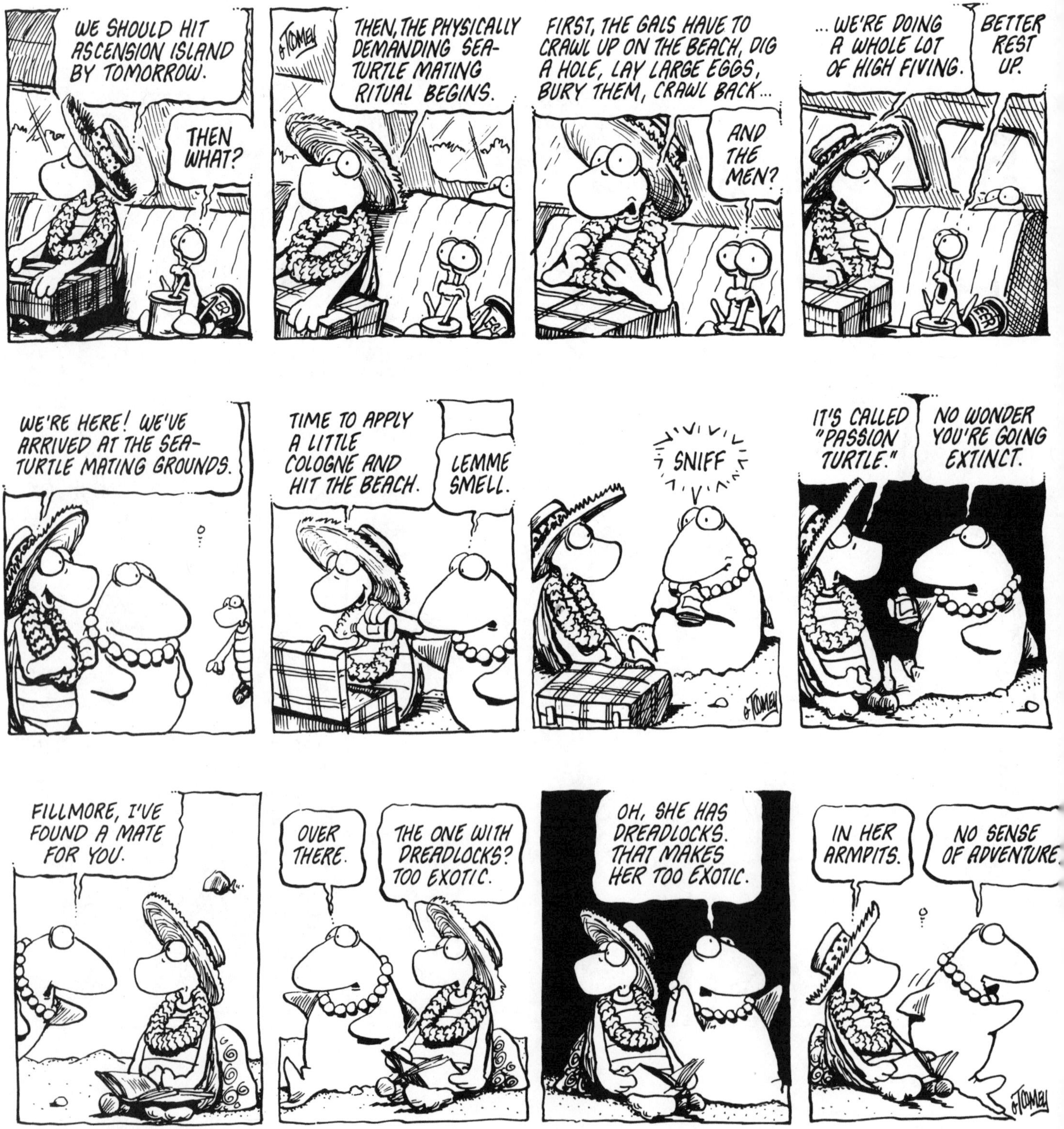

WE SHOULD HIT ASCENSION ISLAND BY TOMORROW.
THEN WHAT?
THEN, THE PHYSICALLY DEMANDING SEA-TURTLE MATING RITUAL BEGINS.
FIRST, THE GALS HAVE TO CRAWL UP ON THE BEACH, DIG A HOLE, LAY LARGE EGGS, BURY THEM, CRAWL BACK...
AND THE MEN?
... WE'RE DOING A WHOLE LOT OF HIGH FIVING.
BETTER REST UP.
WE'RE HERE! WE'VE ARRIVED AT THE SEA-TURTLE MATING GROUNDS.
TIME TO APPLY A LITTLE COLOGNE AND HIT THE BEACH.
LEMME SMELL.
SNIFF
IT'S CALLED "PASSION TURTLE."
NO WONDER YOU'RE GOING EXTINCT.
FILLMORE, I'VE FOUND A MATE FOR YOU.
OVER THERE.
THE ONE WITH DREADLOCKS? TOO EXOTIC.
OH, SHE HAS DREADLOCKS. THAT MAKES HER TOO EXOTIC.
IN HER ARMPITS.
NO SENSE OF ADVENTURE.

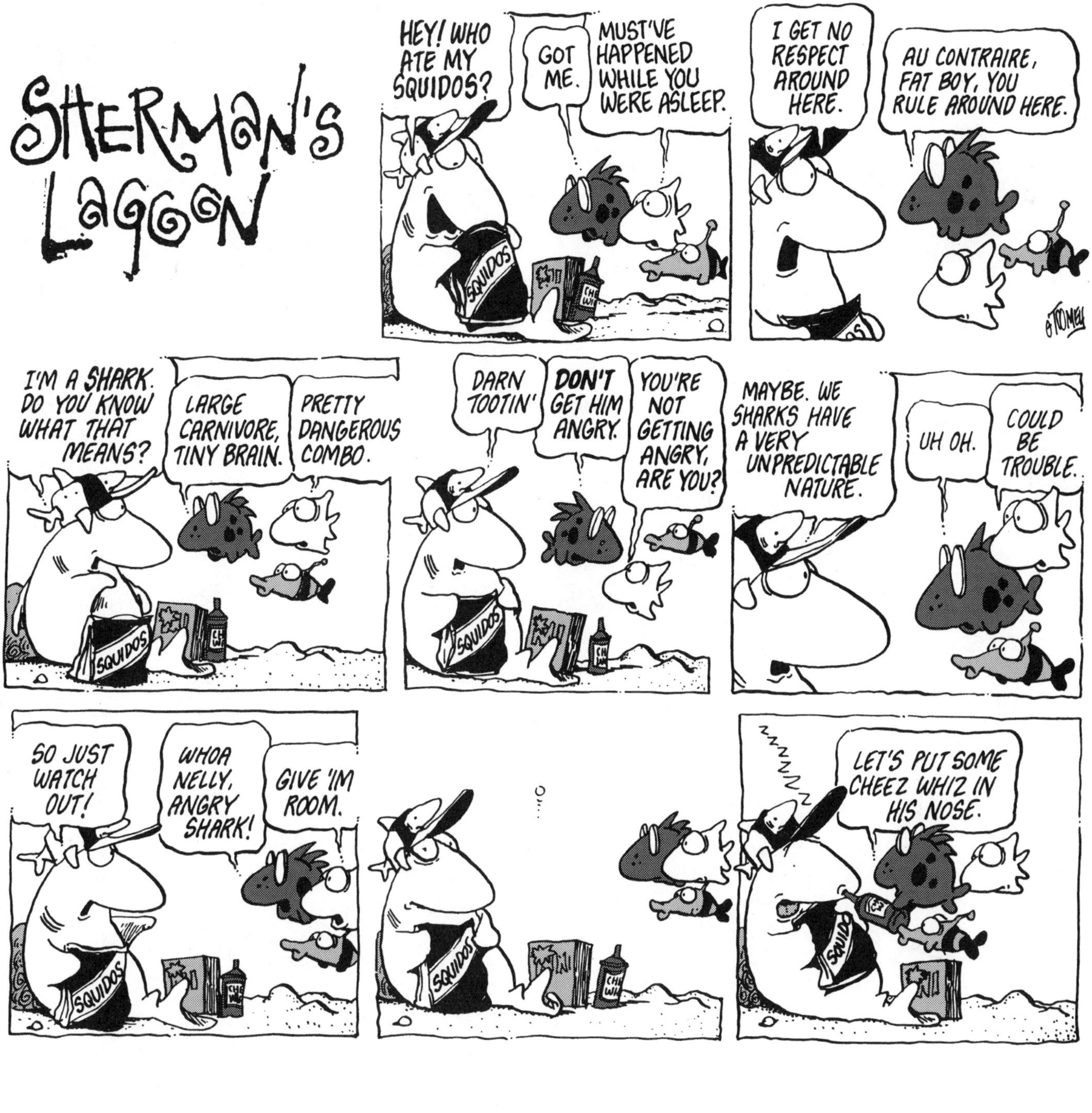
SHERMAN'S LAGOON
HEY! WHO ATE MY SQUIDOS?
GOT ME.
MUST'VE HAPPENED WHILE YOU WERE ASLEEP.
SQUIDOS
I GET NO RESPECT AROUND HERE.
AU CONTRAIRE, FAT BOY, YOU RULE AROUND HERE.
TOOMEY
I'M A SHARK. DO YOU KNOW WHAT THAT MEANS?
LARGE CARNIVORE, TINY BRAIN.
PRETTY DANGEROUS COMBO.
SQUIDOS
DARN TOOTIN'
DON'T GET HIM ANGRY.
YOU'RE NOT GETTING ANGRY, ARE YOU?
SQUIDOS
MAYBE. WE SHARKS HAVE A VERY UNPREDICTABLE NATURE.
UH OH.
COULD BE TROUBLE.
SO JUST WATCH OUT!
WHOA NELLY, ANGRY SHARK!
GIVE 'IM ROOM.
SQUIDOS
SQUIDOS
ZZZZZ
LET'S PUT SOME CHEEZ WHIZ IN HIS NOSE.
SQUIDOS

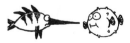

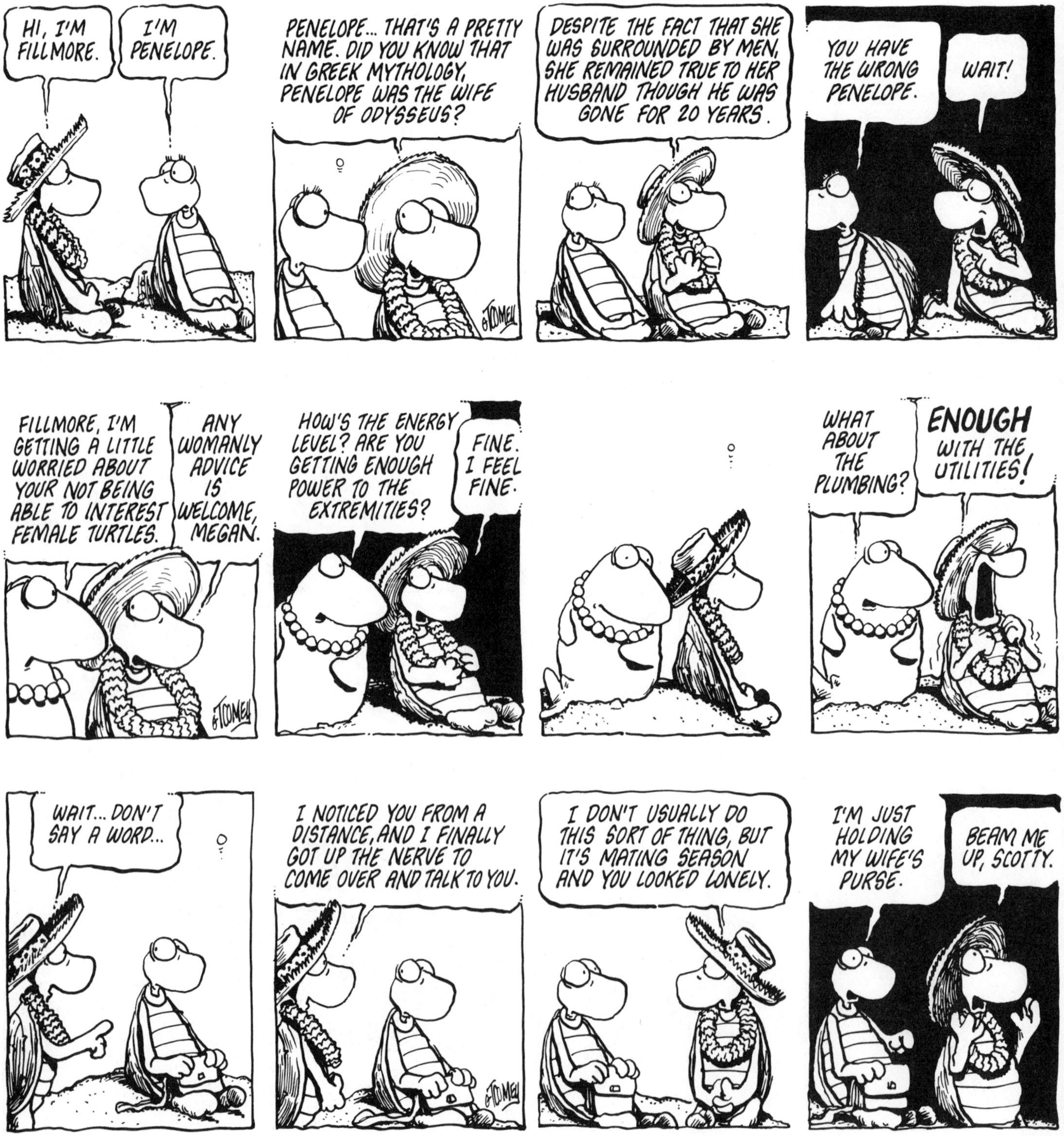
HI, I'M FILLMORE.
I'M PENELOPE.
PENELOPE... THAT'S A PRETTY NAME. DID YOU KNOW THAT IN GREEK MYTHOLOGY, PENELOPE WAS THE WIFE OF ODYSSEUS?
DESPITE THE FACT THAT SHE WAS SURROUNDED BY MEN, SHE REMAINED TRUE TO HER HUSBAND THOUGH HE WAS GONE FOR 20 YEARS.
YOU HAVE THE WRONG PENELOPE.
WAIT!
FILLMORE, I'M GETTING A LITTLE WORRIED ABOUT YOUR NOT BEING ABLE TO INTEREST FEMALE TURTLES.
ANY WOMANLY ADVICE IS WELCOME, MEGAN.
HOW'S THE ENERGY LEVEL? ARE YOU GETTING ENOUGH POWER TO THE EXTREMITIES?
FINE. I FEEL FINE.
WHAT ABOUT THE PLUMBING?
ENOUGH WITH THE UTILITIES!
WAIT... DON'T SAY A WORD...
I NOTICED YOU FROM A DISTANCE, AND I FINALLY GOT UP THE NERVE TO COME OVER AND TALK TO YOU.
I DON'T USUALLY DO THIS SORT OF THING, BUT IT'S MATING SEASON AND YOU LOOKED LONELY.
I'M JUST HOLDING MY WIFE'S PURSE.
BEAM ME UP, SCOTTY.

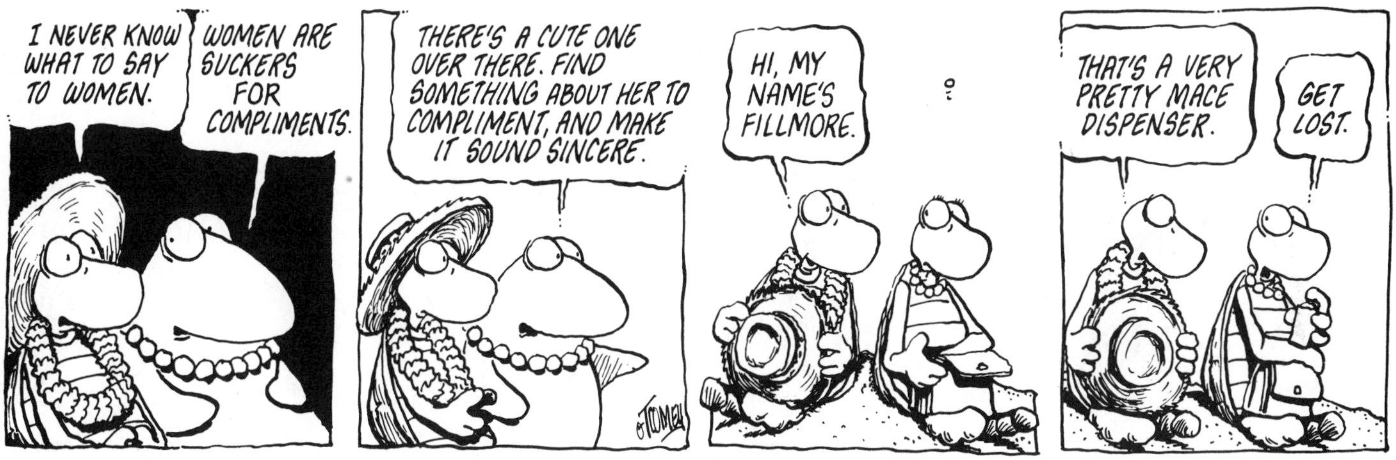
I NEVER KNOW WHAT TO SAY TO WOMEN.
WOMEN ARE SUCKERS FOR COMPLIMENTS.
THERE'S A CUTE ONE OVER THERE. FIND SOMETHING ABOUT HER TO COMPLIMENT, AND MAKE IT SOUND SINCERE.
HI, MY NAME'S FILLMORE.
THAT'S A VERY PRETTY MACE DISPENSER.
GET LOST.

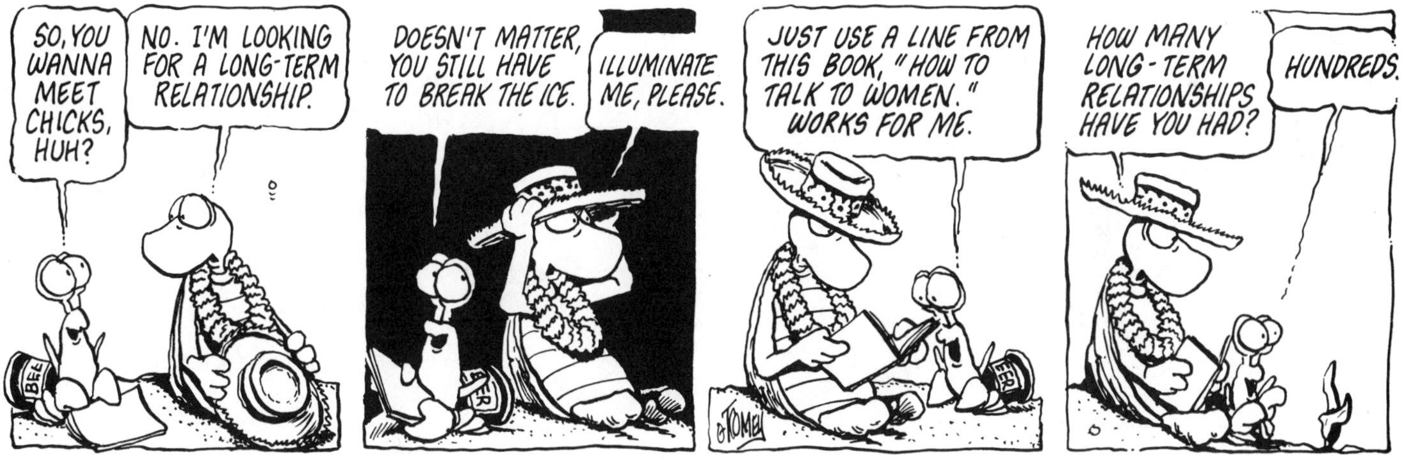
SO, YOU WANNA MEET CHICKS, HUH?
NO. I'M LOOKING FOR A LONG-TERM RELATIONSHIP.
DOESN'T MATTER, YOU STILL HAVE TO BREAK THE ICE.
ILLUMINATE ME, PLEASE.
JUST USE A LINE FROM THIS BOOK, "HOW TO TALK TO WOMEN." WORKS FOR ME.
HOW MANY LONG-TERM RELATIONSHIPS HAVE YOU HAD?
HUNDREDS.

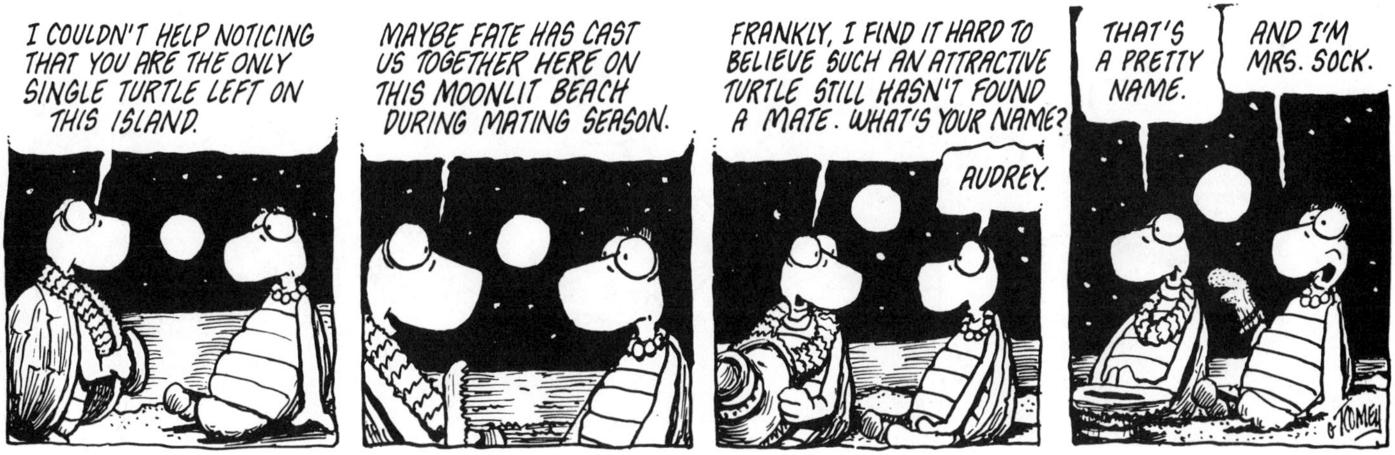
I COULDN'T HELP NOTICING THAT YOU ARE THE ONLY SINGLE TURTLE LEFT ON THIS ISLAND.
MAYBE FATE HAS CAST US TOGETHER HERE ON THIS MOONLIT BEACH DURING MATING SEASON.
FRANKLY, I FIND IT HARD TO BELIEVE SUCH AN ATTRACTIVE TURTLE STILL HASN'T FOUND A MATE. WHAT'S YOUR NAME?
AUDREY.
THAT'S A PRETTY NAME.
AND I'M MRS. SOCK.

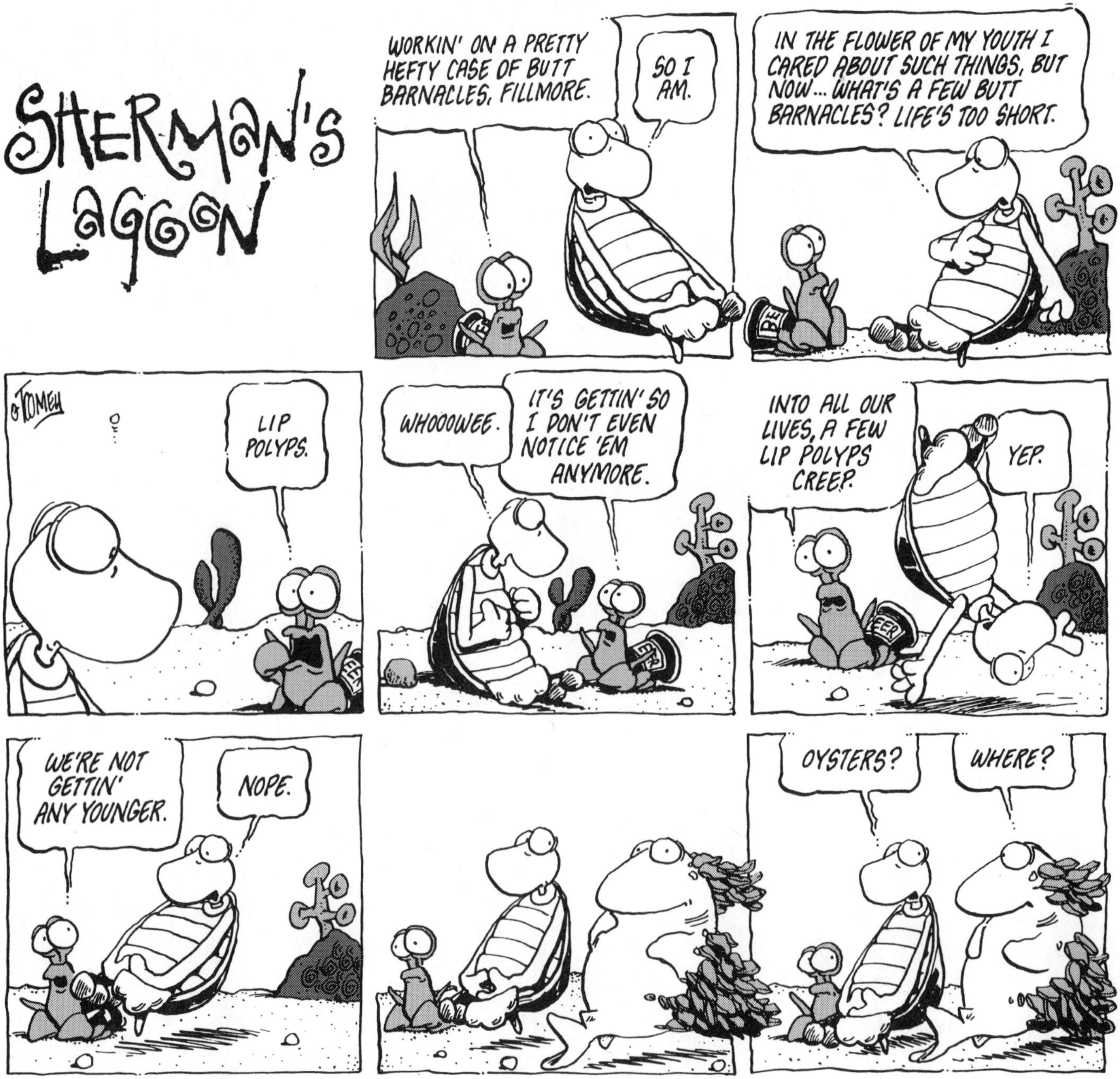
SHERMAN'S LAGOON
WORKIN' ON A PRETTY HEFTY CASE OF BUTT BARNACLES, FILLMORE.
SO I AM.
IN THE FLOWER OF MY YOUTH I CARED ABOUT SUCH THINGS, BUT NOW... WHAT'S A FEW BUTT BARNACLES? LIFE'S TOO SHORT.
TOOMEY
LIP POLYPS.
WHOOOWEE.
IT'S GETTIN' SO I DON'T EVEN NOTICE 'EM ANYMORE.
INTO ALL OUR LIVES, A FEW LIP POLYPS CREEP.
YEP.
WE'RE NOT GETTIN' ANY YOUNGER.
NOPE.
OYSTERS?
WHERE?

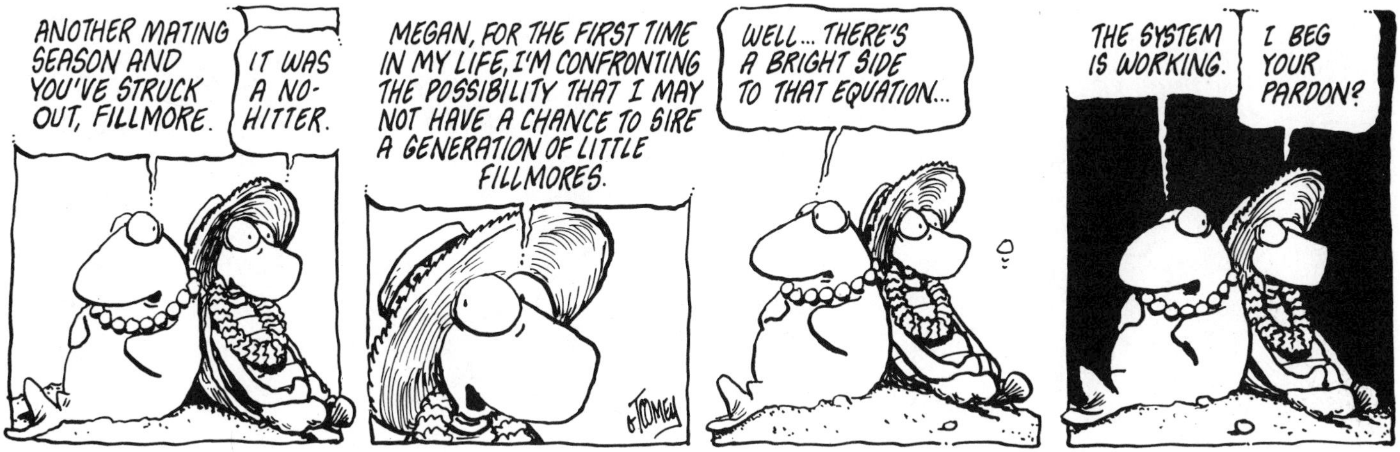
ANOTHER MATING SEASON AND YOU'VE STRUCK OUT, FILLMORE.
IT WAS A NO-HITTER.
MEGAN, FOR THE FIRST TIME IN MY LIFE, I'M CONFRONTING THE POSSIBILITY THAT I MAY NOT HAVE A CHANCE TO SIRE A GENERATION OF LITTLE FILLMORES.
WELL... THERE'S A BRIGHT SIDE TO THAT EQUATION...
THE SYSTEM IS WORKING.
I BEG YOUR PARDON?

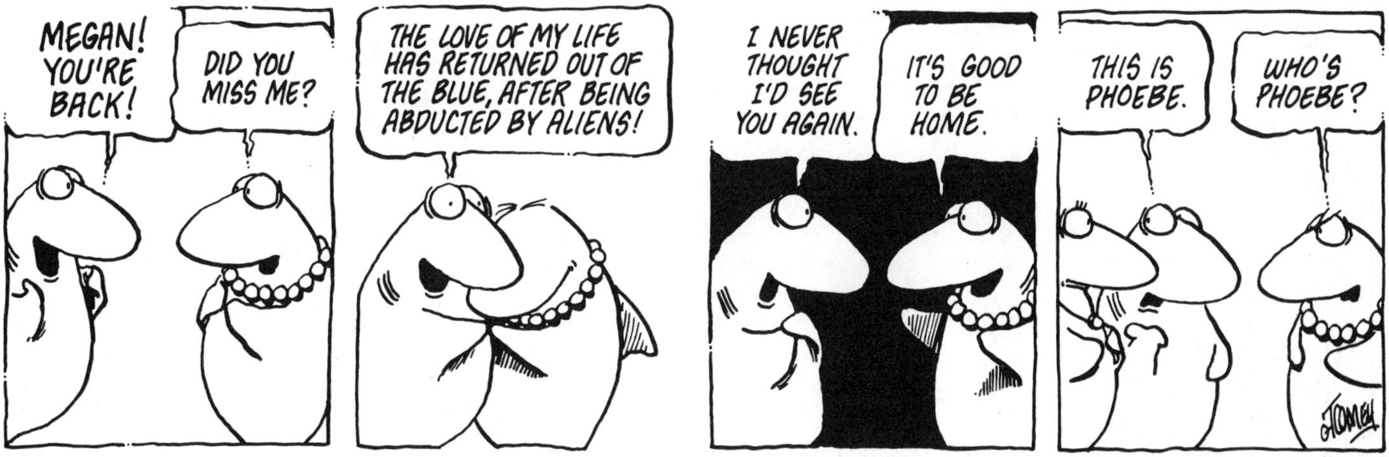
MEGAN! YOU'RE BACK!
DID YOU MISS ME?
THE LOVE OF MY LIFE HAS RETURNED OUT OF THE BLUE, AFTER BEING ABDUCTED BY ALIENS!
I NEVER THOUGHT I'D SEE YOU AGAIN.
IT'S GOOD TO BE HOME.
THIS IS PHOEBE.
WHO'S PHOEBE?

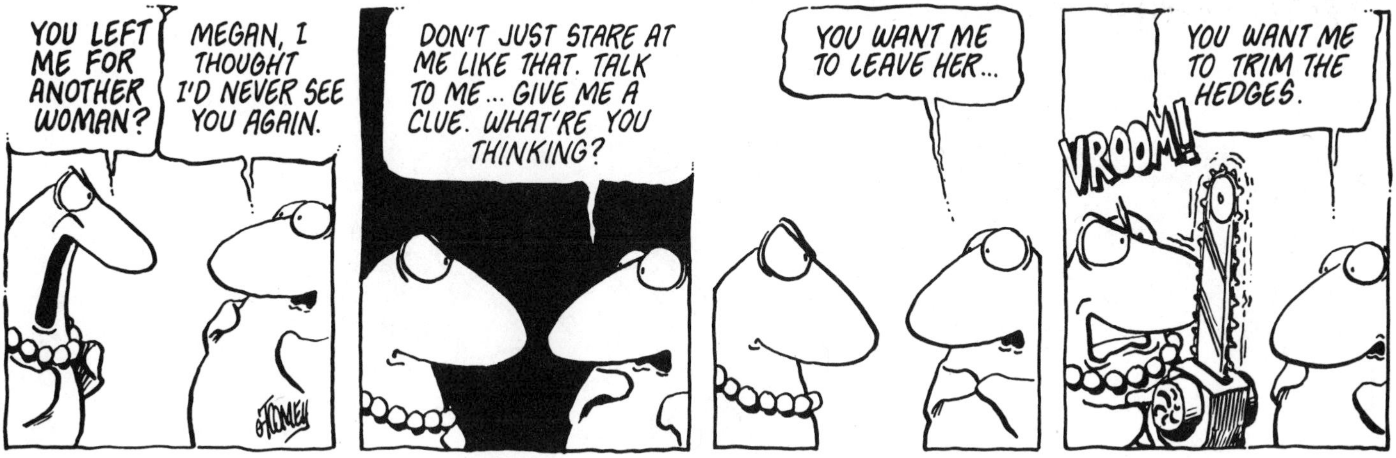
YOU LEFT ME FOR ANOTHER WOMAN?
MEGAN, I THOUGHT I'D NEVER SEE YOU AGAIN.
DON'T JUST STARE AT ME LIKE THAT. TALK TO ME... GIVE ME A CLUE. WHAT'RE YOU THINKING?
YOU WANT ME TO LEAVE HER...
YOU WANT ME TO TRIM THE HEDGES.
VROOM!

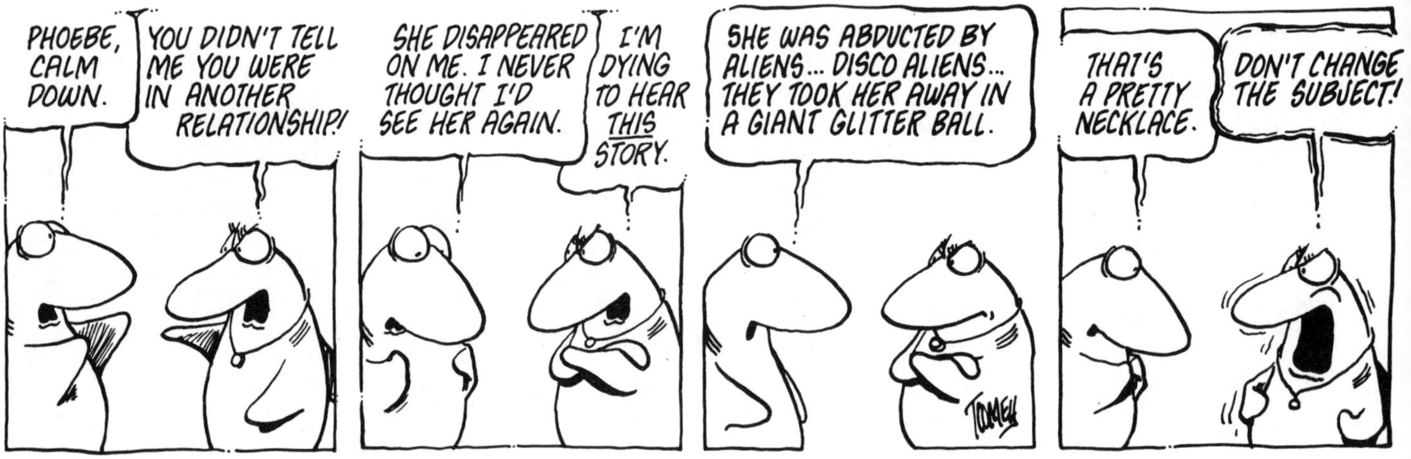
PHOEBE, CALM DOWN.
YOU DIDN'T TELL ME YOU WERE IN ANOTHER RELATIONSHIP!
SHE DISAPPEARED ON ME. I NEVER THOUGHT I'D SEE HER AGAIN.
I'M DYING TO HEAR THIS STORY.
SHE WAS ABDUCTED BY ALIENS... DISCO ALIENS... THEY TOOK HER AWAY IN A GIANT GLITTER BALL.
THAT'S A PRETTY NECKLACE.
DON'T CHANGE THE SUBJECT!
TOOMEY

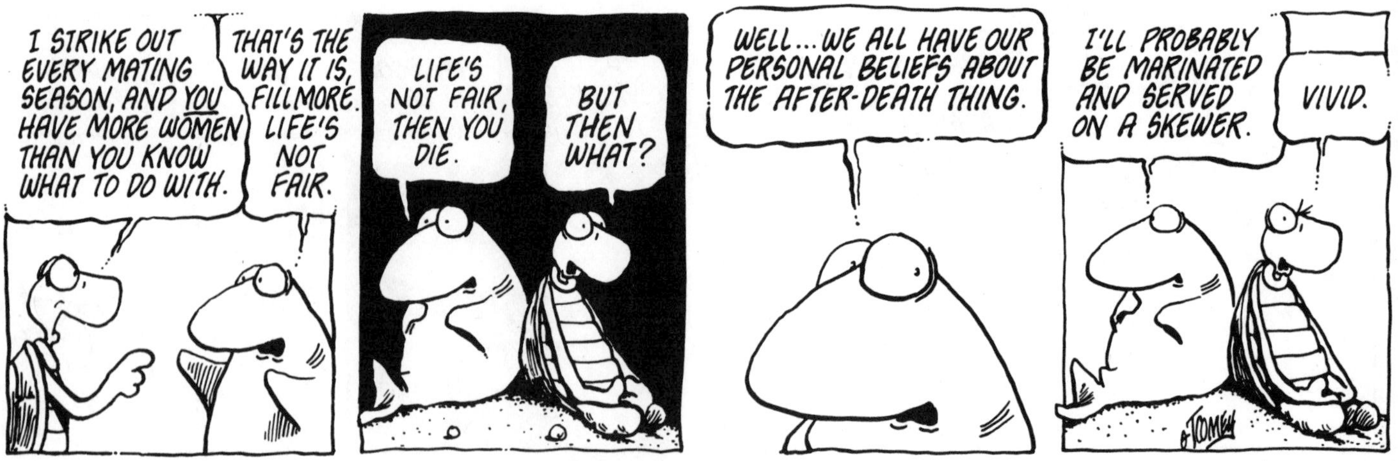
I STRIKE OUT EVERY MATING SEASON, AND YOU HAVE MORE WOMEN THAN YOU KNOW WHAT TO DO WITH.
THAT'S THE WAY IT IS, FILLMORE. LIFE'S NOT FAIR.
LIFE'S NOT FAIR, THEN YOU DIE.
BUT THEN WHAT?
WELL... WE ALL HAVE OUR PERSONAL BELIEFS ABOUT THE AFTER-DEATH THING.
I'LL PROBABLY BE MARINATED AND SERVED ON A SKEWER.
VIVID.
TOOMEY

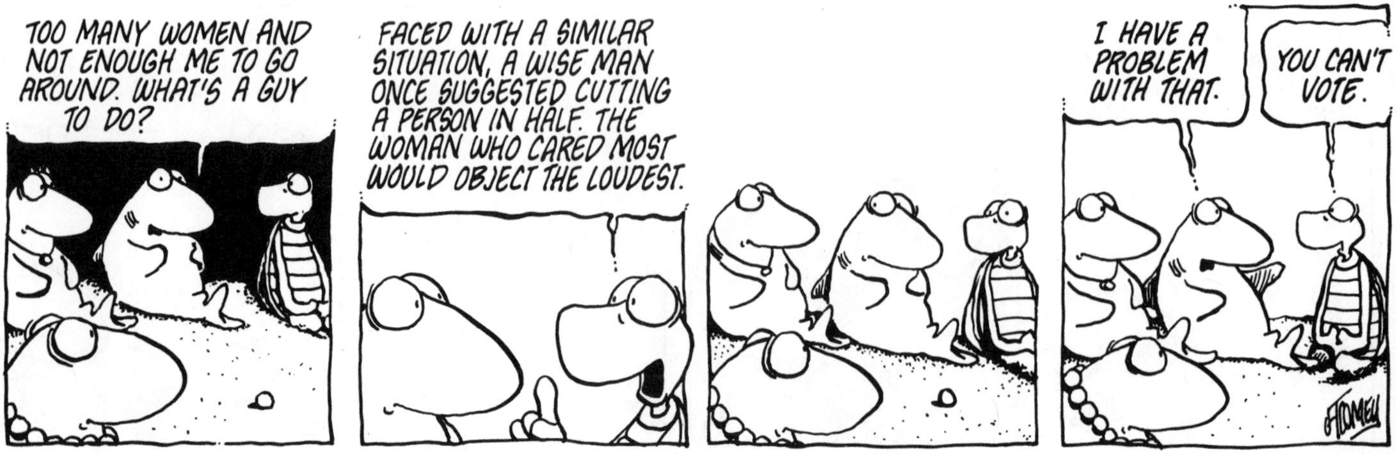
TOO MANY WOMEN AND NOT ENOUGH ME TO GO AROUND. WHAT'S A GUY TO DO?
FACED WITH A SIMILAR SITUATION, A WISE MAN ONCE SUGGESTED CUTTING A PERSON IN HALF. THE WOMAN WHO CARED MOST WOULD OBJECT THE LOUDEST.
I HAVE A PROBLEM WITH THAT.
YOU CAN'T VOTE.
TOOMEY

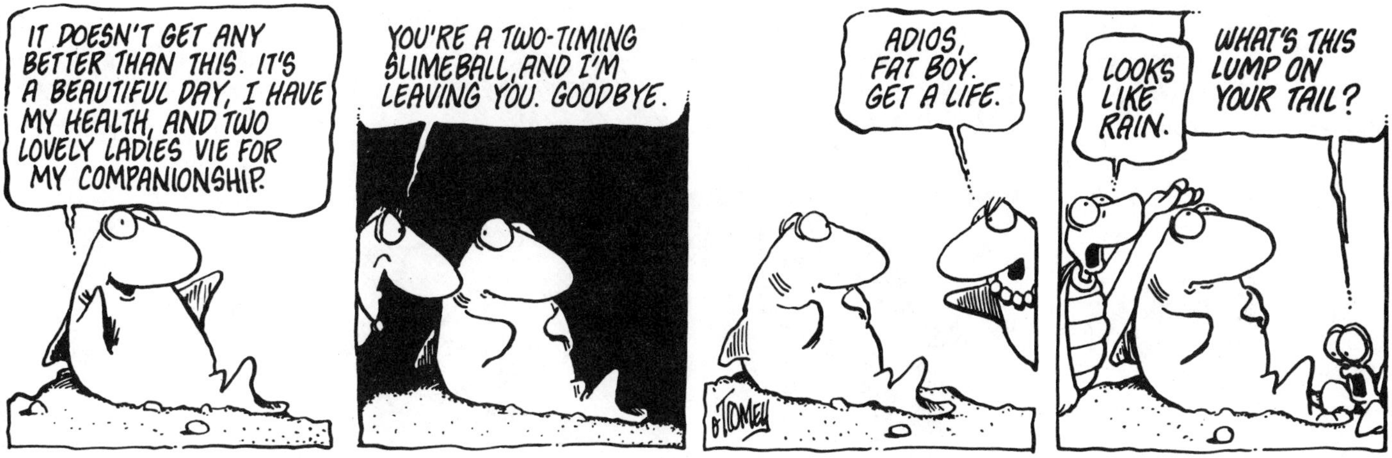
IT DOESN'T GET ANY BETTER THAN THIS. IT'S A BEAUTIFUL DAY, I HAVE MY HEALTH, AND TWO LOVELY LADIES VIE FOR MY COMPANIONSHIP.
YOU'RE A TWO-TIMING SLIMEBALL, AND I'M LEAVING YOU. GOODBYE.
ADIOS, FAT BOY. GET A LIFE.
LOOKS LIKE RAIN.
WHAT'S THIS LUMP ON YOUR TAIL?

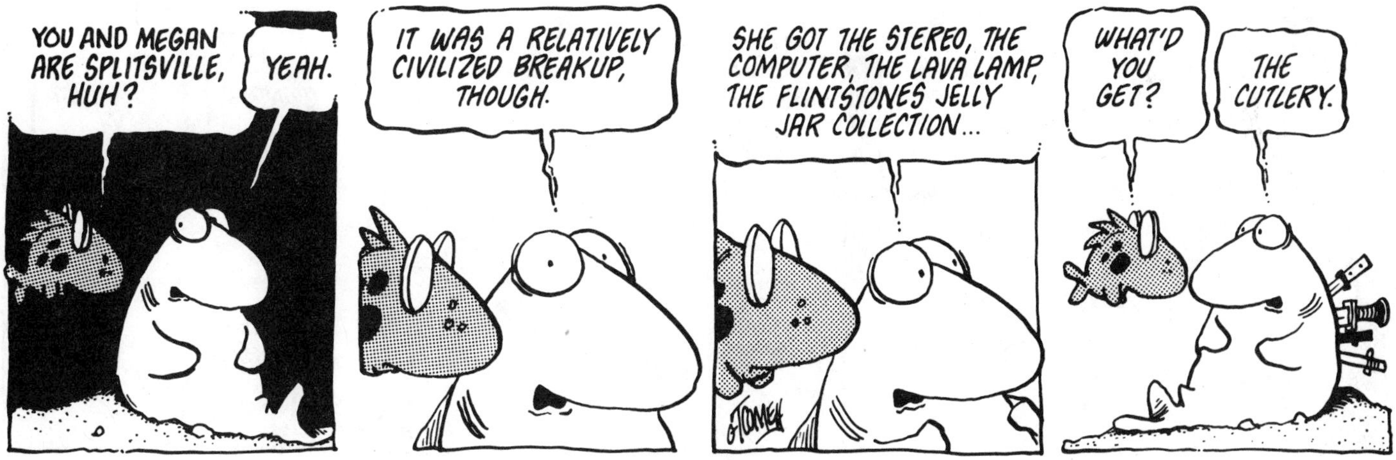
YOU AND MEGAN ARE SPLITSVILLE, HUH?
YEAH.
IT WAS A RELATIVELY CIVILIZED BREAKUP, THOUGH.
SHE GOT THE STEREO, THE COMPUTER, THE LAVA LAMP, THE FLINTSTONES JELLY JAR COLLECTION...
WHAT'D YOU GET?
THE CUTLERY.

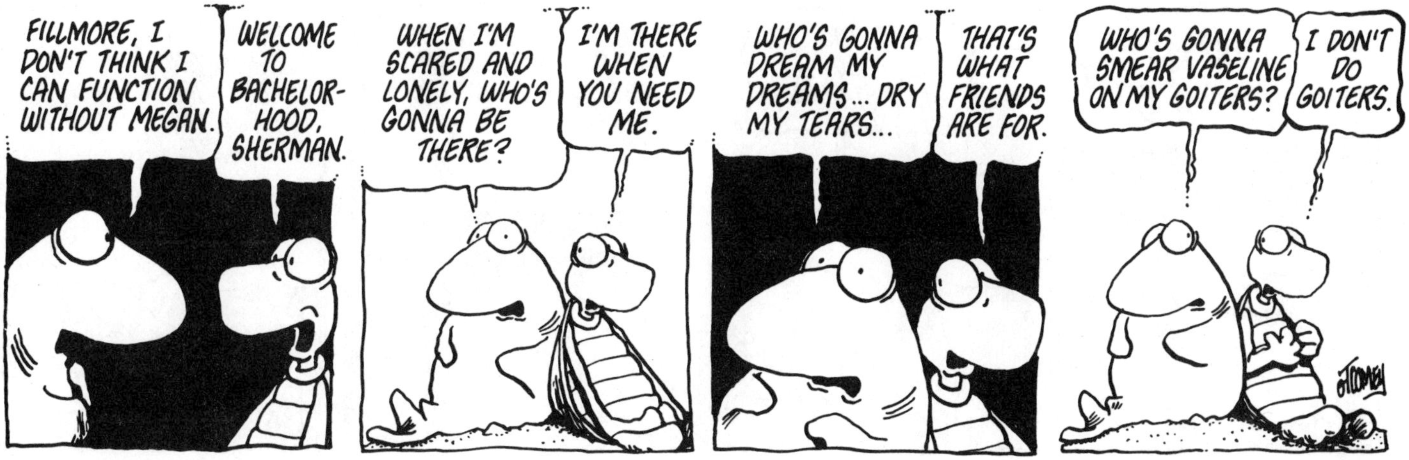
FILLMORE, I DON'T THINK I CAN FUNCTION WITHOUT MEGAN.
WELCOME TO BACHELOR-HOOD, SHERMAN.
WHEN I'M SCARED AND LONELY, WHO'S GONNA BE THERE?
I'M THERE WHEN YOU NEED ME.
WHO'S GONNA DREAM MY DREAMS... DRY MY TEARS...
THAT'S WHAT FRIENDS ARE FOR.
WHO'S GONNA SMEAR VASELINE ON MY GOITERS?
I DON'T DO GOITERS.

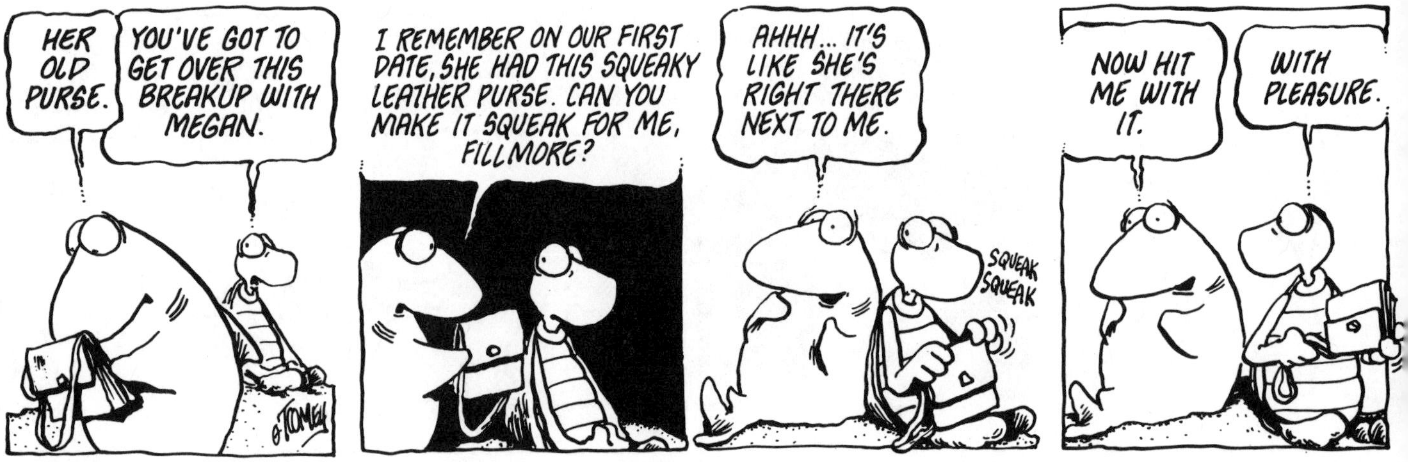
HER OLD PURSE.
YOU'VE GOT TO GET OVER THIS BREAKUP WITH MEGAN.
I REMEMBER ON OUR FIRST DATE, SHE HAD THIS SQUEAKY LEATHER PURSE. CAN YOU MAKE IT SQUEAK FOR ME, FILLMORE?
AHHH... IT'S LIKE SHE'S RIGHT THERE NEXT TO ME.
SQUEAK SQUEAK
NOW HIT ME WITH IT.
WITH PLEASURE.

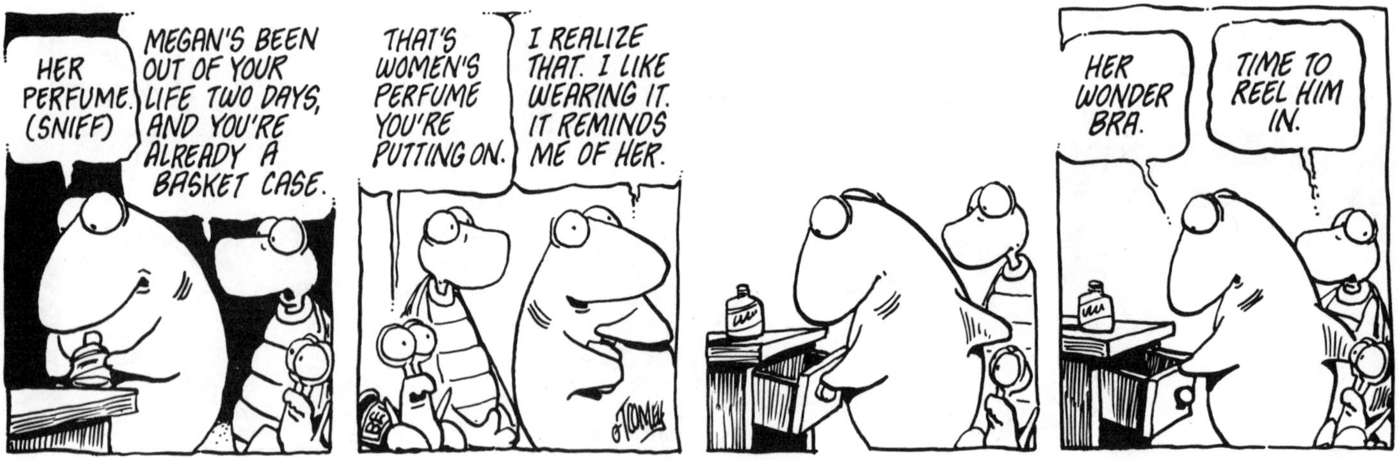
HER PERFUME. (SNIFF)
MEGAN'S BEEN OUT OF YOUR LIFE TWO DAYS, AND YOU'RE ALREADY A BASKET CASE.
THAT'S WOMEN'S PERFUME YOU'RE PUTTING ON.
I REALIZE THAT. I LIKE WEARING IT. IT REMINDS ME OF HER.
HER WONDER BRA.
TIME TO REEL HIM IN.

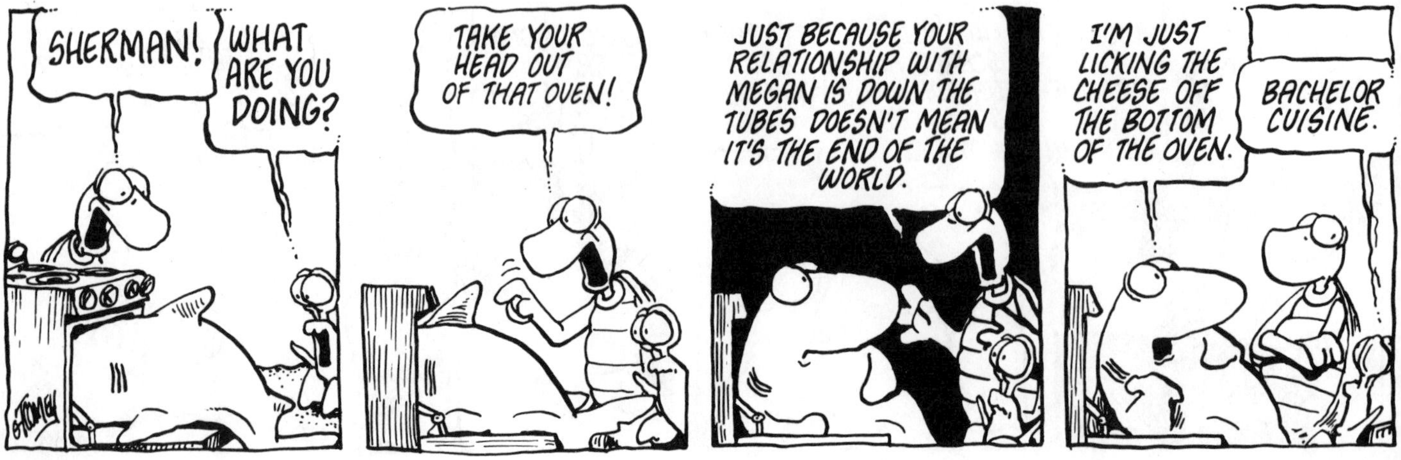
SHERMAN!
WHAT ARE YOU DOING?
TAKE YOUR HEAD OUT OF THAT OVEN!
JUST BECAUSE YOUR RELATIONSHIP WITH MEGAN IS DOWN THE TUBES DOESN'T MEAN IT'S THE END OF THE WORLD.
I'M JUST LICKING THE CHEESE OFF THE BOTTOM OF THE OVEN.
BACHELOR CUISINE.

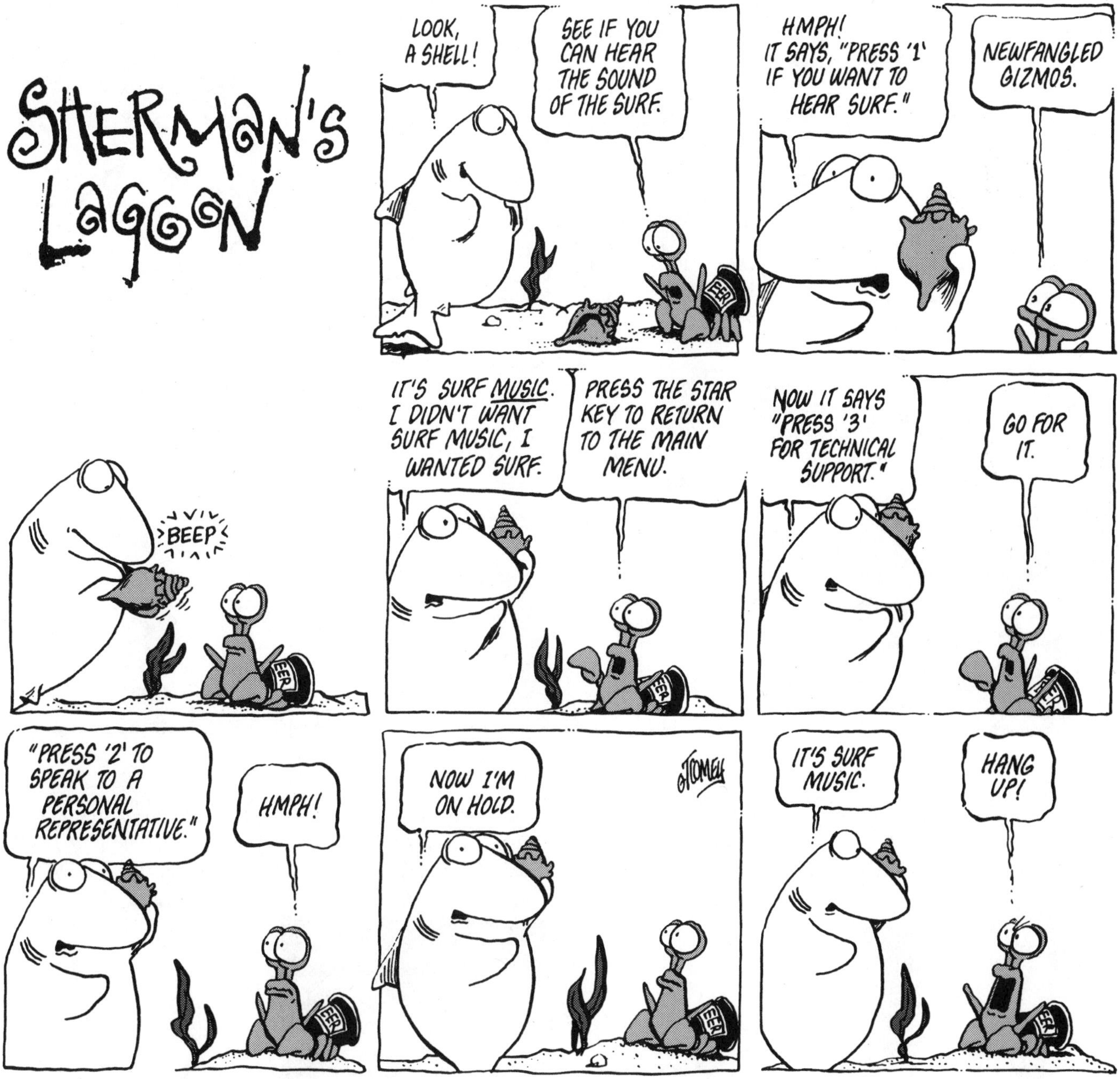
SHERMAN'S LAGOON
LOOK, A SHELL!
SEE IF YOU CAN HEAR THE SOUND OF THE SURF.
HMPH! IT SAYS, "PRESS '1' IF YOU WANT TO HEAR SURF."
NEWFANGLED GIZMOS.
BEEP
IT'S SURF MUSIC. I DIDN'T WANT SURF MUSIC, I WANTED SURF.
PRESS THE STAR KEY TO RETURN TO THE MAIN MENU.
NOW IT SAYS "PRESS '3' FOR TECHNICAL SUPPORT."
GO FOR IT.
"PRESS '2' TO SPEAK TO A PERSONAL REPRESENTATIVE."
HMPH!
NOW I'M ON HOLD.
IT'S SURF MUSIC.
HANG UP!

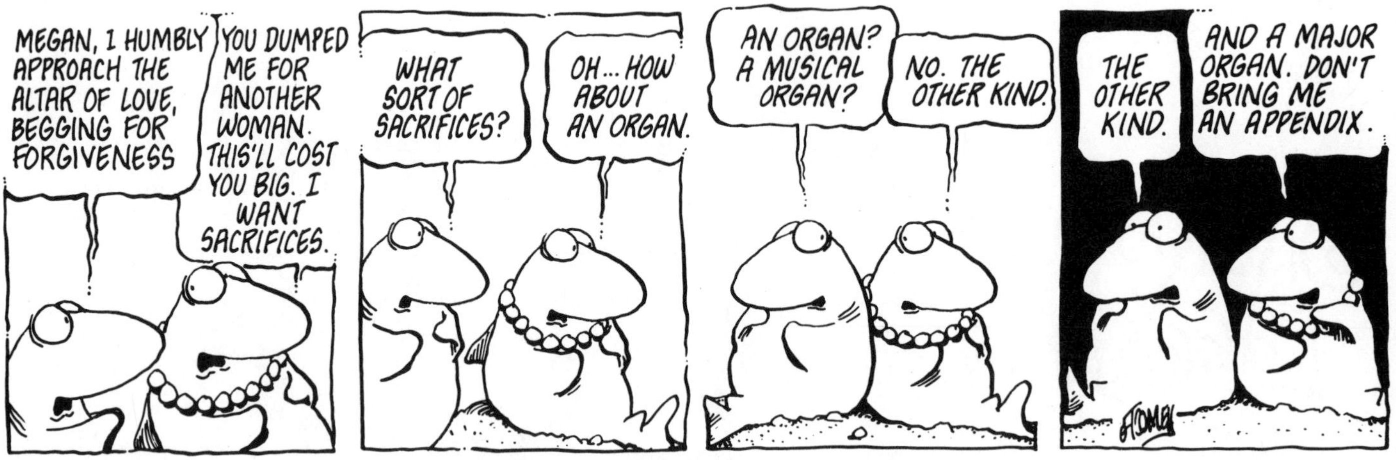
MEGAN, I HUMBLY APPROACH THE ALTAR OF LOVE, BEGGING FOR FORGIVENESS
YOU DUMPED ME FOR ANOTHER WOMAN. THIS'LL COST YOU BIG. I WANT SACRIFICES.
WHAT SORT OF SACRIFICES?
OH... HOW ABOUT AN ORGAN.
AN ORGAN? A MUSICAL ORGAN?
NO. THE OTHER KIND.
THE OTHER KIND.
AND A MAJOR ORGAN. DON'T BRING ME AN APPENDIX.

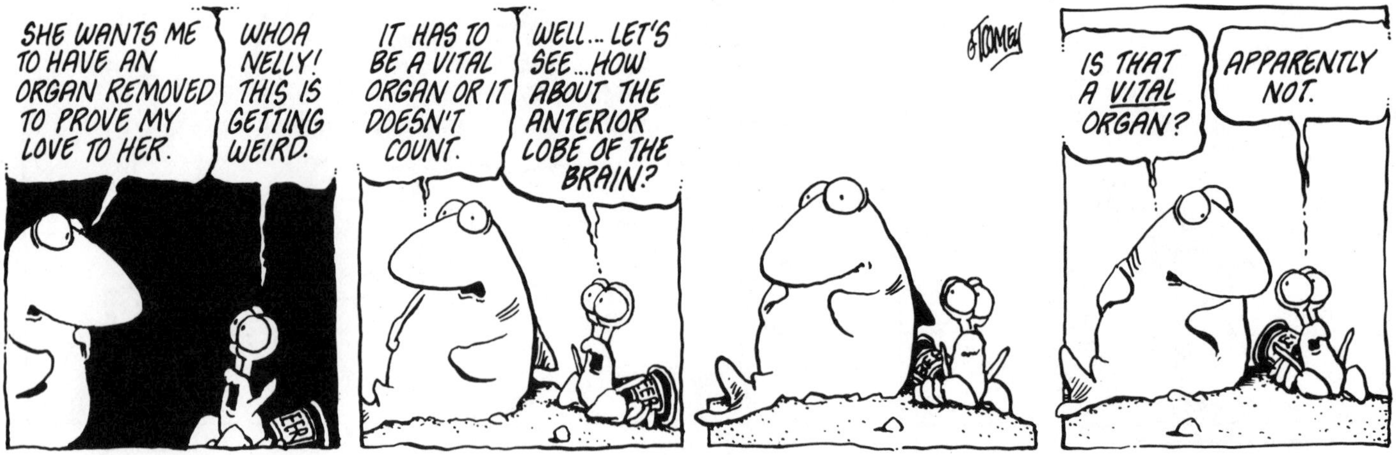
SHE WANTS ME TO HAVE AN ORGAN REMOVED TO PROVE MY LOVE TO HER.
WHOA NELLY! THIS IS GETTING WEIRD.
IT HAS TO BE A VITAL ORGAN OR IT DOESN'T COUNT.
WELL... LET'S SEE... HOW ABOUT THE ANTERIOR LOBE OF THE BRAIN?
IS THAT A VITAL ORGAN?
APPARENTLY NOT.

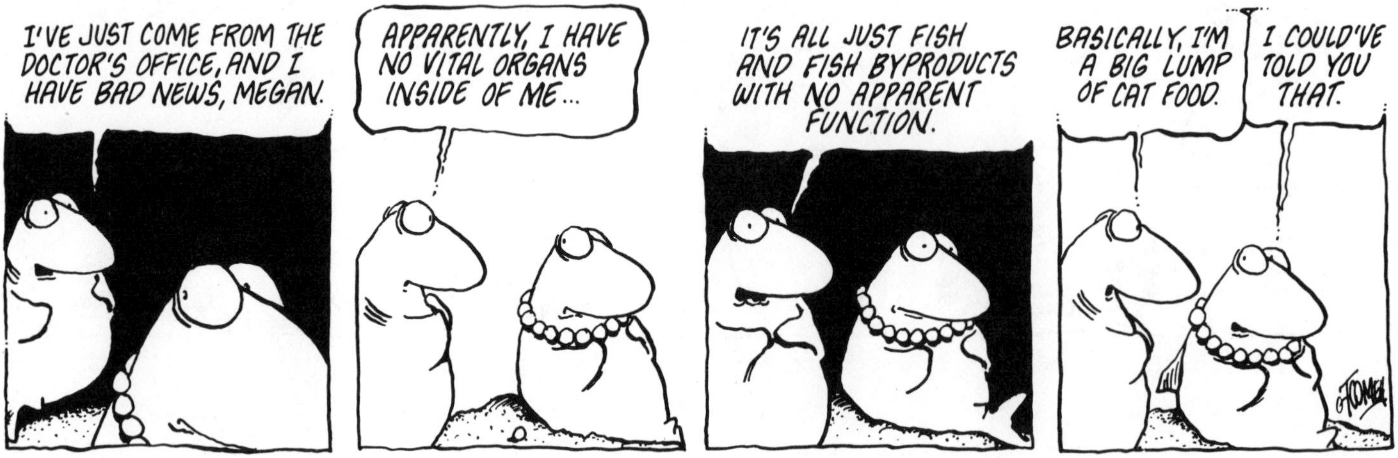
I'VE JUST COME FROM THE DOCTOR'S OFFICE, AND I HAVE BAD NEWS, MEGAN.
APPARENTLY, I HAVE NO VITAL ORGANS INSIDE OF ME...
IT'S ALL JUST FISH AND FISH BYPRODUCTS WITH NO APPARENT FUNCTION.
BASICALLY, I'M A BIG LUMP OF CAT FOOD.
I COULD'VE TOLD YOU THAT.

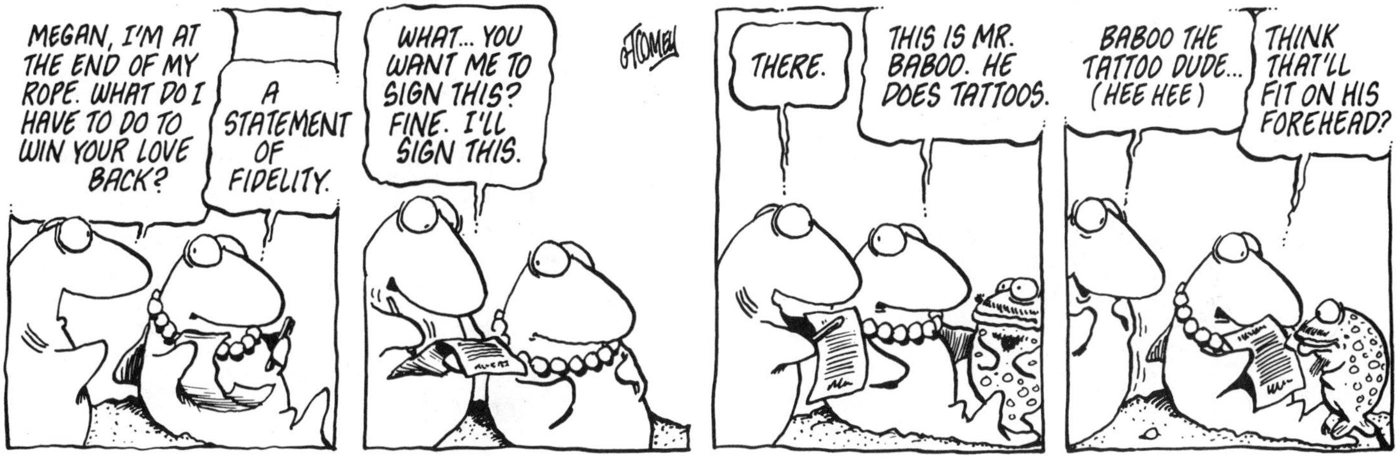
MEGAN, I'M AT THE END OF MY ROPE. WHAT DO I HAVE TO DO TO WIN YOUR LOVE BACK?
A STATEMENT OF FIDELITY.
WHAT... YOU WANT ME TO SIGN THIS? FINE. I'LL SIGN THIS.
THERE.
THIS IS MR. BABOO. HE DOES TATTOOS.
BABOO THE TATTOO DUDE... (HEE HEE)
THINK THAT'LL FIT ON HIS FOREHEAD?

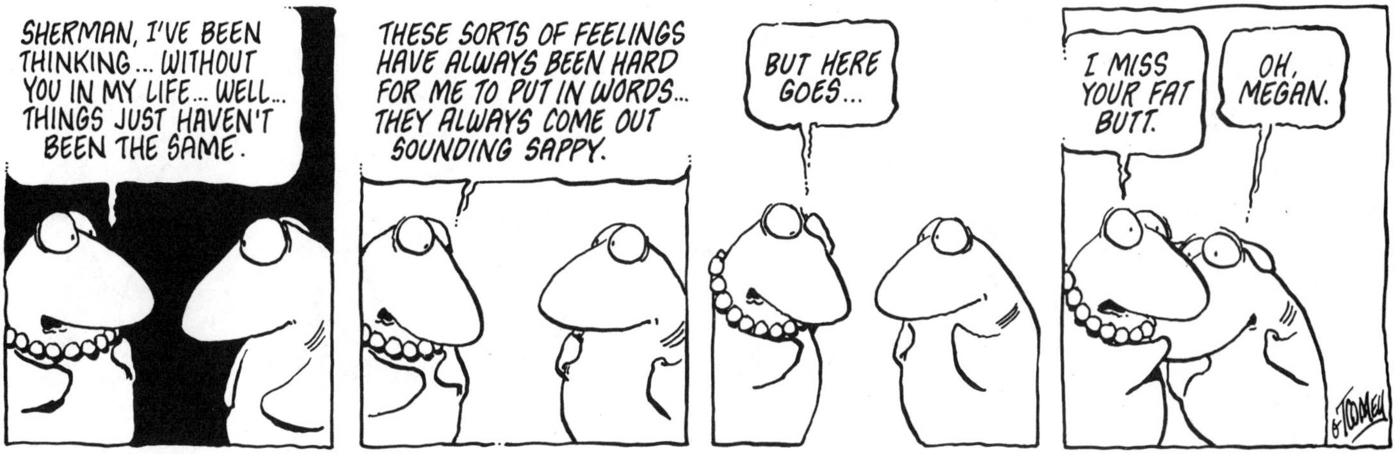
SHERMAN, I'VE BEEN THINKING... WITHOUT YOU IN MY LIFE... WELL... THINGS JUST HAVEN'T BEEN THE SAME.
THESE SORTS OF FEELINGS HAVE ALWAYS BEEN HARD FOR ME TO PUT IN WORDS... THEY ALWAYS COME OUT SOUNDING SAPPY.
BUT HERE GOES...
I MISS YOUR FAT BUTT.
OH, MEGAN.

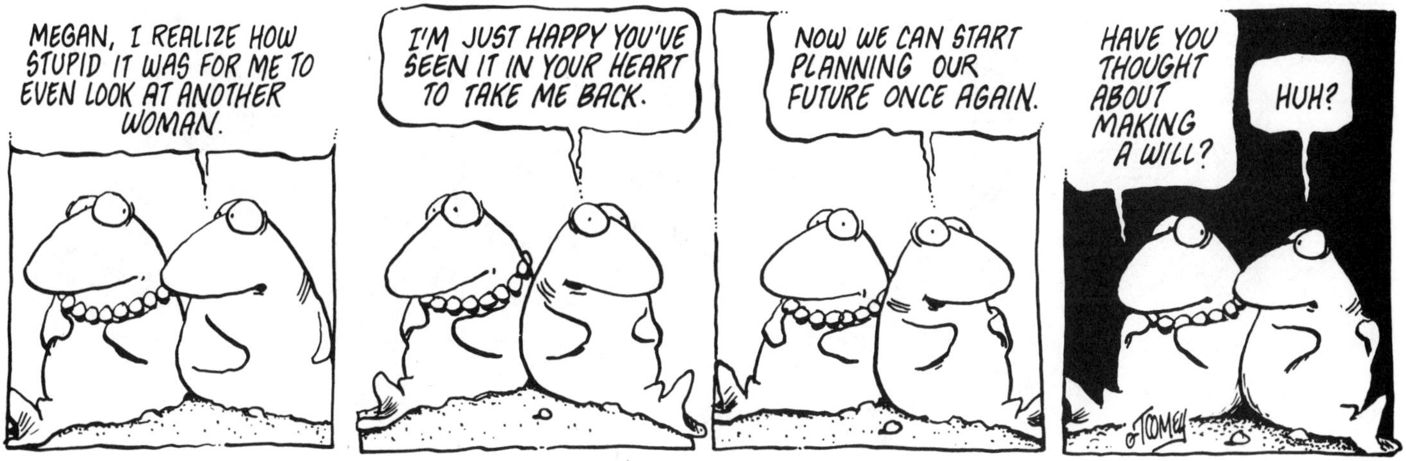
MEGAN, I REALIZE HOW STUPID IT WAS FOR ME TO EVEN LOOK AT ANOTHER WOMAN.
I'M JUST HAPPY YOU'VE SEEN IT IN YOUR HEART TO TAKE ME BACK.
NOW WE CAN START PLANNING OUR FUTURE ONCE AGAIN.
HAVE YOU THOUGHT ABOUT MAKING A WILL?
HUH?

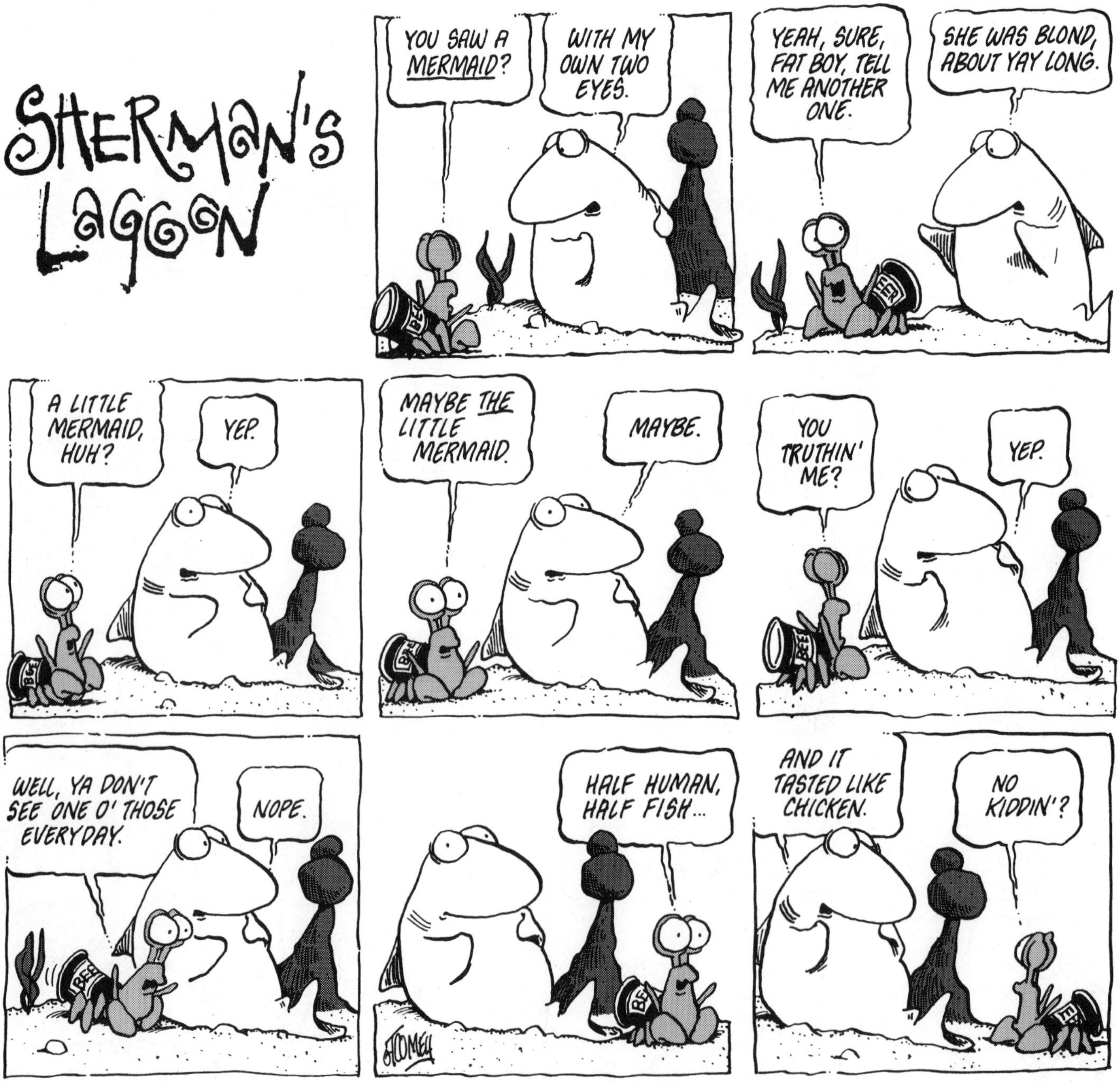
SHERMAN'S LAGOON
YOU SAW A MERMAID?
WITH MY OWN TWO EYES.
YEAH, SURE, FAT BOY, TELL ME ANOTHER ONE.
SHE WAS BLOND, ABOUT YAY LONG.
A LITTLE MERMAID, HUH?
YEP.
MAYBE THE LITTLE MERMAID.
MAYBE.
YOU TRUTHIN' ME?
YEP.
WELL, YA DON'T SEE ONE O' THOSE EVERYDAY.
NOPE.
HALF HUMAN, HALF FISH...
AND IT TASTED LIKE CHICKEN.
NO KIDDIN'?

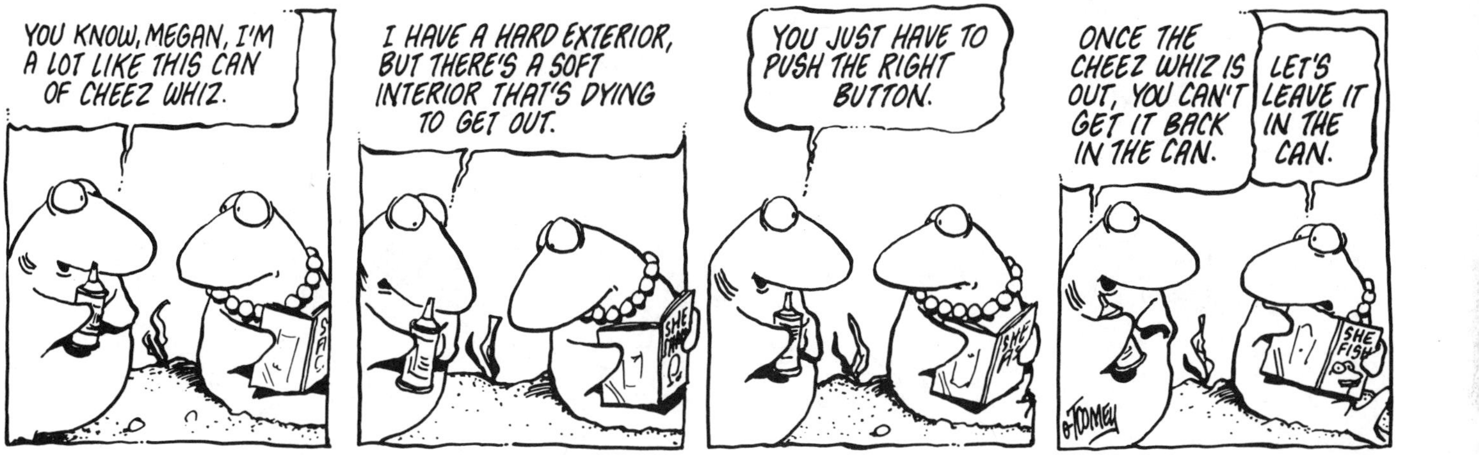
YOU KNOW, MEGAN, I'M A LOT LIKE THIS CAN OF CHEEZ WHIZ.
I HAVE A HARD EXTERIOR, BUT THERE'S A SOFT INTERIOR THAT'S DYING TO GET OUT.
YOU JUST HAVE TO PUSH THE RIGHT BUTTON.
ONCE THE CHEEZ WHIZ IS OUT, YOU CAN'T GET IT BACK IN THE CAN.
LET'S LEAVE IT IN THE CAN.
SHE FISH

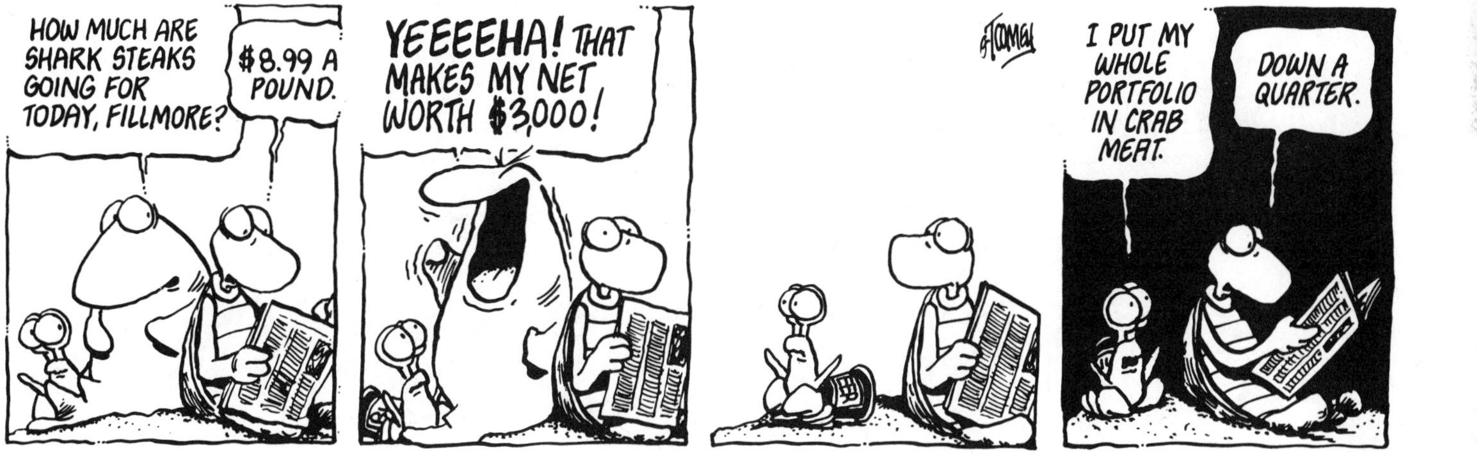
HOW MUCH ARE SHARK STEAKS GOING FOR TODAY, FILLMORE?
$8.99 A POUND.
YEEEEHA! THAT MAKES MY NET WORTH $3,000!
I PUT MY WHOLE PORTFOLIO IN CRAB MEAT.
DOWN A QUARTER.

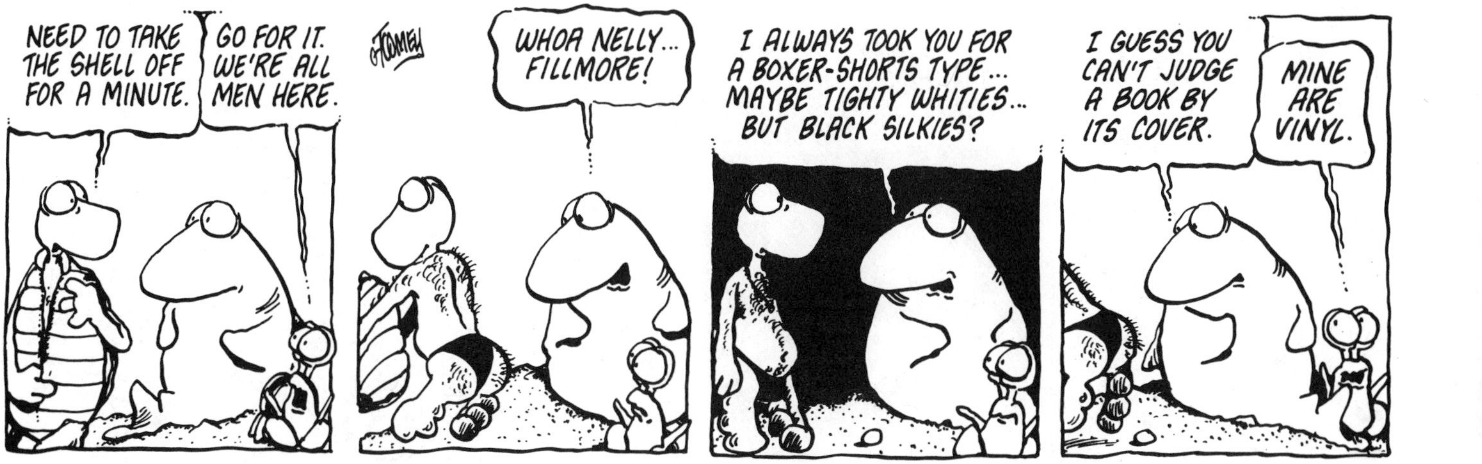
NEED TO TAKE THE SHELL OFF FOR A MINUTE.
GO FOR IT. WE'RE ALL MEN HERE.
WHOA NELLY... FILLMORE!
I ALWAYS TOOK YOU FOR A BOXER-SHORTS TYPE... MAYBE TIGHTY WHITIES... BUT BLACK SILKIES?
I GUESS YOU CAN'T JUDGE A BOOK BY ITS COVER.
MINE ARE VINYL.

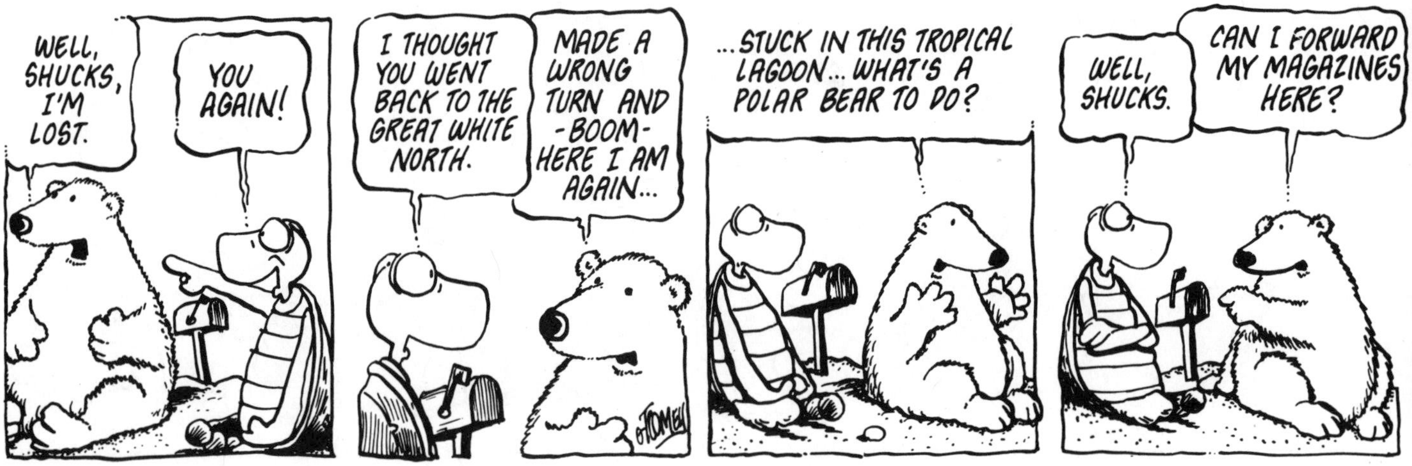
WELL, SHUCKS, I'M LOST.
YOU AGAIN!
I THOUGHT YOU WENT BACK TO THE GREAT WHITE NORTH.
MADE A WRONG TURN AND -BOOM- HERE I AM AGAIN...
...STUCK IN THIS TROPICAL LAGOON... WHAT'S A POLAR BEAR TO DO?
WELL, SHUCKS.
CAN I FORWARD MY MAGAZINES HERE?

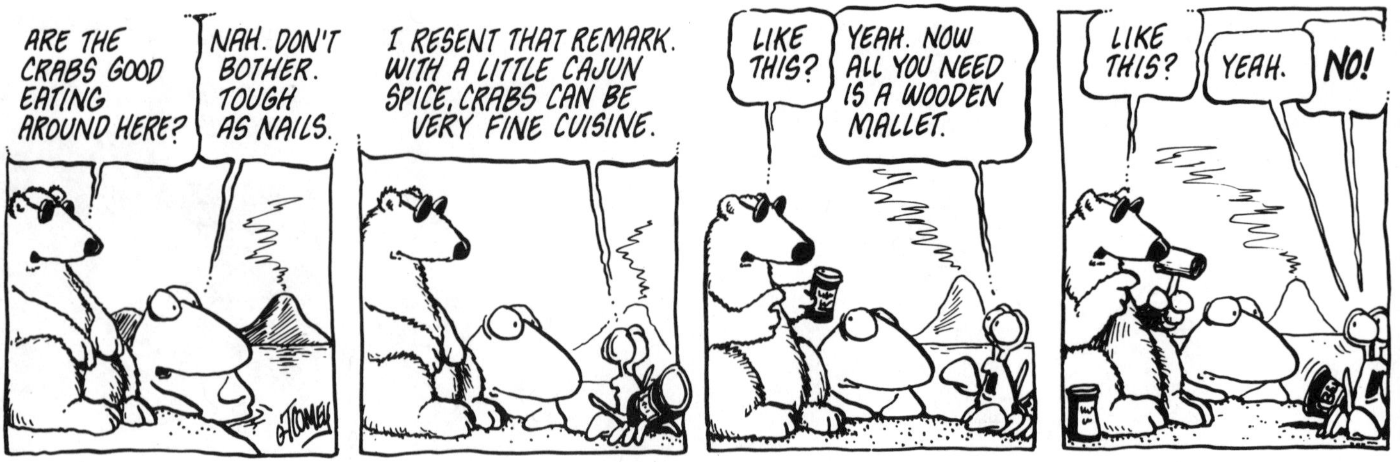
ARE THE CRABS GOOD EATING AROUND HERE?
NAH. DON'T BOTHER. TOUGH AS NAILS.
I RESENT THAT REMARK. WITH A LITTLE CAJUN SPICE, CRABS CAN BE VERY FINE CUISINE.
LIKE THIS?
YEAH. NOW ALL YOU NEED IS A WOODEN MALLET.
LIKE THIS?
YEAH.
NO!

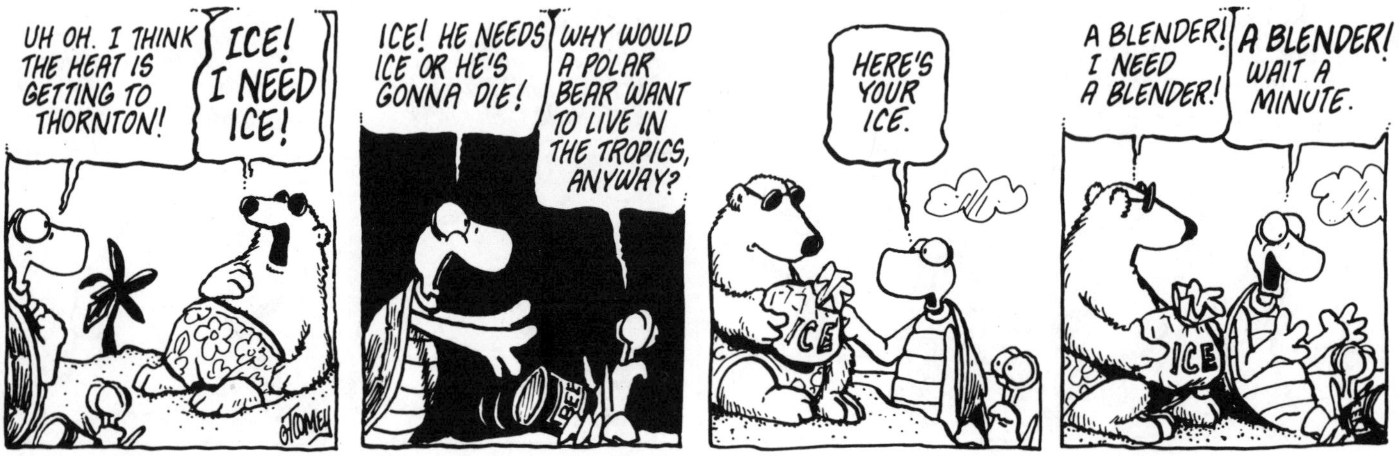
UH OH. I THINK THE HEAT IS GETTING TO THORNTON!
ICE! I NEED ICE!
ICE! HE NEEDS ICE OR HE'S GONNA DIE!
WHY WOULD A POLAR BEAR WANT TO LIVE IN THE TROPICS, ANYWAY?
HERE'S YOUR ICE.
ICE
A BLENDER! I NEED A BLENDER!
A BLENDER! WAIT A MINUTE.
ICE

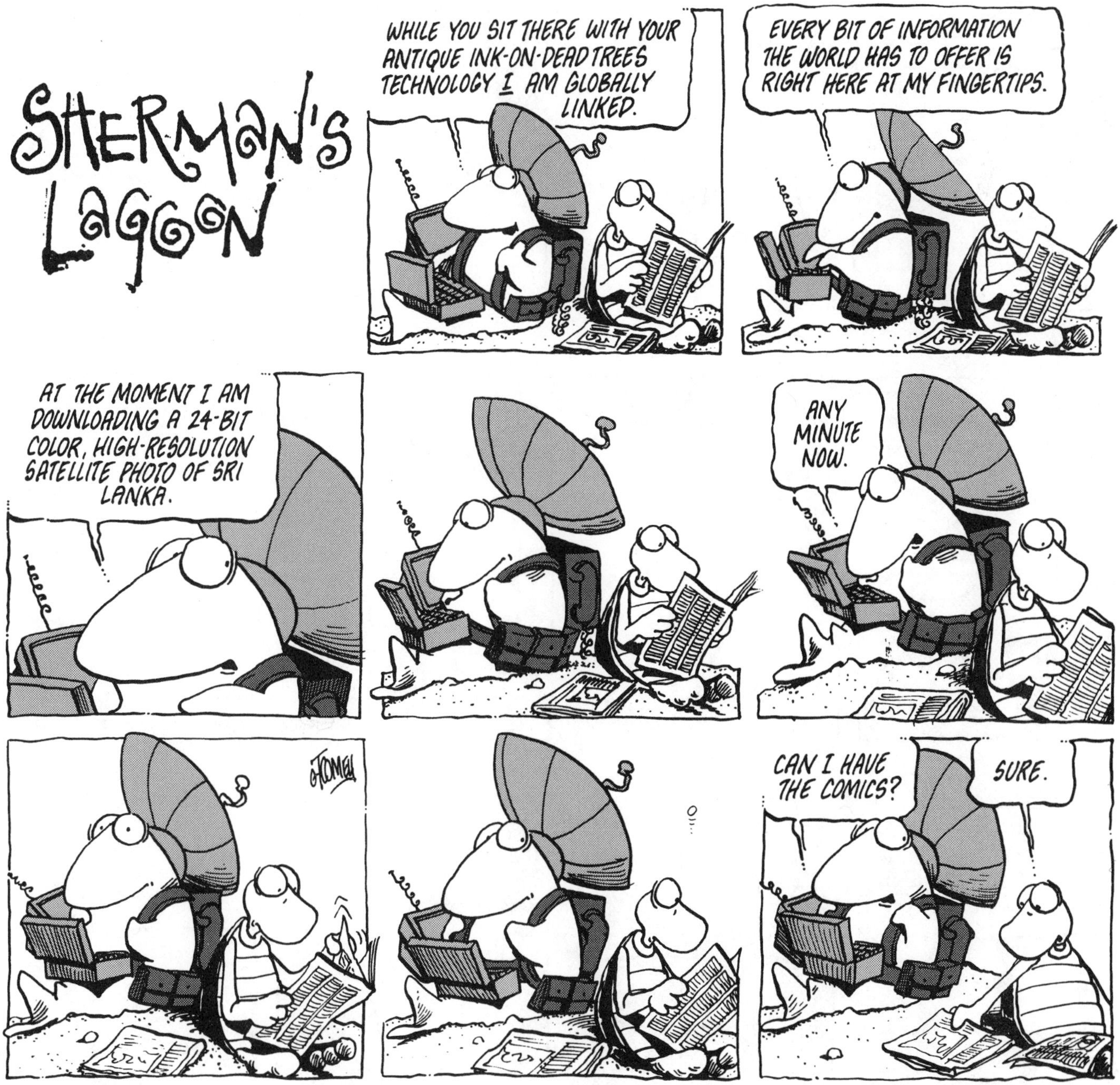
SHERMAN'S LAGOON
WHILE YOU SIT THERE WITH YOUR ANTIQUE INK-ON-DEAD TREES TECHNOLOGY I AM GLOBALLY LINKED.
EVERY BIT OF INFORMATION THE WORLD HAS TO OFFER IS RIGHT HERE AT MY FINGERTIPS.
AT THE MOMENT I AM DOWNLOADING A 24-BIT COLOR, HIGH-RESOLUTION SATELLITE PHOTO OF SRI LANKA.
ANY MINUTE NOW.
CAN I HAVE THE COMICS?
SURE.

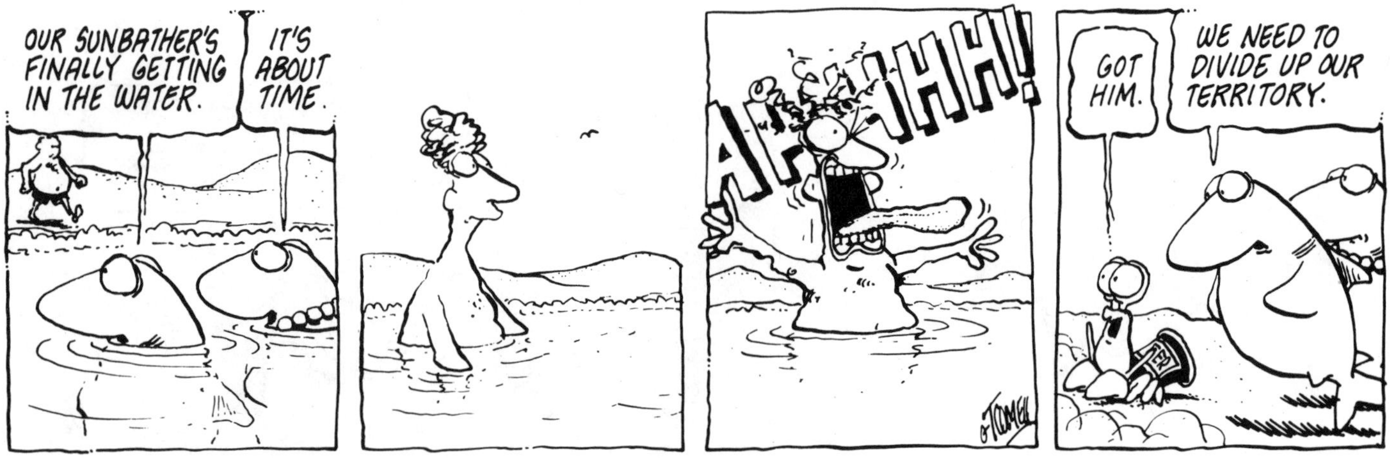
OUR SUNBATHER'S FINALLY GETTING IN THE WATER.
IT'S ABOUT TIME.
GOT HIM.
WE NEED TO DIVIDE UP OUR TERRITORY.

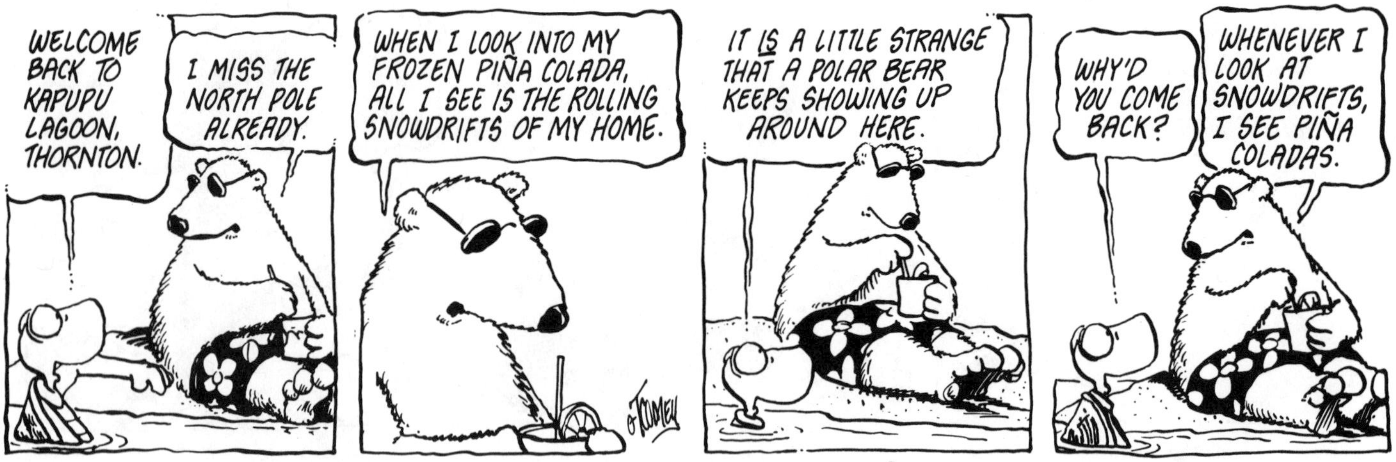
WELCOME BACK TO KAPUPU LAGOON, THORNTON.
I MISS THE NORTH POLE ALREADY.
WHEN I LOOK INTO MY FROZEN PIÑA COLADA, ALL I SEE IS THE ROLLING SNOWDRIFTS OF MY HOME.
IT IS A LITTLE STRANGE THAT A POLAR BEAR KEEPS SHOWING UP AROUND HERE.
WHY'D YOU COME BACK?
WHENEVER I LOOK AT SNOWDRIFTS, I SEE PIÑA COLADAS.

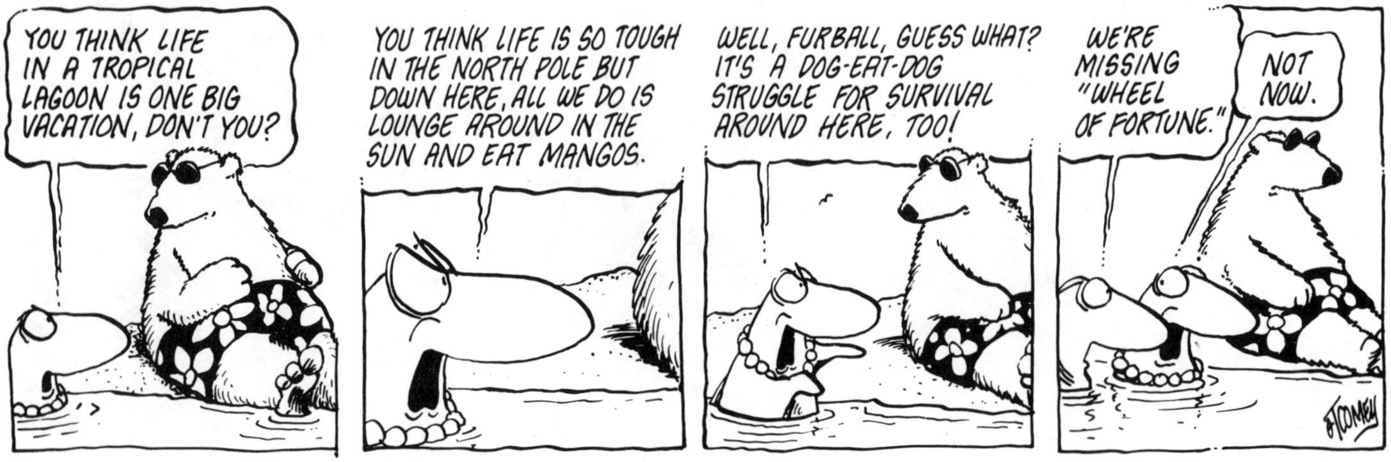
YOU THINK LIFE IN A TROPICAL LAGOON IS ONE BIG VACATION, DON'T YOU?
YOU THINK LIFE IS SO TOUGH IN THE NORTH POLE BUT DOWN HERE, ALL WE DO IS LOUNGE AROUND IN THE SUN AND EAT MANGOS.
WELL, FURBALL, GUESS WHAT? IT'S A DOG-EAT-DOG STRUGGLE FOR SURVIVAL AROUND HERE, TOO!
WE'RE MISSING "WHEEL OF FORTUNE."
NOT NOW.

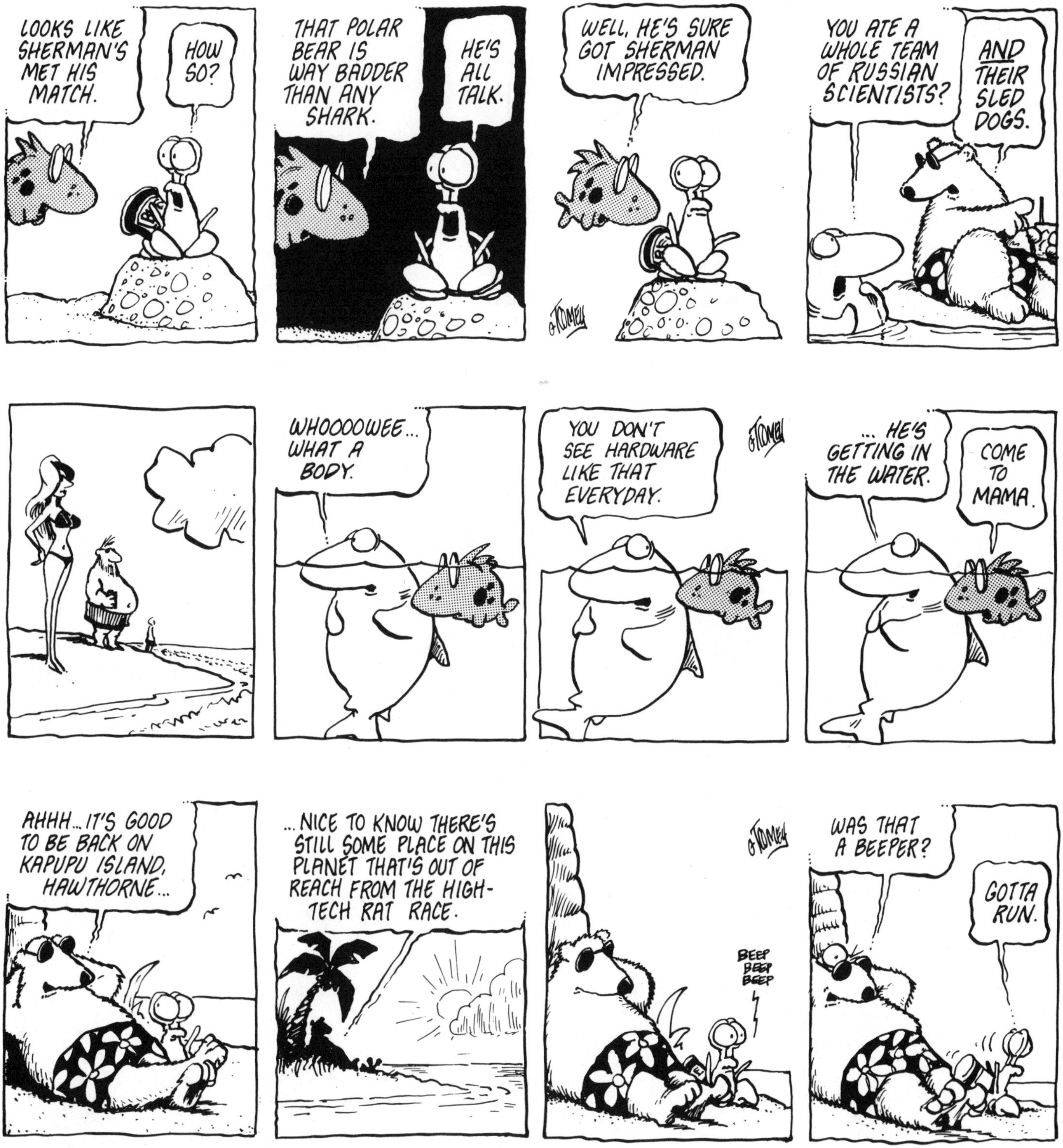
LOOKS LIKE SHERMAN'S MET HIS MATCH.
HOW SO?
THAT POLAR BEAR IS WAY BADDER THAN ANY SHARK.
HE'S ALL TALK.
WELL, HE'S SURE GOT SHERMAN IMPRESSED.
YOU ATE A WHOLE TEAM OF RUSSIAN SCIENTISTS?
AND THEIR SLED DOGS.
WHOOOOWEE... WHAT A BODY.
YOU DON'T SEE HARDWARE LIKE THAT EVERYDAY.
... HE'S GETTING IN THE WATER.
COME TO MAMA.
AHHH... IT'S GOOD TO BE BACK ON KAPUPU ISLAND, HAWTHORNE...
... NICE TO KNOW THERE'S STILL SOME PLACE ON THIS PLANET THAT'S OUT OF REACH FROM THE HIGH-TECH RAT RACE.
BEEP BEEP BEEP
WAS THAT A BEEPER?
GOTTA RUN.

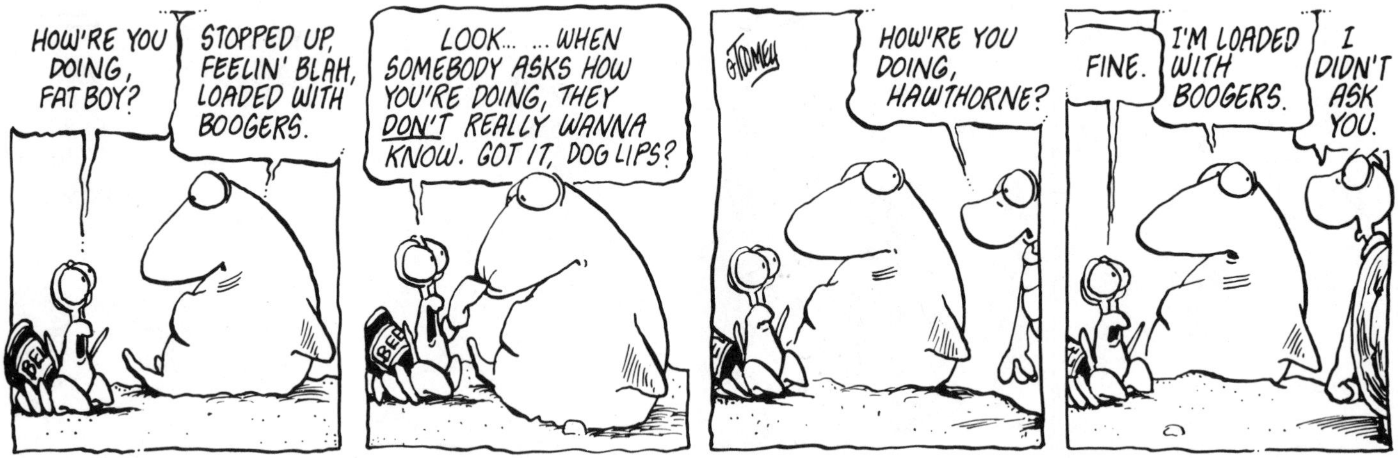
HOW'RE YOU DOING, FAT BOY?
STOPPED UP, FEELIN' BLAH, LOADED WITH BOOGERS.
LOOK... ...WHEN SOMEBODY ASKS HOW YOU'RE DOING, THEY DON'T REALLY WANNA KNOW. GOT IT, DOG LIPS?
HOW'RE YOU DOING, HAWTHORNE?
FINE.
I'M LOADED WITH BOOGERS.
I DIDN'T ASK YOU.

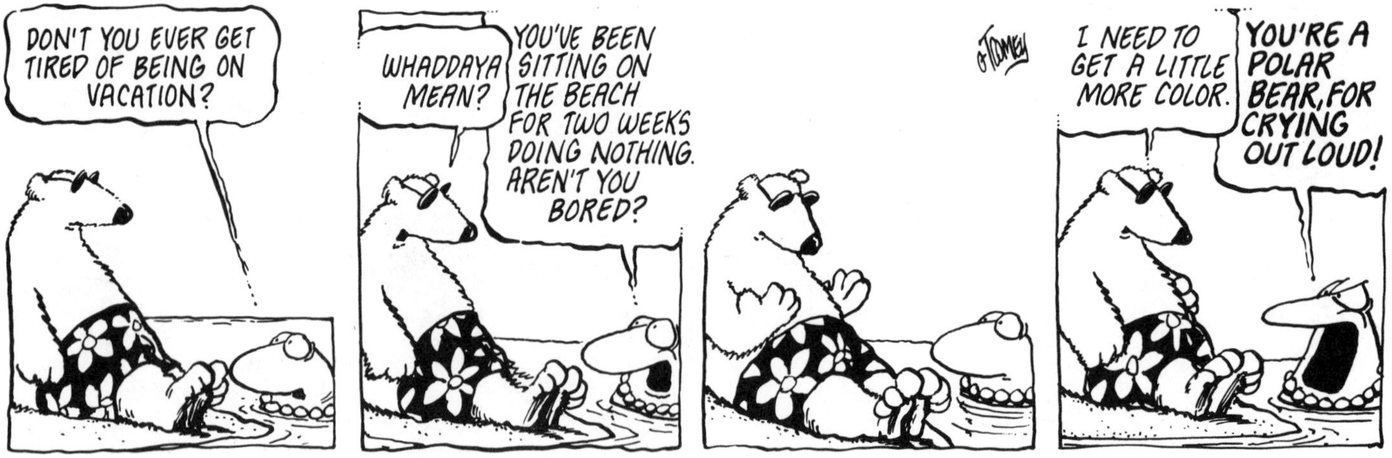
DON'T YOU EVER GET TIRED OF BEING ON VACATION?
WHADDAYA MEAN?
YOU'VE BEEN SITTING ON THE BEACH FOR TWO WEEKS DOING NOTHING. AREN'T YOU BORED?
I NEED TO GET A LITTLE MORE COLOR.
YOU'RE A POLAR BEAR, FOR CRYING OUT LOUD!

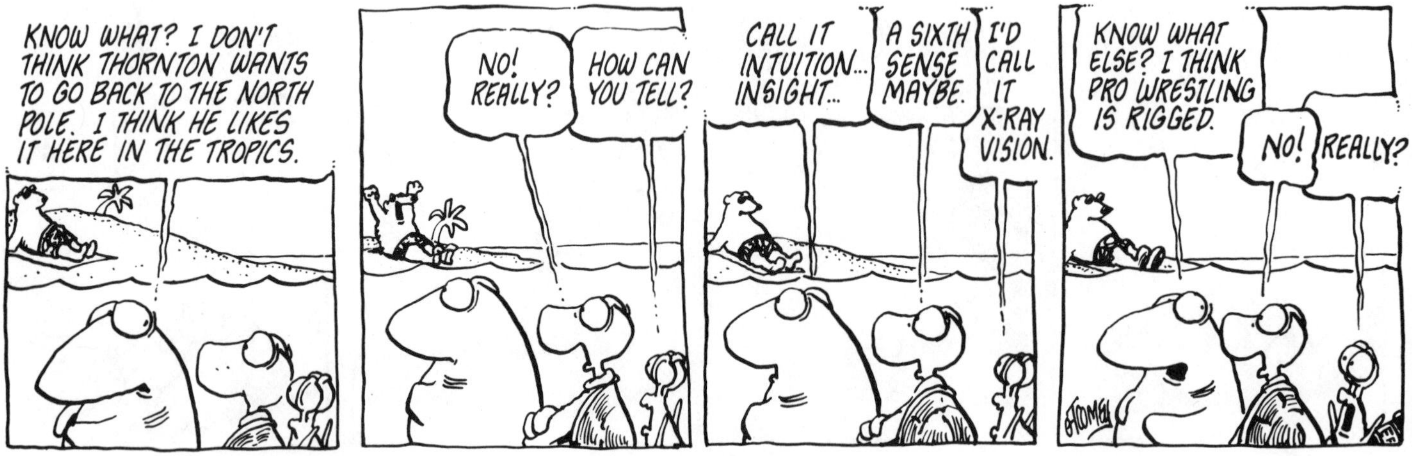
KNOW WHAT? I DON'T THINK THORNTON WANTS TO GO BACK TO THE NORTH POLE. I THINK HE LIKES IT HERE IN THE TROPICS.
NO! REALLY?
HOW CAN YOU TELL?
CALL IT INTUITION... INSIGHT...
A SIXTH SENSE MAYBE.
I'D CALL IT X-RAY VISION.
KNOW WHAT ELSE? I THINK PRO WRESTLING IS RIGGED.
NO!
REALLY?

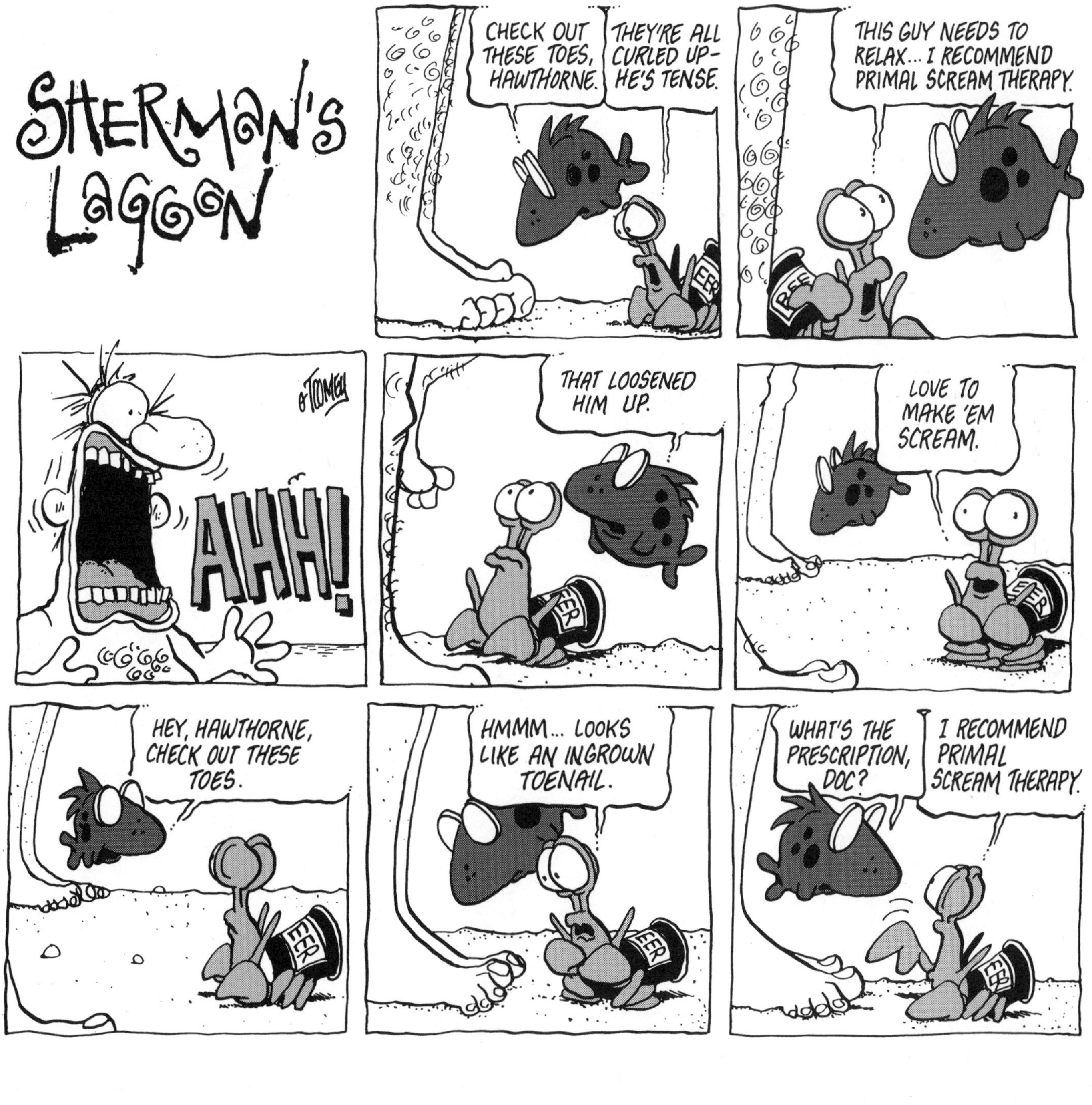
SHERMAN'S LAGOON
CHECK OUT THESE TOES, HAWTHORNE.
THEY'RE ALL CURLED UP– HE'S TENSE.
THIS GUY NEEDS TO RELAX... I RECOMMEND PRIMAL SCREAM THERAPY.
AHHH!
THAT LOOSENED HIM UP.
LOVE TO MAKE 'EM SCREAM.
HEY, HAWTHORNE, CHECK OUT THESE TOES.
HMMM... LOOKS LIKE AN INGROWN TOENAIL.
WHAT'S THE PRESCRIPTION, DOC?
I RECOMMEND PRIMAL SCREAM THERAPY.

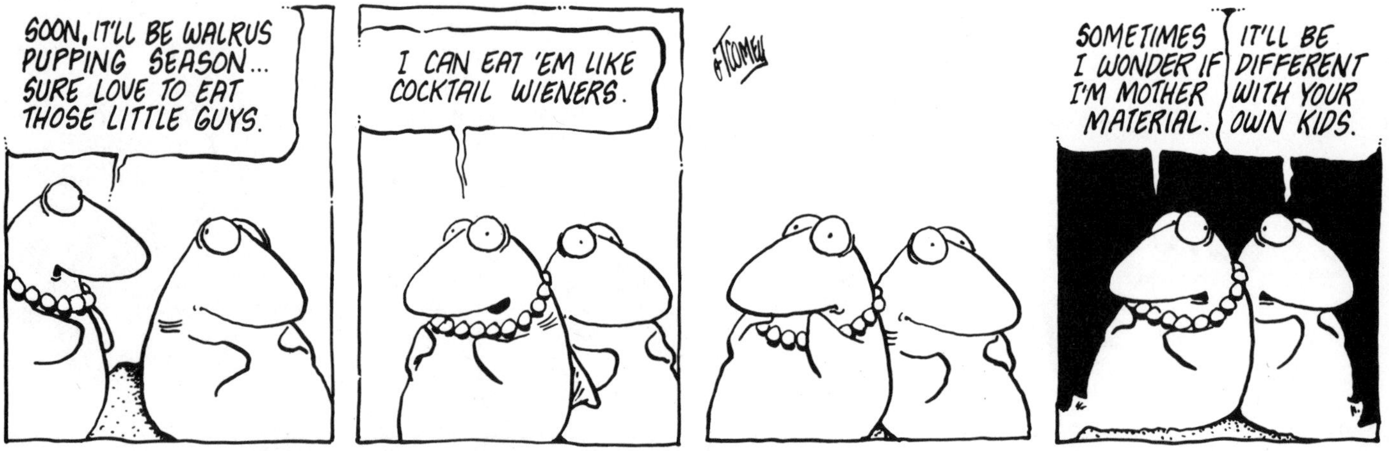
SOON, IT'LL BE WALRUS PUPPING SEASON... SURE LOVE TO EAT THOSE LITTLE GUYS.
I CAN EAT 'EM LIKE COCKTAIL WIENERS.
SOMETIMES I WONDER IF I'M MOTHER MATERIAL.
IT'LL BE DIFFERENT WITH YOUR OWN KIDS.

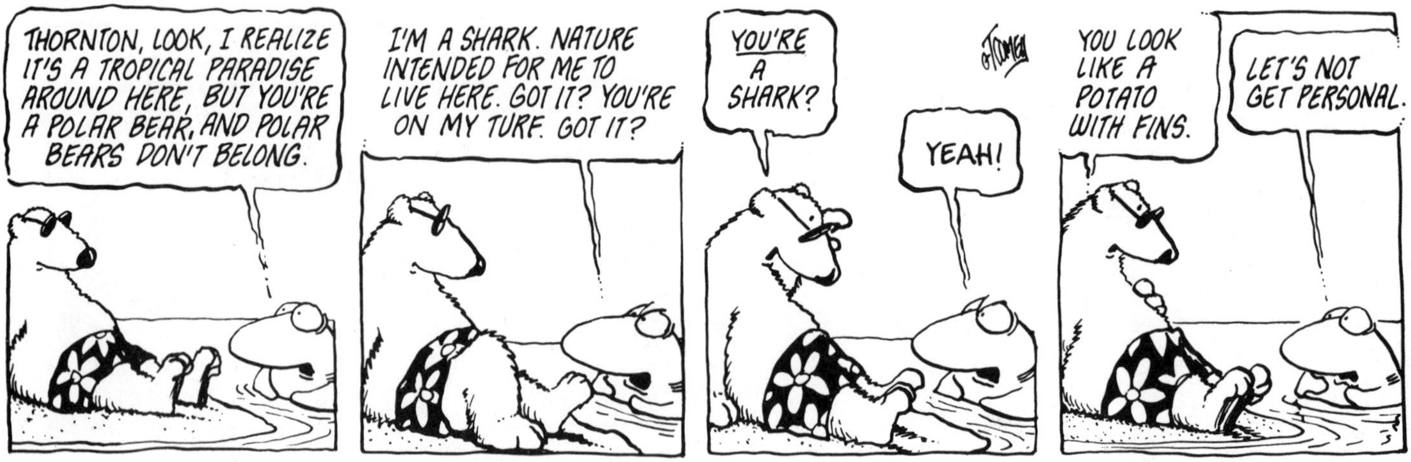
THORNTON, LOOK, I REALIZE IT'S A TROPICAL PARADISE AROUND HERE, BUT YOU'RE A POLAR BEAR, AND POLAR BEARS DON'T BELONG.
I'M A SHARK. NATURE INTENDED FOR ME TO LIVE HERE. GOT IT? YOU'RE ON MY TURF. GOT IT?
YOU'RE A SHARK?
YEAH!
YOU LOOK LIKE A POTATO WITH FINS.
LET'S NOT GET PERSONAL.

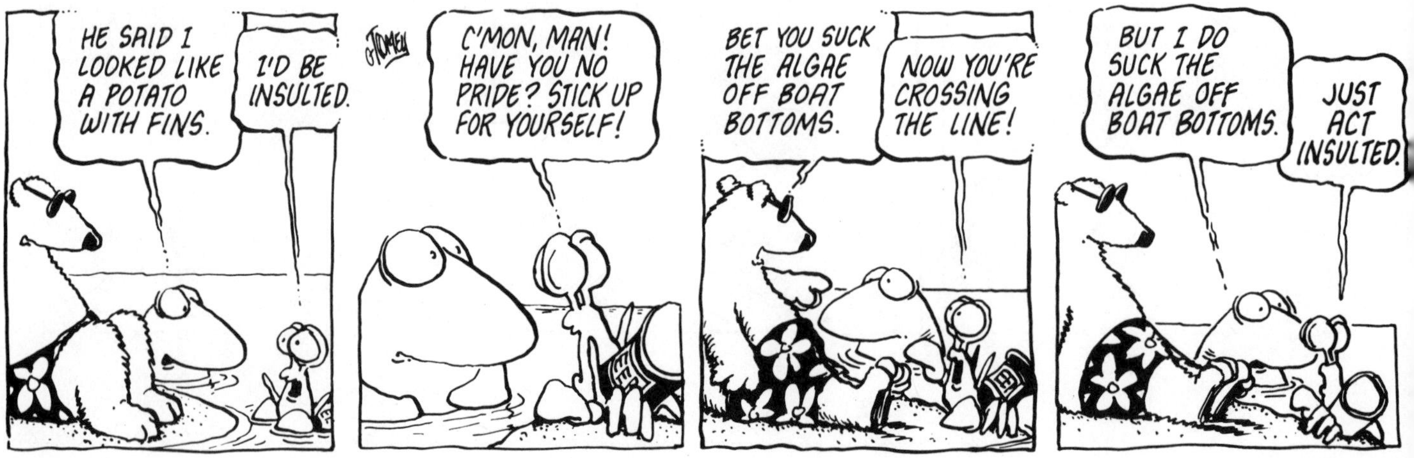
HE SAID I LOOKED LIKE A POTATO WITH FINS.
I'D BE INSULTED.
C'MON, MAN! HAVE YOU NO PRIDE? STICK UP FOR YOURSELF!
BET YOU SUCK THE ALGAE OFF BOAT BOTTOMS.
NOW YOU'RE CROSSING THE LINE!
BUT I DO SUCK THE ALGAE OFF BOAT BOTTOMS.
JUST ACT INSULTED.

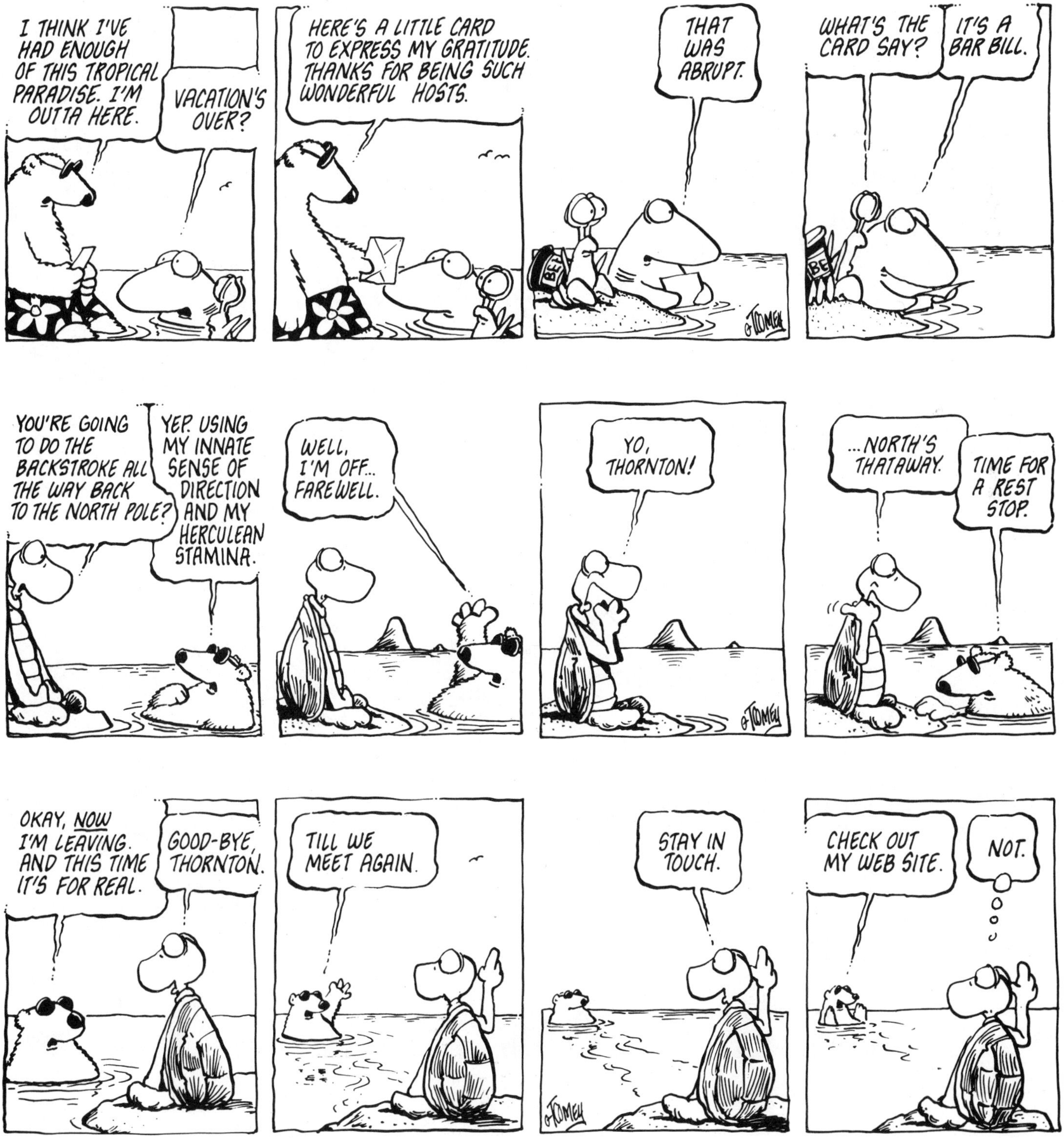
I THINK I'VE HAD ENOUGH OF THIS TROPICAL PARADISE. I'M OUTTA HERE.
VACATION'S OVER?
HERE'S A LITTLE CARD TO EXPRESS MY GRATITUDE. THANKS FOR BEING SUCH WONDERFUL HOSTS.
THAT WAS ABRUPT.
WHAT'S THE CARD SAY?
IT'S A BAR BILL.
YOU'RE GOING TO DO THE BACKSTROKE ALL THE WAY BACK TO THE NORTH POLE?
YEP. USING MY INNATE SENSE OF DIRECTION AND MY HERCULEAN STAMINA.
WELL, I'M OFF... FAREWELL.
YO, THORNTON!
...NORTH'S THATAWAY.
TIME FOR A REST STOP.
OKAY, NOW I'M LEAVING. AND THIS TIME IT'S FOR REAL.
GOOD-BYE, THORNTON.
TILL WE MEET AGAIN.
STAY IN TOUCH.
CHECK OUT MY WEB SITE.
NOT.

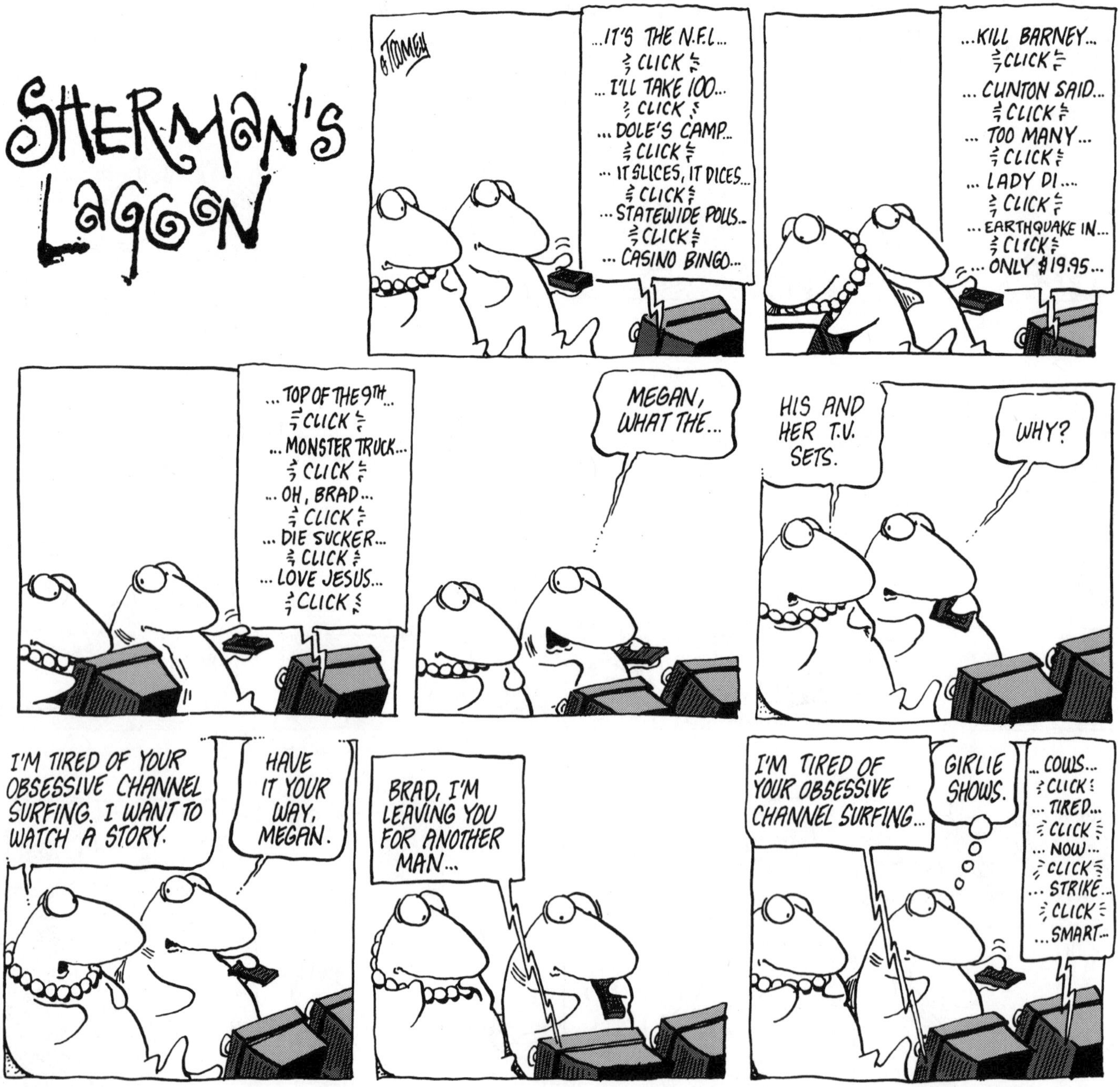
SHERMAN'S LAGOON
...IT'S THE N.F.L... CLICK ...I'LL TAKE 100... CLICK ...DOLE'S CAMP... CLICK ...IT SLICES, IT DICES... CLICK ...STATEWIDE POLLS... CLICK ...CASINO BINGO...
...KILL BARNEY... CLICK ...CLINTON SAID... CLICK ...TOO MANY... CLICK ...LADY DI... CLICK ...EARTHQUAKE IN... CLICK ...ONLY $19.95...
...TOP OF THE 9TH... CLICK ...MONSTER TRUCK... CLICK ...OH, BRAD... CLICK ...DIE SUCKER... CLICK ...LOVE JESUS... CLICK
MEGAN, WHAT THE...
HIS AND HER T.V. SETS.
WHY?
I'M TIRED OF YOUR OBSESSIVE CHANNEL SURFING. I WANT TO WATCH A STORY.
HAVE IT YOUR WAY, MEGAN.
BRAD, I'M LEAVING YOU FOR ANOTHER MAN...
I'M TIRED OF YOUR OBSESSIVE CHANNEL SURFING...
GIRLIE SHOWS.
...COWS... CLICK ...TIRED... CLICK ...NOW... CLICK ...STRIKE... CLICK ...SMART...

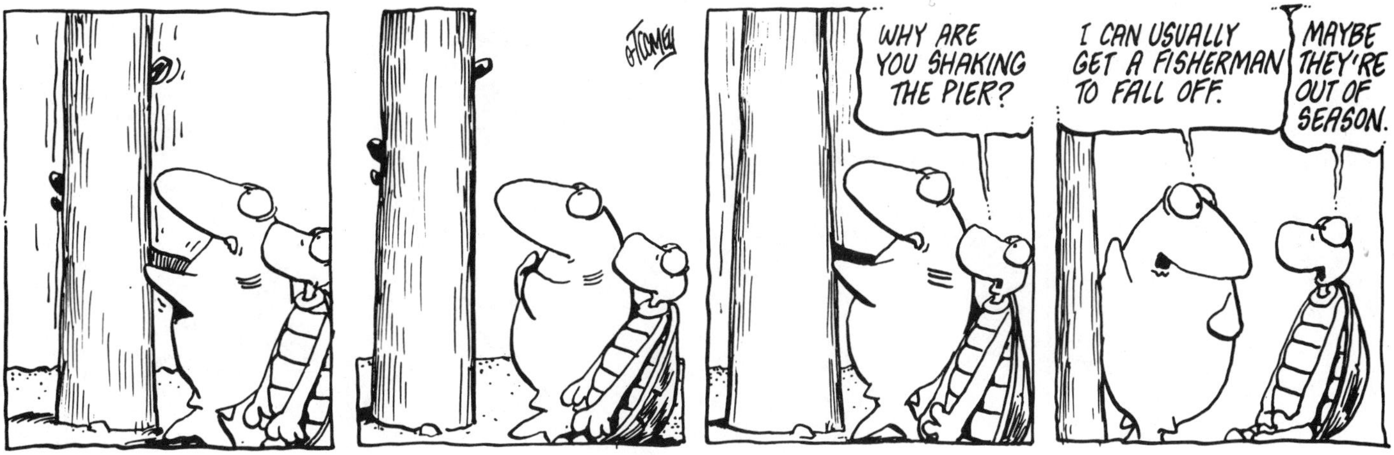
WHY ARE YOU SHAKING THE PIER?
I CAN USUALLY GET A FISHERMAN TO FALL OFF.
MAYBE THEY'RE OUT OF SEASON.

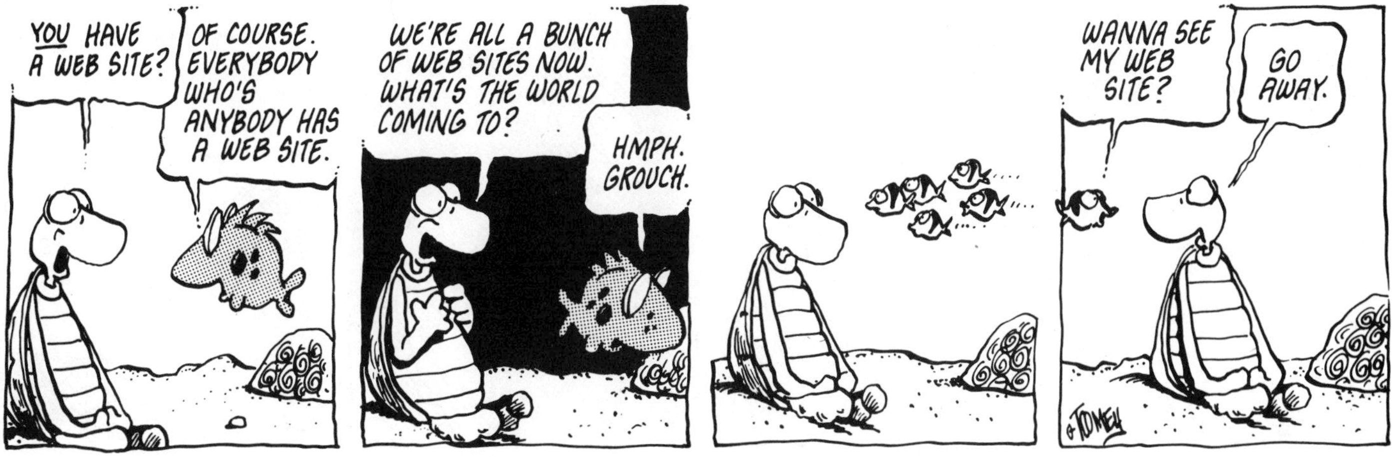
YOU HAVE A WEB SITE?
OF COURSE. EVERYBODY WHO'S ANYBODY HAS A WEB SITE.
WE'RE ALL A BUNCH OF WEB SITES NOW. WHAT'S THE WORLD COMING TO?
HMPH. GROUCH.
WANNA SEE MY WEB SITE?
GO AWAY.

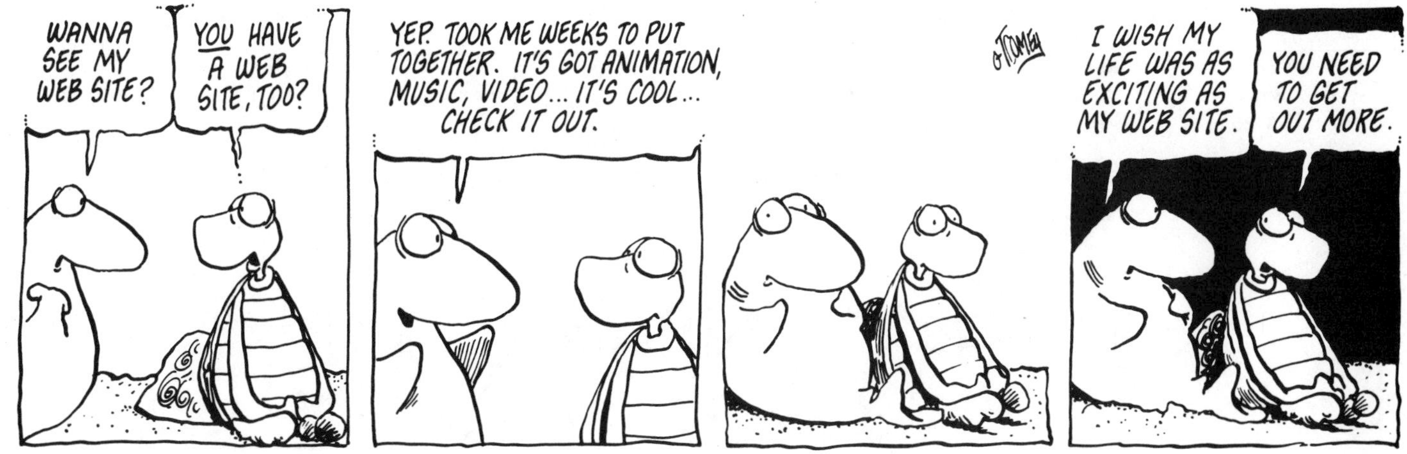
WANNA SEE MY WEB SITE?
YOU HAVE A WEB SITE, TOO?
YEP. TOOK ME WEEKS TO PUT TOGETHER. IT'S GOT ANIMATION, MUSIC, VIDEO... IT'S COOL... CHECK IT OUT.
I WISH MY LIFE WAS AS EXCITING AS MY WEB SITE.
YOU NEED TO GET OUT MORE.

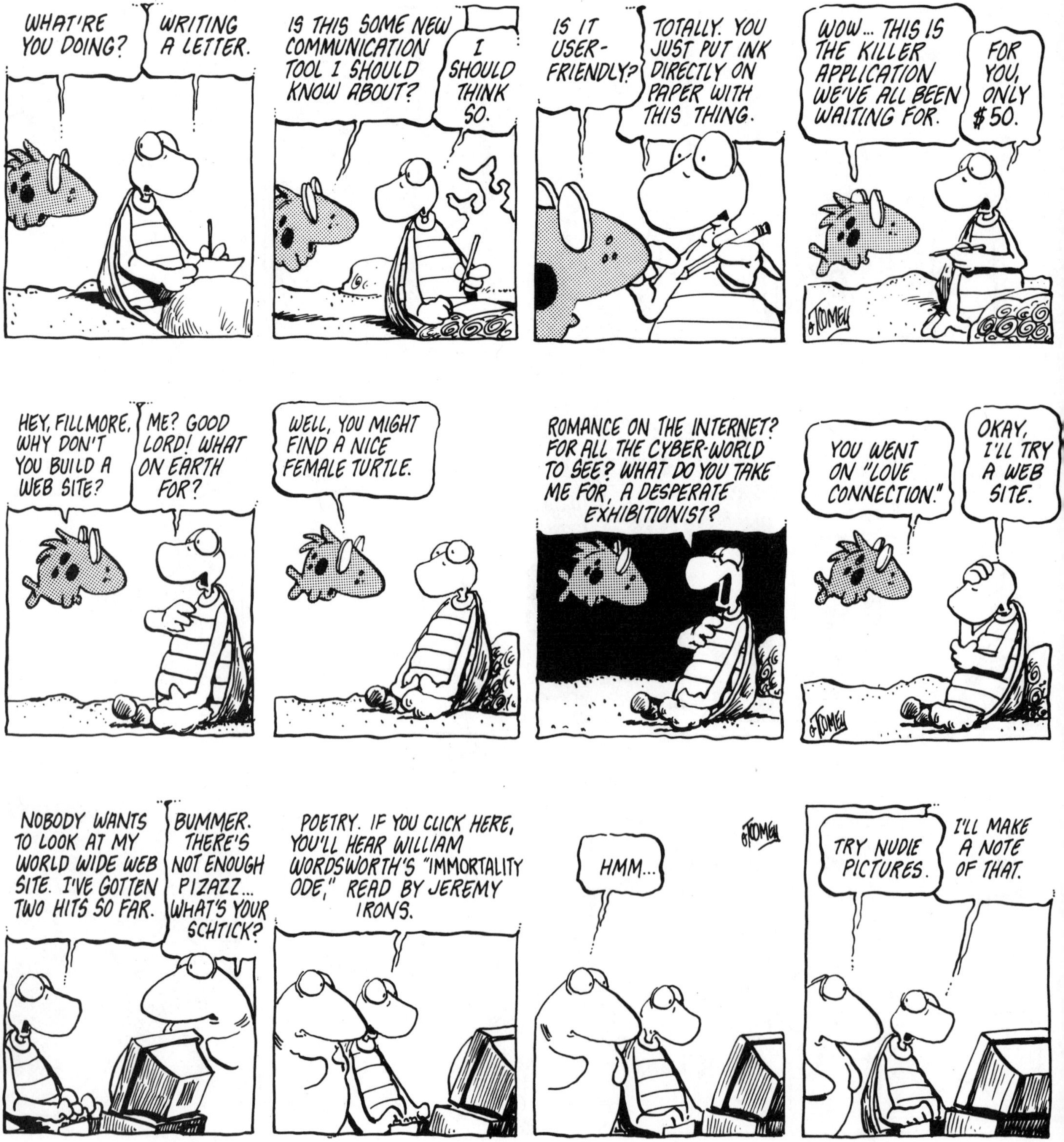
WHAT'RE YOU DOING?
WRITING A LETTER.
IS THIS SOME NEW COMMUNICATION TOOL I SHOULD KNOW ABOUT?
I SHOULD THINK SO.
IS IT USER-FRIENDLY?
TOTALLY. YOU JUST PUT INK DIRECTLY ON PAPER WITH THIS THING.
WOW... THIS IS THE KILLER APPLICATION WE'VE ALL BEEN WAITING FOR.
FOR YOU, ONLY $50.
TOOMEY
HEY, FILLMORE, WHY DON'T YOU BUILD A WEB SITE?
ME? GOOD LORD! WHAT ON EARTH FOR?
WELL, YOU MIGHT FIND A NICE FEMALE TURTLE.
ROMANCE ON THE INTERNET? FOR ALL THE CYBER-WORLD TO SEE? WHAT DO YOU TAKE ME FOR, A DESPERATE EXHIBITIONIST?
YOU WENT ON "LOVE CONNECTION."
OKAY, I'LL TRY A WEB SITE.
TOOMEY
NOBODY WANTS TO LOOK AT MY WORLD WIDE WEB SITE. I'VE GOTTEN TWO HITS SO FAR.
BUMMER. THERE'S NOT ENOUGH PIZAZZ... WHAT'S YOUR SCHTICK?
POETRY. IF YOU CLICK HERE, YOU'LL HEAR WILLIAM WORDSWORTH'S "IMMORTALITY ODE," READ BY JEREMY IRONS.
TOOMEY
HMM...
TRY NUDIE PICTURES.
I'LL MAKE A NOTE OF THAT.

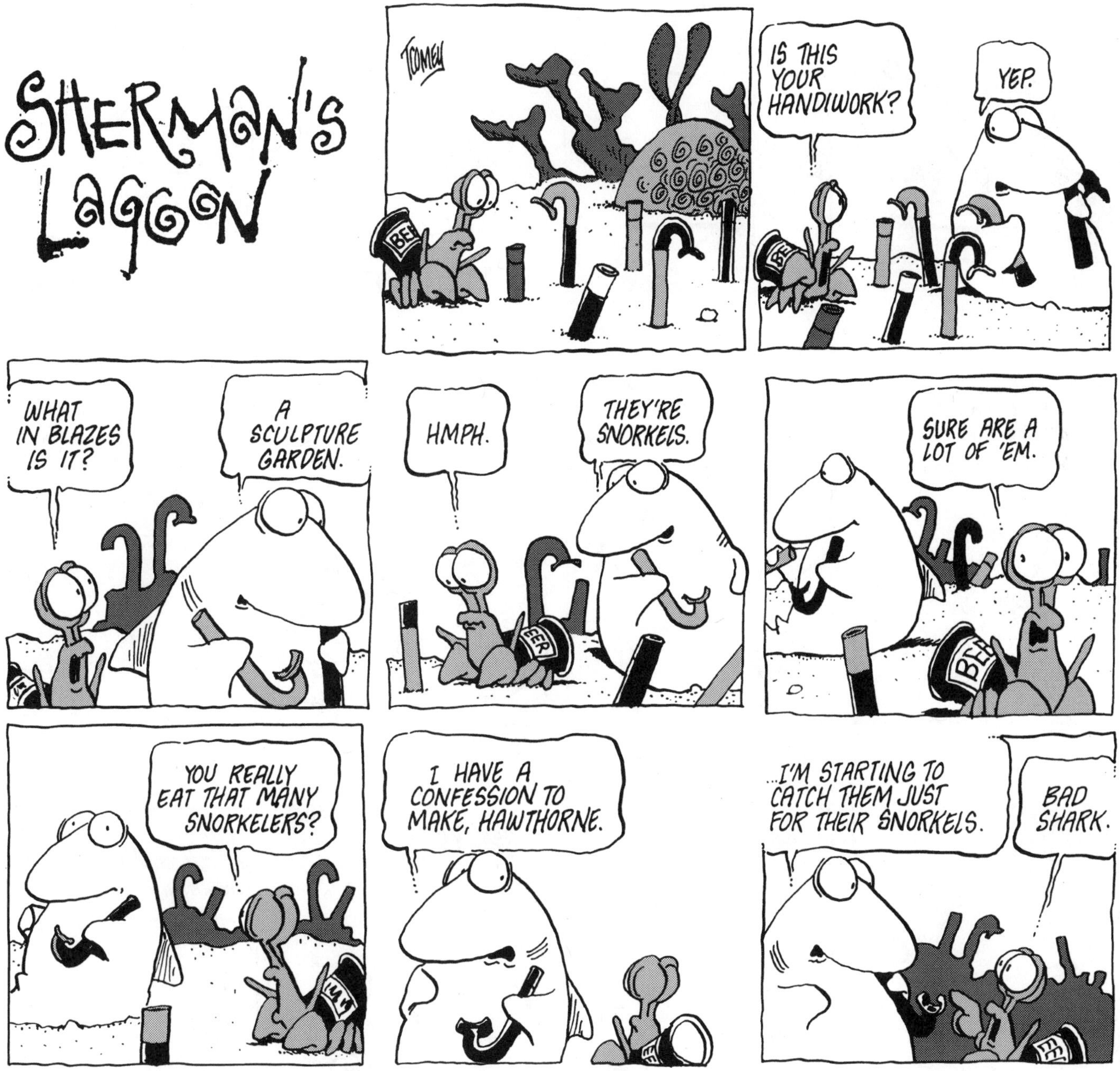
SHERMAN'S LAGOON
TOOMEY
IS THIS YOUR HANDIWORK?
YEP.
WHAT IN BLAZES IS IT?
A SCULPTURE GARDEN.
HMPH.
THEY'RE SNORKELS.
SURE ARE A LOT OF 'EM.
YOU REALLY EAT THAT MANY SNORKELERS?
I HAVE A CONFESSION TO MAKE, HAWTHORNE.
...I'M STARTING TO CATCH THEM JUST FOR THEIR SNORKELS.
BAD SHARK.

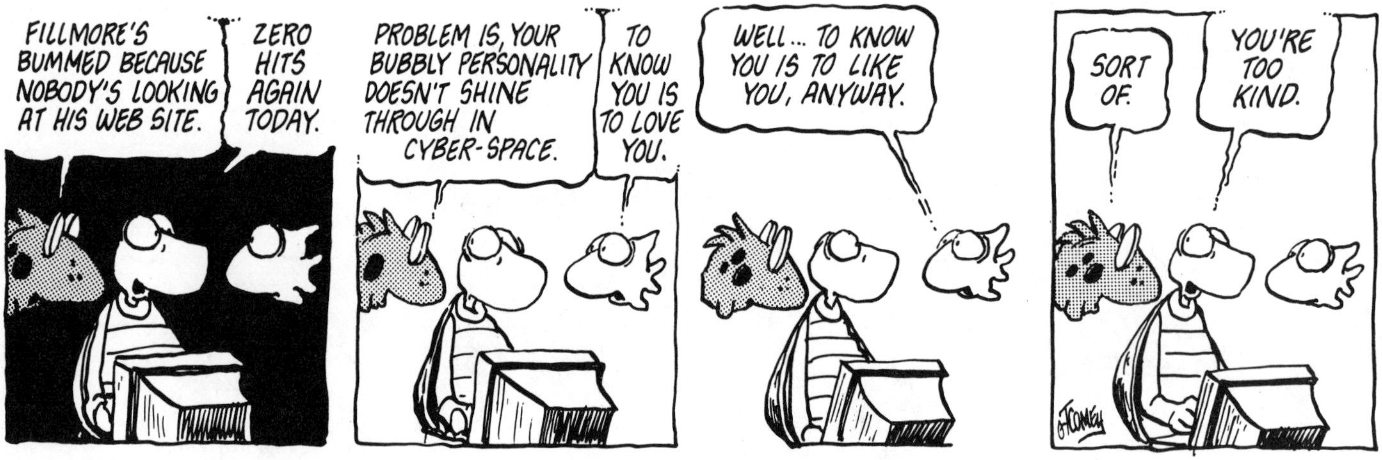
FILLMORE'S BUMMED BECAUSE NOBODY'S LOOKING AT HIS WEB SITE.
ZERO HITS AGAIN TODAY.
PROBLEM IS, YOUR BUBBLY PERSONALITY DOESN'T SHINE THROUGH IN CYBER-SPACE.
TO KNOW YOU IS TO LOVE YOU.
WELL... TO KNOW YOU IS TO LIKE YOU, ANYWAY.
SORT OF.
YOU'RE TOO KIND.

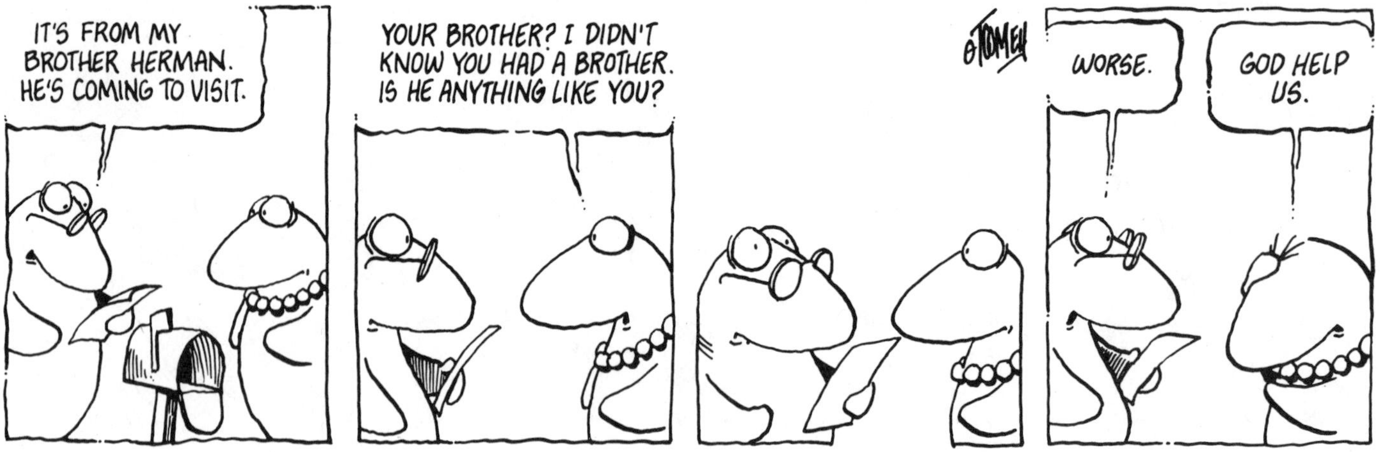
IT'S FROM MY BROTHER HERMAN. HE'S COMING TO VISIT.
YOUR BROTHER? I DIDN'T KNOW YOU HAD A BROTHER. IS HE ANYTHING LIKE YOU?
WORSE.
GOD HELP US.

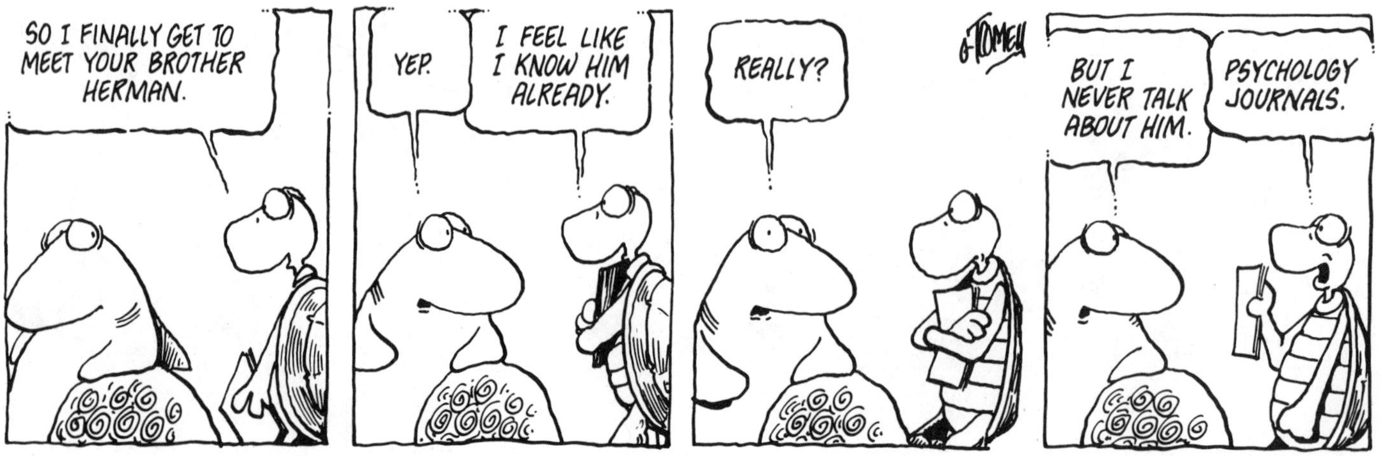
SO I FINALLY GET TO MEET YOUR BROTHER HERMAN.
YEP.
I FEEL LIKE I KNOW HIM ALREADY.
REALLY?
BUT I NEVER TALK ABOUT HIM.
PSYCHOLOGY JOURNALS.

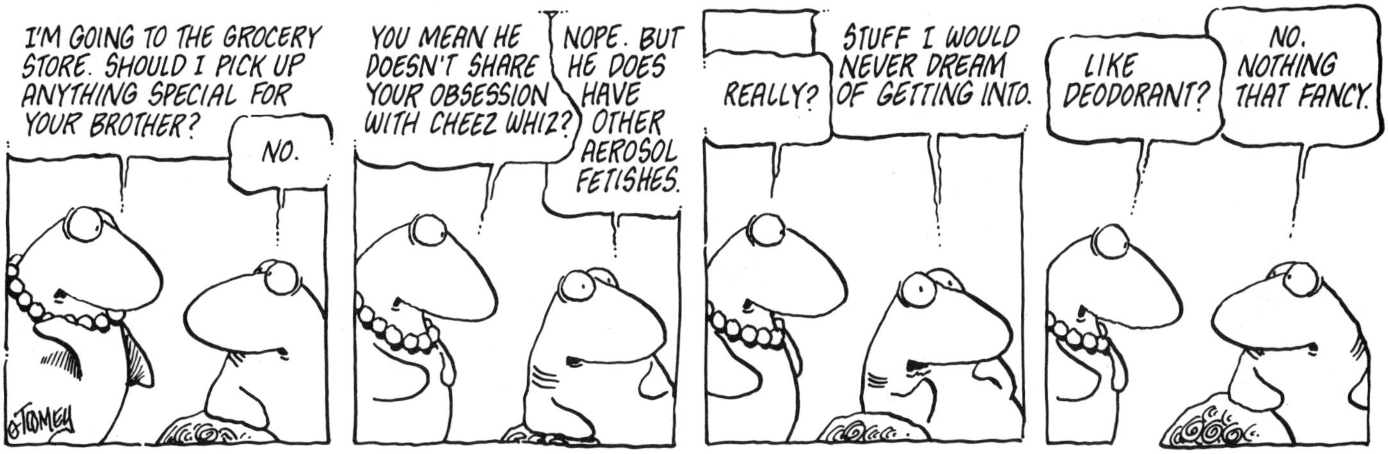
I'M GOING TO THE GROCERY STORE. SHOULD I PICK UP ANYTHING SPECIAL FOR YOUR BROTHER?
NO.
YOU MEAN HE DOESN'T SHARE YOUR OBSESSION WITH CHEEZ WHIZ?
NOPE. BUT HE DOES HAVE OTHER AEROSOL FETISHES.
REALLY?
STUFF I WOULD NEVER DREAM OF GETTING INTO.
LIKE DEODORANT?
NO. NOTHING THAT FANCY.
TOOMEY

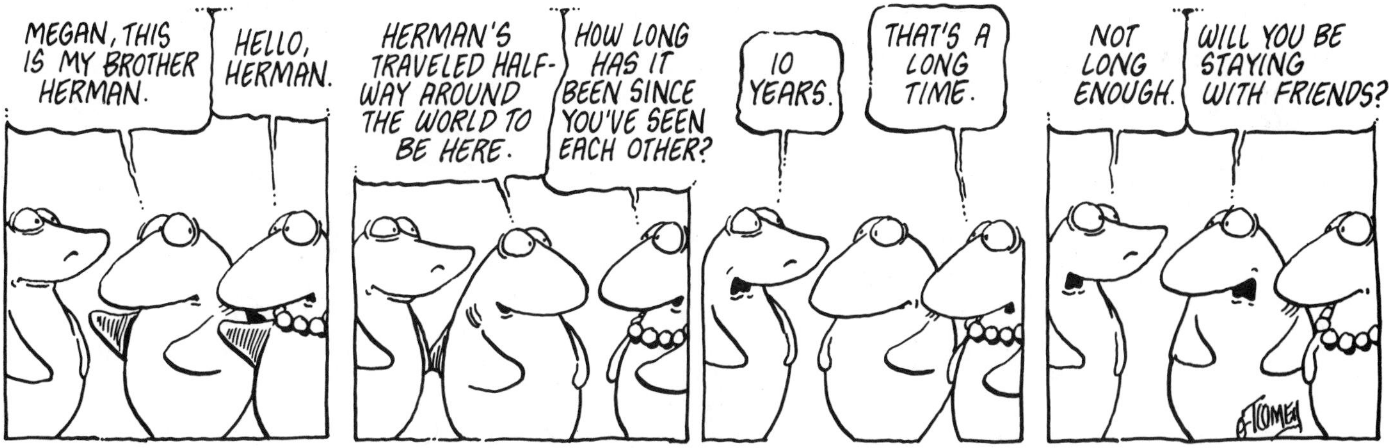
MEGAN, THIS IS MY BROTHER HERMAN.
HELLO, HERMAN.
HERMAN'S TRAVELED HALF-WAY AROUND THE WORLD TO BE HERE.
HOW LONG HAS IT BEEN SINCE YOU'VE SEEN EACH OTHER?
10 YEARS.
THAT'S A LONG TIME.
NOT LONG ENOUGH.
WILL YOU BE STAYING WITH FRIENDS?
TOOMEY

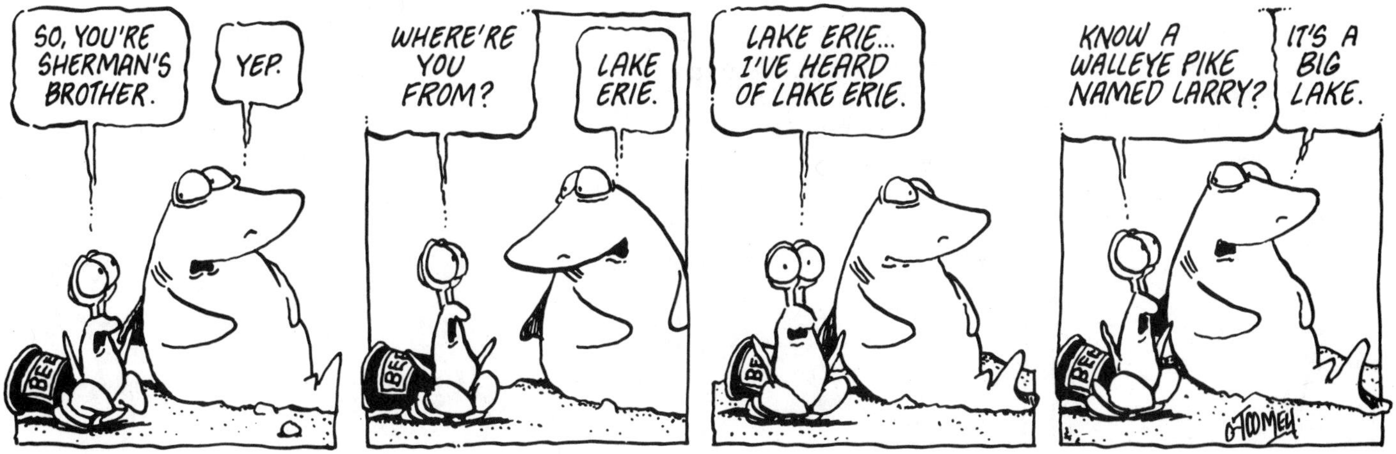
SO, YOU'RE SHERMAN'S BROTHER.
YEP.
WHERE'RE YOU FROM?
LAKE ERIE.
LAKE ERIE... I'VE HEARD OF LAKE ERIE.
KNOW A WALLEYE PIKE NAMED LARRY?
IT'S A BIG LAKE.
TOOMEY

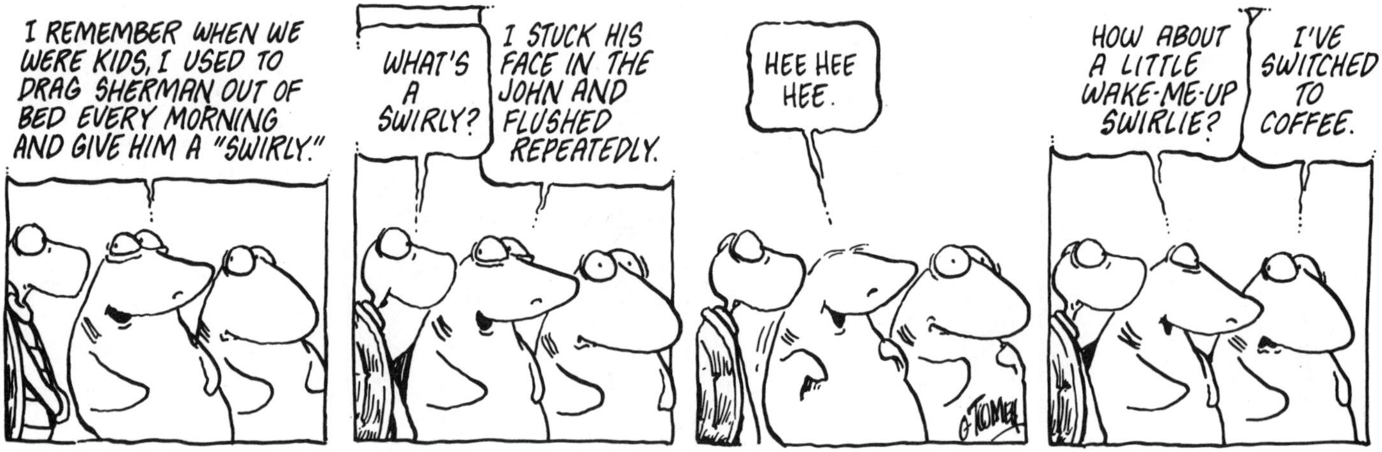
I REMEMBER WHEN WE WERE KIDS, I USED TO DRAG SHERMAN OUT OF BED EVERY MORNING AND GIVE HIM A "SWIRLY."
WHAT'S A SWIRLY?
I STUCK HIS FACE IN THE JOHN AND FLUSHED REPEATEDLY.
HEE HEE HEE.
HOW ABOUT A LITTLE WAKE-ME-UP SWIRLIE?
I'VE SWITCHED TO COFFEE.
TOOMEY

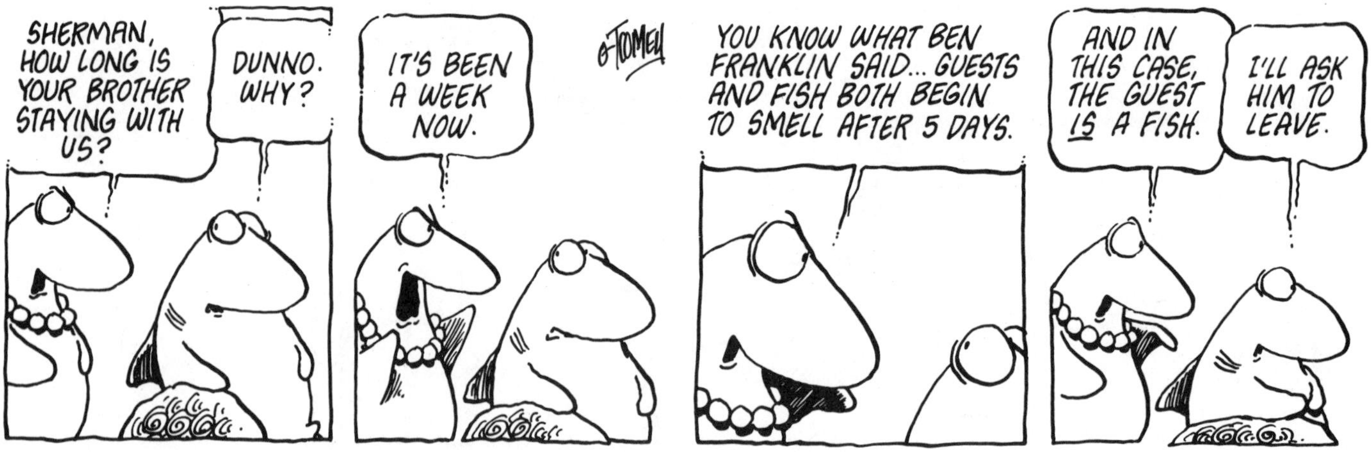
SHERMAN, HOW LONG IS YOUR BROTHER STAYING WITH US?
DUNNO. WHY?
IT'S BEEN A WEEK NOW.
TOOMEY
YOU KNOW WHAT BEN FRANKLIN SAID... GUESTS AND FISH BOTH BEGIN TO SMELL AFTER 5 DAYS.
AND IN THIS CASE, THE GUEST IS A FISH.
I'LL ASK HIM TO LEAVE.

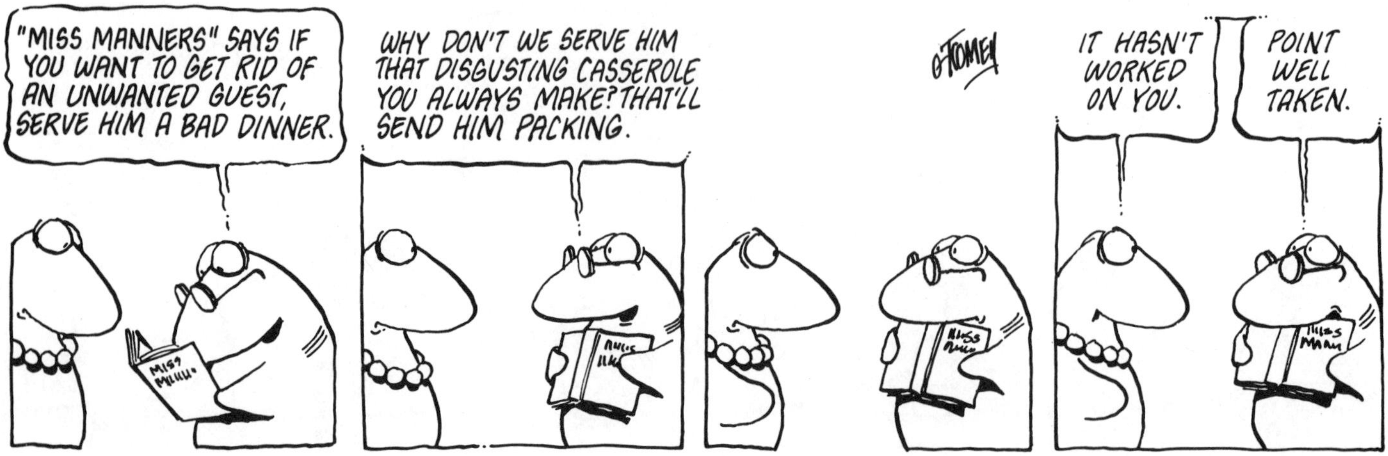
"MISS MANNERS" SAYS IF YOU WANT TO GET RID OF AN UNWANTED GUEST, SERVE HIM A BAD DINNER.
WHY DON'T WE SERVE HIM THAT DISGUSTING CASSEROLE YOU ALWAYS MAKE? THAT'LL SEND HIM PACKING.
TOOMEY
IT HASN'T WORKED ON YOU.
POINT WELL TAKEN.

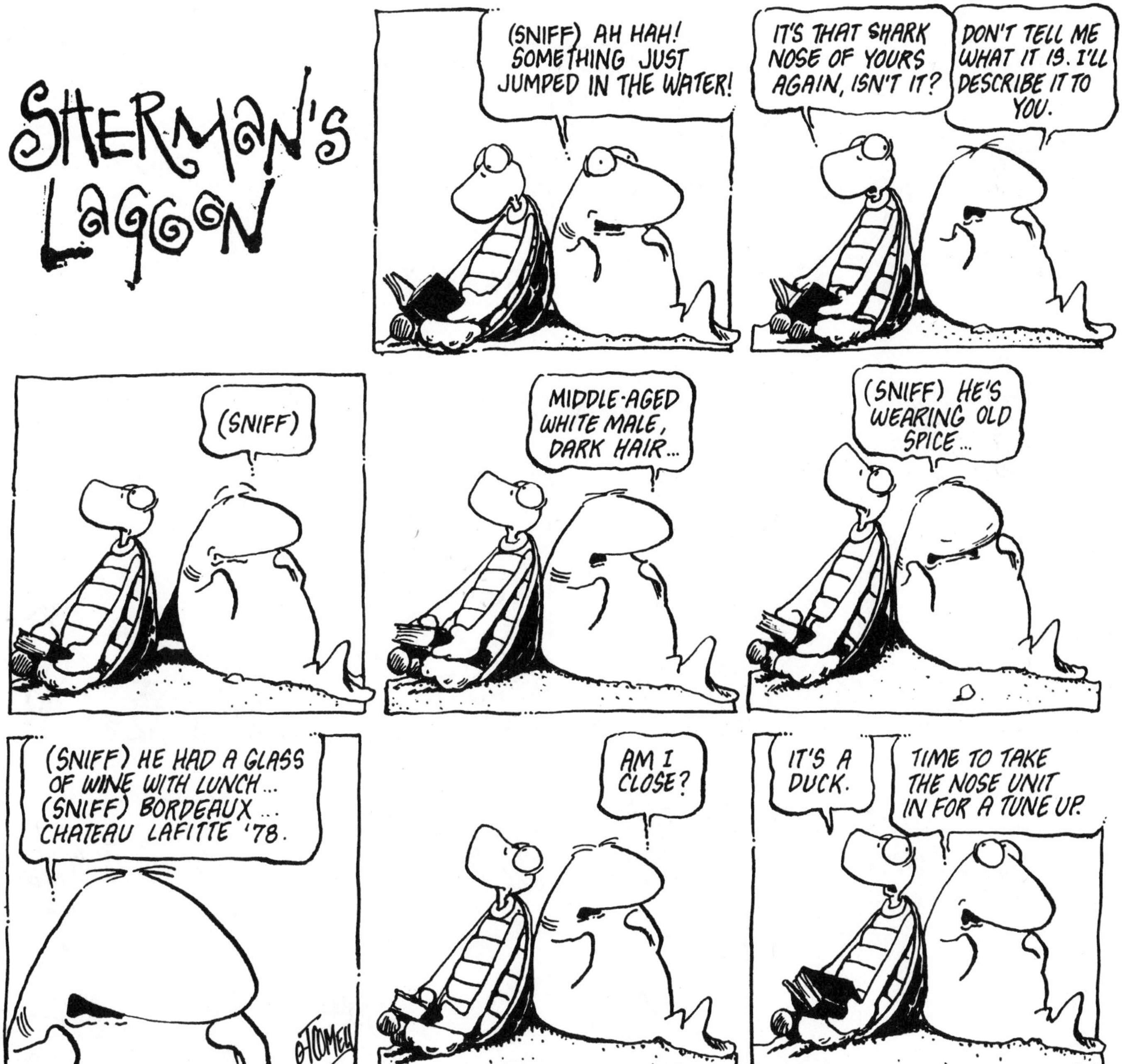
SHERMAN'S LAGOON
(SNIFF) AH HAH! SOMETHING JUST JUMPED IN THE WATER!
IT'S THAT SHARK NOSE OF YOURS AGAIN, ISN'T IT?
DON'T TELL ME WHAT IT IS. I'LL DESCRIBE IT TO YOU.
(SNIFF)
MIDDLE-AGED WHITE MALE, DARK HAIR...
(SNIFF) HE'S WEARING OLD SPICE...
(SNIFF) HE HAD A GLASS OF WINE WITH LUNCH... (SNIFF) BORDEAUX... CHATEAU LAFITTE '78.
AM I CLOSE?
IT'S A DUCK.
TIME TO TAKE THE NOSE UNIT IN FOR A TUNE UP.

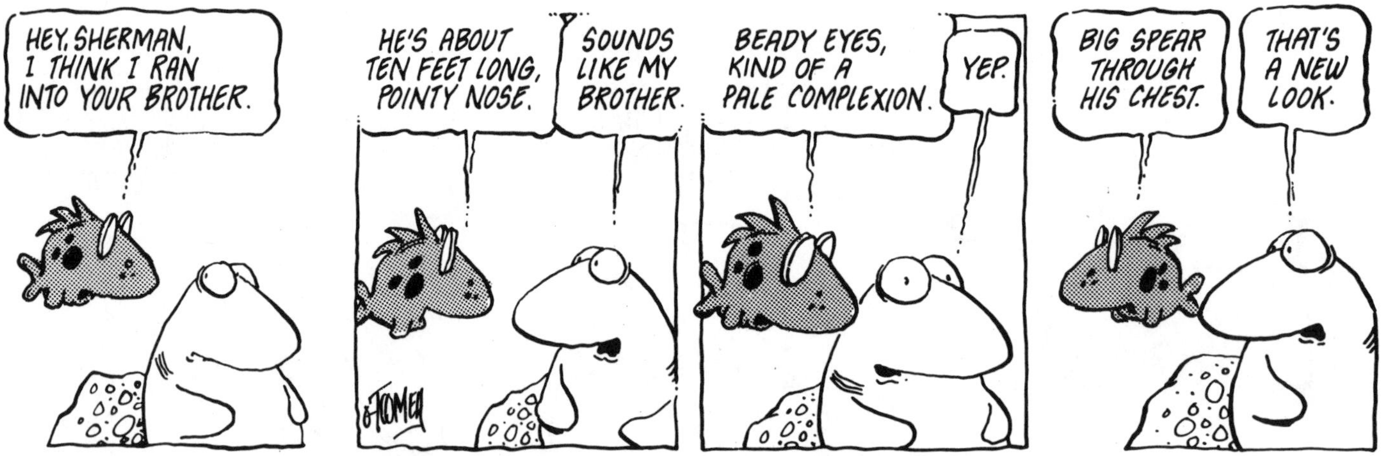
HEY, SHERMAN, I THINK I RAN INTO YOUR BROTHER.
HE'S ABOUT TEN FEET LONG, POINTY NOSE.
SOUNDS LIKE MY BROTHER.
BEADY EYES, KIND OF A PALE COMPLEXION.
YEP.
BIG SPEAR THROUGH HIS CHEST.
THAT'S A NEW LOOK.

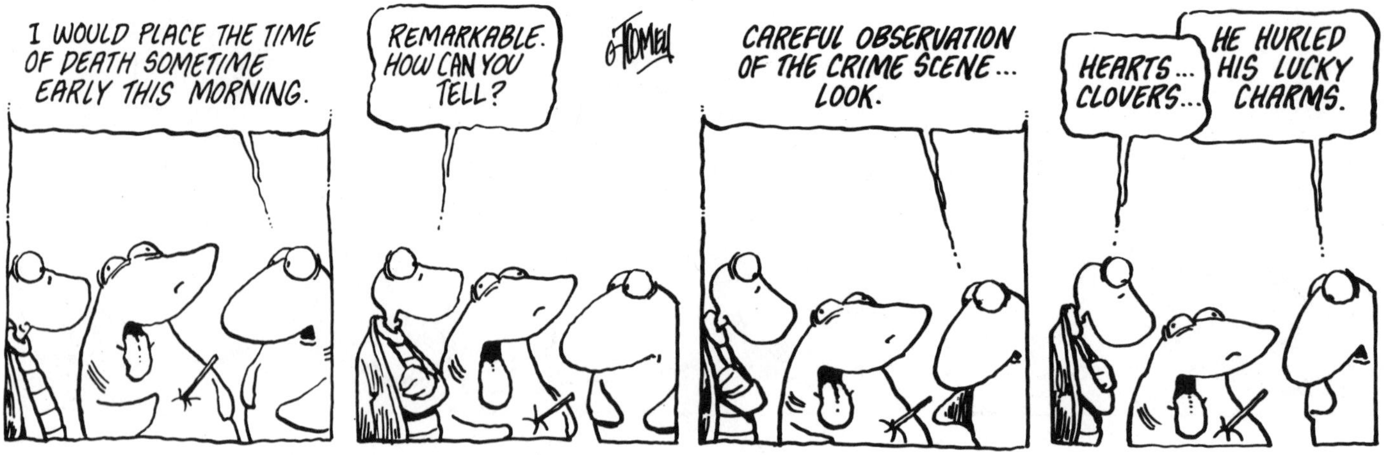
I WOULD PLACE THE TIME OF DEATH SOMETIME EARLY THIS MORNING.
REMARKABLE. HOW CAN YOU TELL?
CAREFUL OBSERVATION OF THE CRIME SCENE... LOOK.
HEARTS... CLOVERS...
HE HURLED HIS LUCKY CHARMS.

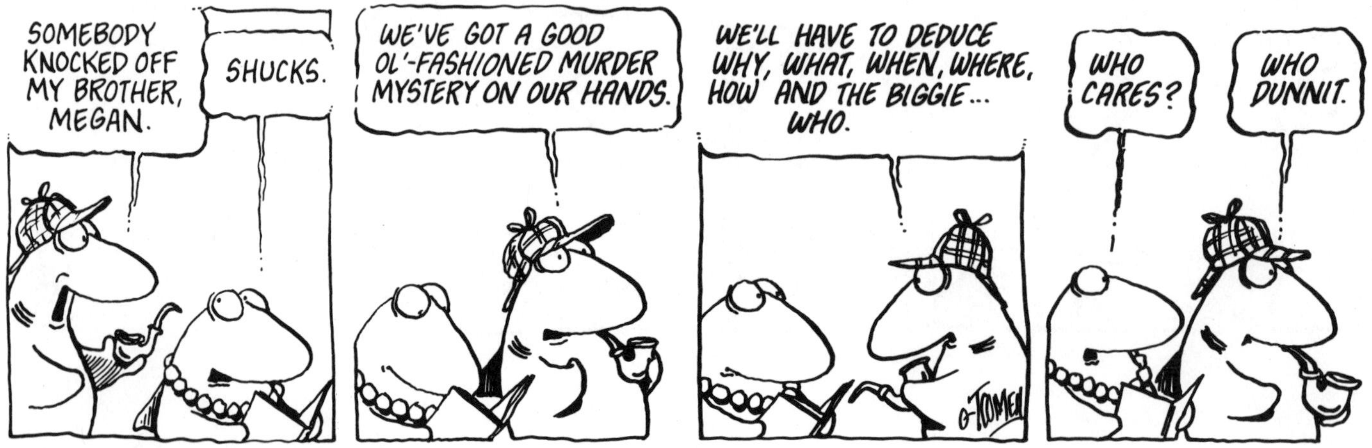
SOMEBODY KNOCKED OFF MY BROTHER, MEGAN.
SHUCKS.
WE'VE GOT A GOOD OL'-FASHIONED MURDER MYSTERY ON OUR HANDS.
WE'LL HAVE TO DEDUCE WHY, WHAT, WHEN, WHERE, HOW AND THE BIGGIE... WHO.
WHO CARES?
WHO DUNNIT.

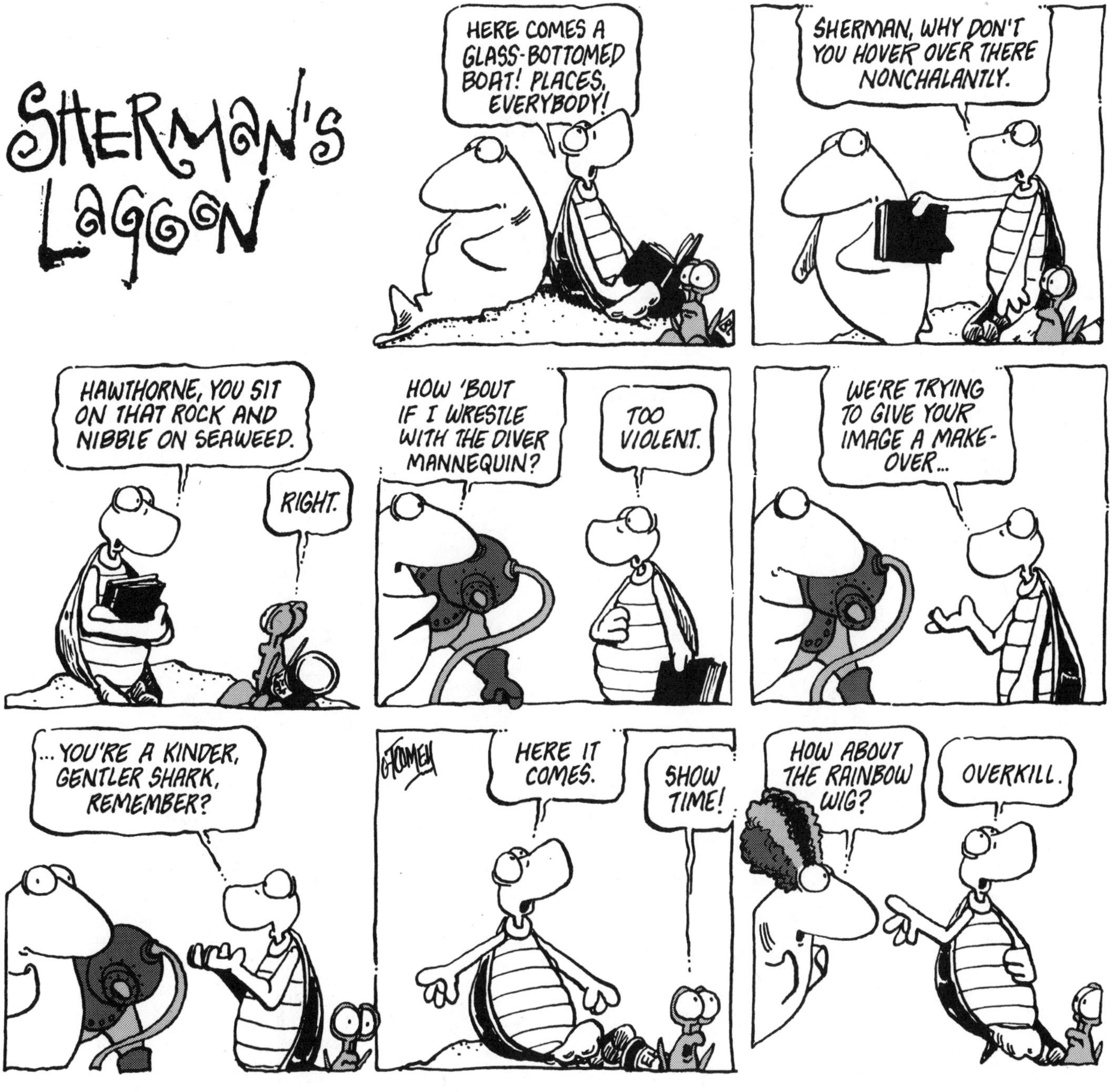
SHERMAN'S LAGOON
HERE COMES A GLASS-BOTTOMED BOAT! PLACES, EVERYBODY!
SHERMAN, WHY DON'T YOU HOVER OVER THERE NONCHALANTLY.
HAWTHORNE, YOU SIT ON THAT ROCK AND NIBBLE ON SEAWEED.
RIGHT.
HOW 'BOUT IF I WRESTLE WITH THE DIVER MANNEQUIN?
TOO VIOLENT.
WE'RE TRYING TO GIVE YOUR IMAGE A MAKE-OVER...
...YOU'RE A KINDER, GENTLER SHARK, REMEMBER?
HERE IT COMES.
SHOW TIME!
HOW ABOUT THE RAINBOW WIG?
OVERKILL.

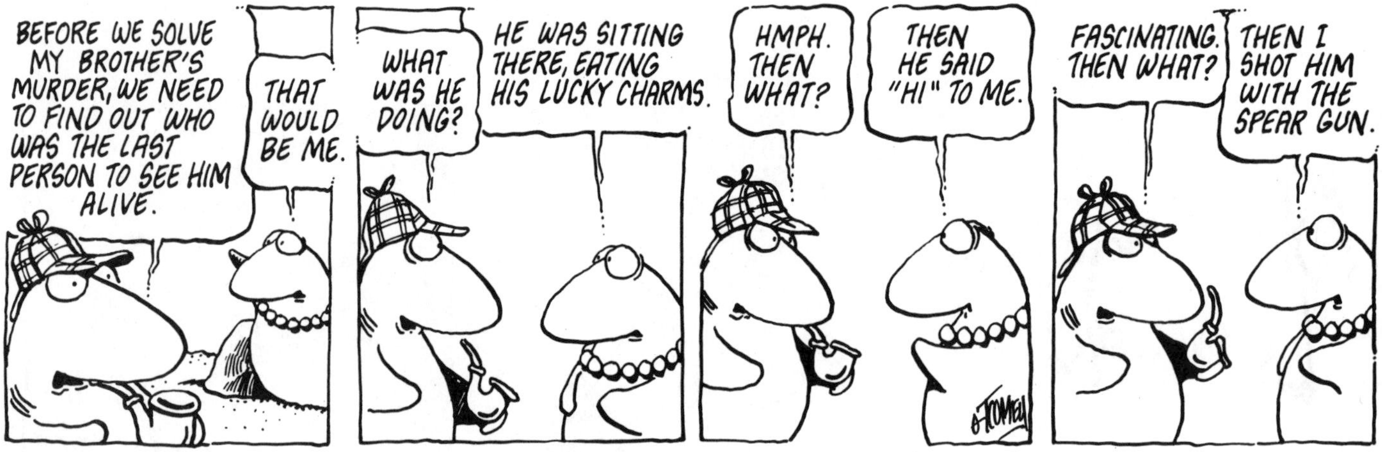
BEFORE WE SOLVE MY BROTHER'S MURDER, WE NEED TO FIND OUT WHO WAS THE LAST PERSON TO SEE HIM ALIVE.
THAT WOULD BE ME.
WHAT WAS HE DOING?
HE WAS SITTING THERE, EATING HIS LUCKY CHARMS.
HMPH. THEN WHAT?
THEN HE SAID "HI" TO ME.
FASCINATING. THEN WHAT?
THEN I SHOT HIM WITH THE SPEAR GUN.

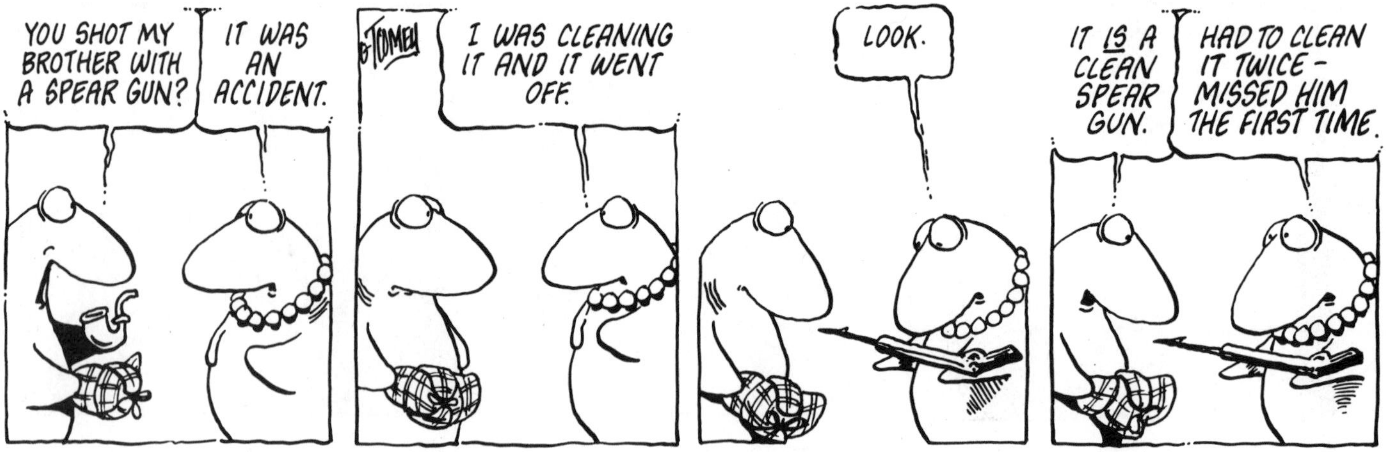
YOU SHOT MY BROTHER WITH A SPEAR GUN?
IT WAS AN ACCIDENT.
I WAS CLEANING IT AND IT WENT OFF.
LOOK.
IT IS A CLEAN SPEAR GUN.
HAD TO CLEAN IT TWICE - MISSED HIM THE FIRST TIME.

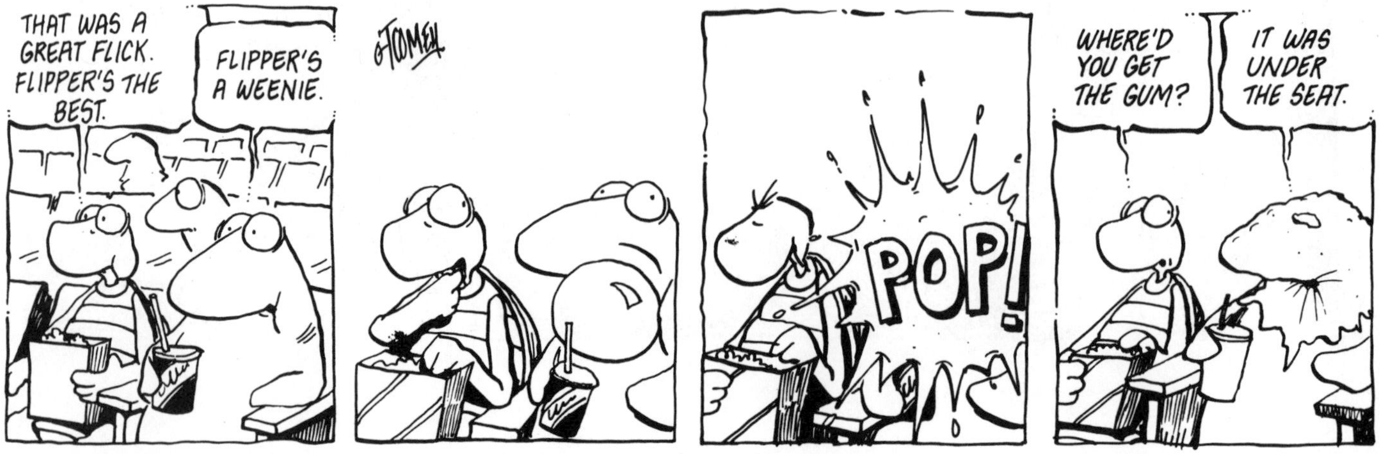
THAT WAS A GREAT FLICK. FLIPPER'S THE BEST.
FLIPPER'S A WEENIE.
POP!
WHERE'D YOU GET THE GUM?
IT WAS UNDER THE SEAT.

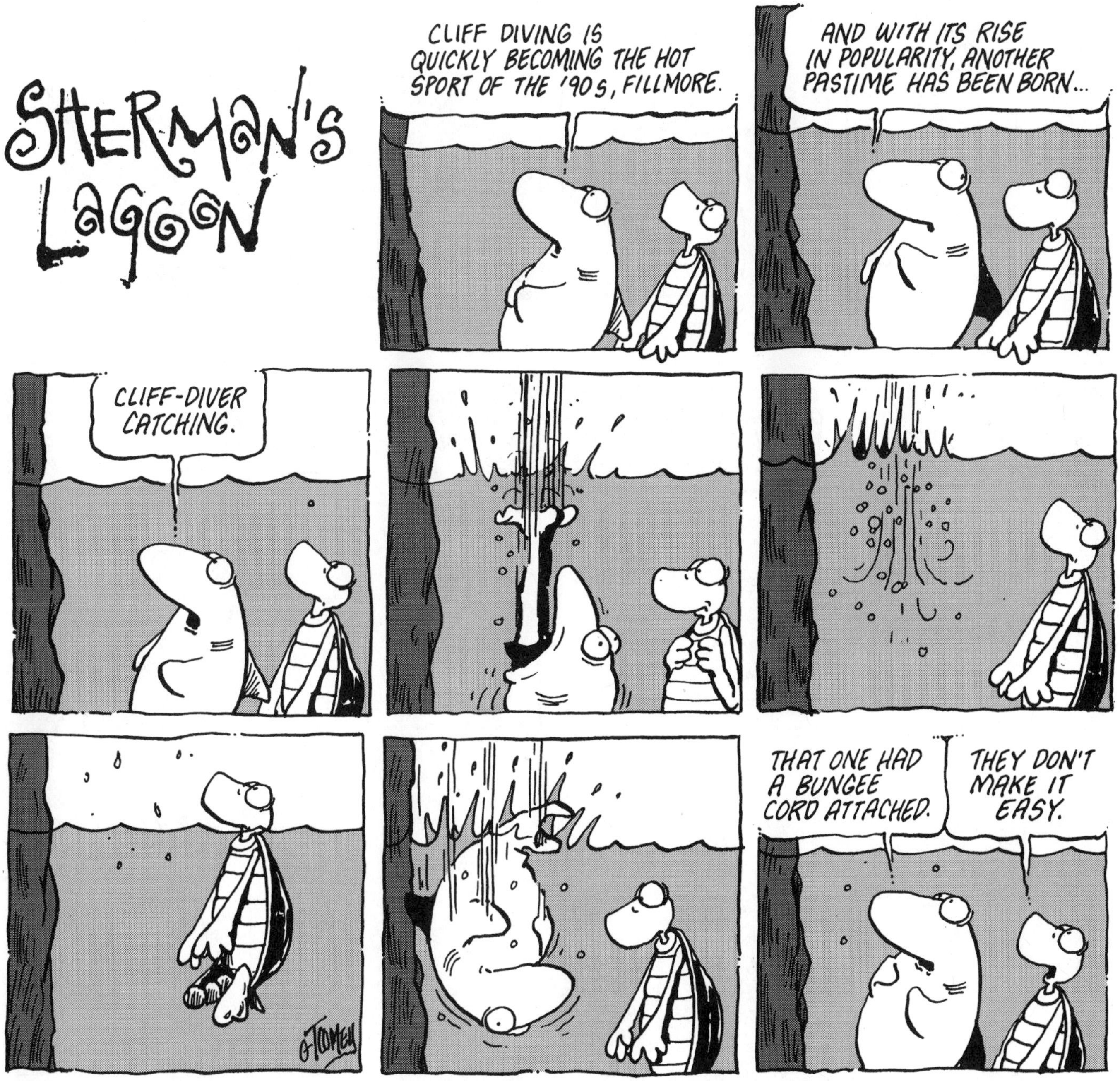
SHERMAN'S LAGOON
CLIFF DIVING IS QUICKLY BECOMING THE HOT SPORT OF THE '90s, FILLMORE.
AND WITH ITS RISE IN POPULARITY, ANOTHER PASTIME HAS BEEN BORN...
CLIFF-DIVER CATCHING.
THAT ONE HAD A BUNGEE CORD ATTACHED.
THEY DON'T MAKE IT EASY.

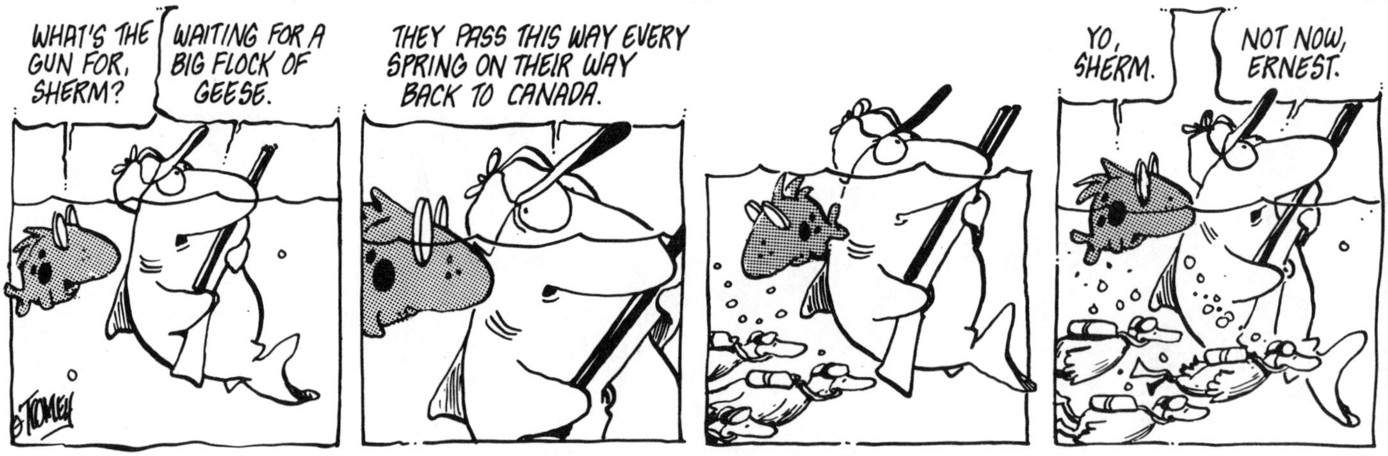
WHAT'S THE GUN FOR, SHERM?
WAITING FOR A BIG FLOCK OF GEESE.
THEY PASS THIS WAY EVERY SPRING ON THEIR WAY BACK TO CANADA.
YO, SHERM.
NOT NOW, ERNEST.

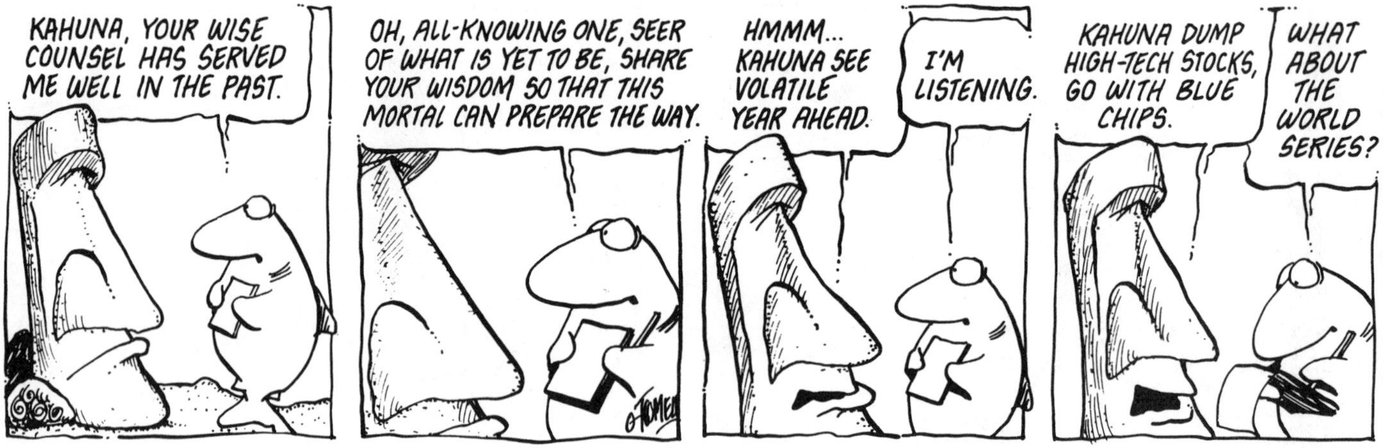
KAHUNA, YOUR WISE COUNSEL HAS SERVED ME WELL IN THE PAST.
OH, ALL-KNOWING ONE, SEER OF WHAT IS YET TO BE, SHARE YOUR WISDOM SO THAT THIS MORTAL CAN PREPARE THE WAY.
HMMM... KAHUNA SEE VOLATILE YEAR AHEAD.
I'M LISTENING.
KAHUNA DUMP HIGH-TECH STOCKS, GO WITH BLUE CHIPS.
WHAT ABOUT THE WORLD SERIES?

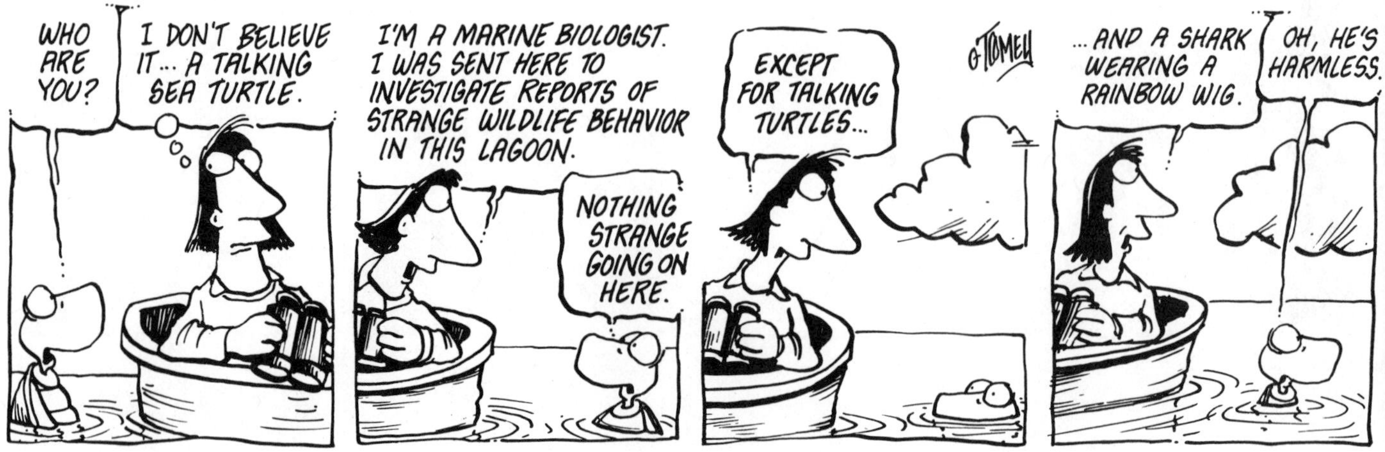
WHO ARE YOU?
I DON'T BELIEVE IT... A TALKING SEA TURTLE.
I'M A MARINE BIOLOGIST. I WAS SENT HERE TO INVESTIGATE REPORTS OF STRANGE WILDLIFE BEHAVIOR IN THIS LAGOON.
NOTHING STRANGE GOING ON HERE.
EXCEPT FOR TALKING TURTLES...
...AND A SHARK WEARING A RAINBOW WIG.
OH, HE'S HARMLESS.

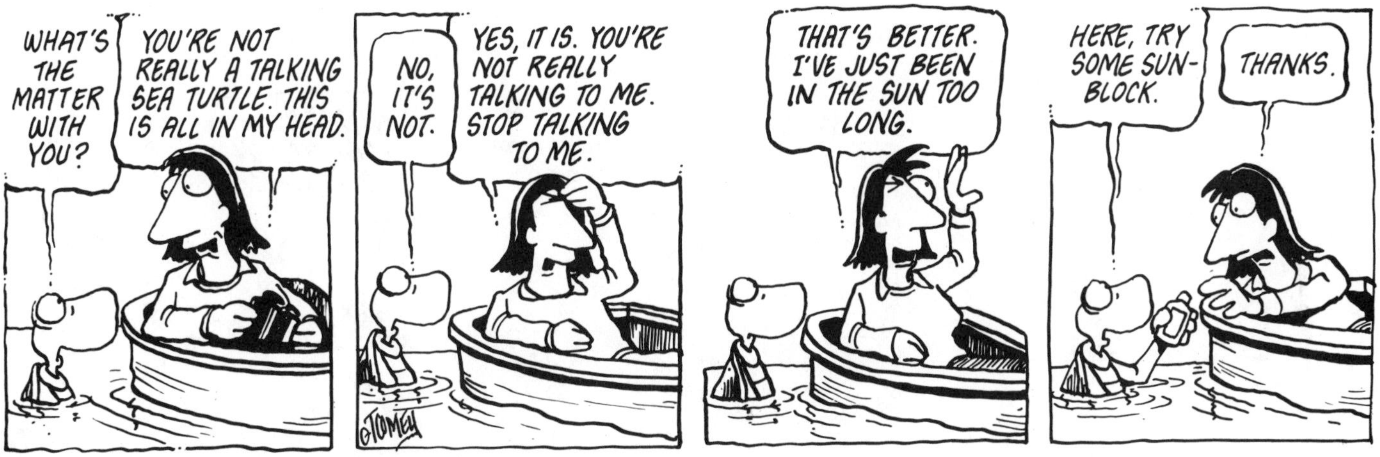
WHAT'S THE MATTER WITH YOU?
YOU'RE NOT REALLY A TALKING SEA TURTLE. THIS IS ALL IN MY HEAD.
NO, IT'S NOT.
YES, IT IS. YOU'RE NOT REALLY TALKING TO ME. STOP TALKING TO ME.
THAT'S BETTER. I'VE JUST BEEN IN THE SUN TOO LONG.
HERE, TRY SOME SUN-BLOCK.
THANKS.

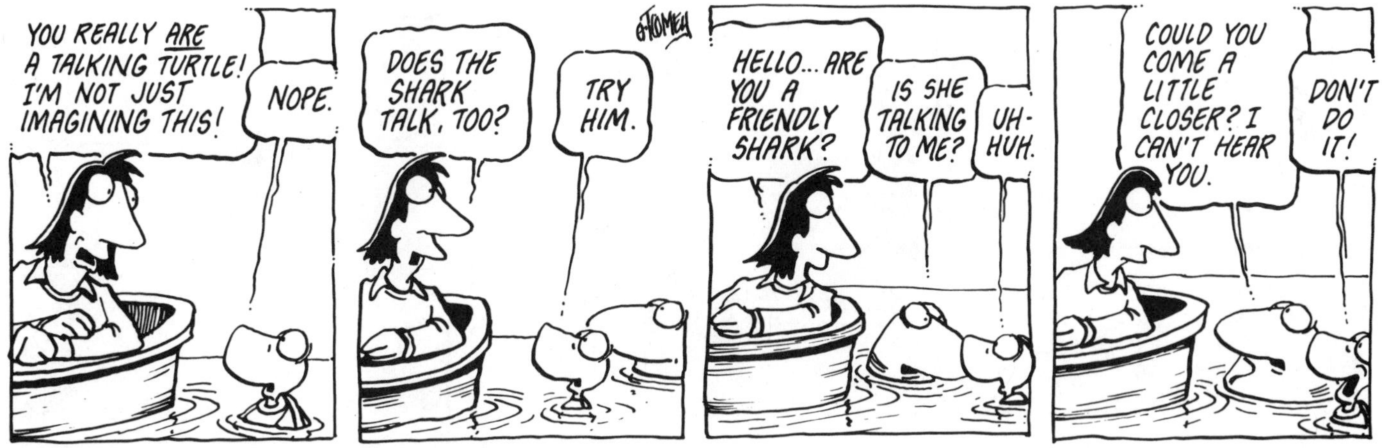
YOU REALLY ARE A TALKING TURTLE! I'M NOT JUST IMAGINING THIS!
NOPE.
DOES THE SHARK TALK, TOO?
TRY HIM.
HELLO... ARE YOU A FRIENDLY SHARK?
IS SHE TALKING TO ME?
UH-HUH.
COULD YOU COME A LITTLE CLOSER? I CAN'T HEAR YOU.
DON'T DO IT!

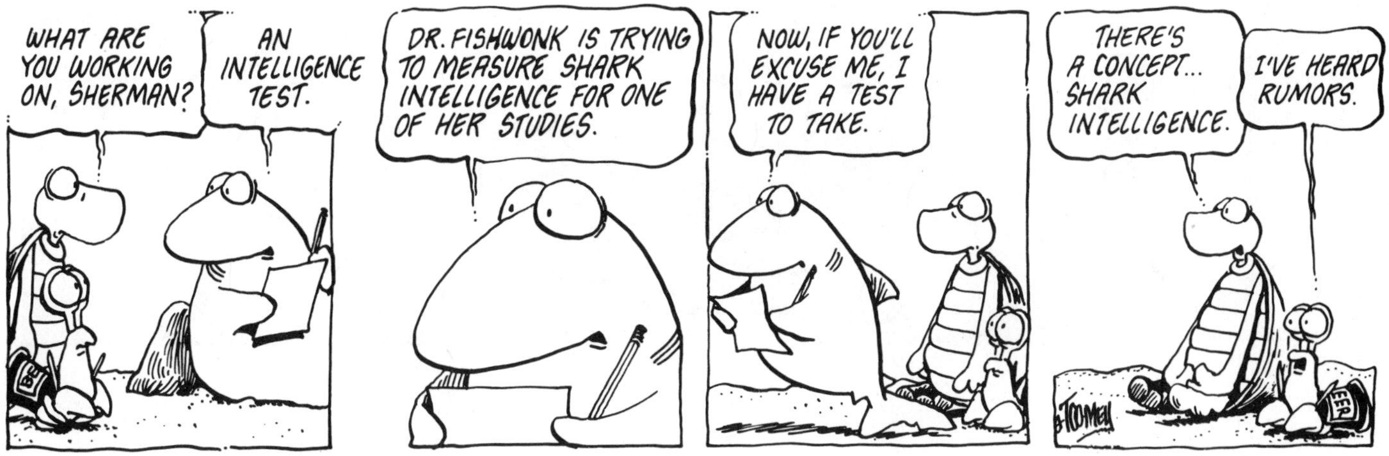
WHAT ARE YOU WORKING ON, SHERMAN?
AN INTELLIGENCE TEST.
DR. FISHWONK IS TRYING TO MEASURE SHARK INTELLIGENCE FOR ONE OF HER STUDIES.
NOW, IF YOU'LL EXCUSE ME, I HAVE A TEST TO TAKE.
THERE'S A CONCEPT... SHARK INTELLIGENCE.
I'VE HEARD RUMORS.

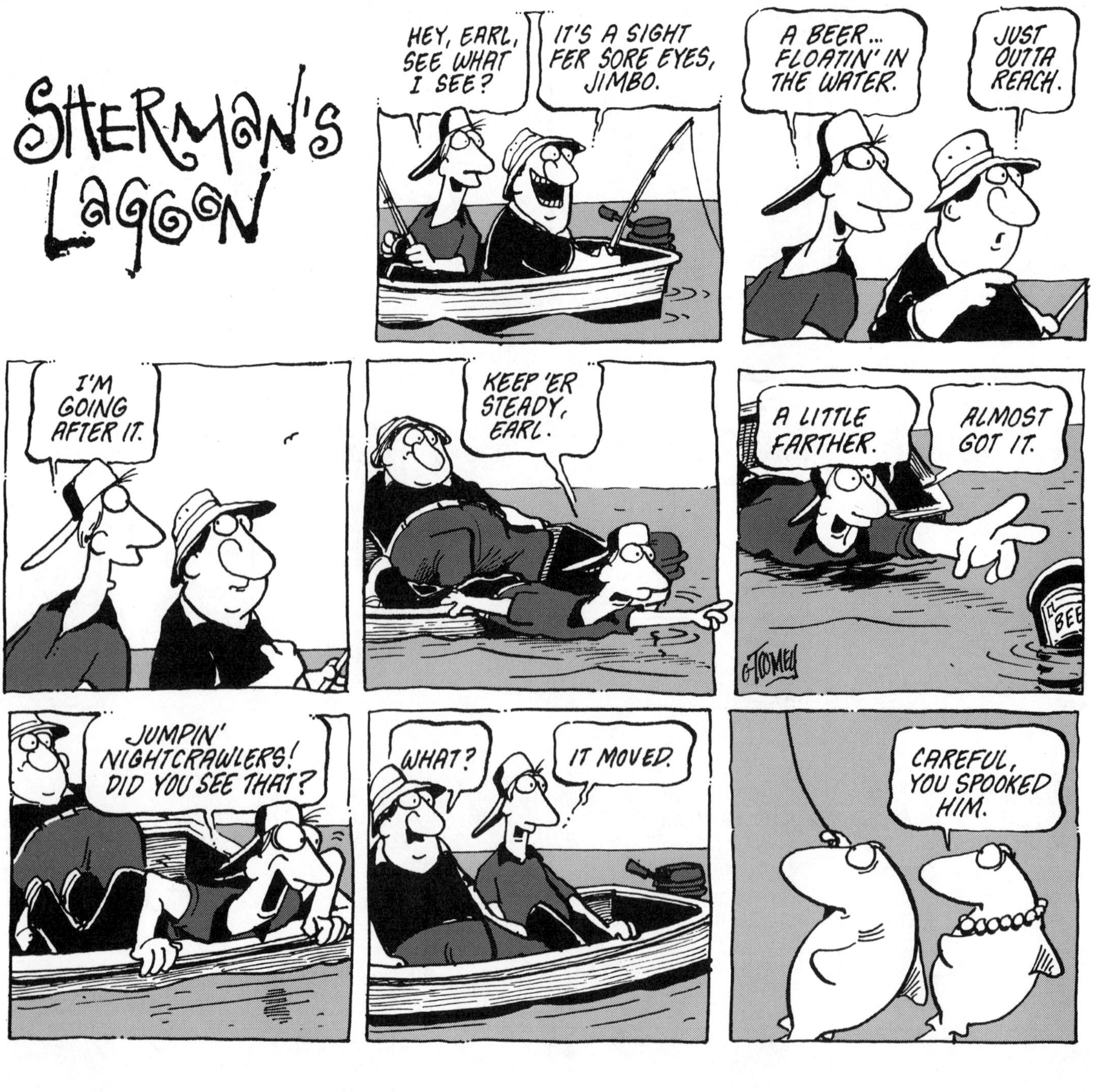
SHERMAN'S LAGOON
HEY, EARL, SEE WHAT I SEE?
IT'S A SIGHT FER SORE EYES, JIMBO.
A BEER... FLOATIN' IN THE WATER.
JUST OUTTA REACH.
I'M GOING AFTER IT.
KEEP 'ER STEADY, EARL.
A LITTLE FARTHER.
ALMOST GOT IT.
BEE
TOOMEY
JUMPIN' NIGHTCRAWLERS! DID YOU SEE THAT?
WHAT?
IT MOVED.
CAREFUL, YOU SPOOKED HIM.

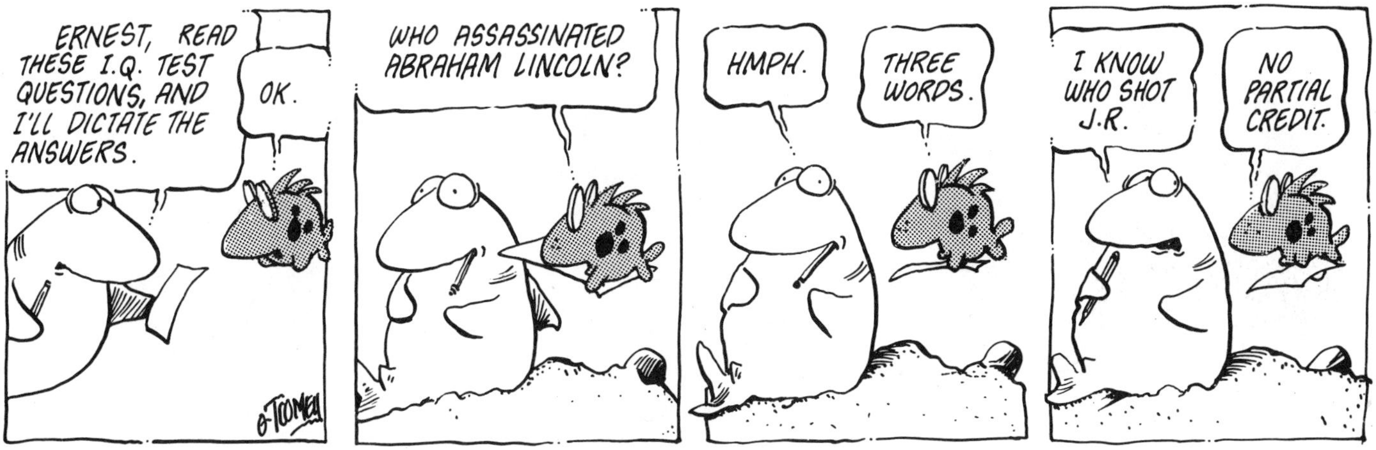
ERNEST, READ THESE I.Q. TEST QUESTIONS, AND I'LL DICTATE THE ANSWERS.
OK.
WHO ASSASSINATED ABRAHAM LINCOLN?
HMPH.
THREE WORDS.
I KNOW WHO SHOT J.R.
NO PARTIAL CREDIT.

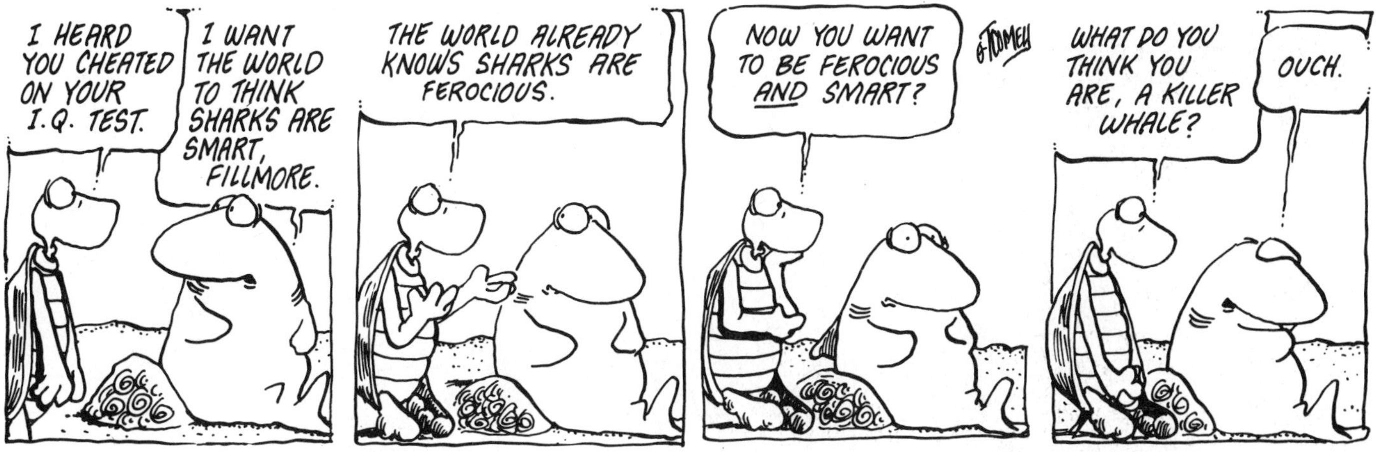
I HEARD YOU CHEATED ON YOUR I.Q. TEST.
I WANT THE WORLD TO THINK SHARKS ARE SMART, FILLMORE.
THE WORLD ALREADY KNOWS SHARKS ARE FEROCIOUS.
NOW YOU WANT TO BE FEROCIOUS AND SMART?
WHAT DO YOU THINK YOU ARE, A KILLER WHALE?
OUCH.

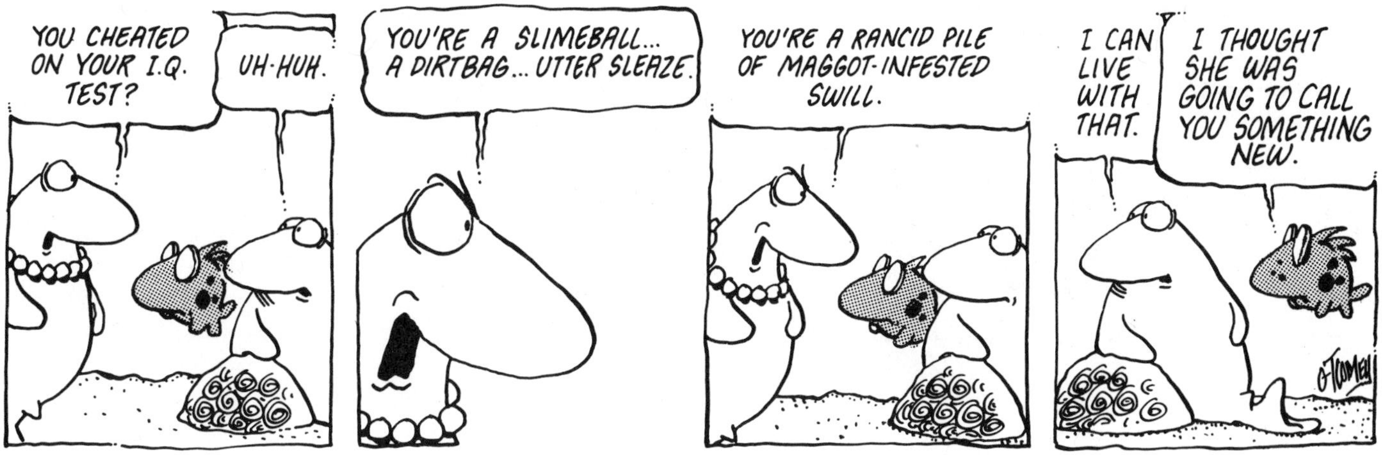
YOU CHEATED ON YOUR I.Q. TEST?
UH-HUH.
YOU'RE A SLIMEBALL... A DIRTBAG... UTTER SLEAZE.
YOU'RE A RANCID PILE OF MAGGOT-INFESTED SWILL.
I CAN LIVE WITH THAT.
I THOUGHT SHE WAS GOING TO CALL YOU SOMETHING NEW.

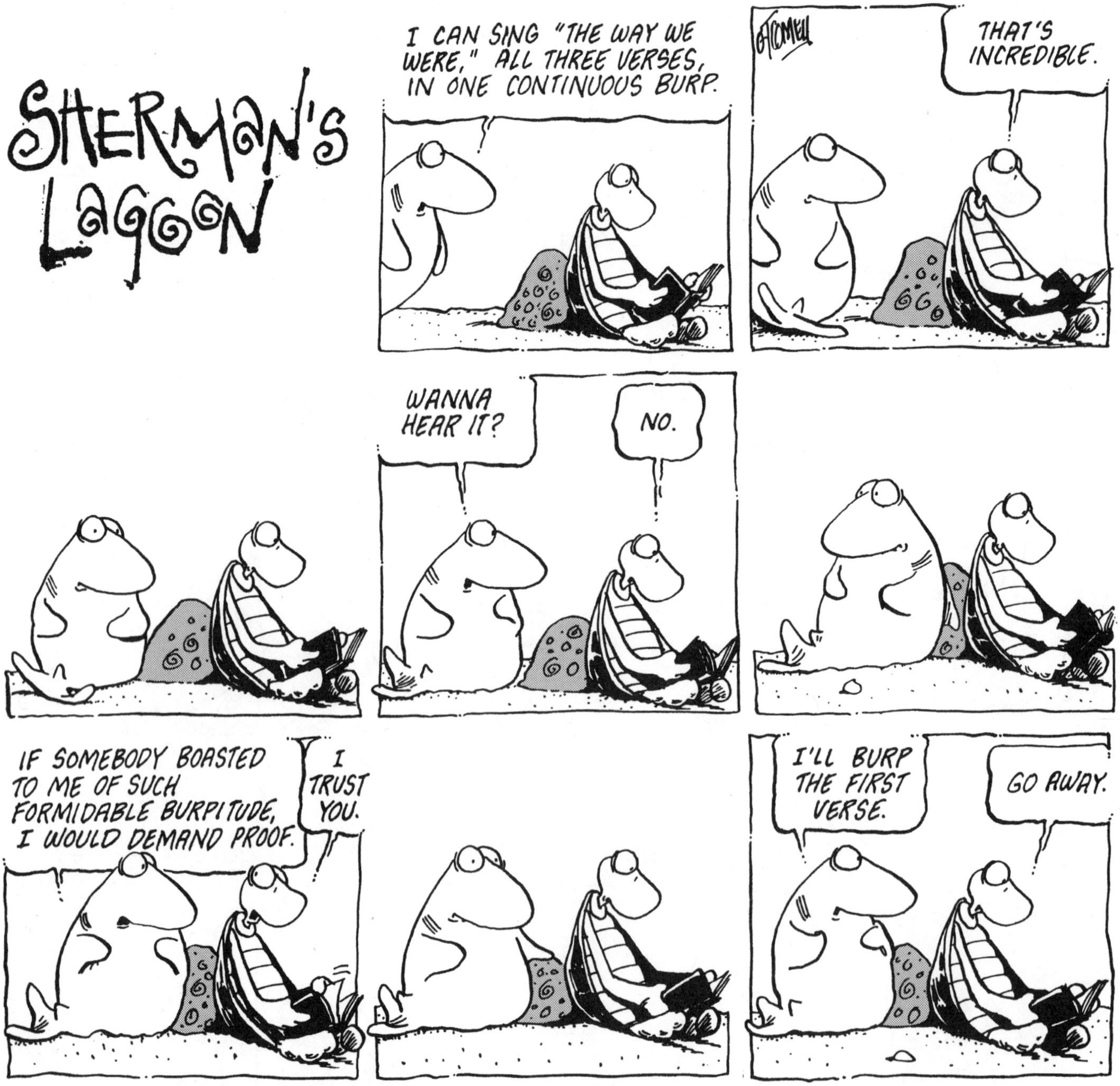
SHERMAN'S LAGOON
I CAN SING "THE WAY WE WERE," ALL THREE VERSES, IN ONE CONTINUOUS BURP.
THAT'S INCREDIBLE.
WANNA HEAR IT?
NO.
IF SOMEBODY BOASTED TO ME OF SUCH FORMIDABLE BURPITUDE, I WOULD DEMAND PROOF.
I TRUST YOU.
I'LL BURP THE FIRST VERSE.
GO AWAY.

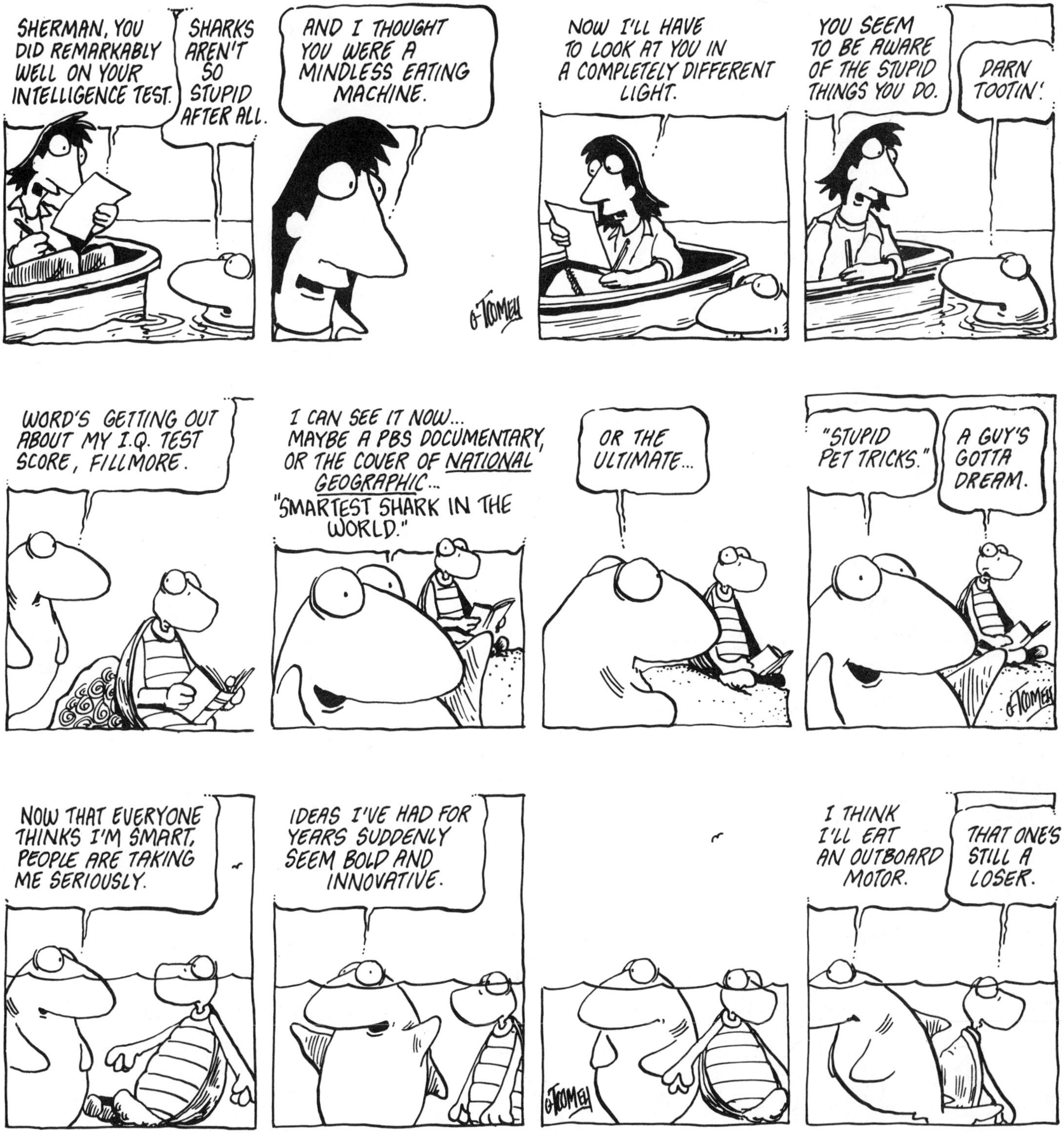
SHERMAN, YOU DID REMARKABLY WELL ON YOUR INTELLIGENCE TEST.
SHARKS AREN'T SO STUPID AFTER ALL.
AND I THOUGHT YOU WERE A MINDLESS EATING MACHINE.
NOW I'LL HAVE TO LOOK AT YOU IN A COMPLETELY DIFFERENT LIGHT.
YOU SEEM TO BE AWARE OF THE STUPID THINGS YOU DO.
DARN TOOTIN'!
WORD'S GETTING OUT ABOUT MY I.Q. TEST SCORE, FILLMORE.
I CAN SEE IT NOW... MAYBE A PBS DOCUMENTARY, OR THE COVER OF NATIONAL GEOGRAPHIC... "SMARTEST SHARK IN THE WORLD."
OR THE ULTIMATE...
"STUPID PET TRICKS."
A GUY'S GOTTA DREAM.
NOW THAT EVERYONE THINKS I'M SMART, PEOPLE ARE TAKING ME SERIOUSLY.
IDEAS I'VE HAD FOR YEARS SUDDENLY SEEM BOLD AND INNOVATIVE.
I THINK I'LL EAT AN OUTBOARD MOTOR.
THAT ONE'S STILL A LOSER.

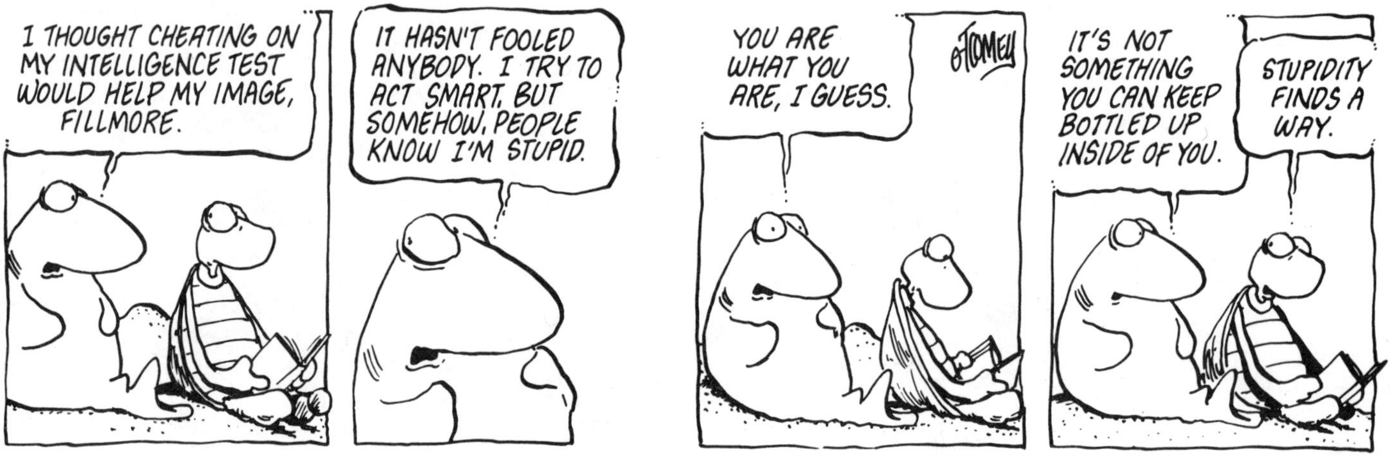
I THOUGHT CHEATING ON MY INTELLIGENCE TEST WOULD HELP MY IMAGE, FILLMORE.
IT HASN'T FOOLED ANYBODY. I TRY TO ACT SMART, BUT SOMEHOW, PEOPLE KNOW I'M STUPID.
YOU ARE WHAT YOU ARE, I GUESS.
IT'S NOT SOMETHING YOU CAN KEEP BOTTLED UP INSIDE OF YOU.
STUPIDITY FINDS A WAY.

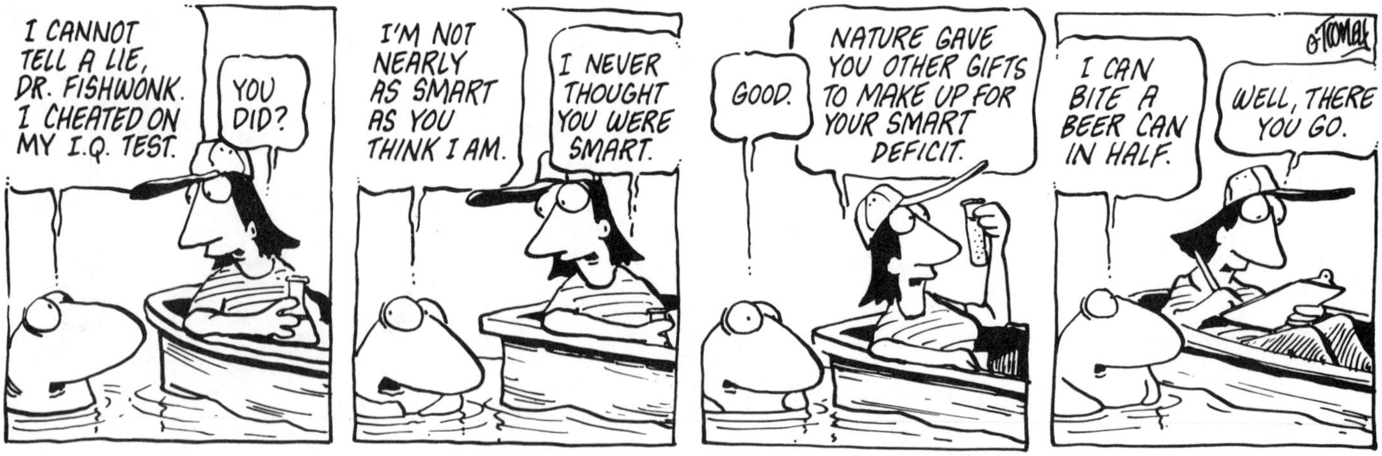
I CANNOT TELL A LIE, DR. FISHWONK. I CHEATED ON MY I.Q. TEST.
YOU DID?
I'M NOT NEARLY AS SMART AS YOU THINK I AM.
I NEVER THOUGHT YOU WERE SMART.
GOOD.
NATURE GAVE YOU OTHER GIFTS TO MAKE UP FOR YOUR SMART DEFICIT.
I CAN BITE A BEER CAN IN HALF.
WELL, THERE YOU GO.

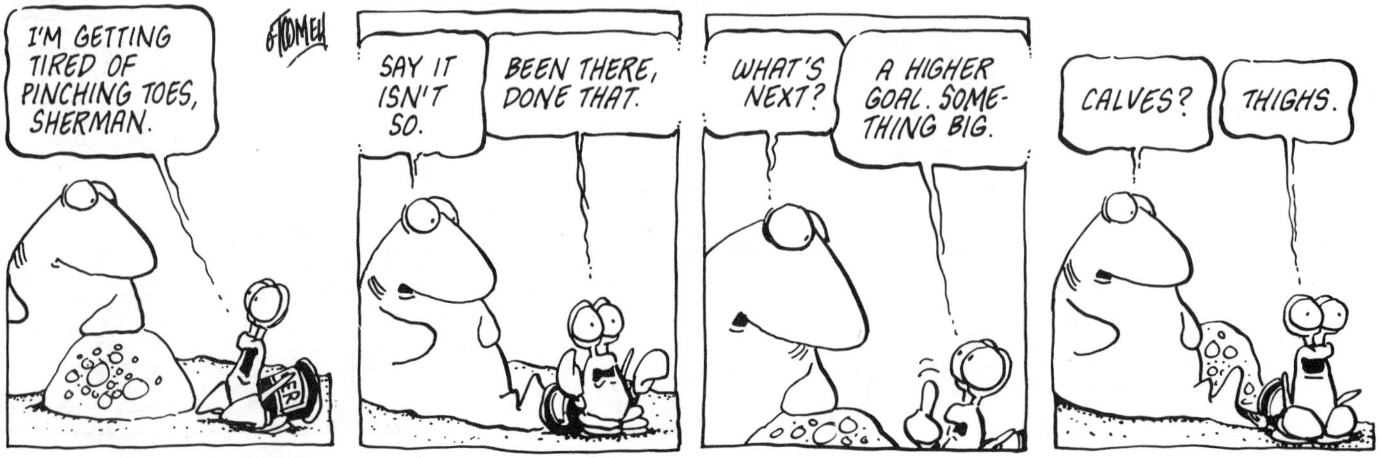
I'M GETTING TIRED OF PINCHING TOES, SHERMAN.
SAY IT ISN'T SO.
BEEN THERE, DONE THAT.
WHAT'S NEXT?
A HIGHER GOAL. SOMETHING BIG.
CALVES?
THIGHS.

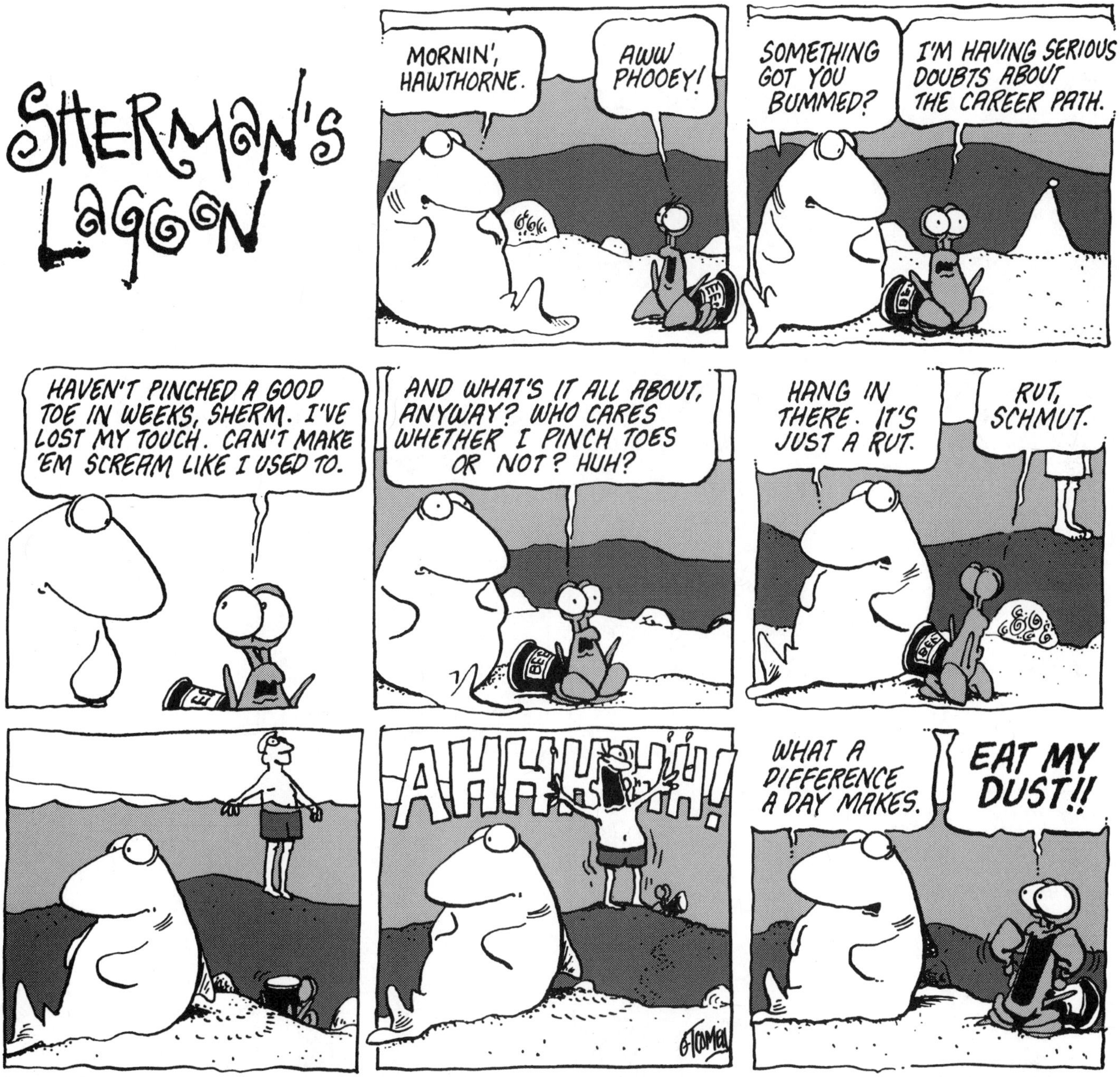
SHERMAN'S LAGOON
MORNIN', HAWTHORNE.
AWW PHOOEY!
SOMETHING GOT YOU BUMMED?
I'M HAVING SERIOUS DOUBTS ABOUT THE CAREER PATH.
HAVEN'T PINCHED A GOOD TOE IN WEEKS, SHERM. I'VE LOST MY TOUCH. CAN'T MAKE 'EM SCREAM LIKE I USED TO.
AND WHAT'S IT ALL ABOUT, ANYWAY? WHO CARES WHETHER I PINCH TOES OR NOT? HUH?
HANG IN THERE. IT'S JUST A RUT.
RUT, SCHMUT.
AHHHHHH!
WHAT A DIFFERENCE A DAY MAKES.
EAT MY DUST!!

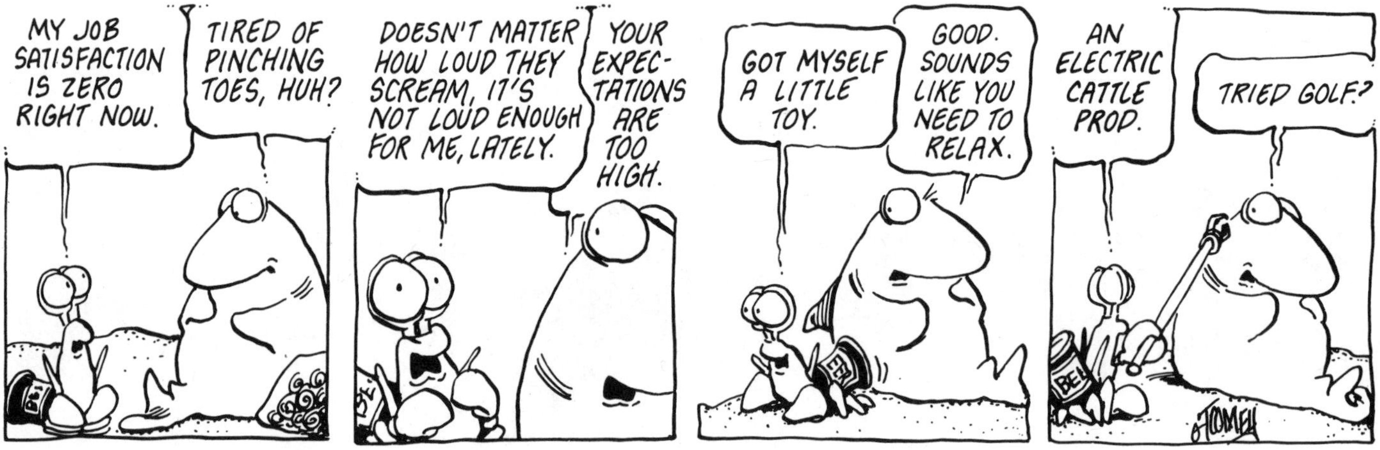
MY JOB SATISFACTION IS ZERO RIGHT NOW.
TIRED OF PINCHING TOES, HUH?
DOESN'T MATTER HOW LOUD THEY SCREAM, IT'S NOT LOUD ENOUGH FOR ME, LATELY.
YOUR EXPECTATIONS ARE TOO HIGH.
GOT MYSELF A LITTLE TOY.
GOOD. SOUNDS LIKE YOU NEED TO RELAX.
AN ELECTRIC CATTLE PROD.
TRIED GOLF?
TOOMEY

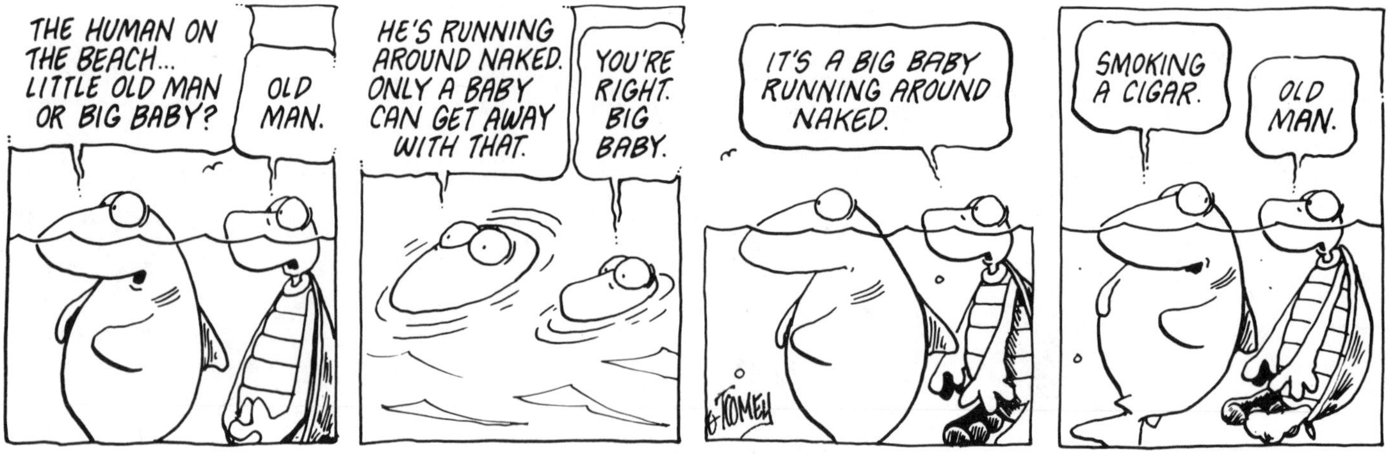
THE HUMAN ON THE BEACH... LITTLE OLD MAN OR BIG BABY?
OLD MAN.
HE'S RUNNING AROUND NAKED. ONLY A BABY CAN GET AWAY WITH THAT.
YOU'RE RIGHT. BIG BABY.
IT'S A BIG BABY RUNNING AROUND NAKED.
TOOMEY
SMOKING A CIGAR.
OLD MAN.

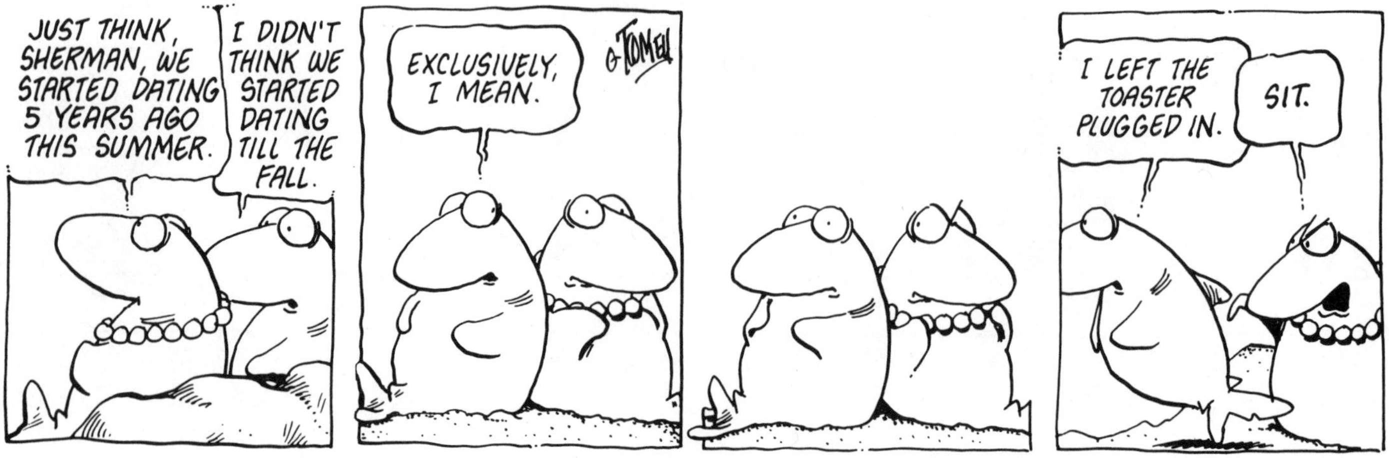
JUST THINK, SHERMAN, WE STARTED DATING 5 YEARS AGO THIS SUMMER.
I DIDN'T THINK WE STARTED DATING TILL THE FALL.
EXCLUSIVELY, I MEAN.
TOOMEY
I LEFT THE TOASTER PLUGGED IN.
SIT.

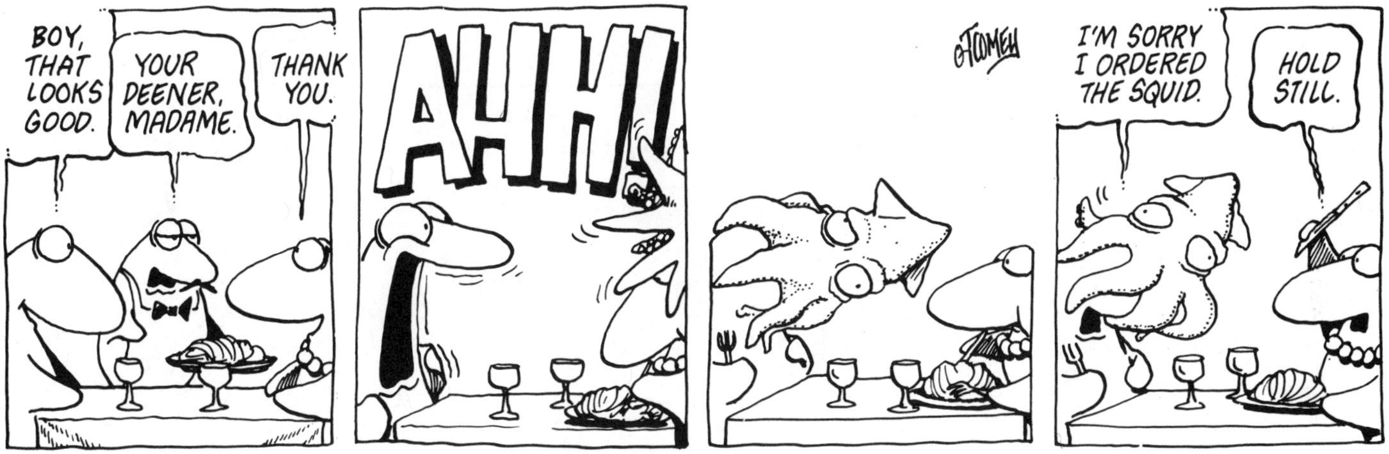
BOY, THAT LOOKS GOOD.
YOUR DEENER, MADAME.
THANK YOU.
AHH!
I'M SORRY I ORDERED THE SQUID.
HOLD STILL.

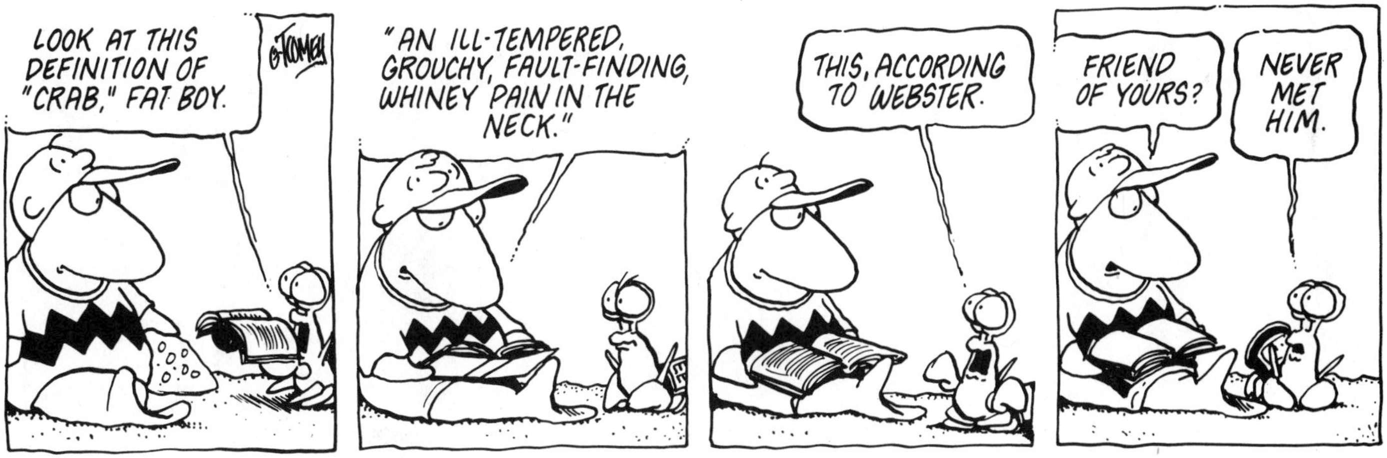
LOOK AT THIS DEFINITION OF "CRAB," FAT BOY.
"AN ILL-TEMPERED, GROUCHY, FAULT-FINDING, WHINEY PAIN IN THE NECK."
THIS, ACCORDING TO WEBSTER.
FRIEND OF YOURS?
NEVER MET HIM.

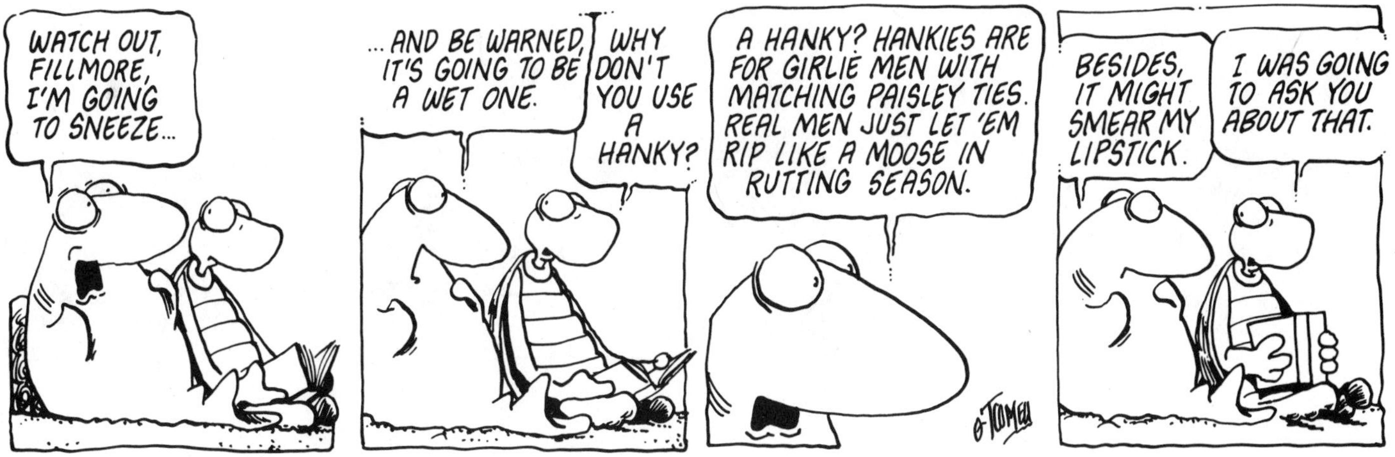
WATCH OUT, FILLMORE, I'M GOING TO SNEEZE...
... AND BE WARNED, IT'S GOING TO BE A WET ONE.
WHY DON'T YOU USE A HANKY?
A HANKY? HANKIES ARE FOR GIRLIE MEN WITH MATCHING PAISLEY TIES. REAL MEN JUST LET 'EM RIP LIKE A MOOSE IN RUTTING SEASON.
BESIDES, IT MIGHT SMEAR MY LIPSTICK.
I WAS GOING TO ASK YOU ABOUT THAT.

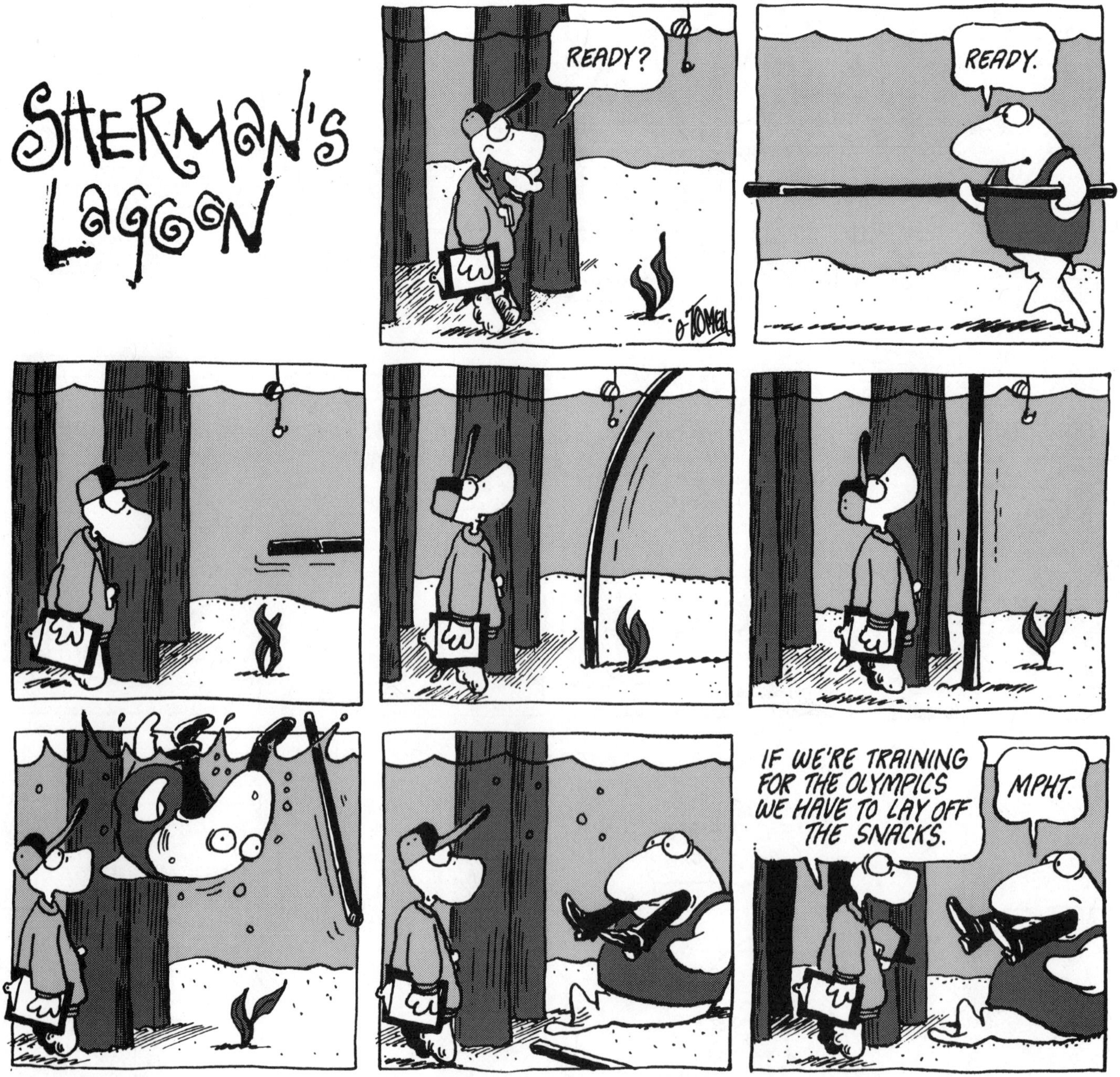
SHERMAN'S LAGOON
READY?
READY.
IF WE'RE TRAINING FOR THE OLYMPICS WE HAVE TO LAY OFF THE SNACKS.
MPHT.

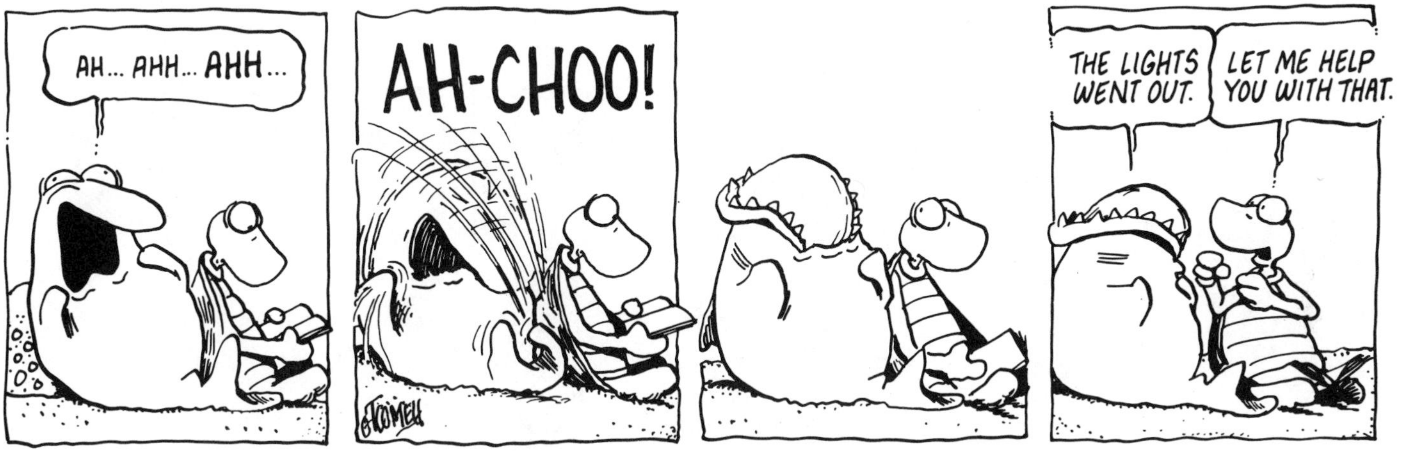
AH... AHH... AHH...
AH-CHOO!
THE LIGHTS WENT OUT.
LET ME HELP YOU WITH THAT.

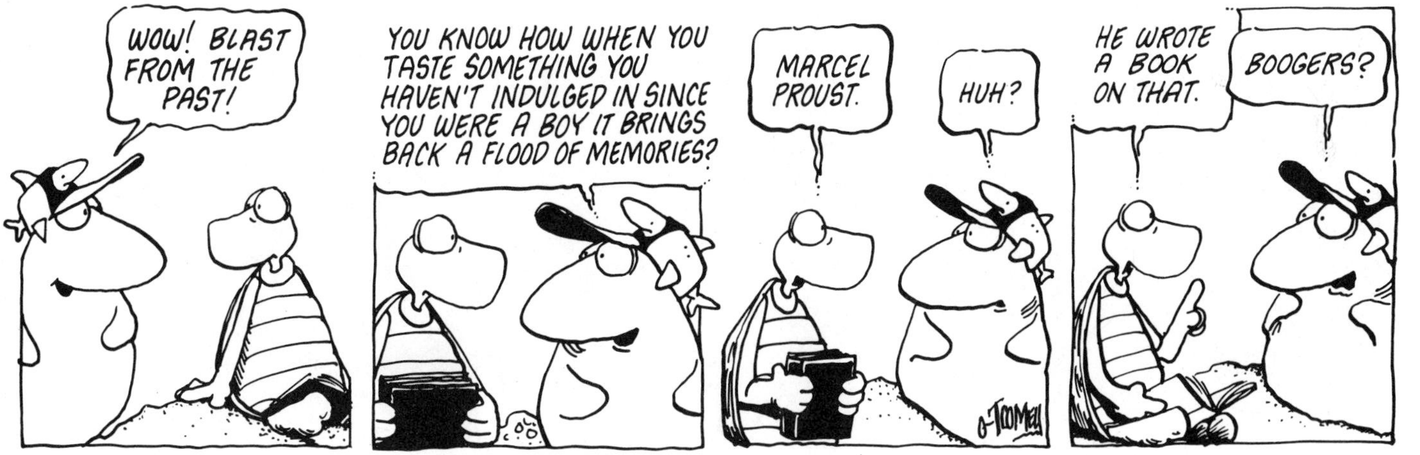
WOW! BLAST FROM THE PAST!
YOU KNOW HOW WHEN YOU TASTE SOMETHING YOU HAVEN'T INDULGED IN SINCE YOU WERE A BOY IT BRINGS BACK A FLOOD OF MEMORIES?
MARCEL PROUST.
HUH?
HE WROTE A BOOK ON THAT.
BOOGERS?

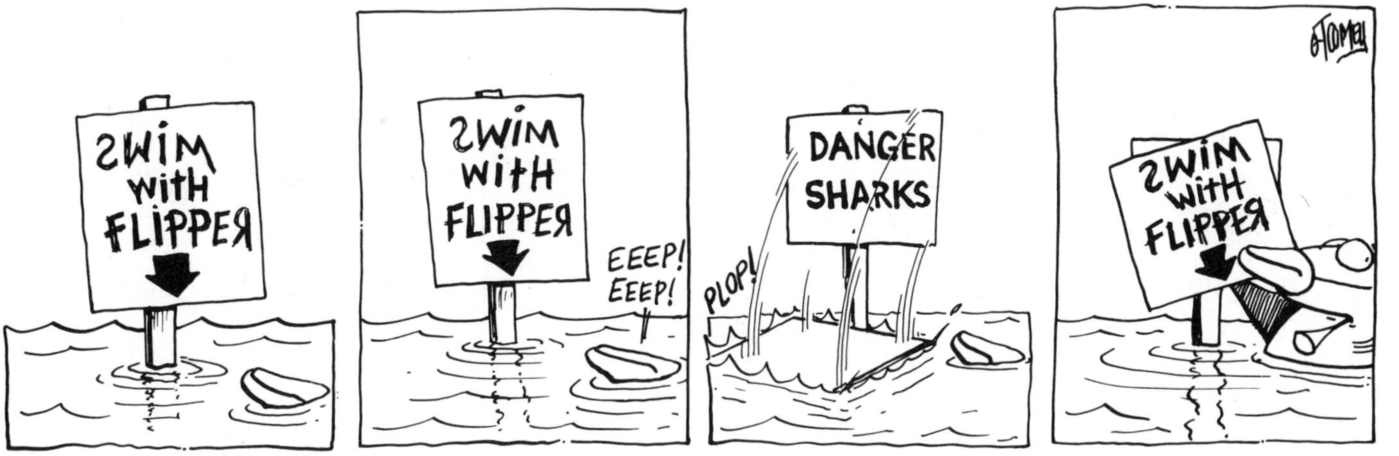
SWIM with FLIPPER
SWIM with FLIPPER
EEEP! EEEP!
PLOP!
DANGER SHARKS
SWIM with FLIPPER

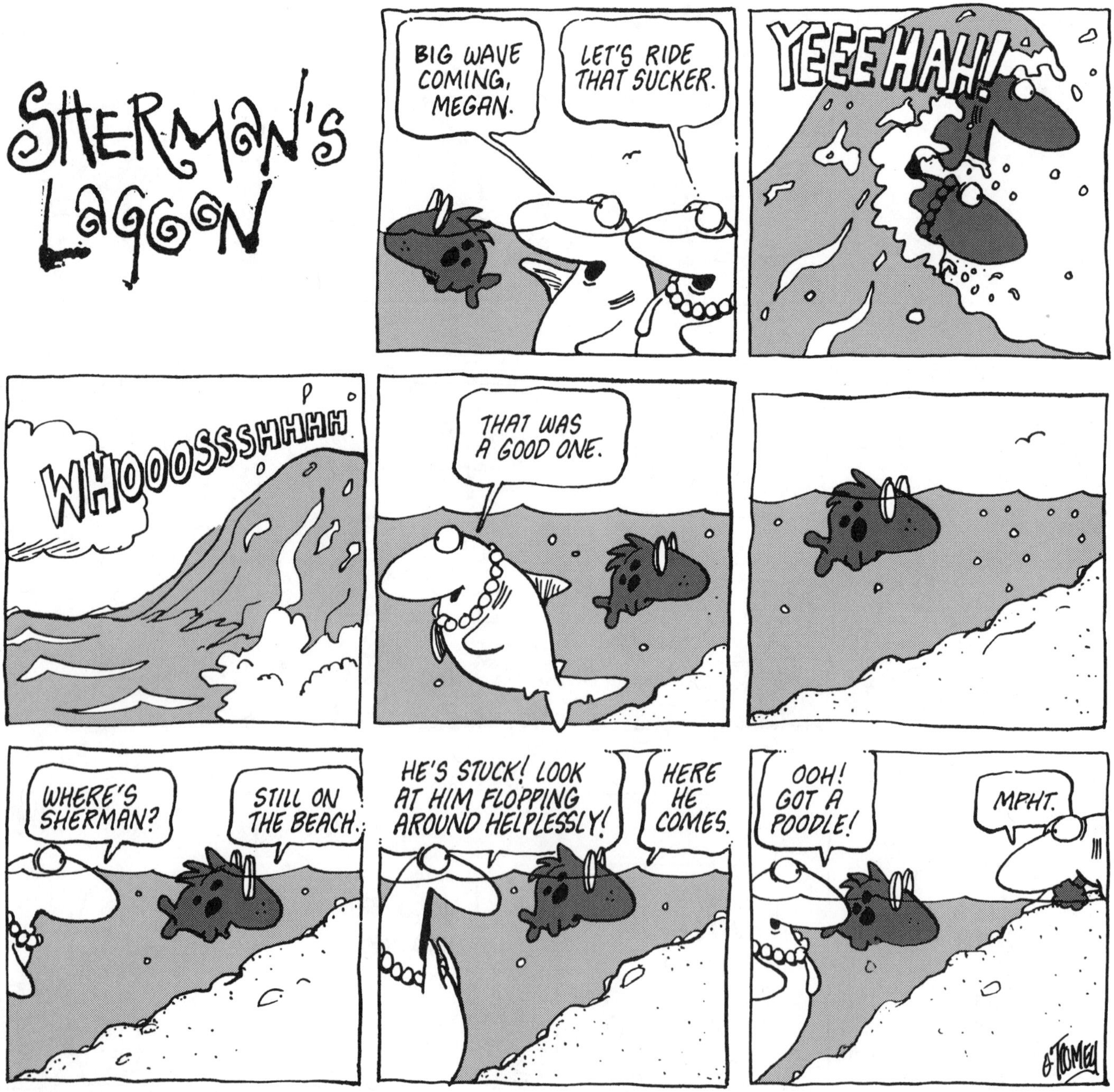
SHERMAN'S LAGOON
BIG WAVE COMING, MEGAN.
LET'S RIDE THAT SUCKER.
YEEEHAH!
WHOOOOSSSHHHHH
THAT WAS A GOOD ONE.
WHERE'S SHERMAN?
STILL ON THE BEACH.
HE'S STUCK! LOOK AT HIM FLOPPING AROUND HELPLESSLY!
HERE HE COMES.
OOH! GOT A POODLE!
MPHT.
TOOMEY

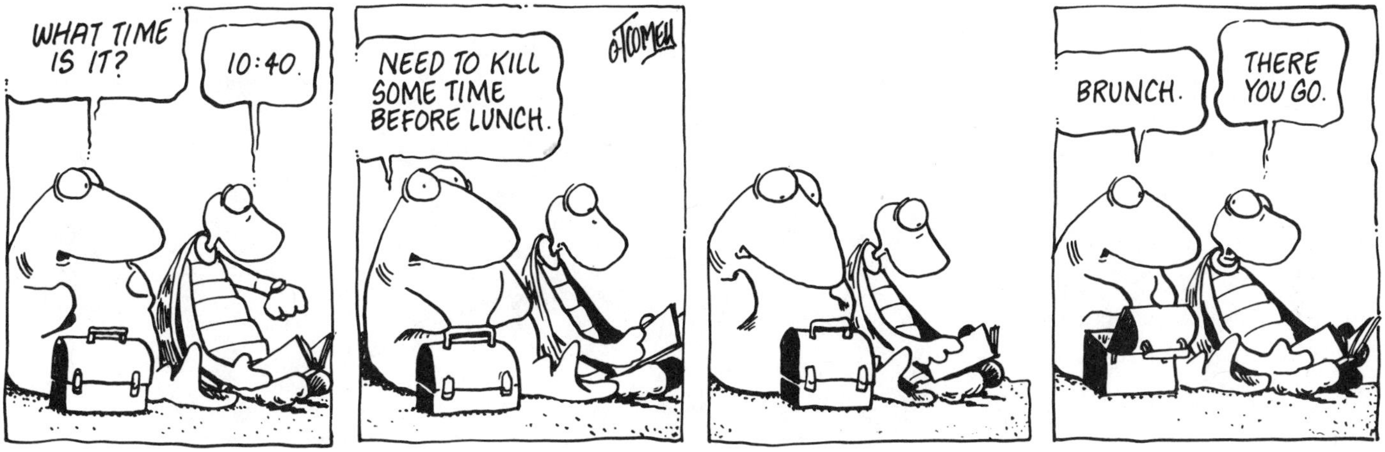
WHAT TIME IS IT?
10:40.
NEED TO KILL SOME TIME BEFORE LUNCH.
BRUNCH.
THERE YOU GO.

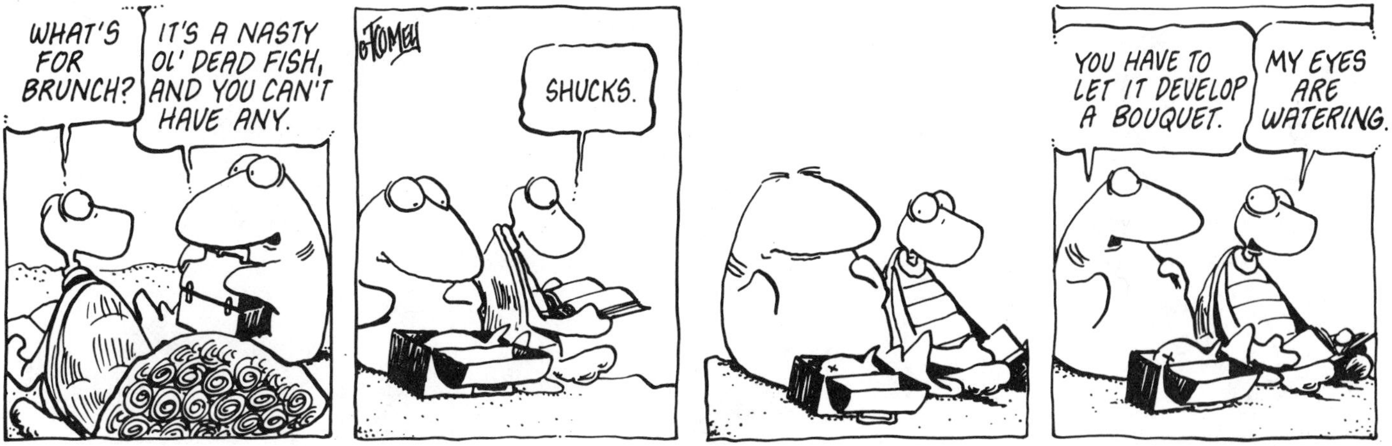
WHAT'S FOR BRUNCH?
IT'S A NASTY OL' DEAD FISH, AND YOU CAN'T HAVE ANY.
SHUCKS.
YOU HAVE TO LET IT DEVELOP A BOUQUET.
MY EYES ARE WATERING.

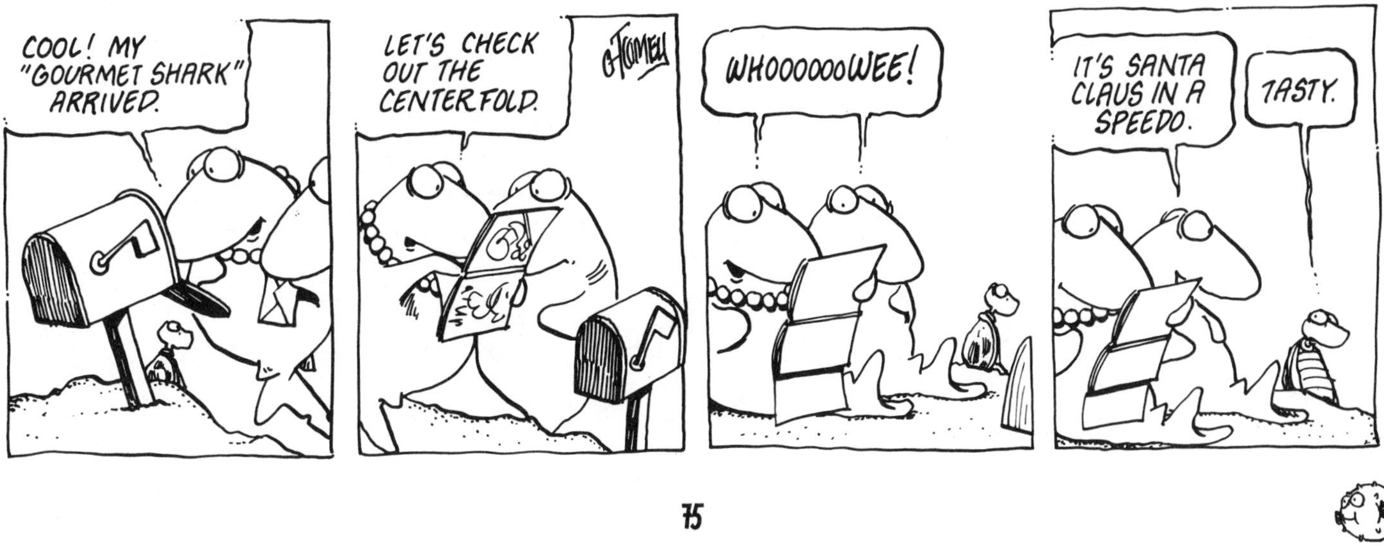
COOL! MY "GOURMET SHARK" ARRIVED.
LET'S CHECK OUT THE CENTERFOLD.
WHOOOOOOOWEE!
IT'S SANTA CLAUS IN A SPEEDO.
TASTY.

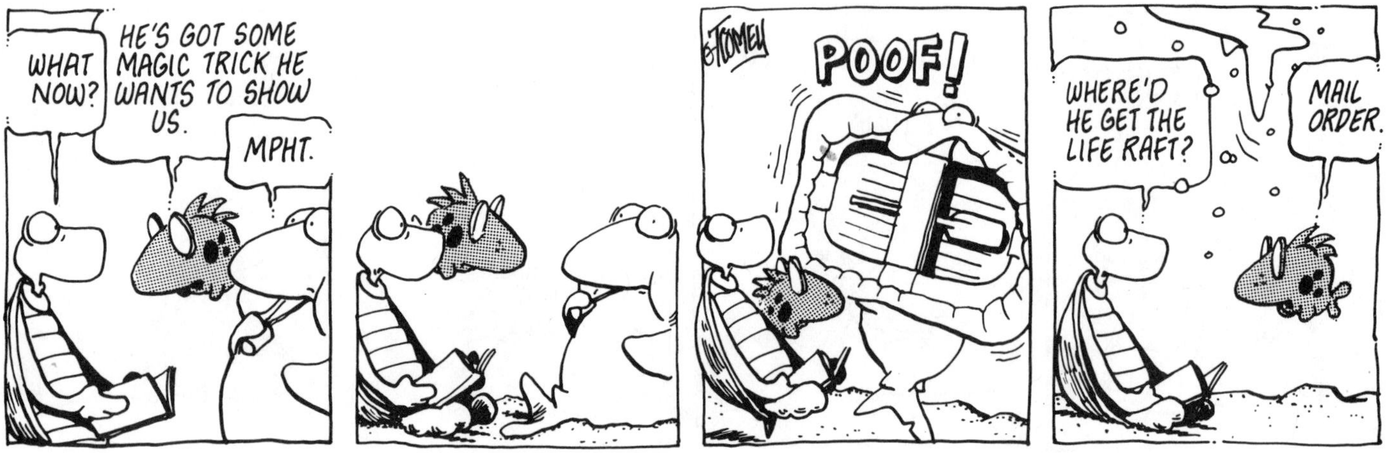
WHAT NOW?
HE'S GOT SOME MAGIC TRICK HE WANTS TO SHOW US.
MPHT.
TOOMEY
POOF!
WHERE'D HE GET THE LIFE RAFT?
MAIL ORDER.

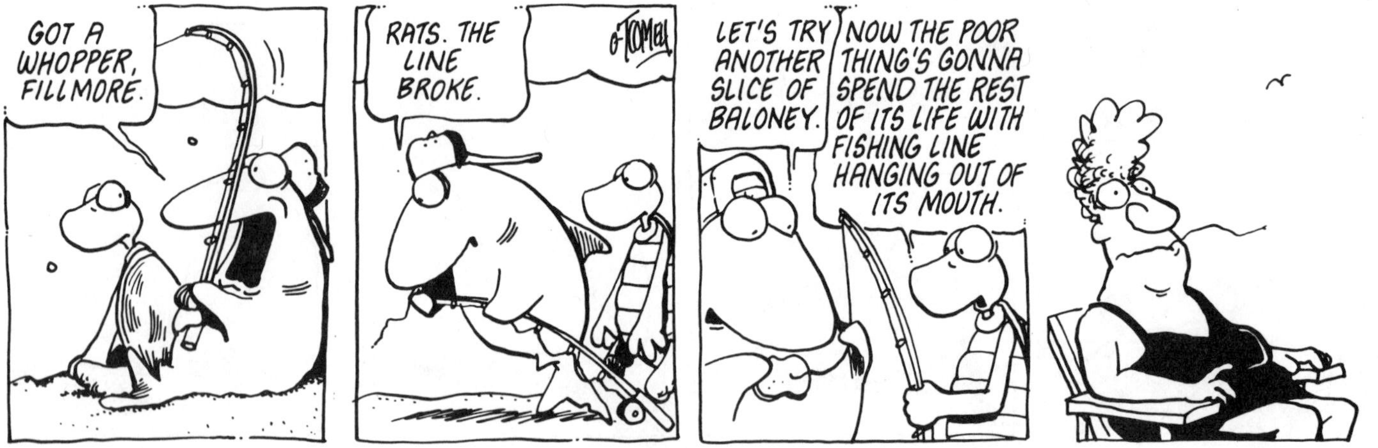
GOT A WHOPPER, FILLMORE.
RATS. THE LINE BROKE.
TOOMEY
LET'S TRY ANOTHER SLICE OF BALONEY.
NOW THE POOR THING'S GONNA SPEND THE REST OF ITS LIFE WITH FISHING LINE HANGING OUT OF ITS MOUTH.

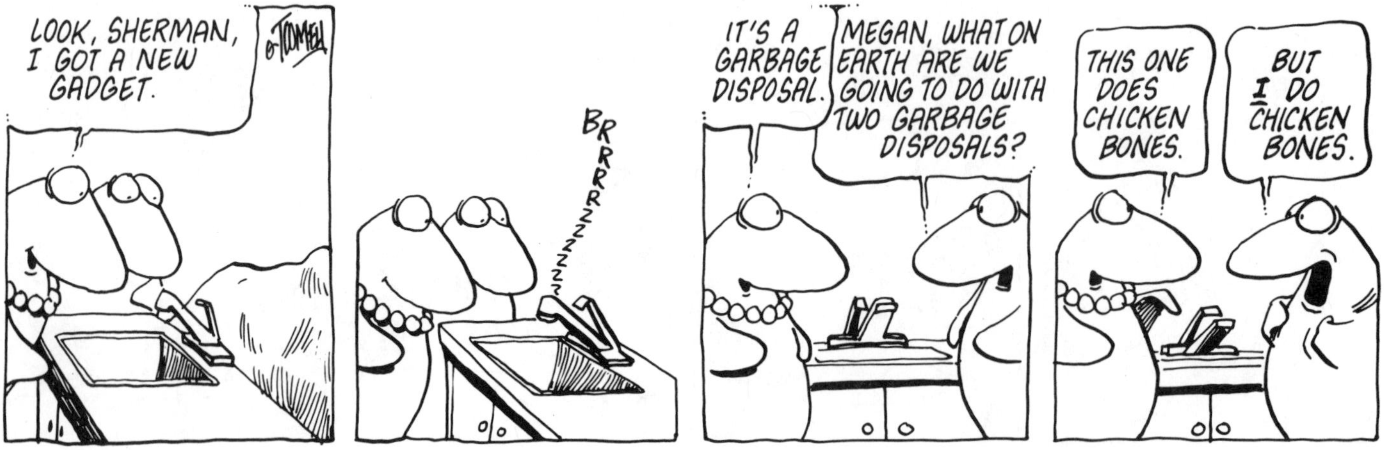
LOOK, SHERMAN, I GOT A NEW GADGET.
TOOMEY
BRRRZZZZZZ
IT'S A GARBAGE DISPOSAL.
MEGAN, WHAT ON EARTH ARE WE GOING TO DO WITH TWO GARBAGE DISPOSALS?
THIS ONE DOES CHICKEN BONES.
BUT **I** DO CHICKEN BONES.

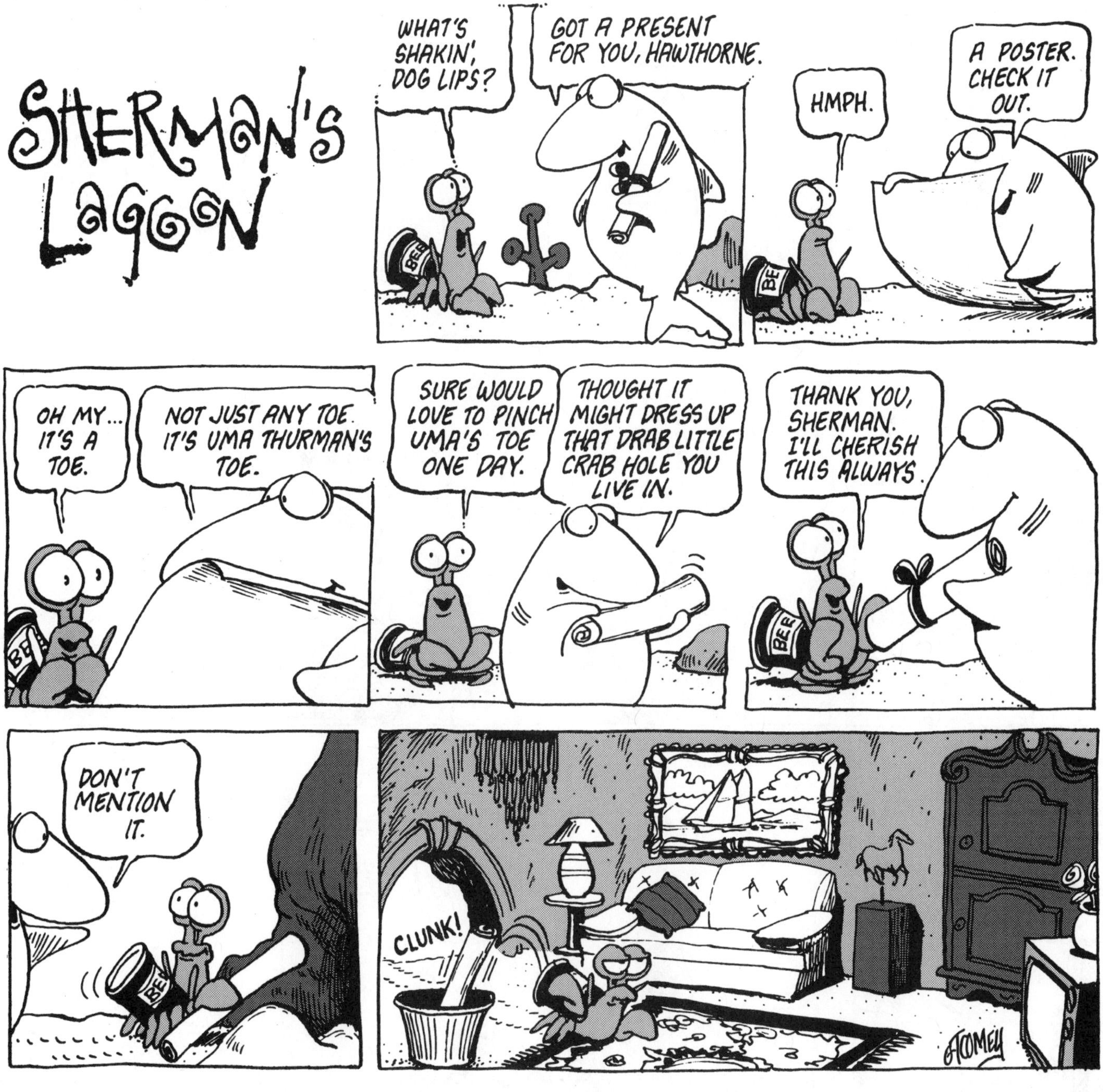
SHERMAN'S LAGOON
WHAT'S SHAKIN', DOG LIPS?
GOT A PRESENT FOR YOU, HAWTHORNE.
HMPH.
A POSTER. CHECK IT OUT.
OH MY... IT'S A TOE.
NOT JUST ANY TOE. IT'S UMA THURMAN'S TOE.
SURE WOULD LOVE TO PINCH UMA'S TOE ONE DAY.
THOUGHT IT MIGHT DRESS UP THAT DRAB LITTLE CRAB HOLE YOU LIVE IN.
THANK YOU, SHERMAN. I'LL CHERISH THIS ALWAYS.
DON'T MENTION IT.
CLUNK!
TOOMEY

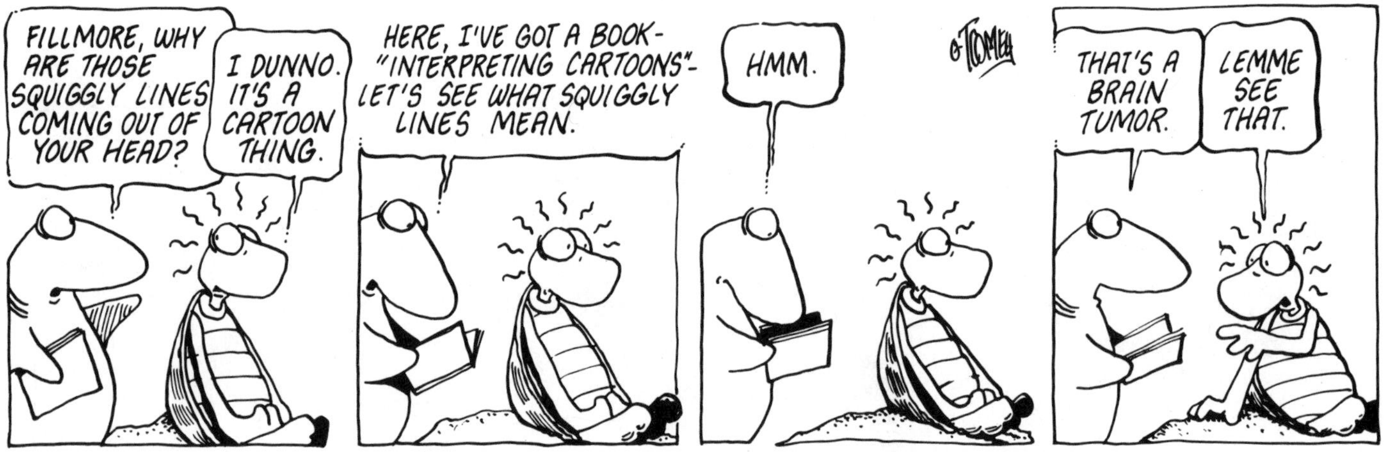
FILLMORE, WHY ARE THOSE SQUIGGLY LINES COMING OUT OF YOUR HEAD?
I DUNNO. IT'S A CARTOON THING.
HERE, I'VE GOT A BOOK- "INTERPRETING CARTOONS"- LET'S SEE WHAT SQUIGGLY LINES MEAN.
HMM.
THAT'S A BRAIN TUMOR.
LEMME SEE THAT.

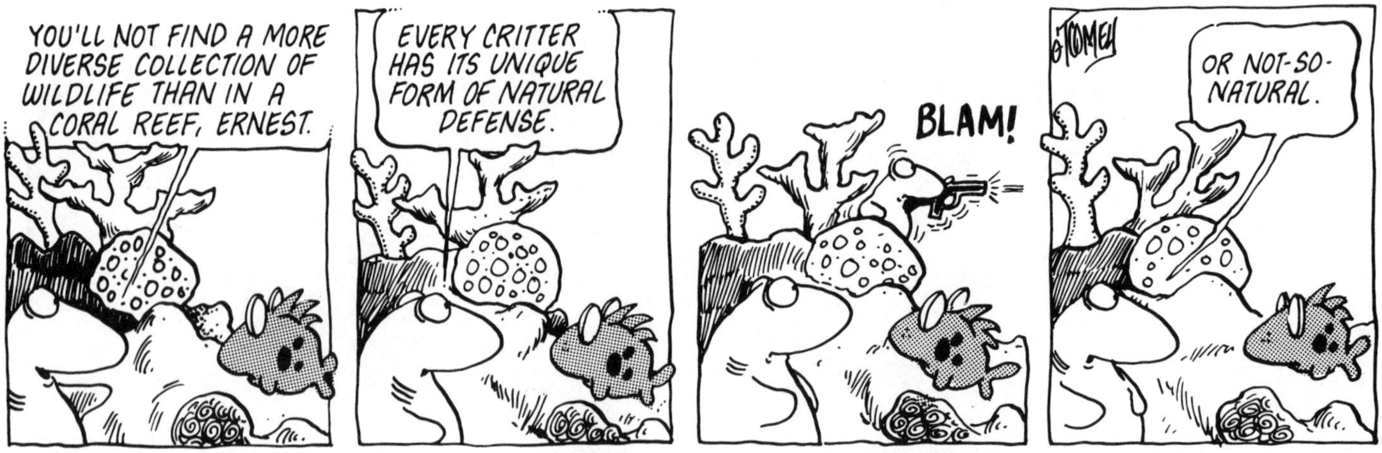
YOU'LL NOT FIND A MORE DIVERSE COLLECTION OF WILDLIFE THAN IN A CORAL REEF, ERNEST.
EVERY CRITTER HAS ITS UNIQUE FORM OF NATURAL DEFENSE.
BLAM!
OR NOT-SO-NATURAL.

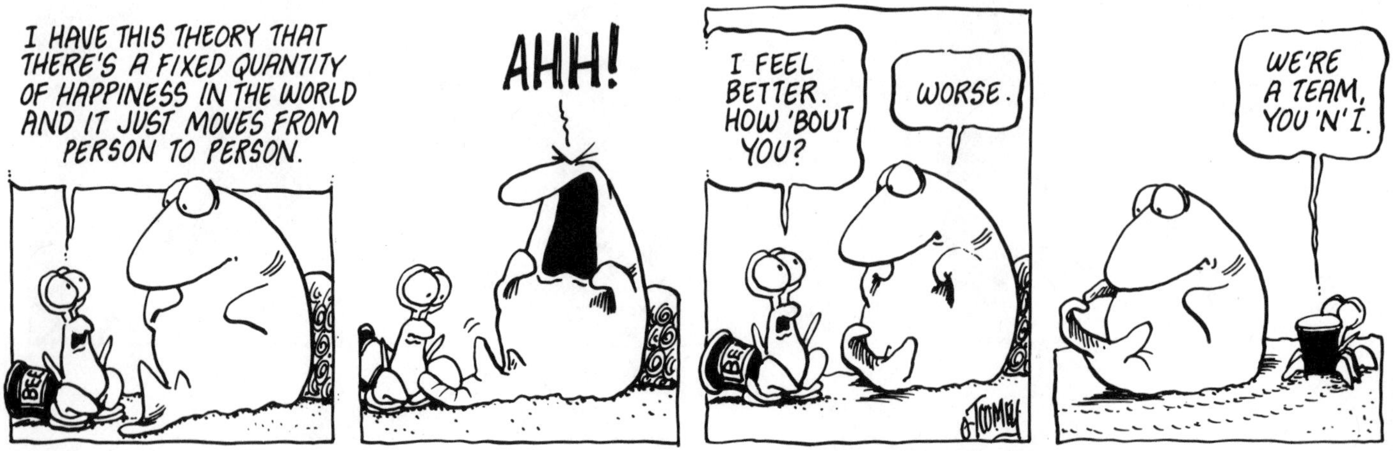
I HAVE THIS THEORY THAT THERE'S A FIXED QUANTITY OF HAPPINESS IN THE WORLD AND IT JUST MOVES FROM PERSON TO PERSON.
AHH!
I FEEL BETTER. HOW 'BOUT YOU?
WORSE.
WE'RE A TEAM, YOU 'N' I.

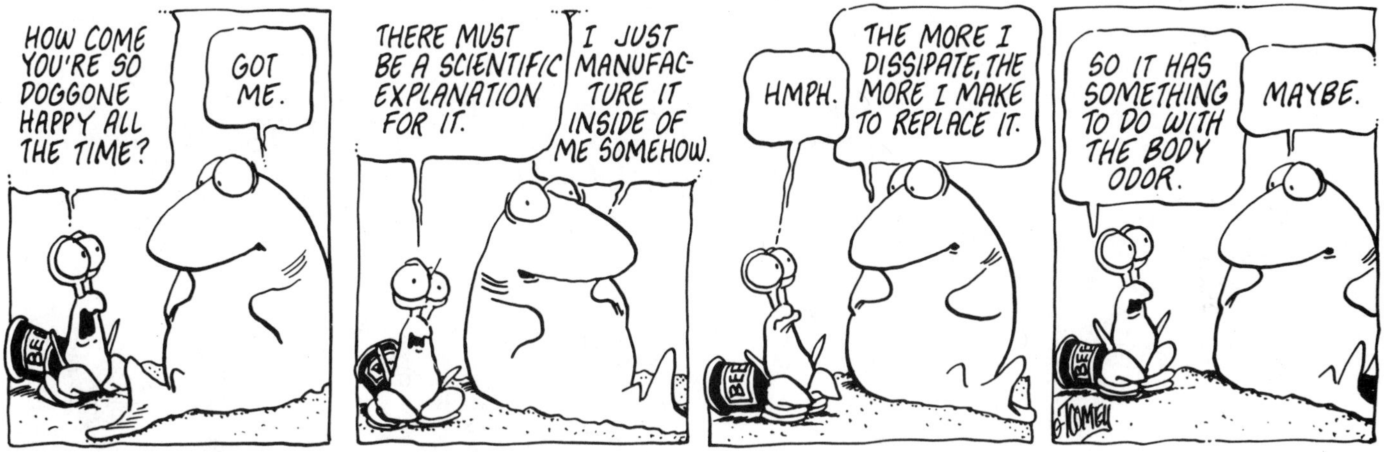
HOW COME YOU'RE SO DOGGONE HAPPY ALL THE TIME?
GOT ME.
THERE MUST BE A SCIENTIFIC EXPLANATION FOR IT.
I JUST MANUFACTURE IT INSIDE OF ME SOMEHOW.
HMPH.
THE MORE I DISSIPATE, THE MORE I MAKE TO REPLACE IT.
SO IT HAS SOMETHING TO DO WITH THE BODY ODOR.
MAYBE.

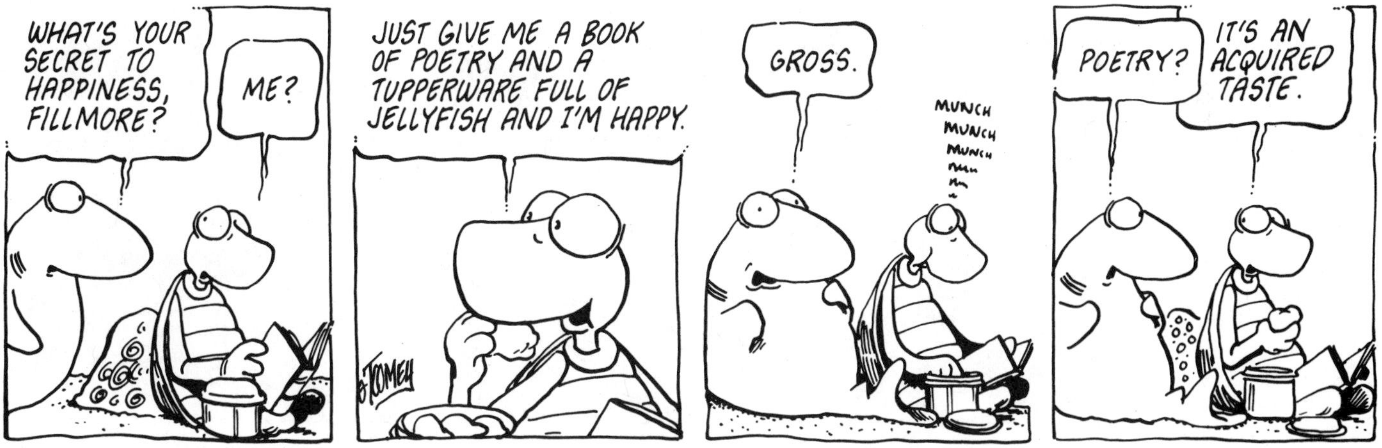
WHAT'S YOUR SECRET TO HAPPINESS, FILLMORE?
ME?
JUST GIVE ME A BOOK OF POETRY AND A TUPPERWARE FULL OF JELLYFISH AND I'M HAPPY.
GROSS.
MUNCH MUNCH MUNCH
POETRY?
IT'S AN ACQUIRED TASTE.

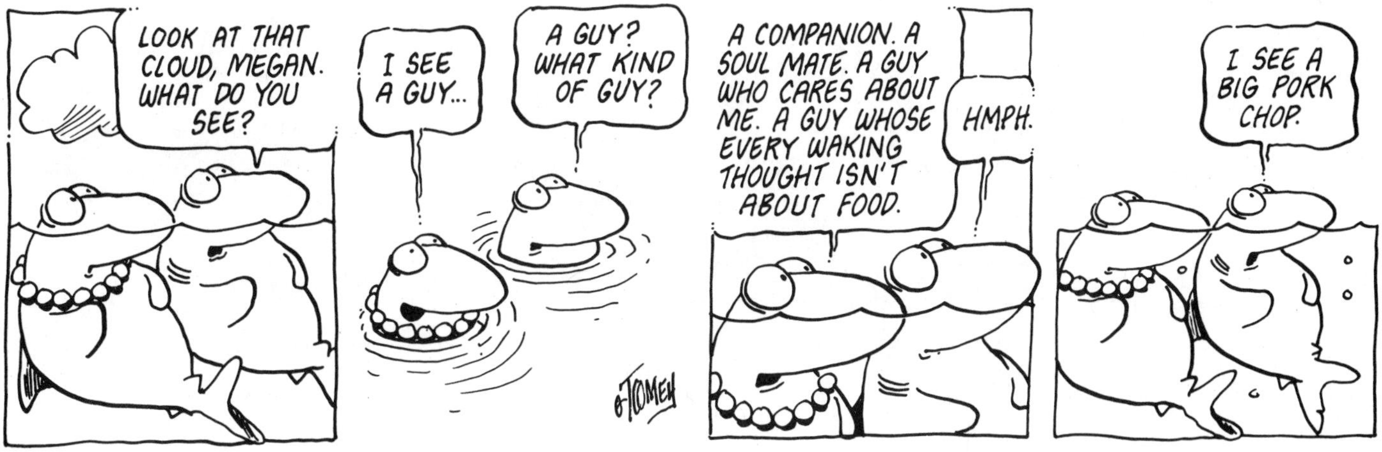
LOOK AT THAT CLOUD, MEGAN. WHAT DO YOU SEE?
I SEE A GUY...
A GUY? WHAT KIND OF GUY?
A COMPANION. A SOUL MATE. A GUY WHO CARES ABOUT ME. A GUY WHOSE EVERY WAKING THOUGHT ISN'T ABOUT FOOD.
HMPH.
I SEE A BIG PORK CHOP.

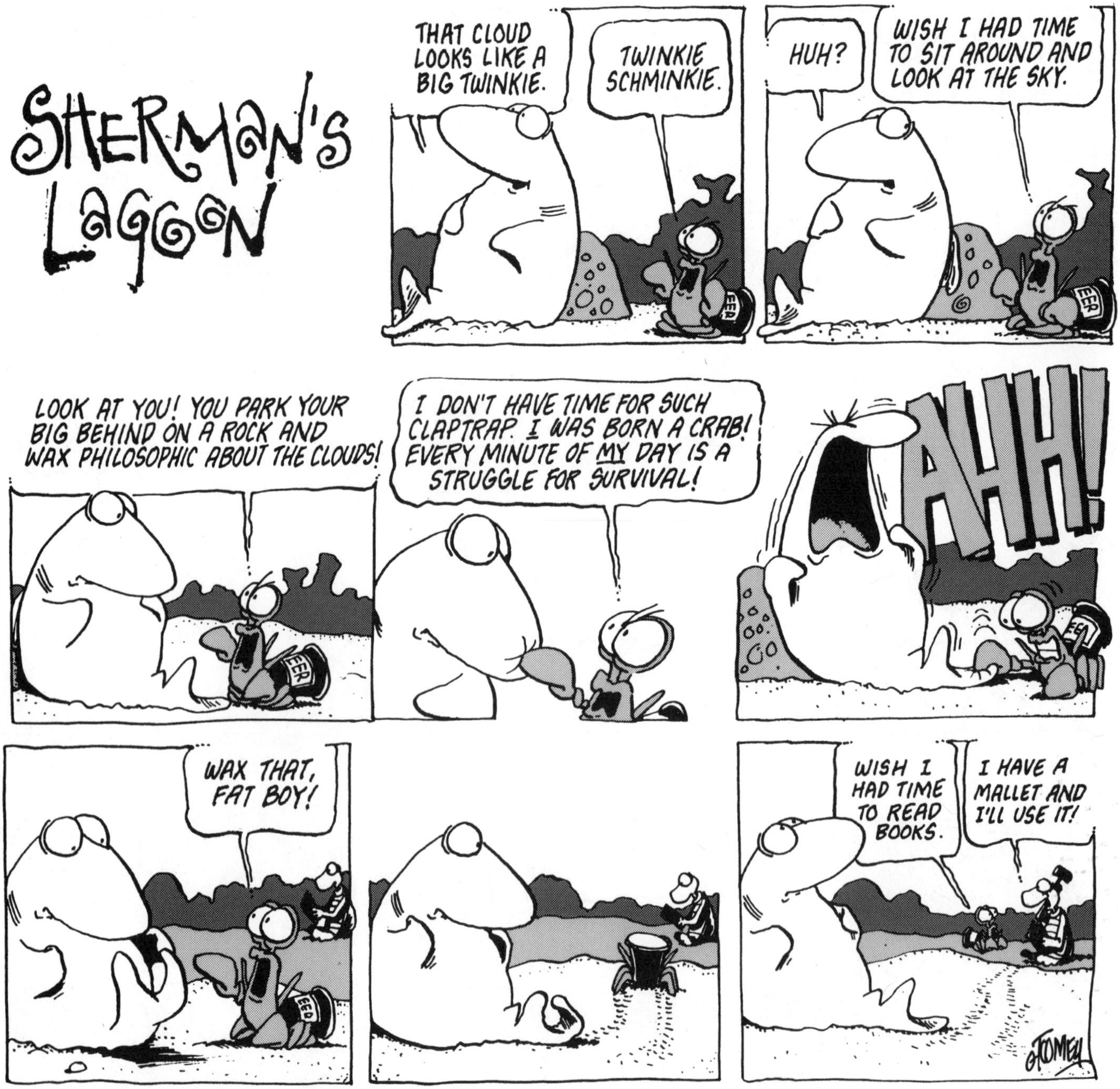
SHERMAN'S LAGOON
THAT CLOUD LOOKS LIKE A BIG TWINKIE.
TWINKIE SCHMINKIE.
HUH?
WISH I HAD TIME TO SIT AROUND AND LOOK AT THE SKY.
LOOK AT YOU! YOU PARK YOUR BIG BEHIND ON A ROCK AND WAX PHILOSOPHIC ABOUT THE CLOUDS!
I DON'T HAVE TIME FOR SUCH CLAPTRAP. I WAS BORN A CRAB! EVERY MINUTE OF MY DAY IS A STRUGGLE FOR SURVIVAL!
AHH!
WAX THAT, FAT BOY!
WISH I HAD TIME TO READ BOOKS.
I HAVE A MALLET AND I'LL USE IT!

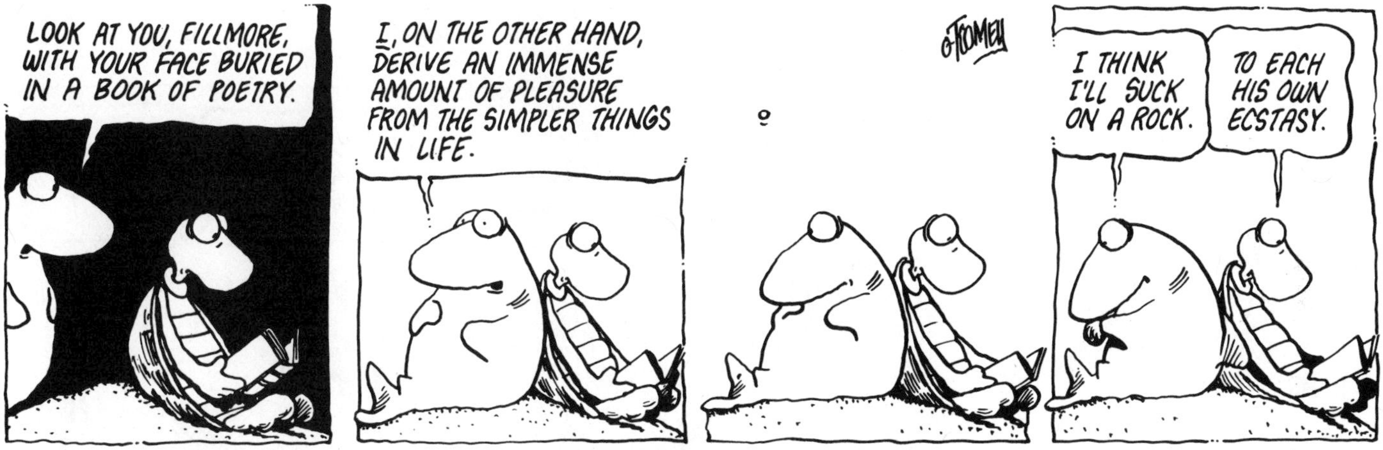
LOOK AT YOU, FILLMORE, WITH YOUR FACE BURIED IN A BOOK OF POETRY.
I, ON THE OTHER HAND, DERIVE AN IMMENSE AMOUNT OF PLEASURE FROM THE SIMPLER THINGS IN LIFE.
I THINK I'LL SUCK ON A ROCK.
TO EACH HIS OWN ECSTASY.

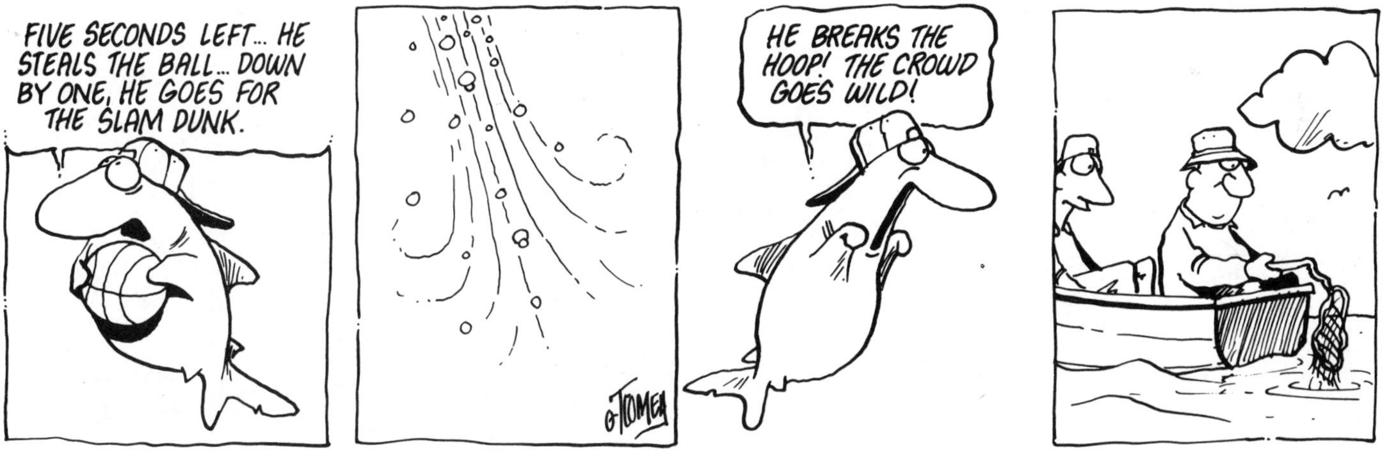
FIVE SECONDS LEFT... HE STEALS THE BALL... DOWN BY ONE, HE GOES FOR THE SLAM DUNK.
HE BREAKS THE HOOP! THE CROWD GOES WILD!

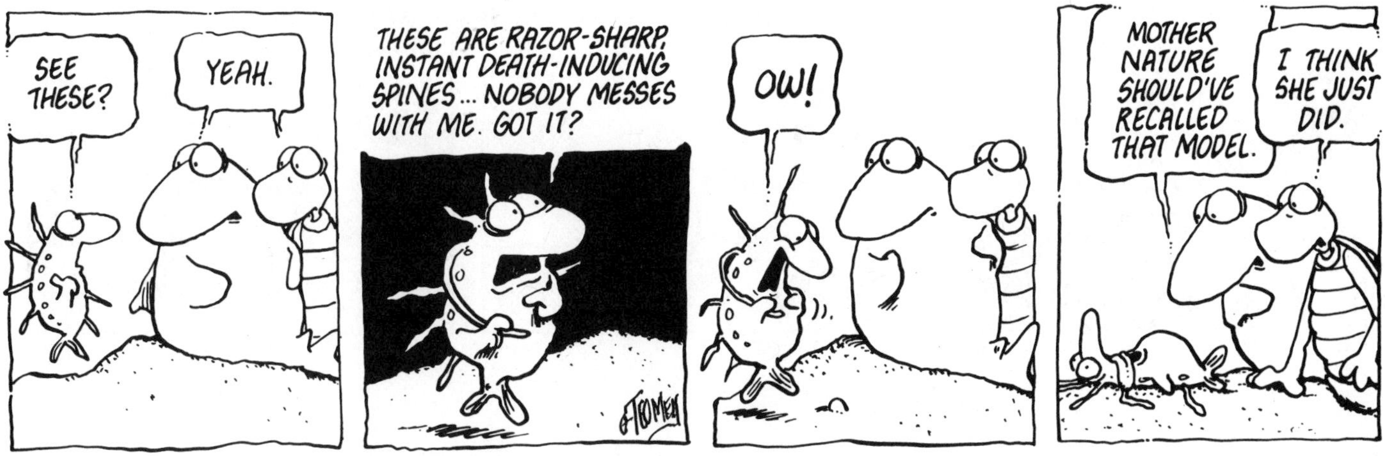
SEE THESE?
YEAH.
THESE ARE RAZOR-SHARP, INSTANT DEATH-INDUCING SPINES... NOBODY MESSES WITH ME. GOT IT?
OW!
MOTHER NATURE SHOULD'VE RECALLED THAT MODEL.
I THINK SHE JUST DID.

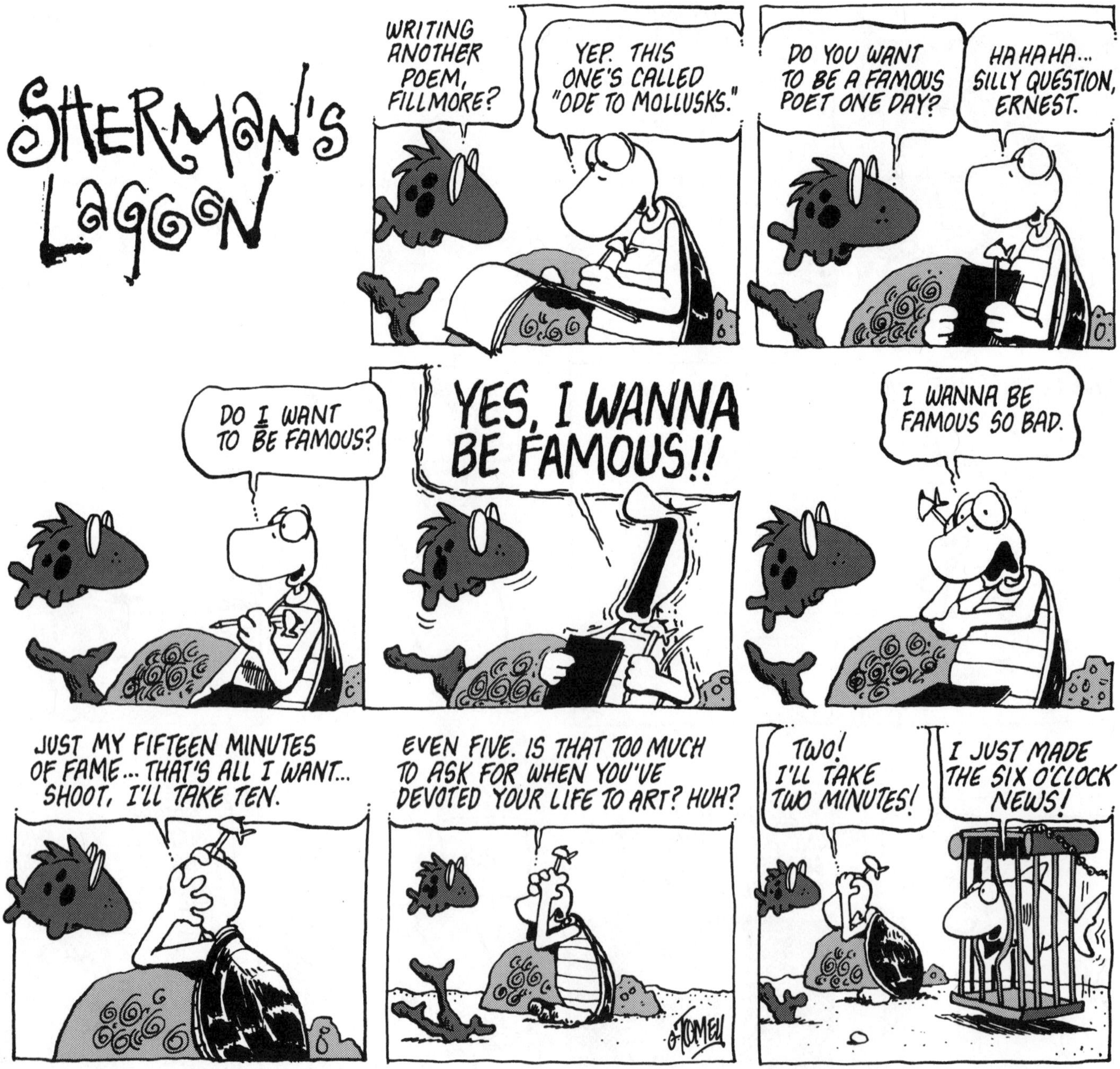
SHERMAN'S LAGOON
WRITING ANOTHER POEM, FILLMORE?
YEP. THIS ONE'S CALLED "ODE TO MOLLUSKS."
DO YOU WANT TO BE A FAMOUS POET ONE DAY?
HA HA HA... SILLY QUESTION, ERNEST.
DO I WANT TO BE FAMOUS?
YES, I WANNA BE FAMOUS!!
I WANNA BE FAMOUS SO BAD.
JUST MY FIFTEEN MINUTES OF FAME... THAT'S ALL I WANT... SHOOT, I'LL TAKE TEN.
EVEN FIVE. IS THAT TOO MUCH TO ASK FOR WHEN YOU'VE DEVOTED YOUR LIFE TO ART? HUH?
TWO! I'LL TAKE TWO MINUTES!
I JUST MADE THE SIX O'CLOCK NEWS!

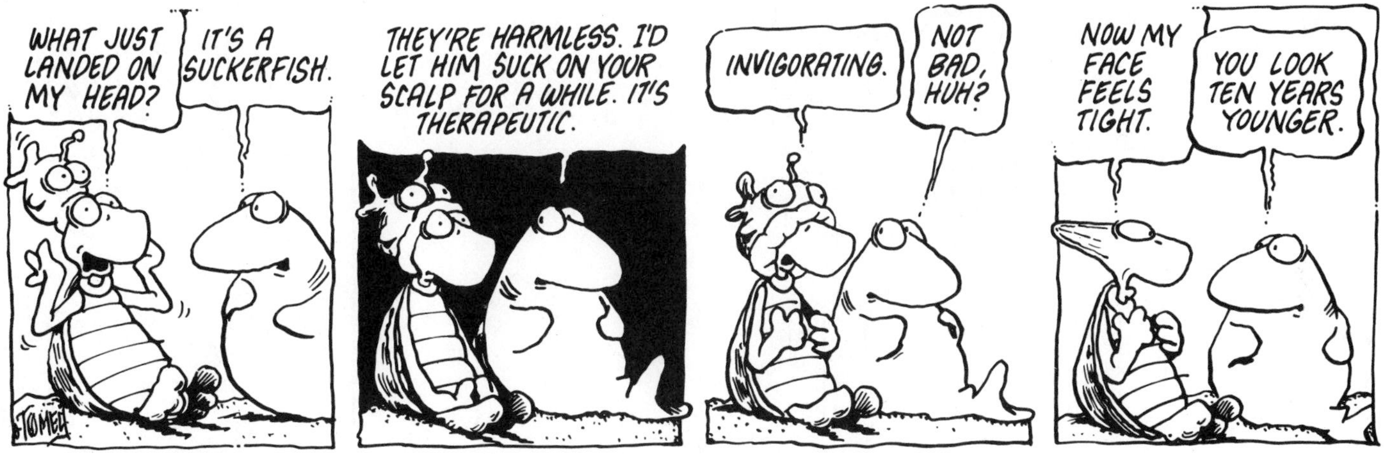
WHAT JUST LANDED ON MY HEAD?
IT'S A SUCKERFISH.
THEY'RE HARMLESS. I'D LET HIM SUCK ON YOUR SCALP FOR A WHILE. IT'S THERAPEUTIC.
INVIGORATING.
NOT BAD, HUH?
NOW MY FACE FEELS TIGHT.
YOU LOOK TEN YEARS YOUNGER.
TOOMEY

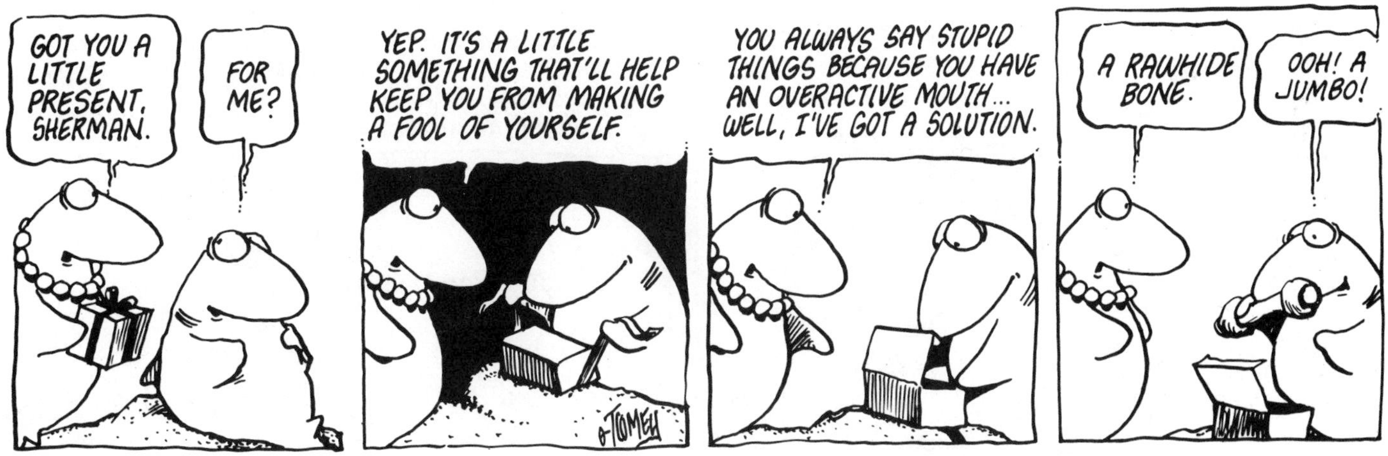
GOT YOU A LITTLE PRESENT, SHERMAN.
FOR ME?
YEP. IT'S A LITTLE SOMETHING THAT'LL HELP KEEP YOU FROM MAKING A FOOL OF YOURSELF.
YOU ALWAYS SAY STUPID THINGS BECAUSE YOU HAVE AN OVERACTIVE MOUTH... WELL, I'VE GOT A SOLUTION.
A RAWHIDE BONE.
OOH! A JUMBO!
TOOMEY

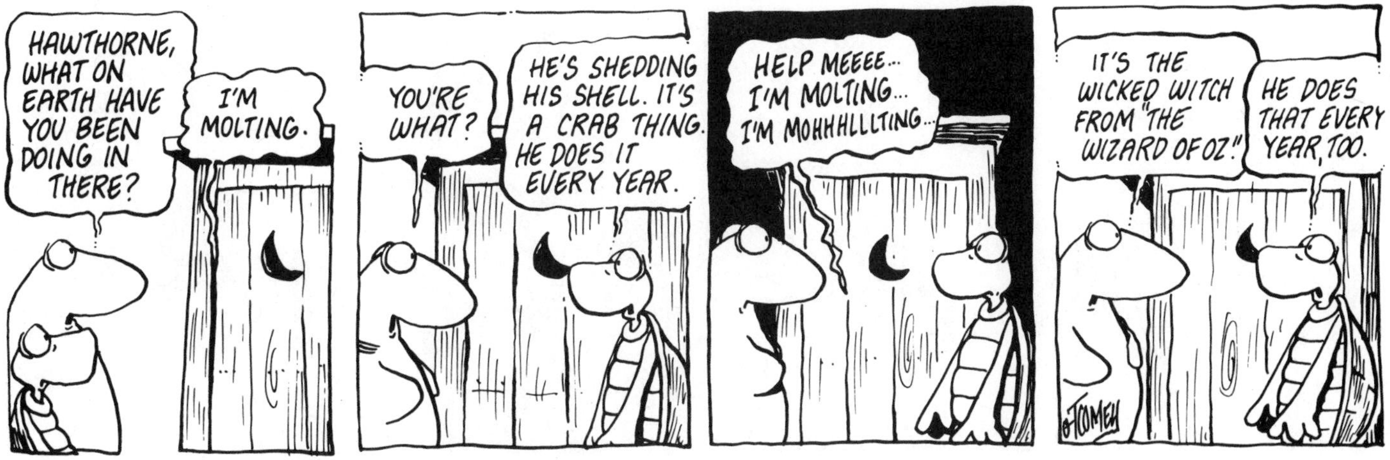
HAWTHORNE, WHAT ON EARTH HAVE YOU BEEN DOING IN THERE?
I'M MOLTING.
YOU'RE WHAT?
HE'S SHEDDING HIS SHELL. IT'S A CRAB THING. HE DOES IT EVERY YEAR.
HELP MEEEE... I'M MOLTING... I'M MOHHHLLLTING...
IT'S THE WICKED WITCH FROM "THE WIZARD OF OZ."
HE DOES THAT EVERY YEAR, TOO.
TOOMEY

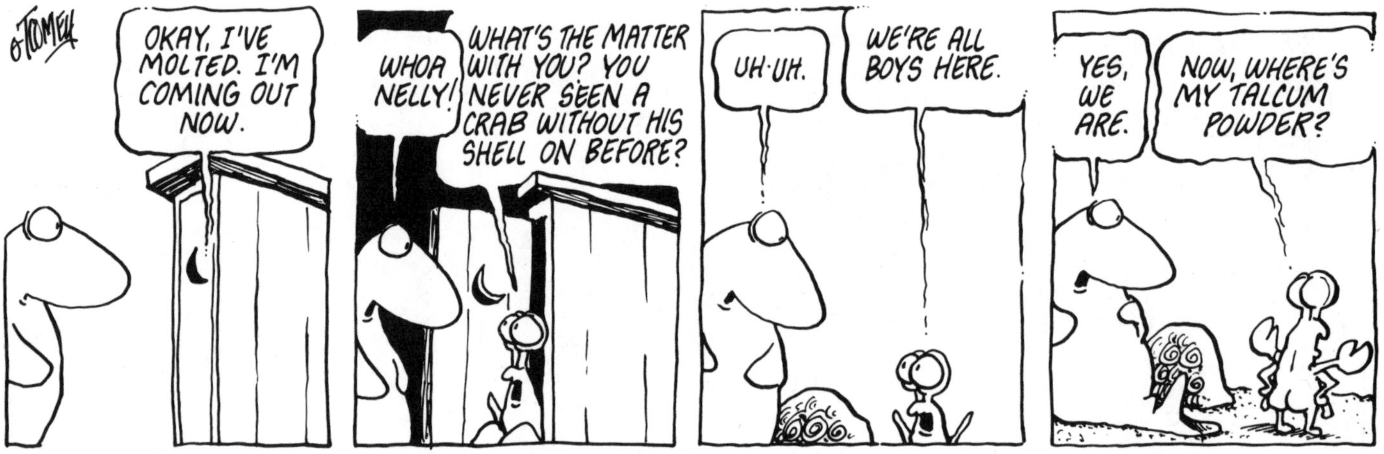
OKAY, I'VE MOLTED. I'M COMING OUT NOW.
WHOA NELLY!
WHAT'S THE MATTER WITH YOU? YOU NEVER SEEN A CRAB WITHOUT HIS SHELL ON BEFORE?
UH-UH.
WE'RE ALL BOYS HERE.
YES, WE ARE.
NOW, WHERE'S MY TALCUM POWDER?

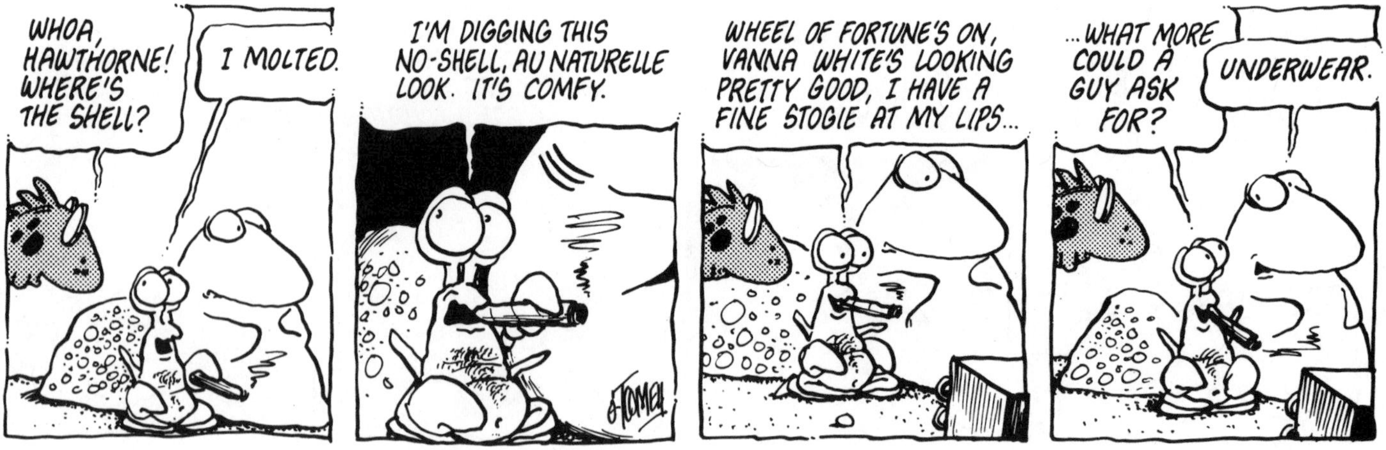
WHOA, HAWTHORNE! WHERE'S THE SHELL?
I MOLTED.
I'M DIGGING THIS NO-SHELL, AU NATURELLE LOOK. IT'S COMFY.
WHEEL OF FORTUNE'S ON, VANNA WHITE'S LOOKING PRETTY GOOD, I HAVE A FINE STOGIE AT MY LIPS...
...WHAT MORE COULD A GUY ASK FOR?
UNDERWEAR.

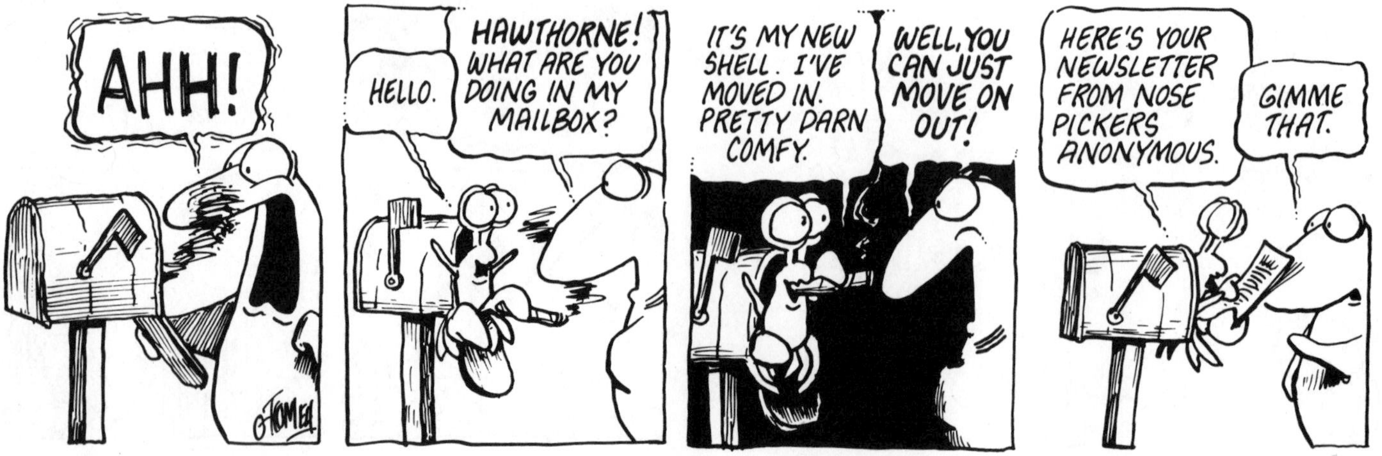
AHH!
HELLO.
HAWTHORNE! WHAT ARE YOU DOING IN MY MAILBOX?
IT'S MY NEW SHELL. I'VE MOVED IN. PRETTY DARN COMFY.
WELL, YOU CAN JUST MOVE ON OUT!
HERE'S YOUR NEWSLETTER FROM NOSE PICKERS ANONYMOUS.
GIMME THAT.

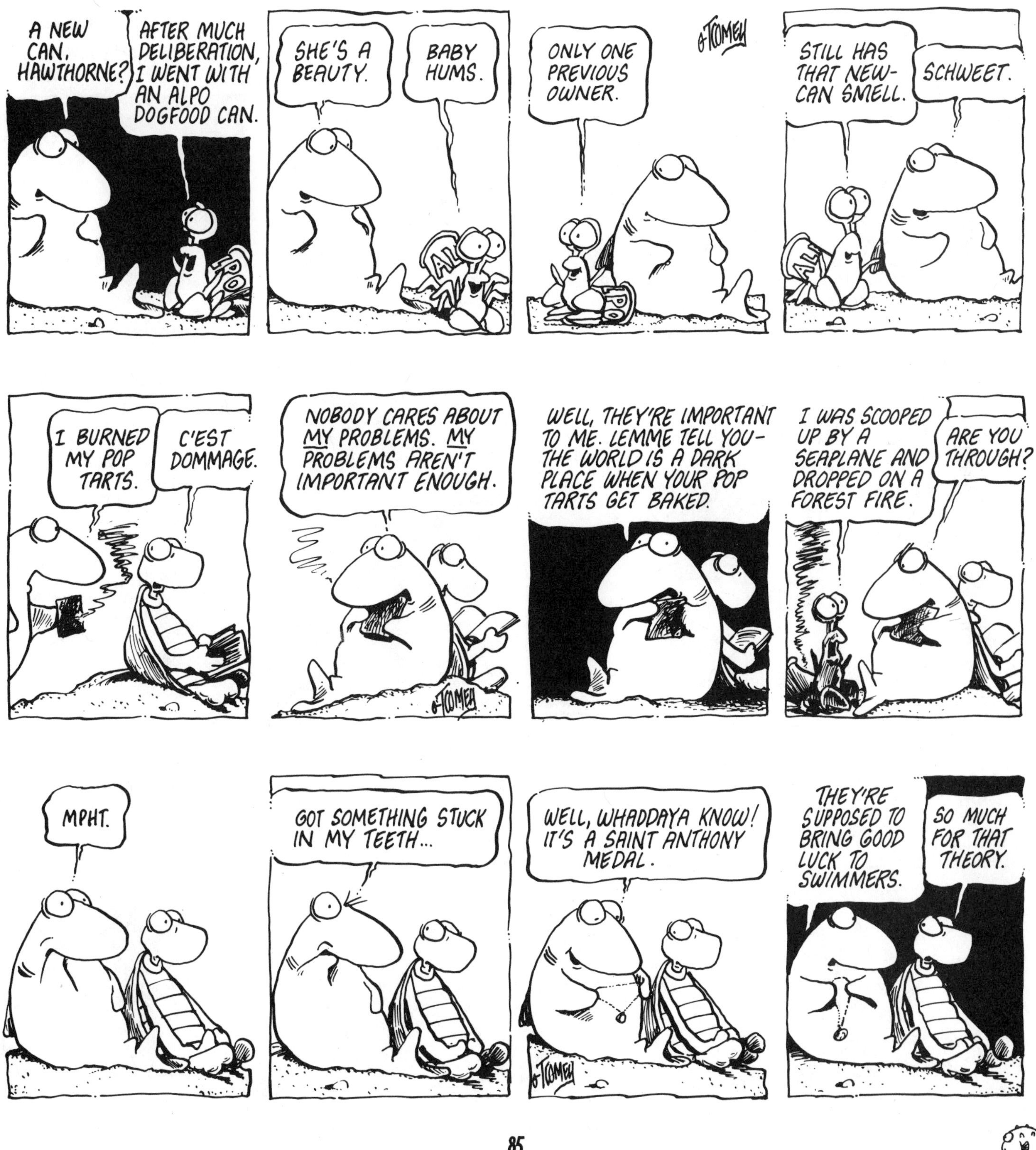
A NEW CAN, HAWTHORNE?
AFTER MUCH DELIBERATION, I WENT WITH AN ALPO DOGFOOD CAN.
SHE'S A BEAUTY.
BABY HUMS.
ONLY ONE PREVIOUS OWNER.
STILL HAS THAT NEW-CAN SMELL.
SCHWEET.
I BURNED MY POP TARTS.
C'EST DOMMAGE.
NOBODY CARES ABOUT MY PROBLEMS. MY PROBLEMS AREN'T IMPORTANT ENOUGH.
WELL, THEY'RE IMPORTANT TO ME. LEMME TELL YOU- THE WORLD IS A DARK PLACE WHEN YOUR POP TARTS GET BAKED.
I WAS SCOOPED UP BY A SEAPLANE AND DROPPED ON A FOREST FIRE.
ARE YOU THROUGH?
MPHT.
GOT SOMETHING STUCK IN MY TEETH...
WELL, WHADDAYA KNOW! IT'S A SAINT ANTHONY MEDAL.
THEY'RE SUPPOSED TO BRING GOOD LUCK TO SWIMMERS.
SO MUCH FOR THAT THEORY.

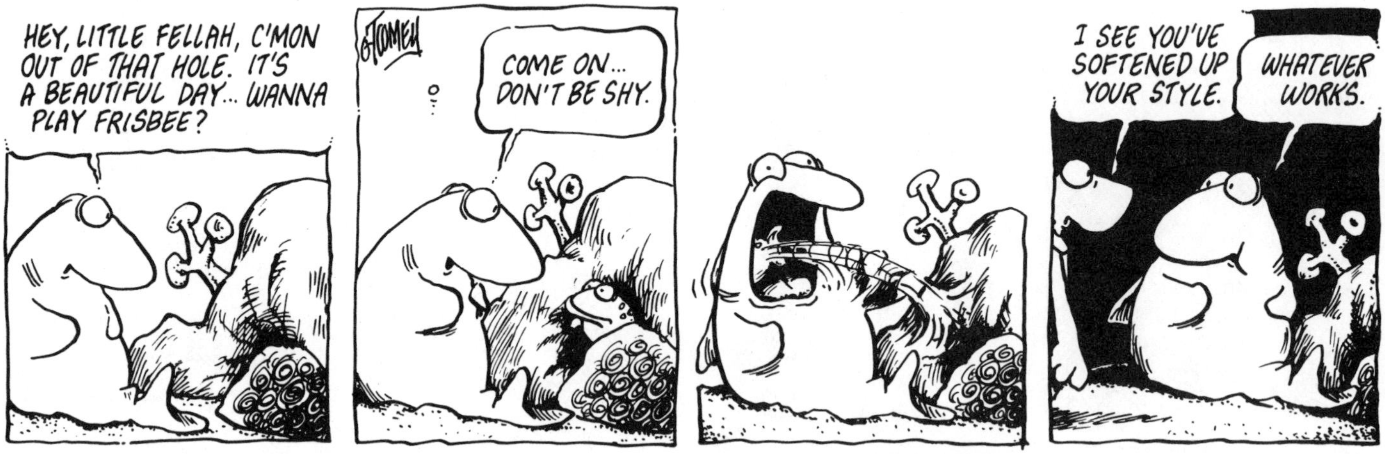
HEY, LITTLE FELLAH, C'MON OUT OF THAT HOLE. IT'S A BEAUTIFUL DAY... WANNA PLAY FRISBEE?
COME ON... DON'T BE SHY.
I SEE YOU'VE SOFTENED UP YOUR STYLE.
WHATEVER WORKS.

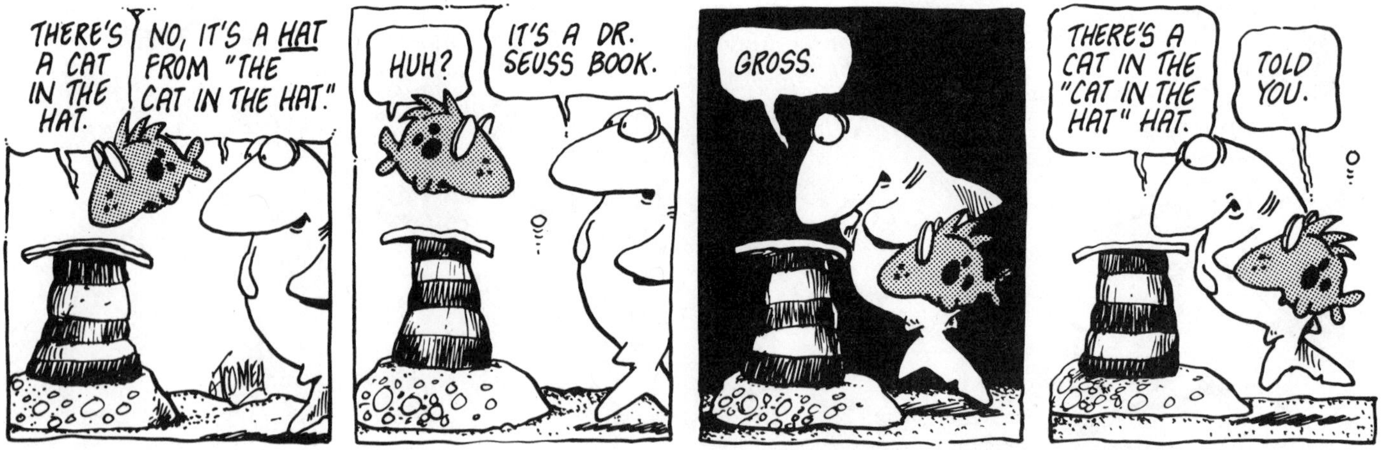
THERE'S A CAT IN THE HAT.
NO, IT'S A HAT FROM "THE CAT IN THE HAT."
HUH?
IT'S A DR. SEUSS BOOK.
GROSS.
THERE'S A CAT IN THE "CAT IN THE HAT" HAT.
TOLD YOU.

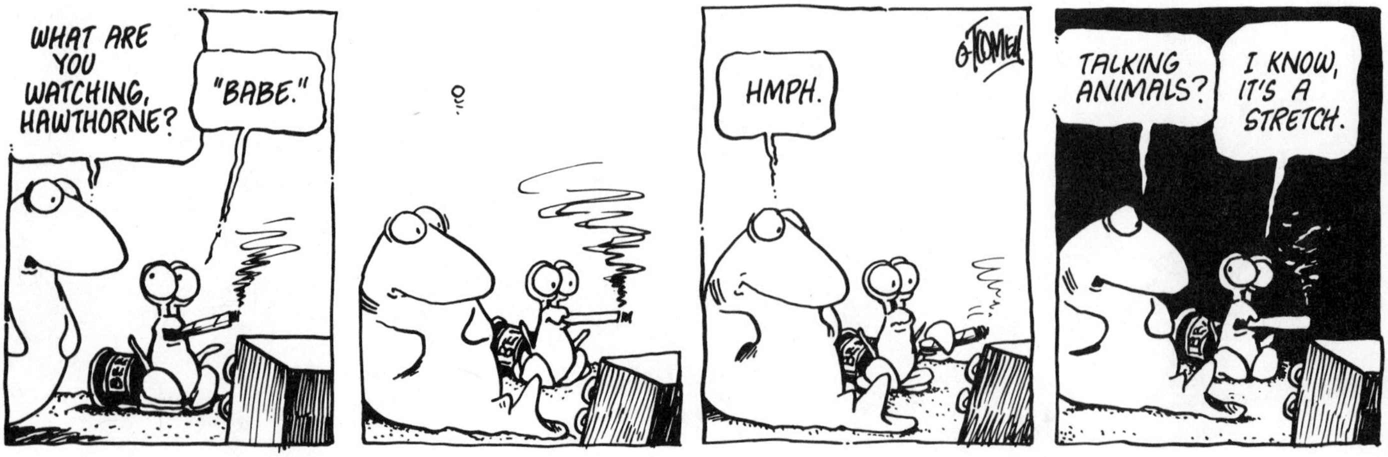
WHAT ARE YOU WATCHING, HAWTHORNE?
"BABE."
HMPH.
TALKING ANIMALS?
I KNOW, IT'S A STRETCH.

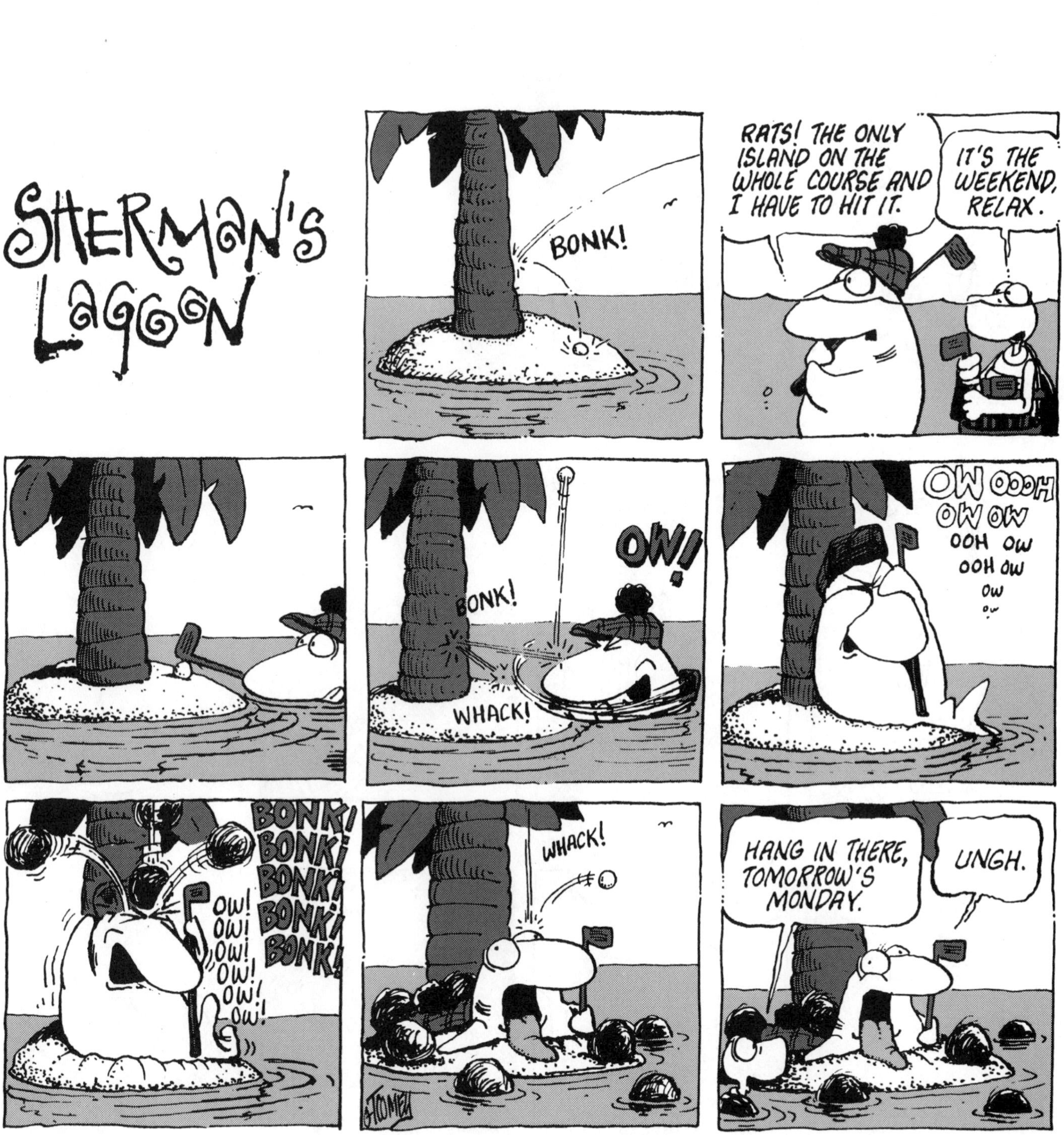
SHERMAN'S LAGOON
BONK!
RATS! THE ONLY ISLAND ON THE WHOLE COURSE AND I HAVE TO HIT IT.
IT'S THE WEEKEND, RELAX.
OW!
BONK!
WHACK!
OW OW
OOH OW
OOH OW
OW
OW! OW! OW! OW! OW! OW!
BONK! BONK! BONK! BONK! BONK!
WHACK!
TOOMEY
HANG IN THERE, TOMORROW'S MONDAY.
UNGH.

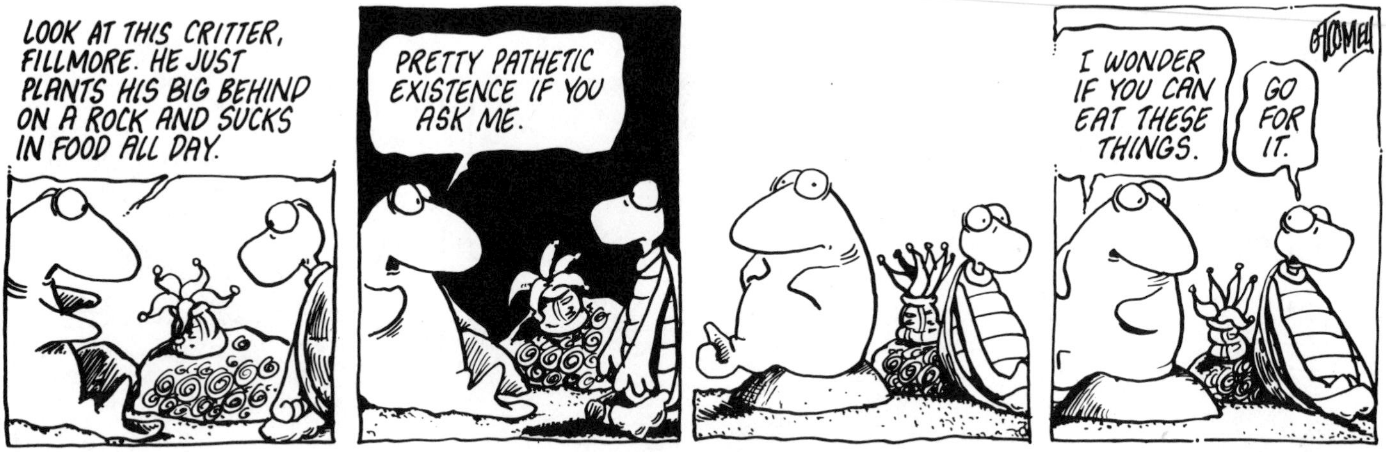
LOOK AT THIS CRITTER, FILLMORE. HE JUST PLANTS HIS BIG BEHIND ON A ROCK AND SUCKS IN FOOD ALL DAY.
PRETTY PATHETIC EXISTENCE IF YOU ASK ME.
I WONDER IF YOU CAN EAT THESE THINGS.
GO FOR IT.

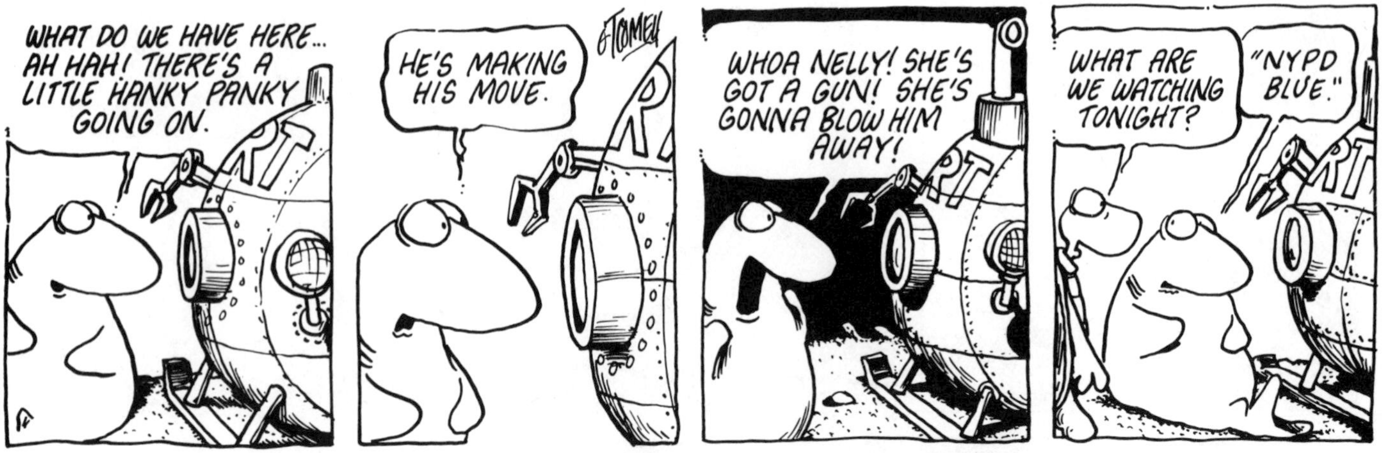
WHAT DO WE HAVE HERE... AH HAH! THERE'S A LITTLE HANKY PANKY GOING ON.
HE'S MAKING HIS MOVE.
WHOA NELLY! SHE'S GOT A GUN! SHE'S GONNA BLOW HIM AWAY!
WHAT ARE WE WATCHING TONIGHT?
"NYPD BLUE."

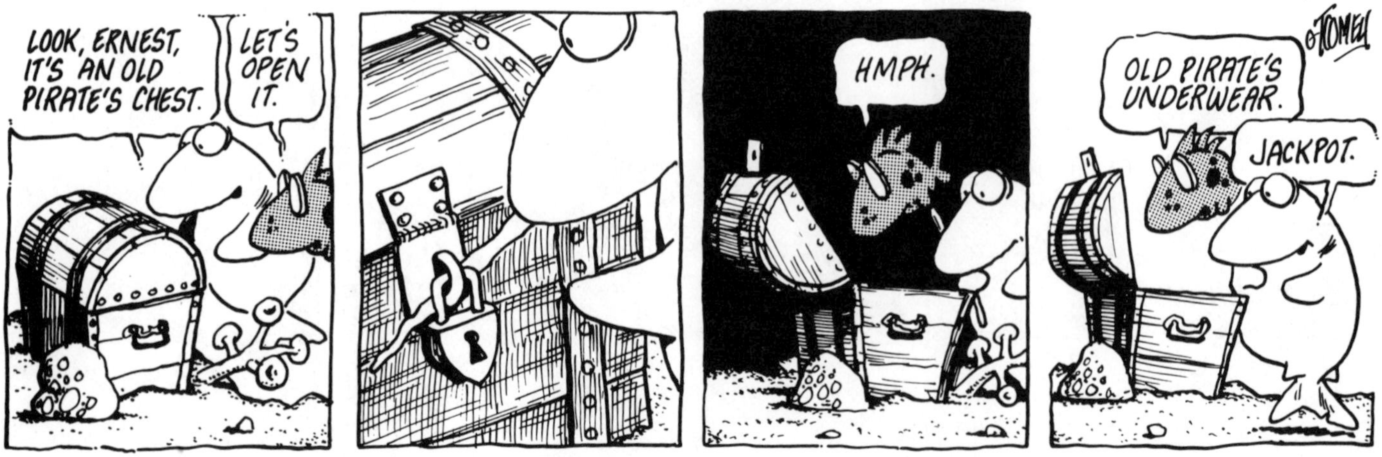
LOOK, ERNEST, IT'S AN OLD PIRATE'S CHEST.
LET'S OPEN IT.
HMPH.
OLD PIRATE'S UNDERWEAR.
JACKPOT.

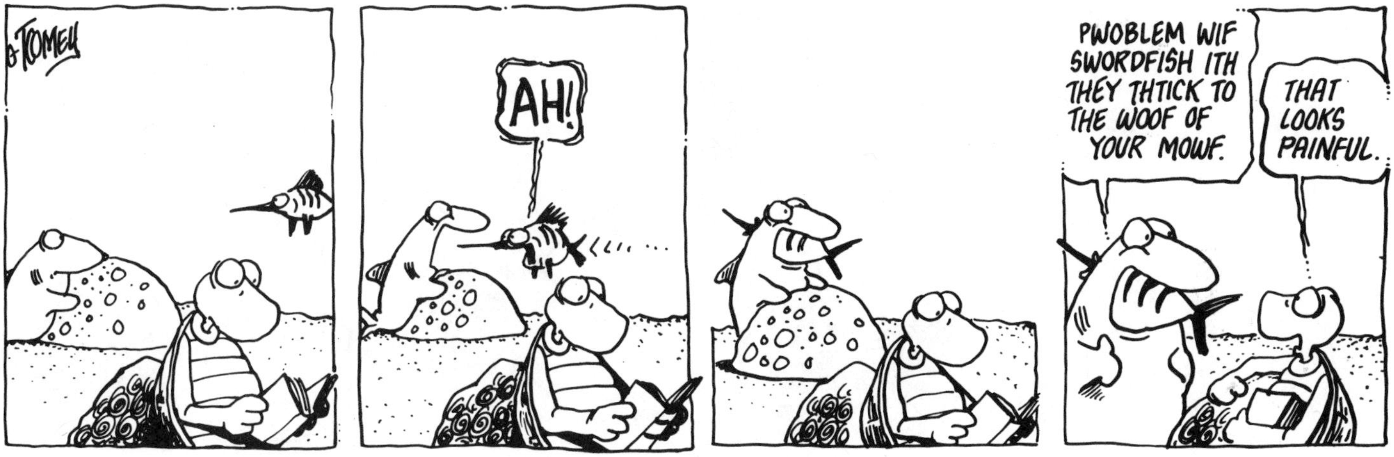

AH!
PWOBLEM WIF SWORDFISH ITH THEY THTICK TO THE WOOF OF YOUR MOWF.
THAT LOOKS PAINFUL.

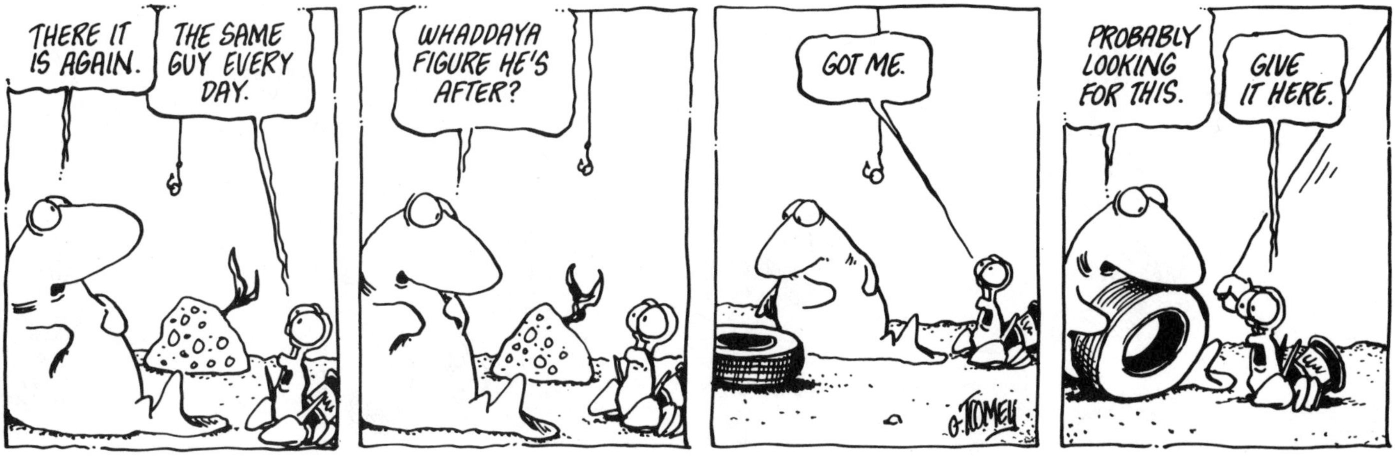

THERE IT IS AGAIN.
THE SAME GUY EVERY DAY.
WHADDAYA FIGURE HE'S AFTER?
GOT ME.
PROBABLY LOOKING FOR THIS.
GIVE IT HERE.

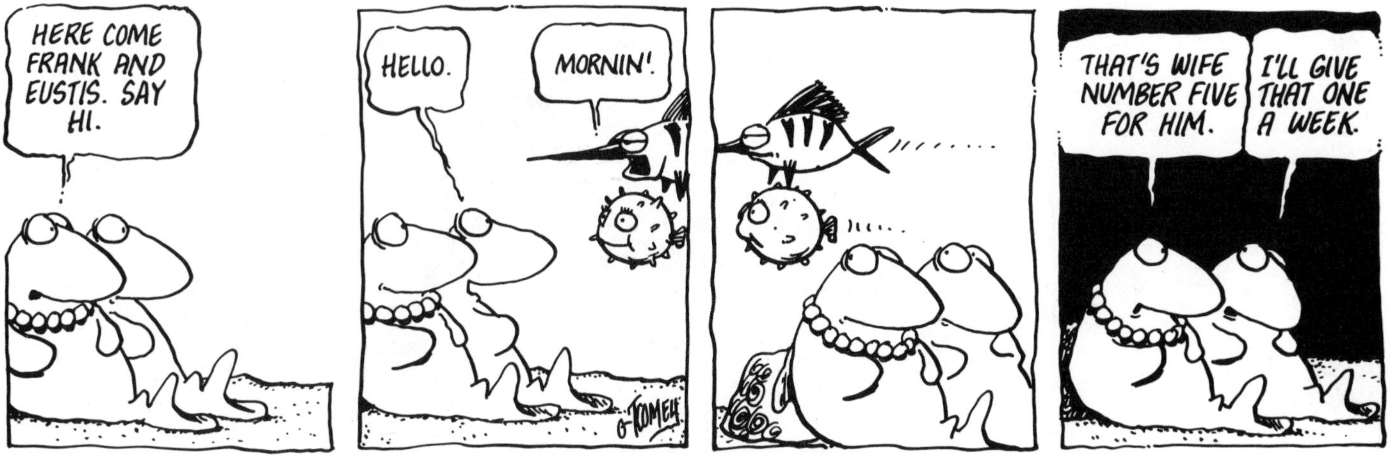

HERE COME FRANK AND EUSTIS. SAY HI.
HELLO.
MORNIN'.
THAT'S WIFE NUMBER FIVE FOR HIM.
I'LL GIVE THAT ONE A WEEK.

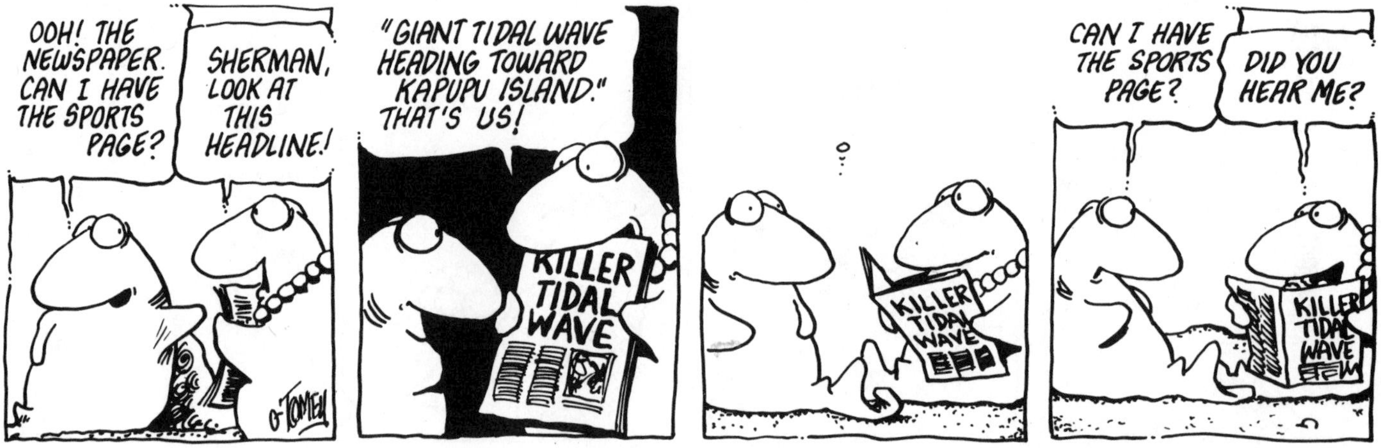
OOH! THE NEWSPAPER. CAN I HAVE THE SPORTS PAGE?
SHERMAN, LOOK AT THIS HEADLINE!
"GIANT TIDAL WAVE HEADING TOWARD KAPUPU ISLAND." THAT'S US!
KILLER TIDAL WAVE
KILLER TIDAL WAVE
CAN I HAVE THE SPORTS PAGE?
DID YOU HEAR ME?
KILLER TIDAL WAVE

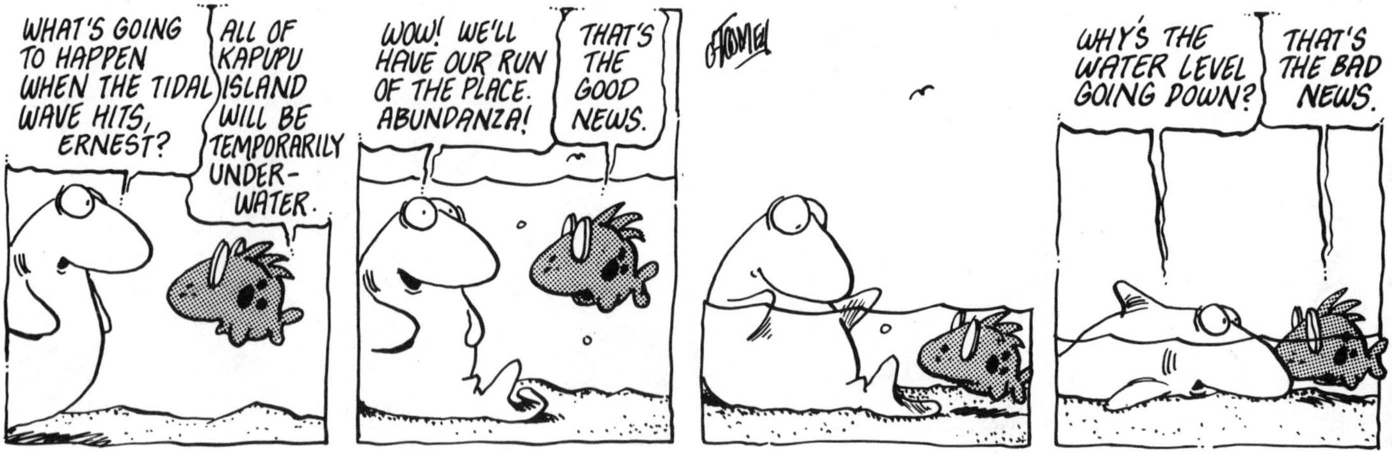
WHAT'S GOING TO HAPPEN WHEN THE TIDAL WAVE HITS, ERNEST?
ALL OF KAPUPU ISLAND WILL BE TEMPORARILY UNDER-WATER.
WOW! WE'LL HAVE OUR RUN OF THE PLACE. ABUNDANZA!
THAT'S THE GOOD NEWS.
WHY'S THE WATER LEVEL GOING DOWN?
THAT'S THE BAD NEWS.

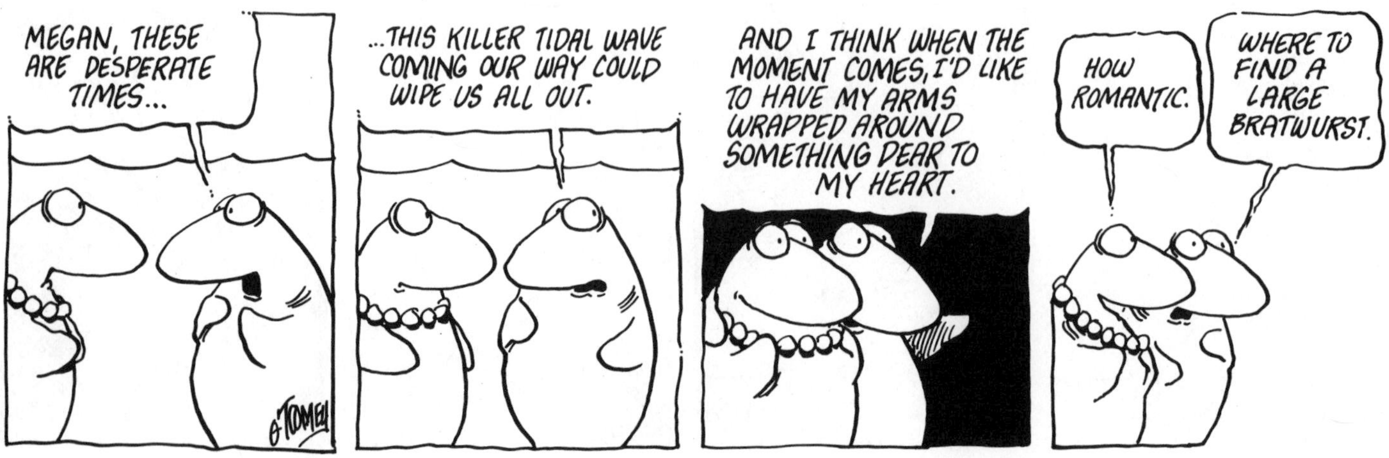
MEGAN, THESE ARE DESPERATE TIMES...
...THIS KILLER TIDAL WAVE COMING OUR WAY COULD WIPE US ALL OUT.
AND I THINK WHEN THE MOMENT COMES, I'D LIKE TO HAVE MY ARMS WRAPPED AROUND SOMETHING DEAR TO MY HEART.
HOW ROMANTIC.
WHERE TO FIND A LARGE BRATWURST.

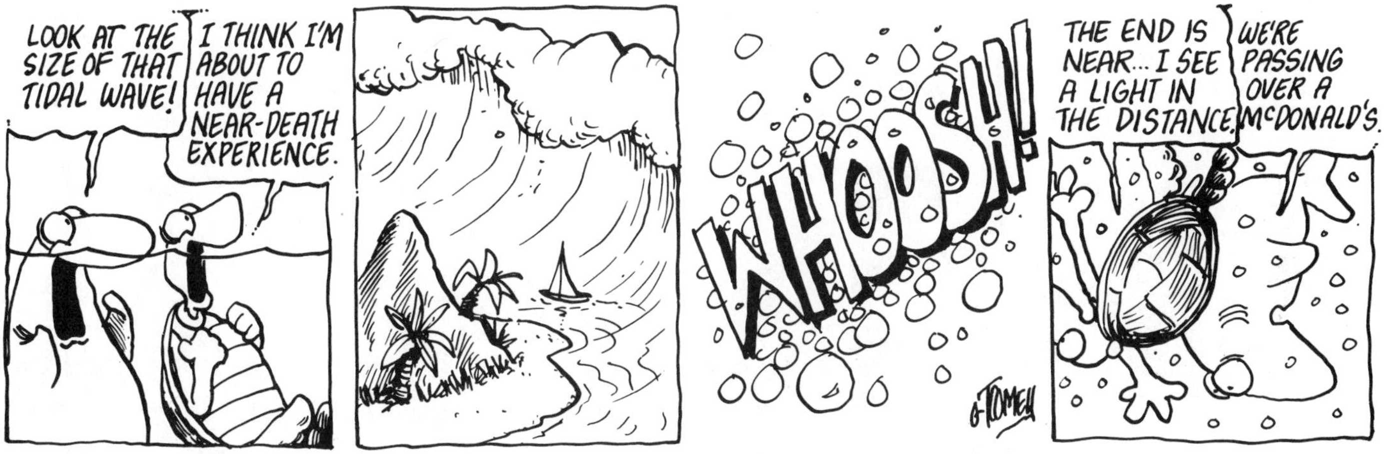
LOOK AT THE SIZE OF THAT TIDAL WAVE!
I THINK I'M ABOUT TO HAVE A NEAR-DEATH EXPERIENCE.
WHOOSH!!
THE END IS NEAR... I SEE A LIGHT IN THE DISTANCE.
WE'RE PASSING OVER A McDONALD'S.

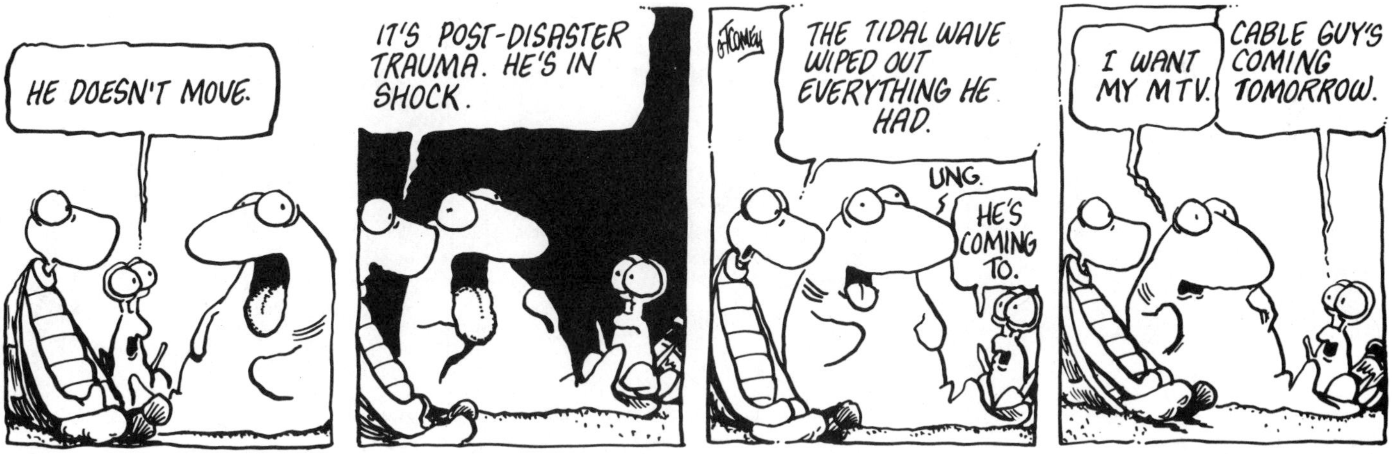
HE DOESN'T MOVE.
IT'S POST-DISASTER TRAUMA. HE'S IN SHOCK.
THE TIDAL WAVE WIPED OUT EVERYTHING HE HAD.
UNG.
HE'S COMING TO.
I WANT MY MTV.
CABLE GUY'S COMING TOMORROW.

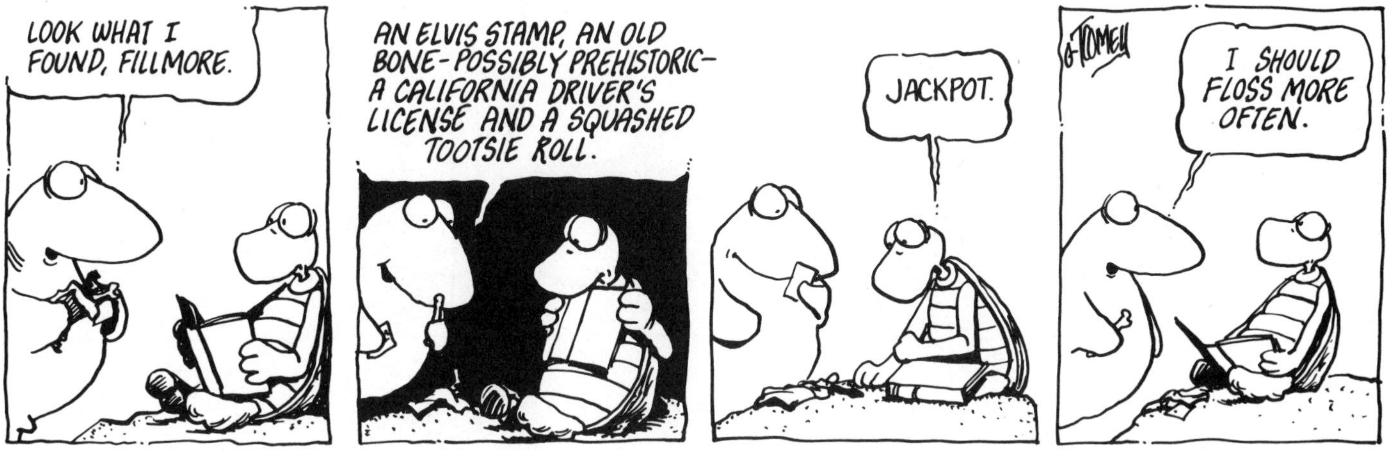
LOOK WHAT I FOUND, FILLMORE.
AN ELVIS STAMP, AN OLD BONE-POSSIBLY PREHISTORIC-A CALIFORNIA DRIVER'S LICENSE AND A SQUASHED TOOTSIE ROLL.
JACKPOT.
I SHOULD FLOSS MORE OFTEN.

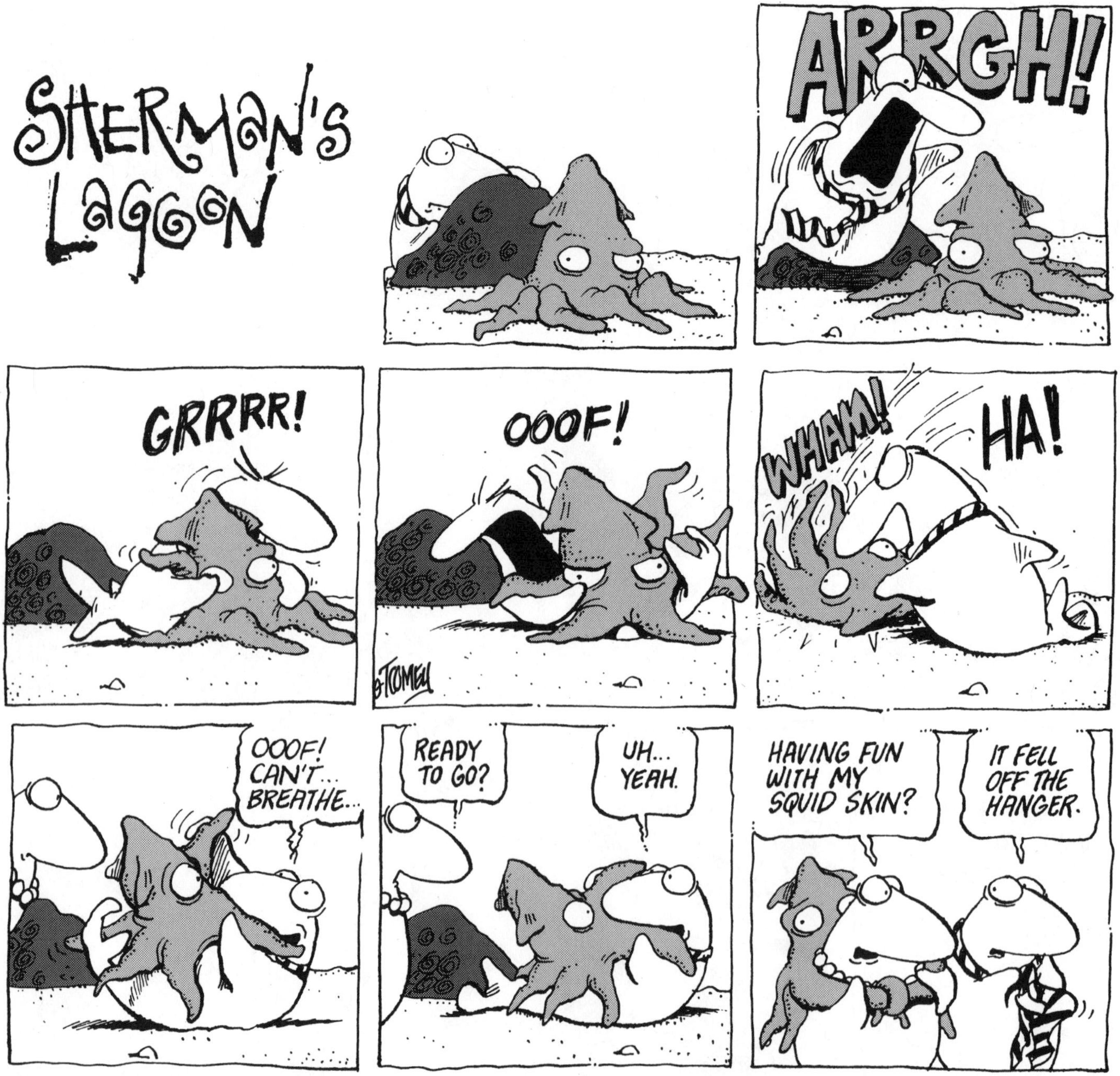
SHERMAN'S LAGOON
ARRGH!
GRRRR!
OOOF!
TOOMEY
WHAM!
HA!
OOOF! CAN'T... BREATHE...
READY TO GO?
UH... YEAH.
HAVING FUN WITH MY SQUID SKIN?
IT FELL OFF THE HANGER.

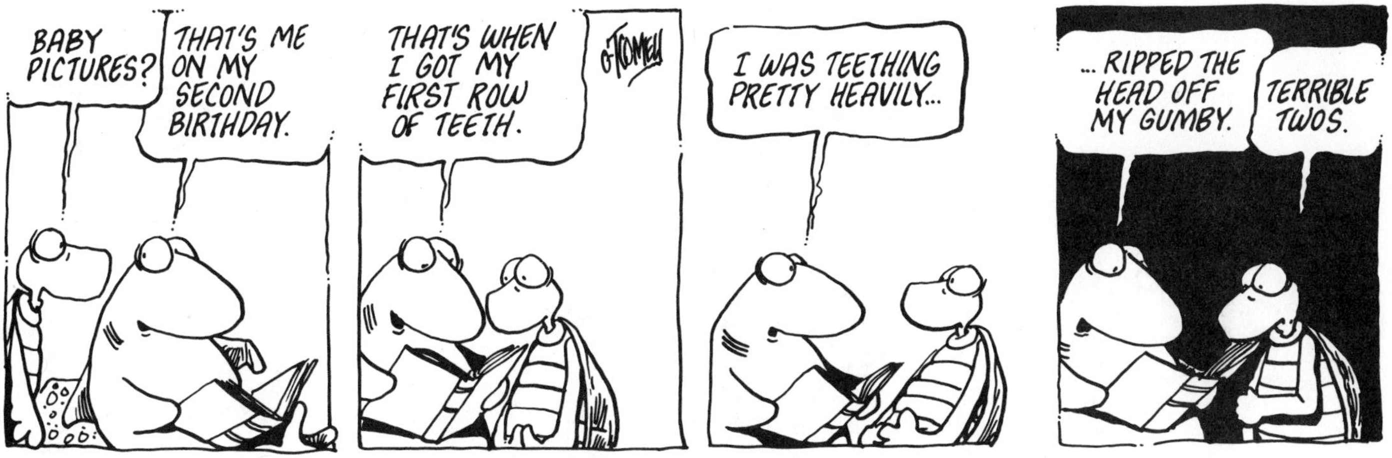
BABY PICTURES?
THAT'S ME ON MY SECOND BIRTHDAY.
THAT'S WHEN I GOT MY FIRST ROW OF TEETH.
I WAS TEETHING PRETTY HEAVILY...
... RIPPED THE HEAD OFF MY GUMBY.
TERRIBLE TWOS.

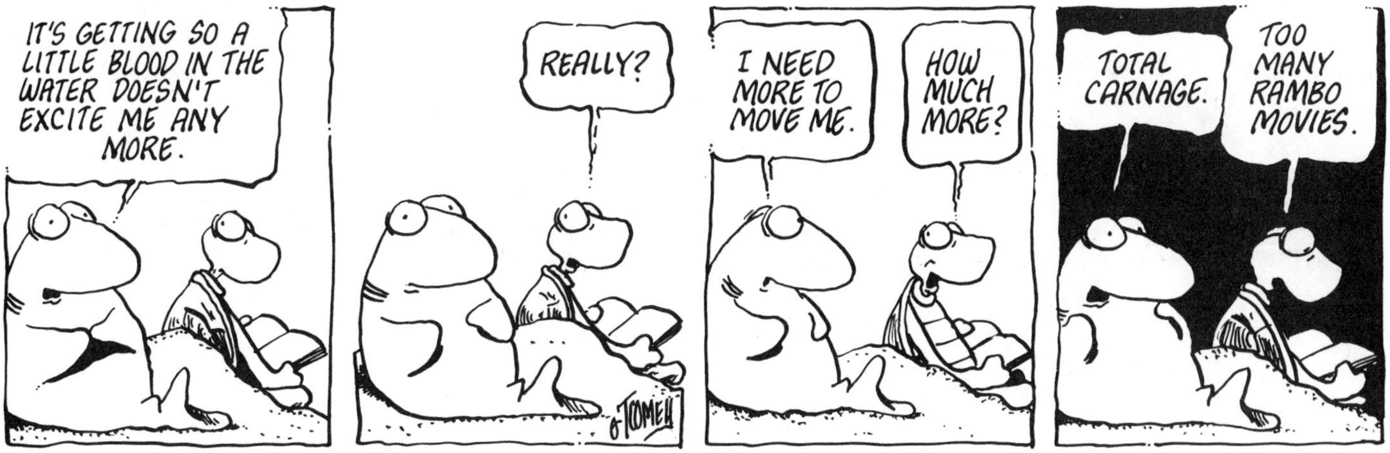
IT'S GETTING SO A LITTLE BLOOD IN THE WATER DOESN'T EXCITE ME ANY MORE.
REALLY?
I NEED MORE TO MOVE ME.
HOW MUCH MORE?
TOTAL CARNAGE.
TOO MANY RAMBO MOVIES.

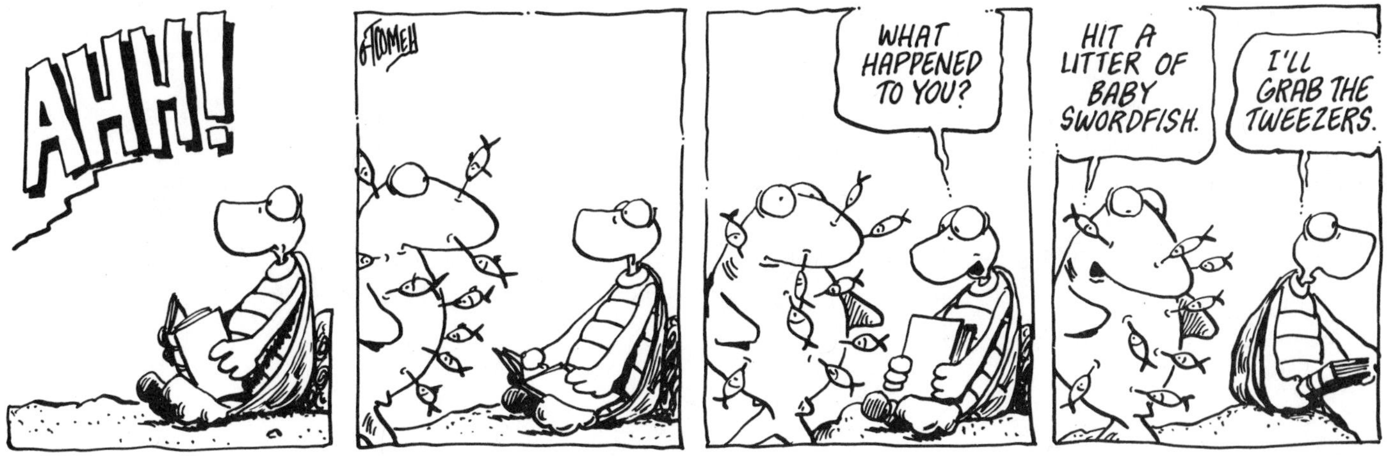
AHH!
WHAT HAPPENED TO YOU?
HIT A LITTER OF BABY SWORDFISH.
I'LL GRAB THE TWEEZERS.

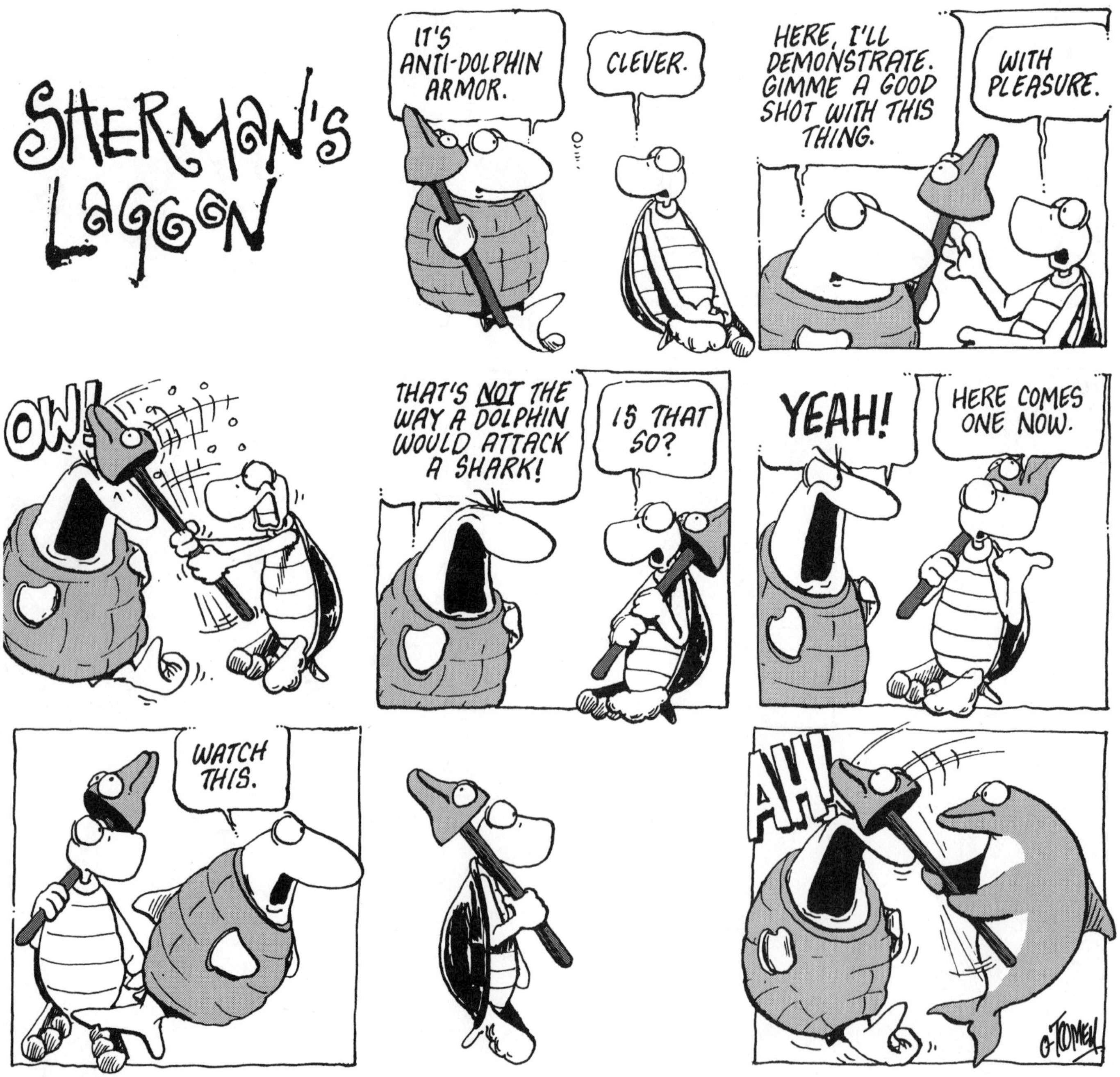
SHERMAN'S LAGOON
IT'S ANTI-DOLPHIN ARMOR.
CLEVER.
HERE, I'LL DEMONSTRATE. GIMME A GOOD SHOT WITH THIS THING.
WITH PLEASURE.
OW!
THAT'S NOT THE WAY A DOLPHIN WOULD ATTACK A SHARK!
IS THAT SO?
YEAH!
HERE COMES ONE NOW.
WATCH THIS.
AH!
TOOMEY

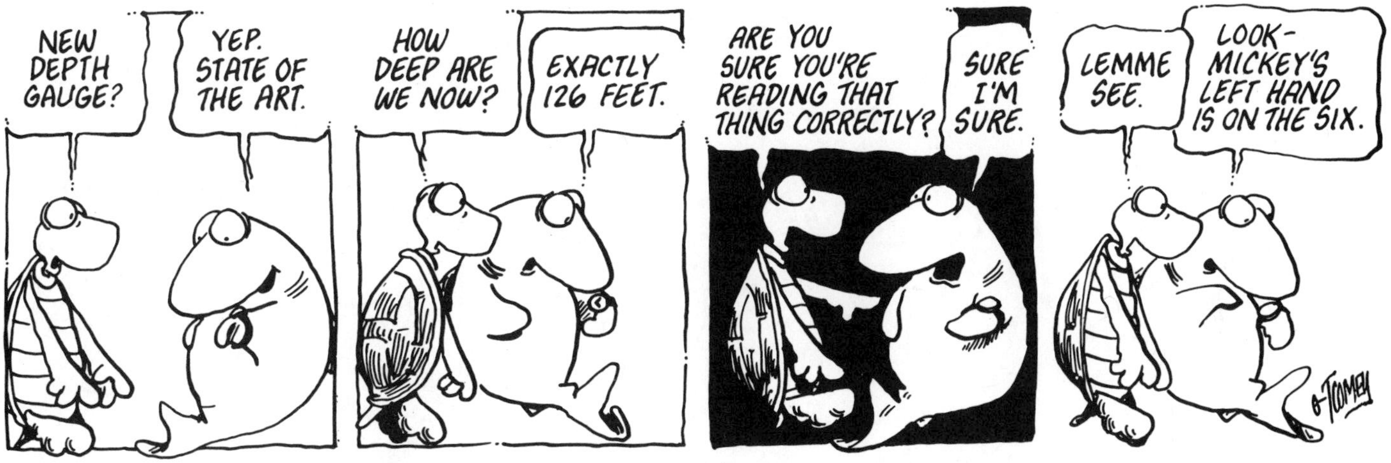
NEW DEPTH GAUGE?
YEP. STATE OF THE ART.
HOW DEEP ARE WE NOW?
EXACTLY 126 FEET.
ARE YOU SURE YOU'RE READING THAT THING CORRECTLY?
SURE I'M SURE.
LEMME SEE.
LOOK- MICKEY'S LEFT HAND IS ON THE SIX.
TOOMEY

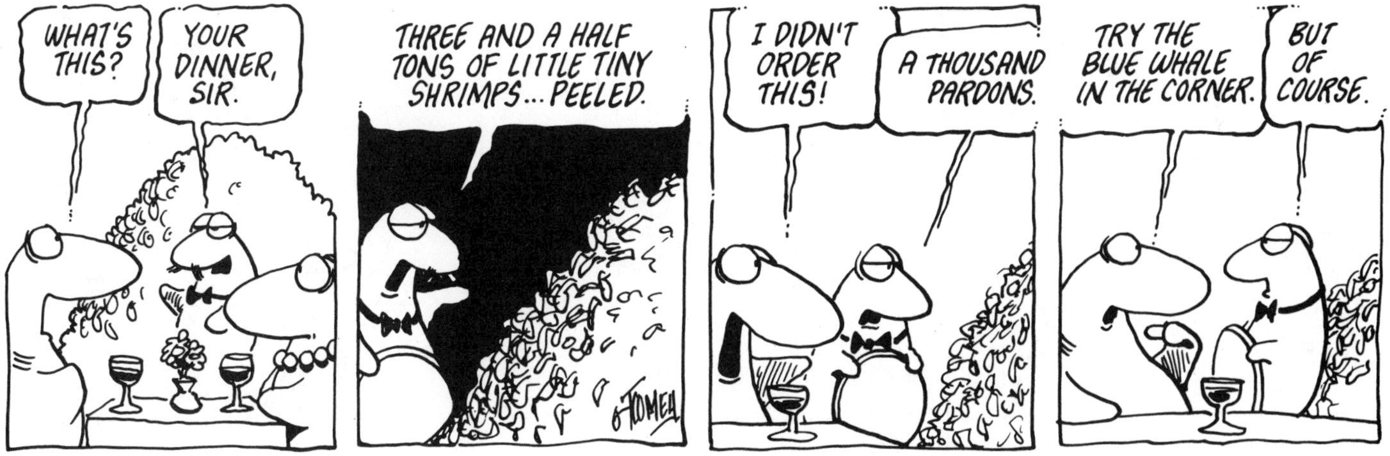
WHAT'S THIS?
YOUR DINNER, SIR.
THREE AND A HALF TONS OF LITTLE TINY SHRIMPS... PEELED.
TOOMEY
I DIDN'T ORDER THIS!
A THOUSAND PARDONS.
TRY THE BLUE WHALE IN THE CORNER.
BUT OF COURSE.

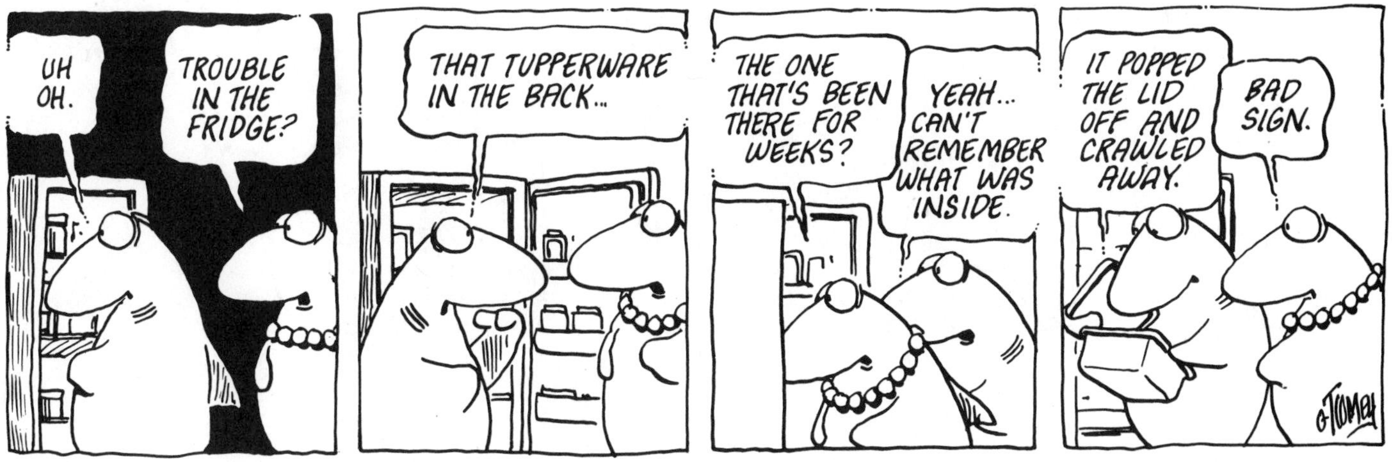
UH OH.
TROUBLE IN THE FRIDGE?
THAT TUPPERWARE IN THE BACK...
THE ONE THAT'S BEEN THERE FOR WEEKS?
YEAH... CAN'T REMEMBER WHAT WAS INSIDE.
IT POPPED THE LID OFF AND CRAWLED AWAY.
BAD SIGN.
TOOMEY

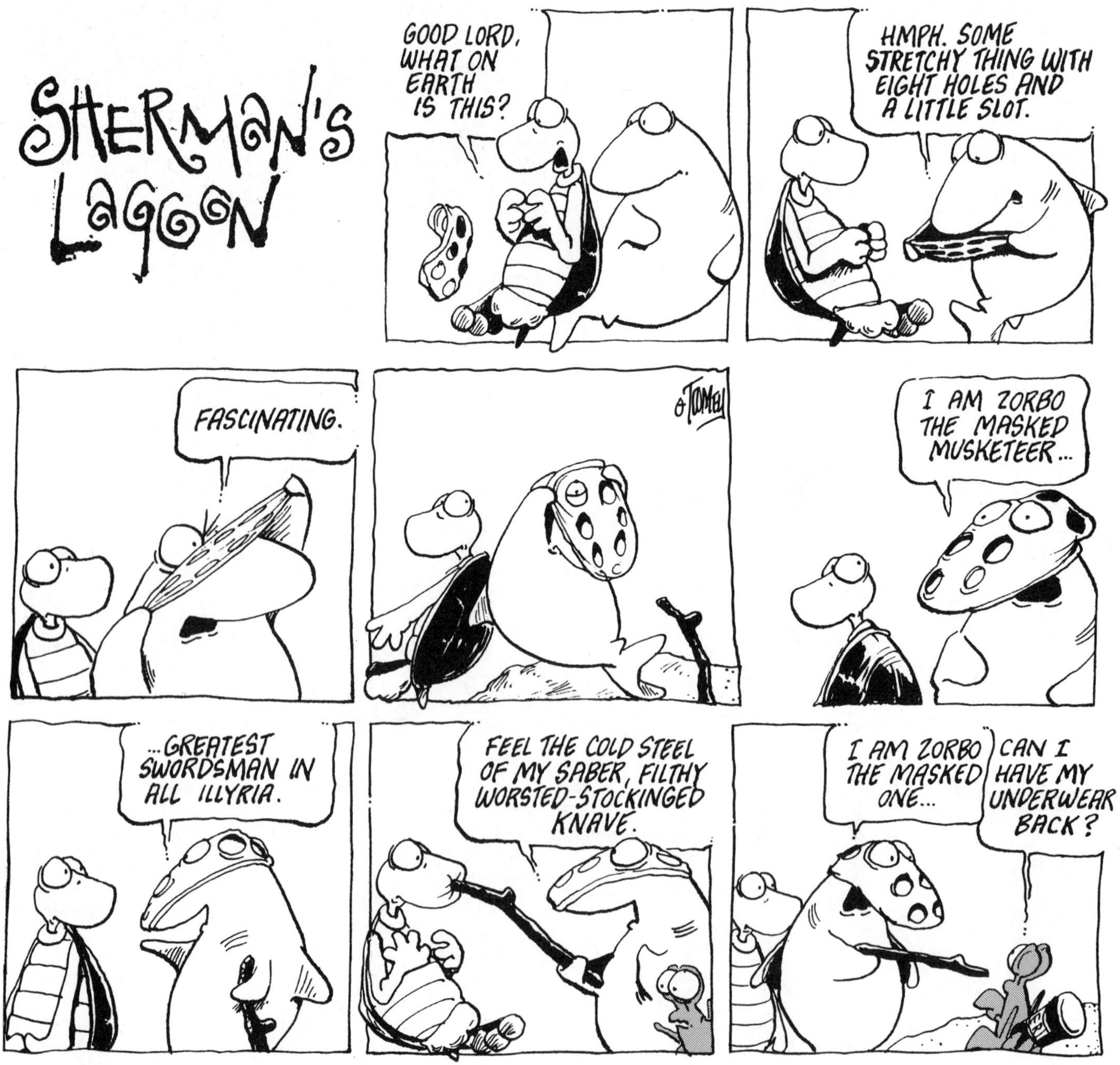
SHERMAN'S LAGOON
GOOD LORD, WHAT ON EARTH IS THIS?
HMPH. SOME STRETCHY THING WITH EIGHT HOLES AND A LITTLE SLOT.
FASCINATING.
I AM ZORBO THE MASKED MUSKETEER...
...GREATEST SWORDSMAN IN ALL ILLYRIA.
FEEL THE COLD STEEL OF MY SABER, FILTHY WORSTED-STOCKINGED KNAVE.
I AM ZORBO THE MASKED ONE...
CAN I HAVE MY UNDERWEAR BACK?

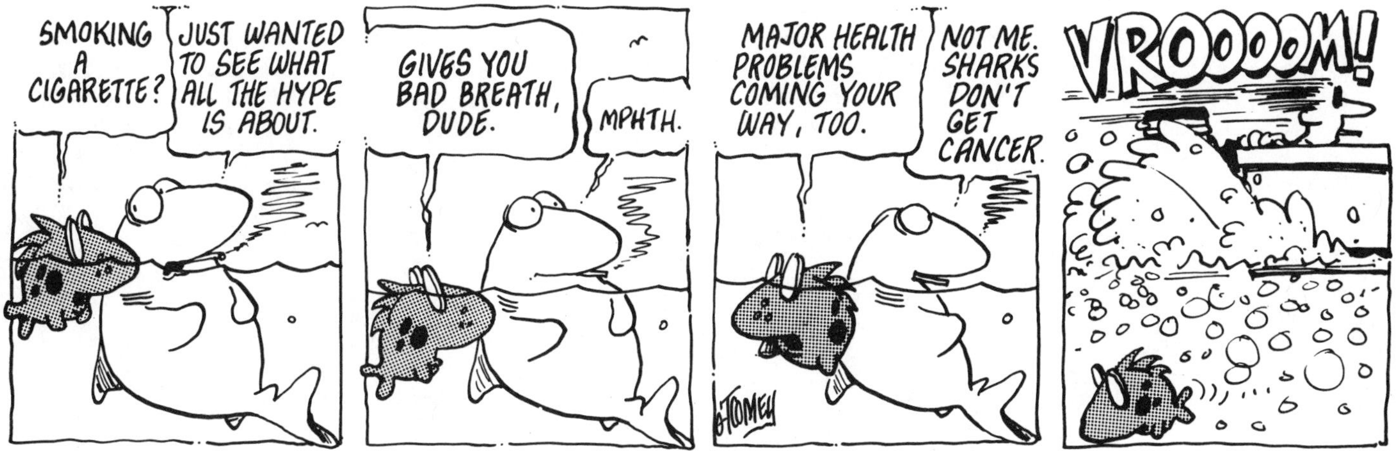
SMOKING A CIGARETTE?
JUST WANTED TO SEE WHAT ALL THE HYPE IS ABOUT.
GIVES YOU BAD BREATH, DUDE.
MPHTH.
MAJOR HEALTH PROBLEMS COMING YOUR WAY, TOO.
NOT ME. SHARKS DON'T GET CANCER.
VROOOOM!
TOOMEY

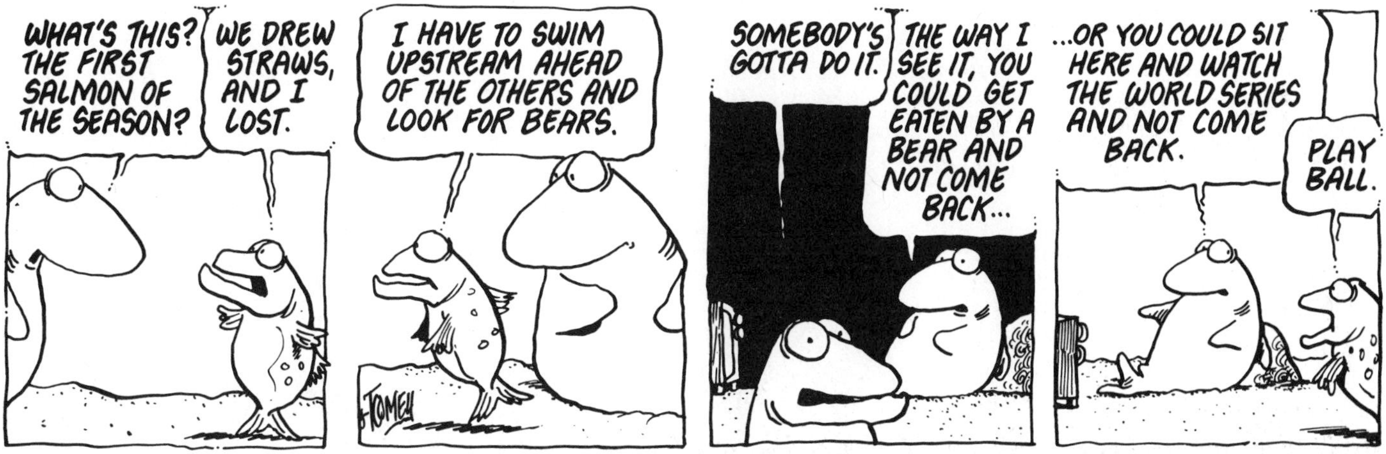
WHAT'S THIS? THE FIRST SALMON OF THE SEASON?
WE DREW STRAWS, AND I LOST.
I HAVE TO SWIM UPSTREAM AHEAD OF THE OTHERS AND LOOK FOR BEARS.
SOMEBODY'S GOTTA DO IT.
THE WAY I SEE IT, YOU COULD GET EATEN BY A BEAR AND NOT COME BACK...
...OR YOU COULD SIT HERE AND WATCH THE WORLD SERIES AND NOT COME BACK.
PLAY BALL.
TOOMEY

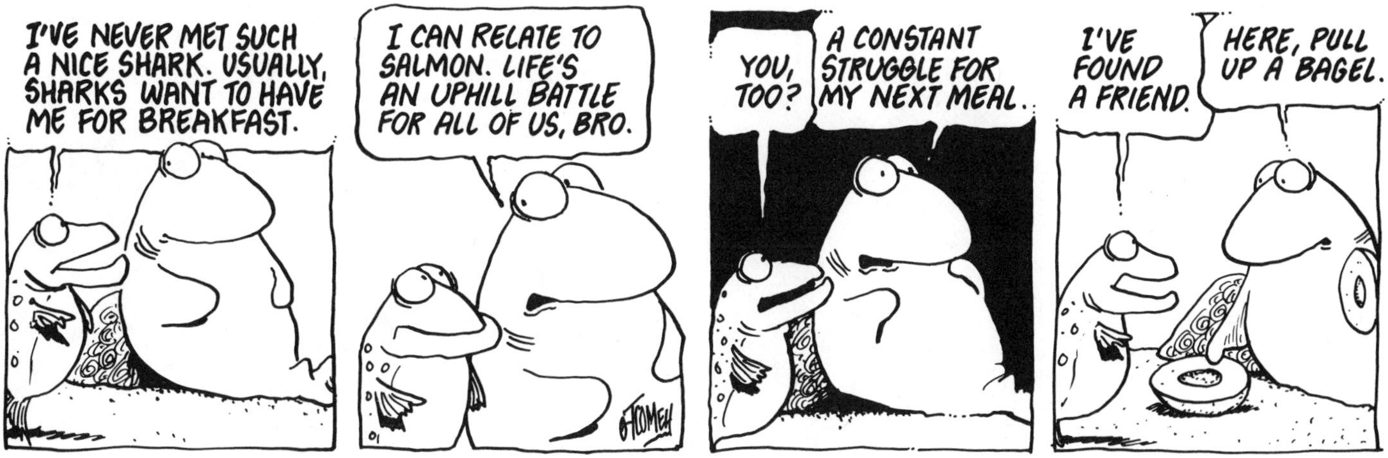
I'VE NEVER MET SUCH A NICE SHARK. USUALLY, SHARKS WANT TO HAVE ME FOR BREAKFAST.
I CAN RELATE TO SALMON. LIFE'S AN UPHILL BATTLE FOR ALL OF US, BRO.
YOU, TOO?
A CONSTANT STRUGGLE FOR MY NEXT MEAL.
I'VE FOUND A FRIEND.
HERE, PULL UP A BAGEL.
TOOMEY

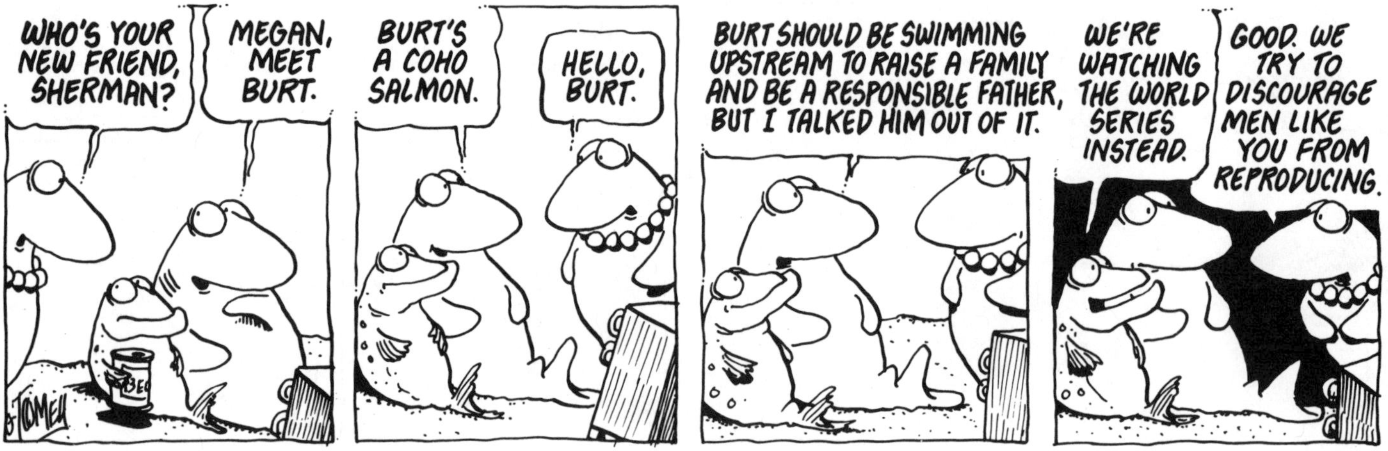
WHO'S YOUR NEW FRIEND, SHERMAN?
MEGAN, MEET BURT.
BURT'S A COHO SALMON.
HELLO, BURT.
BURT SHOULD BE SWIMMING UPSTREAM TO RAISE A FAMILY AND BE A RESPONSIBLE FATHER, BUT I TALKED HIM OUT OF IT.
WE'RE WATCHING THE WORLD SERIES INSTEAD.
GOOD. WE TRY TO DISCOURAGE MEN LIKE YOU FROM REPRODUCING.
TOOMEY

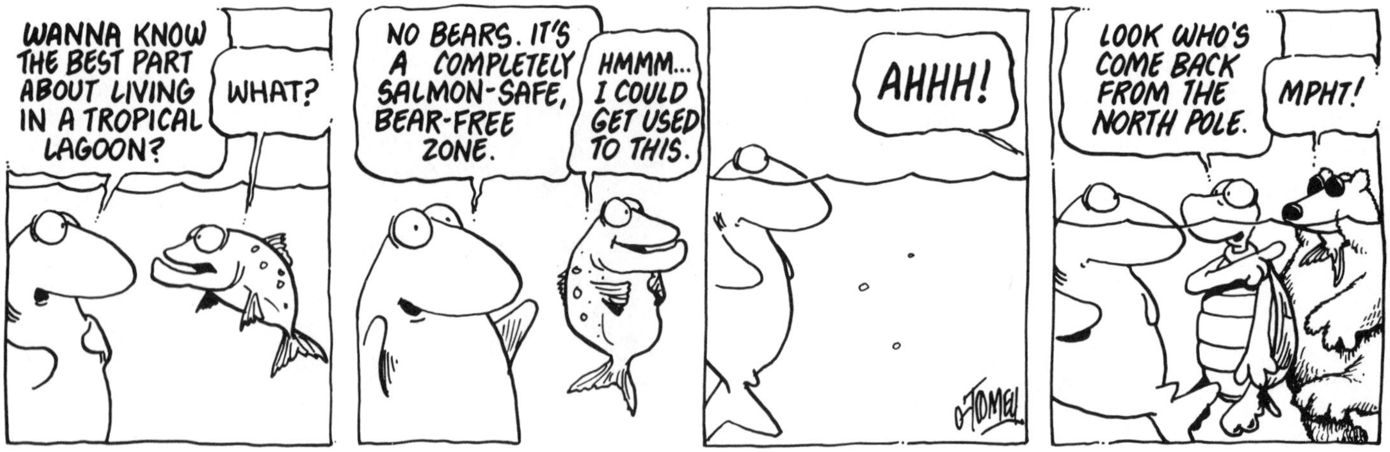
WANNA KNOW THE BEST PART ABOUT LIVING IN A TROPICAL LAGOON?
WHAT?
NO BEARS. IT'S A COMPLETELY SALMON-SAFE, BEAR-FREE ZONE.
HMMM... I COULD GET USED TO THIS.
AHHH!
TOOMEY
LOOK WHO'S COME BACK FROM THE NORTH POLE.
MPHT!

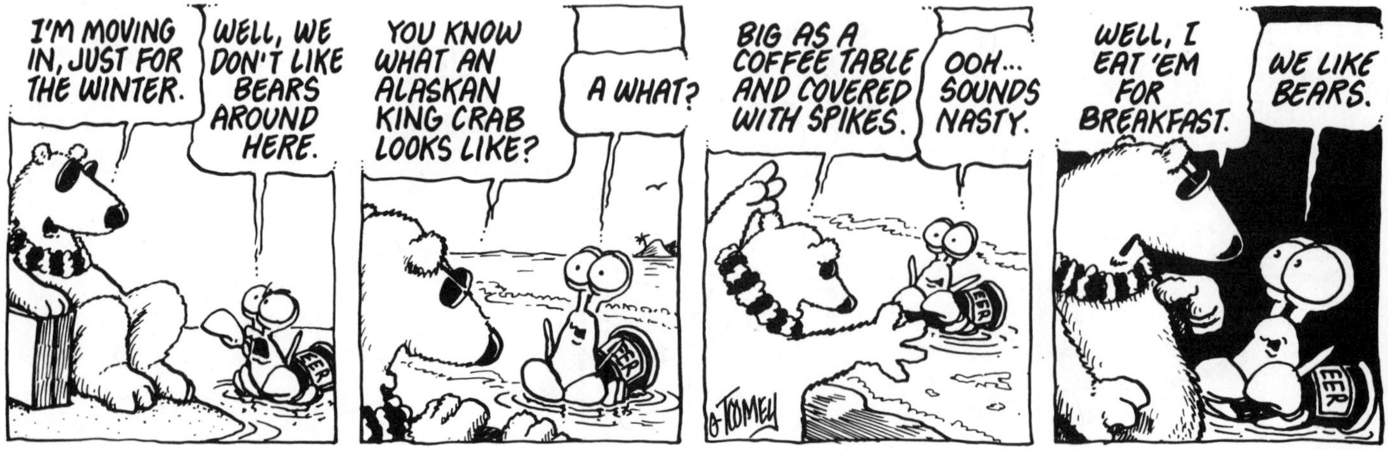
I'M MOVING IN, JUST FOR THE WINTER.
WELL, WE DON'T LIKE BEARS AROUND HERE.
YOU KNOW WHAT AN ALASKAN KING CRAB LOOKS LIKE?
A WHAT?
BIG AS A COFFEE TABLE AND COVERED WITH SPIKES.
OOH... SOUNDS NASTY.
TOOMEY
WELL, I EAT 'EM FOR BREAKFAST.
WE LIKE BEARS.

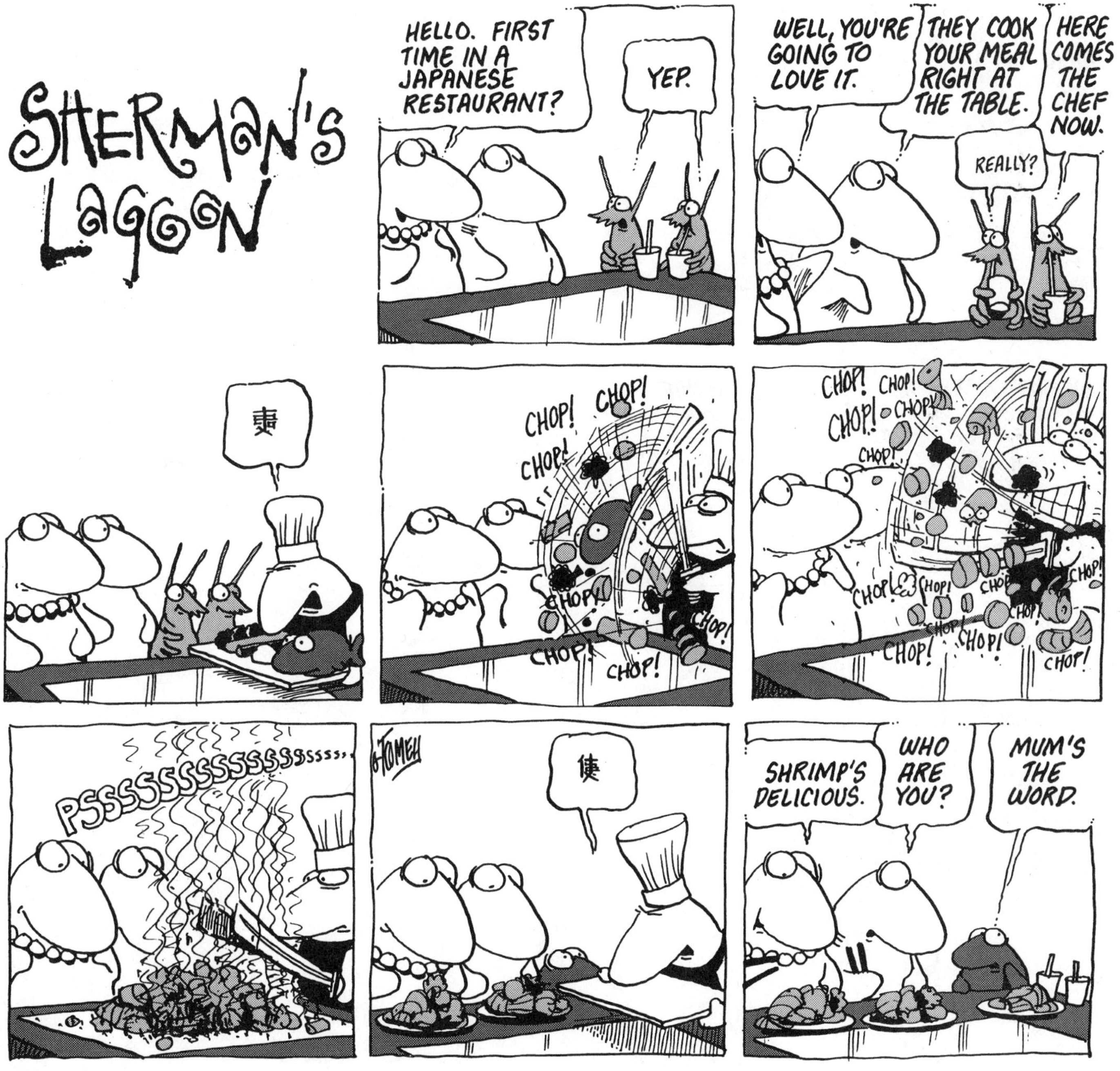
SHERMAN'S LAGOON
HELLO. FIRST TIME IN A JAPANESE RESTAURANT?
YEP.
WELL, YOU'RE GOING TO LOVE IT.
THEY COOK YOUR MEAL RIGHT AT THE TABLE.
HERE COMES THE CHEF NOW.
REALLY?
CHOP! CHOP! CHOP! CHOP! CHOP! CHOP!
CHOP! CHOP! CHOP! CHOP! CHOP! CHOP! CHOP! CHOP! CHOP! CHOP! CHOP! CHOP! CHOP! CHOP!
PSSSSSSSSSSSSSSSsssss..
SHRIMP'S DELICIOUS.
WHO ARE YOU?
MUM'S THE WORD.

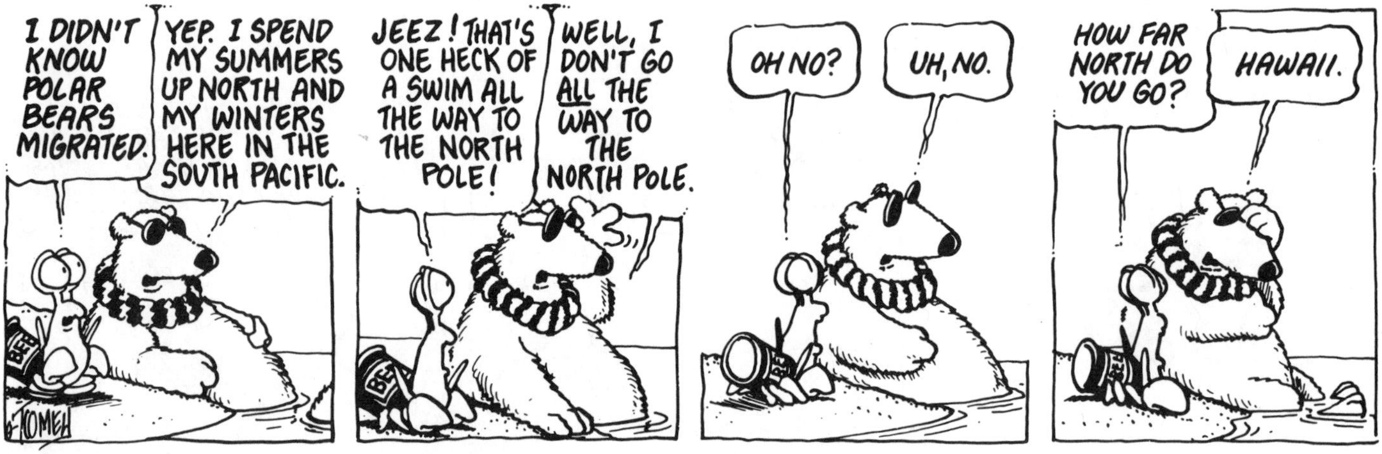
I DIDN'T KNOW POLAR BEARS MIGRATED.
YEP. I SPEND MY SUMMERS UP NORTH AND MY WINTERS HERE IN THE SOUTH PACIFIC.
JEEZ! THAT'S ONE HECK OF A SWIM ALL THE WAY TO THE NORTH POLE!
WELL, I DON'T GO ALL THE WAY TO THE NORTH POLE.
OH NO?
UH, NO.
HOW FAR NORTH DO YOU GO?
HAWAII.

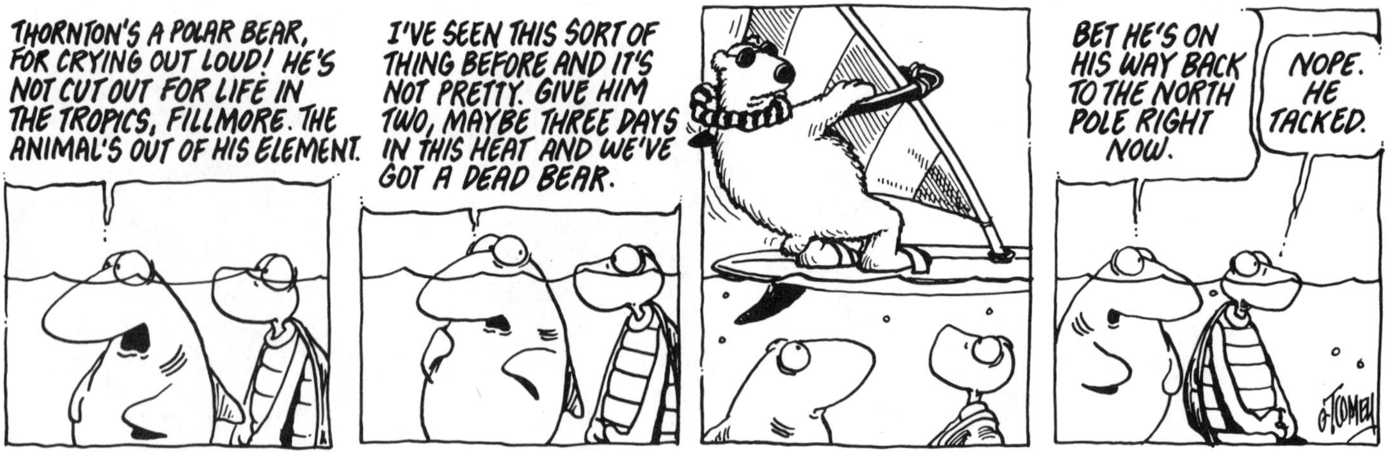
THORNTON'S A POLAR BEAR, FOR CRYING OUT LOUD! HE'S NOT CUT OUT FOR LIFE IN THE TROPICS, FILLMORE. THE ANIMAL'S OUT OF HIS ELEMENT.
I'VE SEEN THIS SORT OF THING BEFORE AND IT'S NOT PRETTY. GIVE HIM TWO, MAYBE THREE DAYS IN THIS HEAT AND WE'VE GOT A DEAD BEAR.
BET HE'S ON HIS WAY BACK TO THE NORTH POLE RIGHT NOW.
NOPE. HE TACKED.

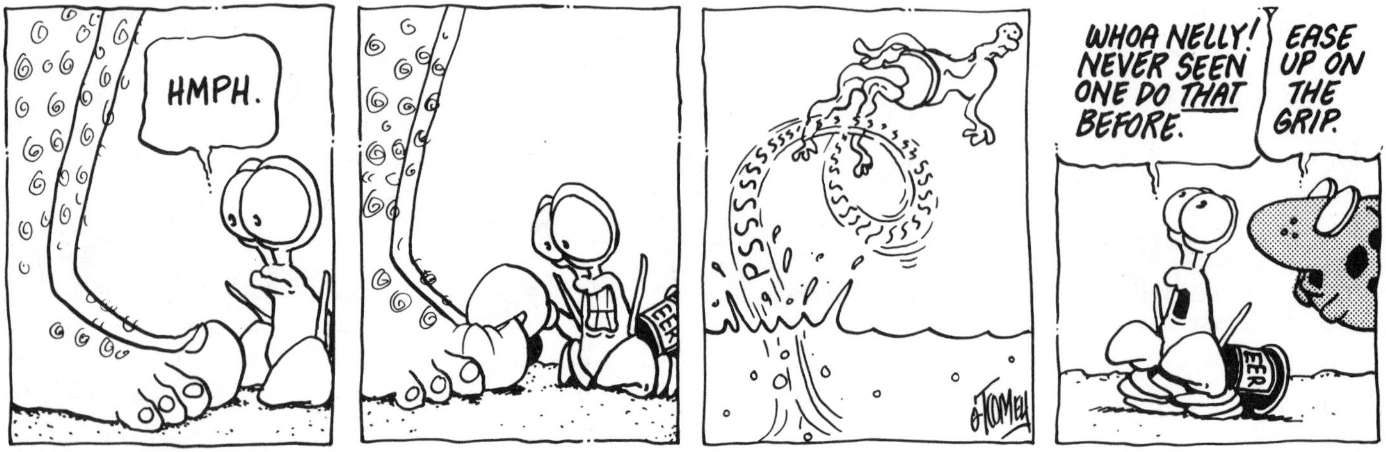
HMPH.
WHOA NELLY! NEVER SEEN ONE DO THAT BEFORE.
EASE UP ON THE GRIP.

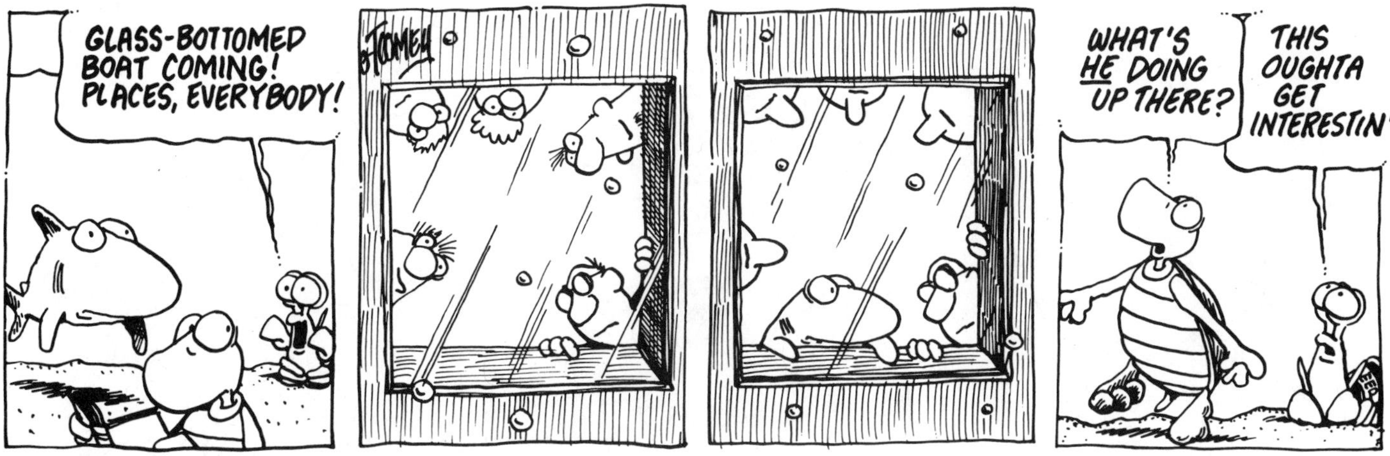
GLASS-BOTTOMED BOAT COMING! PLACES, EVERYBODY!
WHAT'S HE DOING UP THERE?
THIS OUGHTA GET INTERESTIN'.

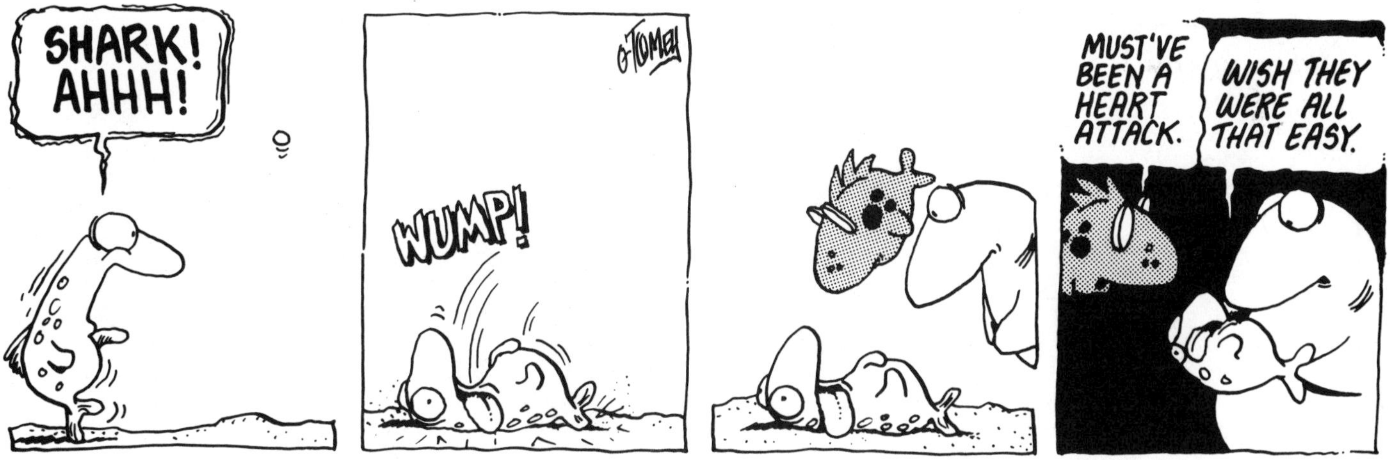
SHARK! AHHH!
WUMP!
MUST'VE BEEN A HEART ATTACK.
WISH THEY WERE ALL THAT EASY.

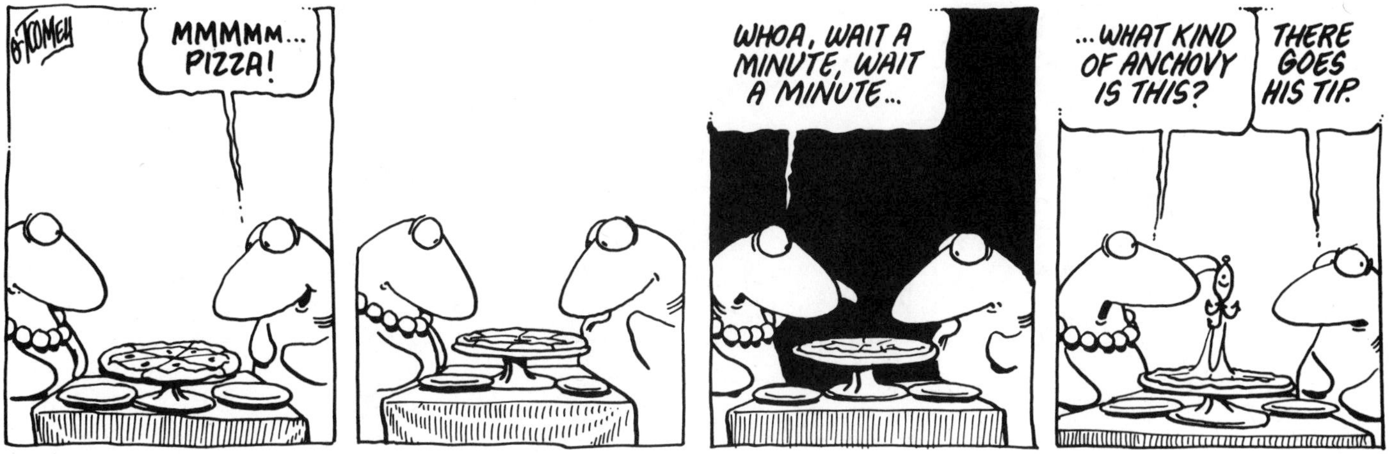
MMMMM... PIZZA!
WHOA, WAIT A MINUTE, WAIT A MINUTE...
...WHAT KIND OF ANCHOVY IS THIS?
THERE GOES HIS TIP.

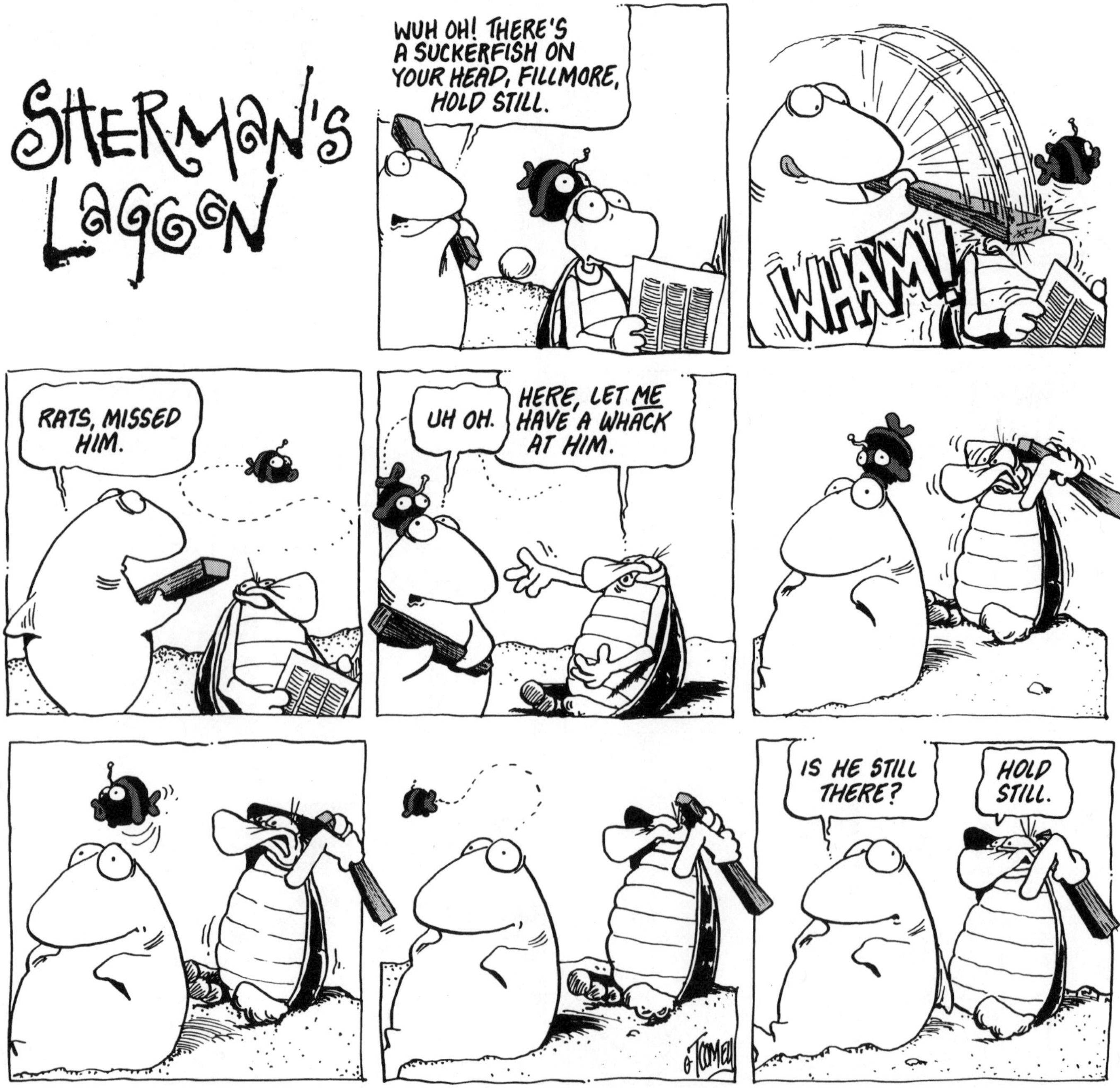
SHERMAN'S LAGOON
WUH OH! THERE'S A SUCKERFISH ON YOUR HEAD, FILLMORE, HOLD STILL.
WHAM!
RATS, MISSED HIM.
UH OH.
HERE, LET ME HAVE A WHACK AT HIM.
IS HE STILL THERE?
HOLD STILL.
TOOMEY

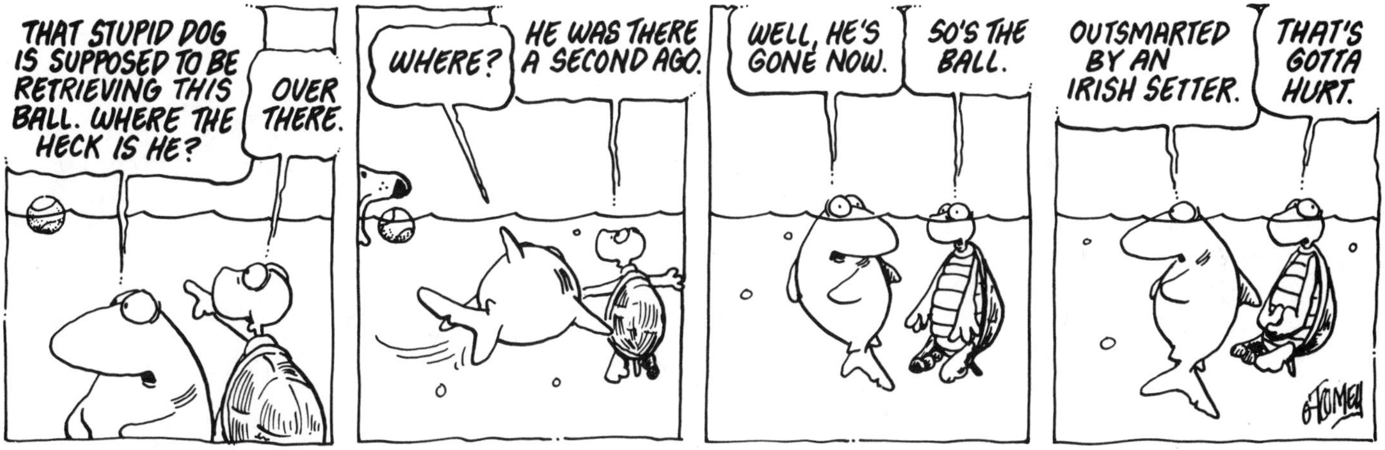
THAT STUPID DOG IS SUPPOSED TO BE RETRIEVING THIS BALL. WHERE THE HECK IS HE?
OVER THERE.
WHERE?
HE WAS THERE A SECOND AGO.
WELL, HE'S GONE NOW.
SO'S THE BALL.
OUTSMARTED BY AN IRISH SETTER.
THAT'S GOTTA HURT.

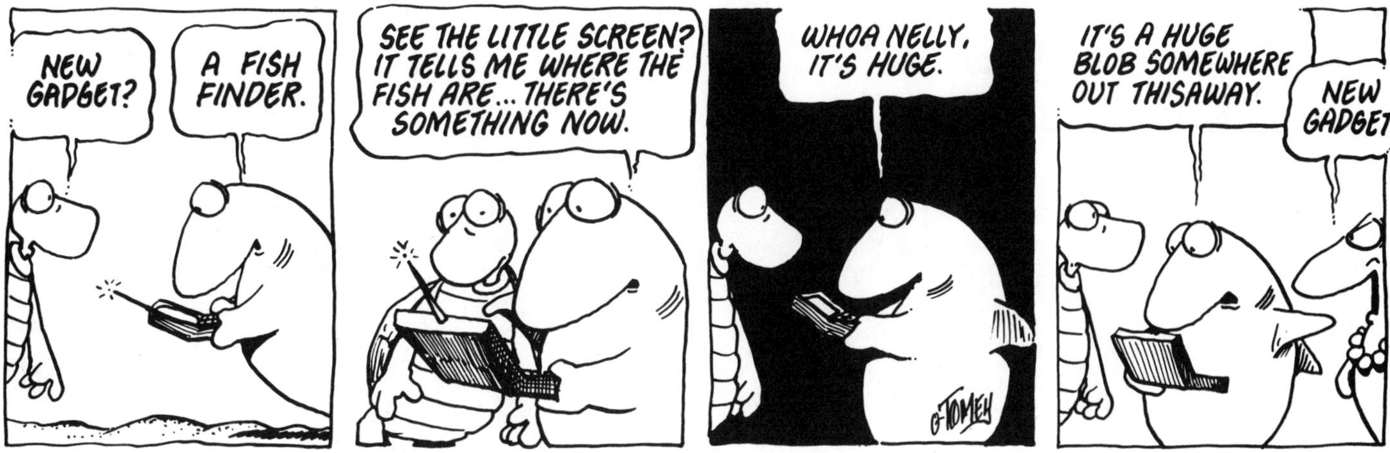
NEW GADGET?
A FISH FINDER.
SEE THE LITTLE SCREEN? IT TELLS ME WHERE THE FISH ARE... THERE'S SOMETHING NOW.
WHOA NELLY, IT'S HUGE.
IT'S A HUGE BLOB SOMEWHERE OUT THISAWAY.
NEW GADGET?

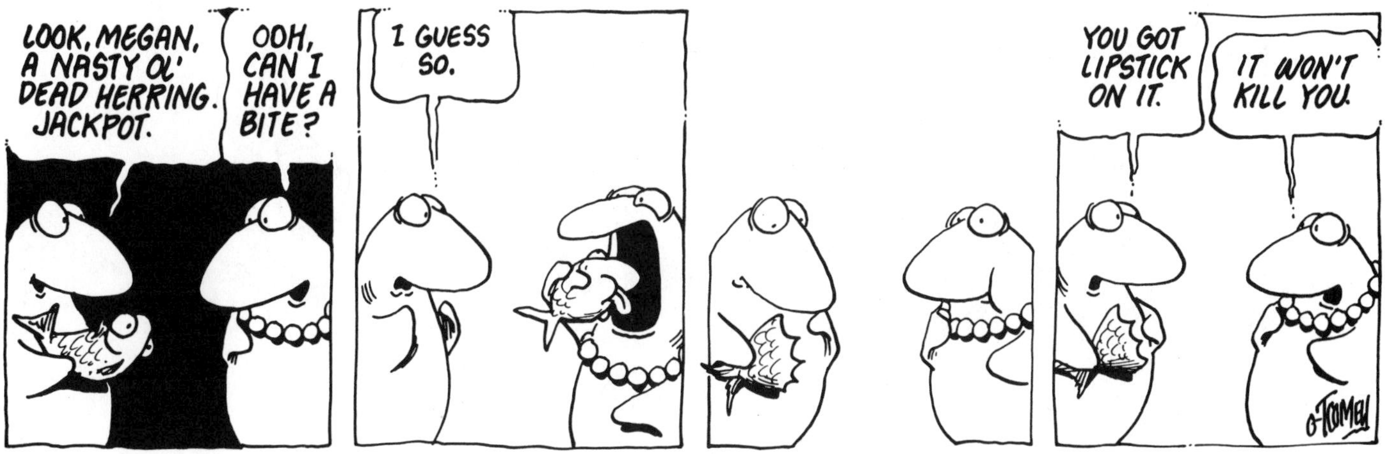
LOOK, MEGAN, A NASTY OL' DEAD HERRING. JACKPOT.
OOH, CAN I HAVE A BITE?
I GUESS SO.
YOU GOT LIPSTICK ON IT.
IT WON'T KILL YOU.

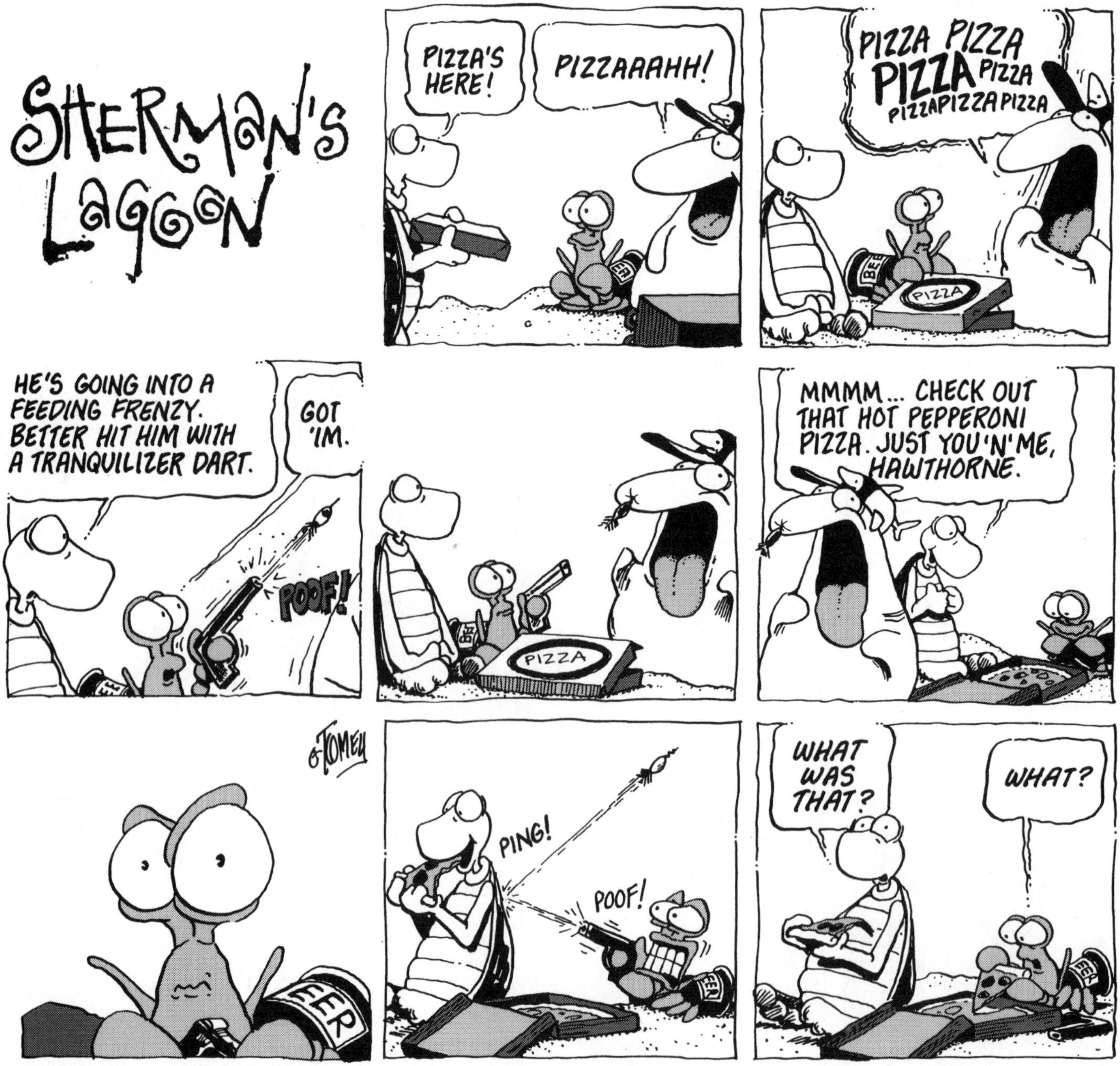
SHERMAN'S LAGOON
PIZZA'S HERE!
PIZZAAAHH!
PIZZA PIZZA PIZZA PIZZA PIZZAPIZZAPIZZA
PIZZA
HE'S GOING INTO A FEEDING FRENZY. BETTER HIT HIM WITH A TRANQUILIZER DART.
GOT 'IM.
POOF!
PIZZA
MMMM... CHECK OUT THAT HOT PEPPERONI PIZZA. JUST YOU'N'ME, HAWTHORNE.
PING!
POOF!
WHAT WAS THAT?
WHAT?

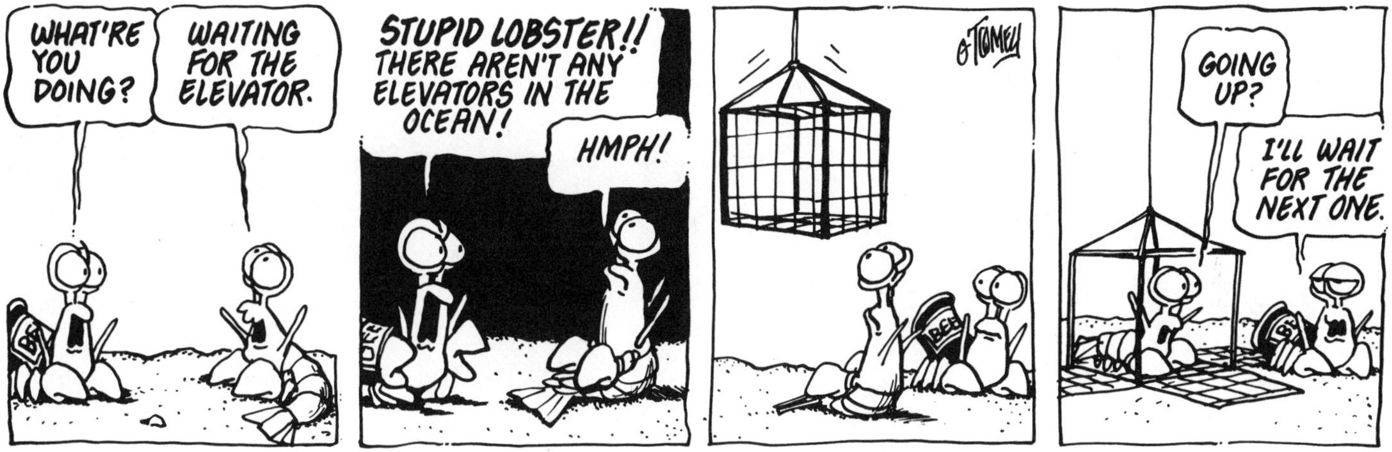
WHAT'RE YOU DOING?
WAITING FOR THE ELEVATOR.
STUPID LOBSTER!! THERE AREN'T ANY ELEVATORS IN THE OCEAN!
HMPH!
GOING UP?
I'LL WAIT FOR THE NEXT ONE.

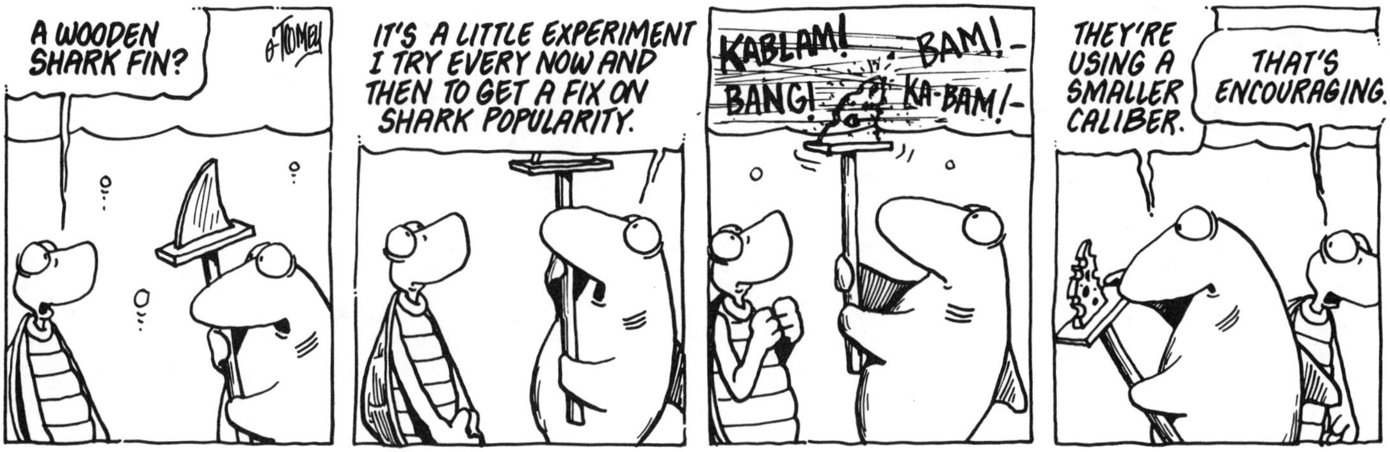
A WOODEN SHARK FIN?
IT'S A LITTLE EXPERIMENT I TRY EVERY NOW AND THEN TO GET A FIX ON SHARK POPULARITY.
KABLAM! BAM! BANG! KA-BAM!
THEY'RE USING A SMALLER CALIBER.
THAT'S ENCOURAGING.

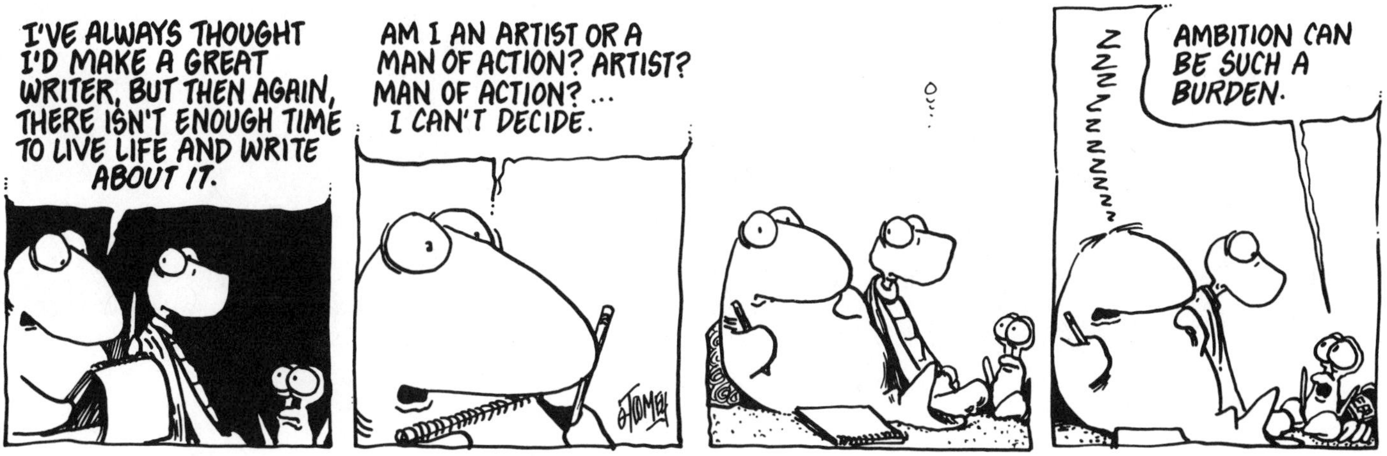
I'VE ALWAYS THOUGHT I'D MAKE A GREAT WRITER, BUT THEN AGAIN, THERE ISN'T ENOUGH TIME TO LIVE LIFE AND WRITE ABOUT IT.
AM I AN ARTIST OR A MAN OF ACTION? ARTIST? MAN OF ACTION? ... I CAN'T DECIDE.
AMBITION CAN BE SUCH A BURDEN.

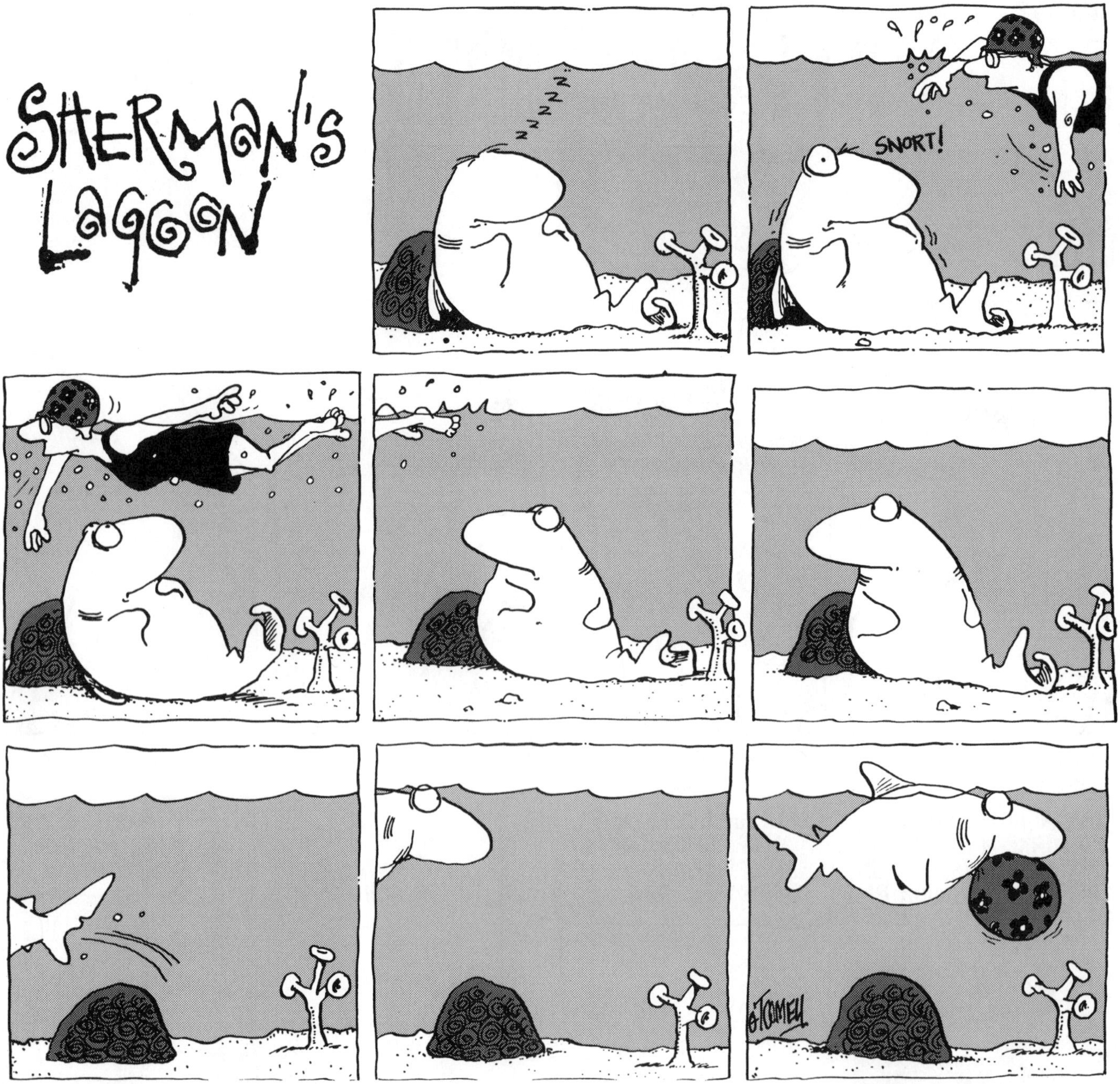
SHERMAN'S LAGOON
ZZZZZ
SNORT!
©TOOMEY

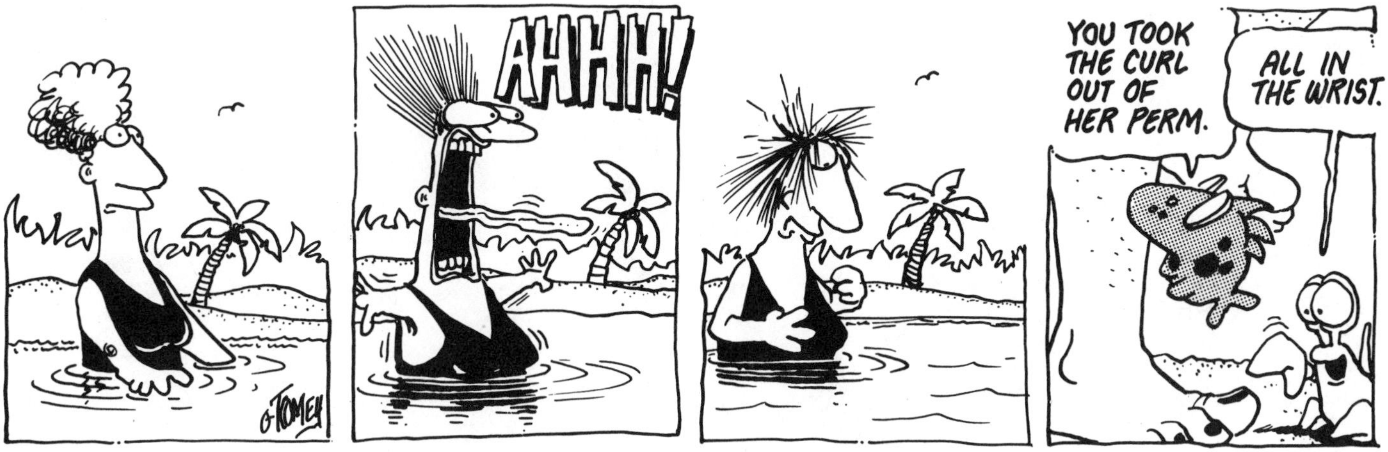
AHHH!
YOU TOOK THE CURL OUT OF HER PERM.
ALL IN THE WRIST.

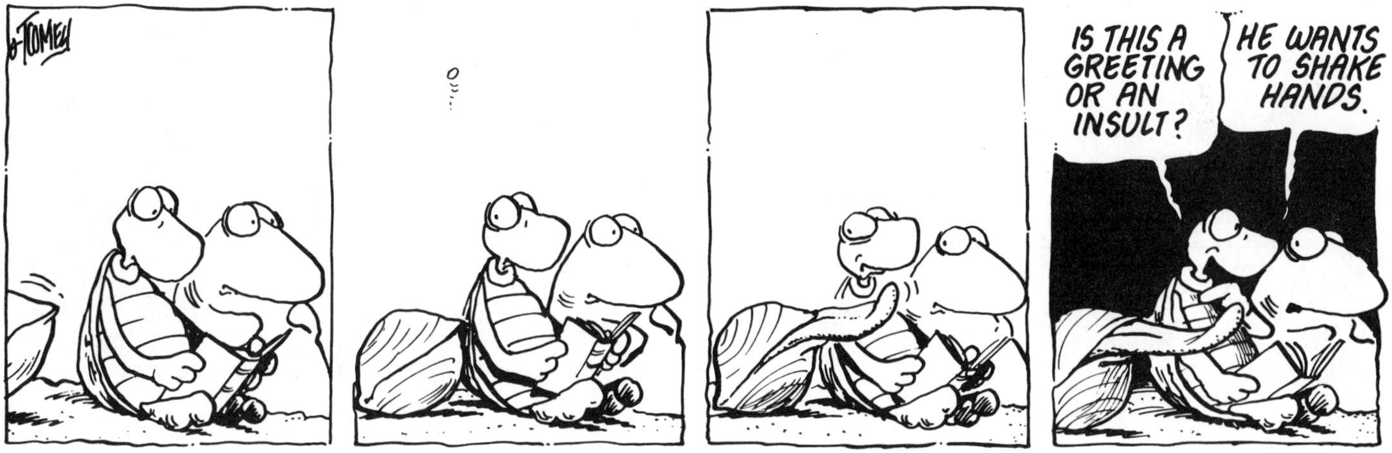
IS THIS A GREETING OR AN INSULT?
HE WANTS TO SHAKE HANDS.

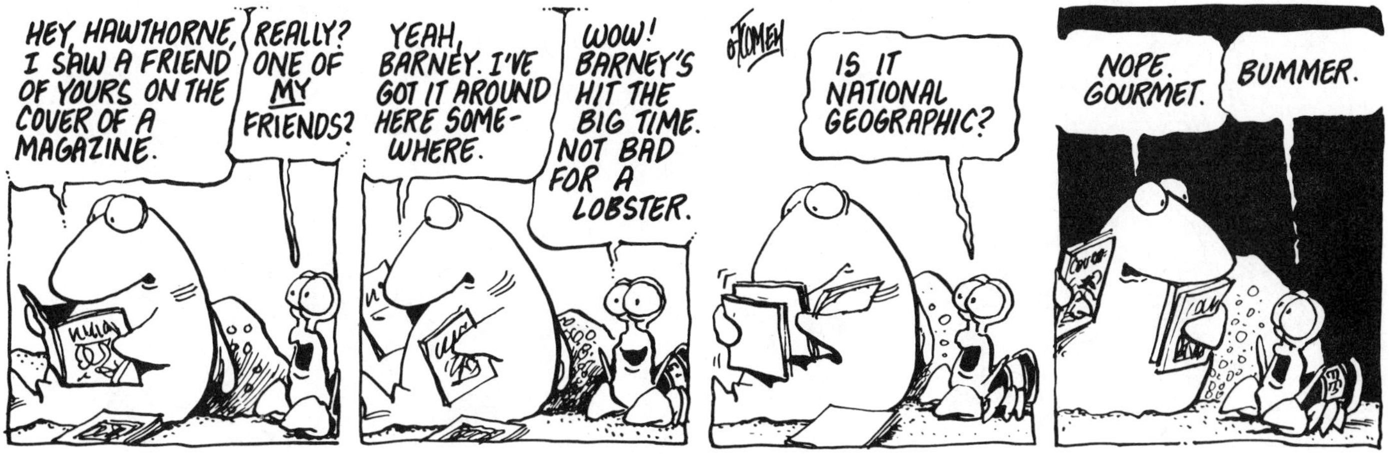
HEY, HAWTHORNE, I SAW A FRIEND OF YOURS ON THE COVER OF A MAGAZINE.
REALLY? ONE OF MY FRIENDS?
YEAH, BARNEY. I'VE GOT IT AROUND HERE SOMEWHERE.
WOW! BARNEY'S HIT THE BIG TIME. NOT BAD FOR A LOBSTER.
IS IT NATIONAL GEOGRAPHIC?
NOPE. GOURMET.
BUMMER.

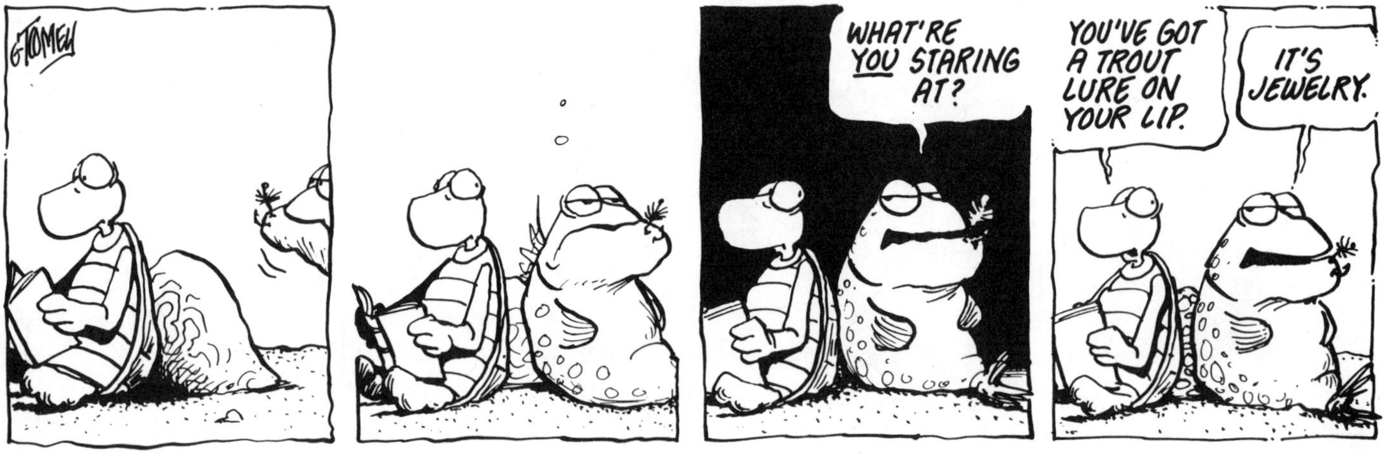
WHAT'RE YOU STARING AT?
YOU'VE GOT A TROUT LURE ON YOUR LIP.
IT'S JEWELRY.

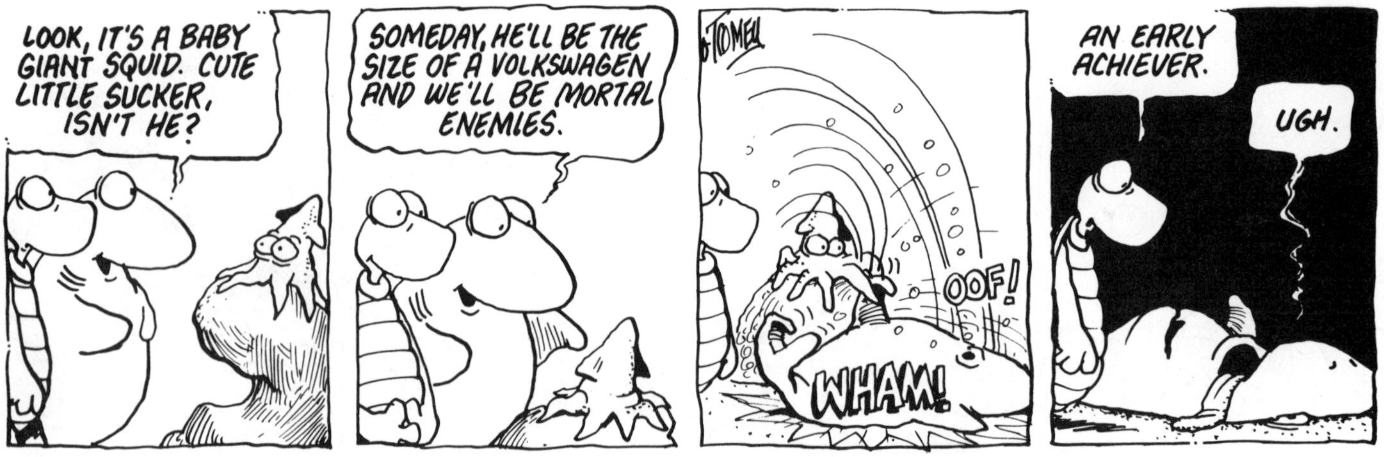
LOOK, IT'S A BABY GIANT SQUID. CUTE LITTLE SUCKER, ISN'T HE?
SOMEDAY, HE'LL BE THE SIZE OF A VOLKSWAGEN AND WE'LL BE MORTAL ENEMIES.
OOF!
WHAM!
AN EARLY ACHIEVER.
UGH.

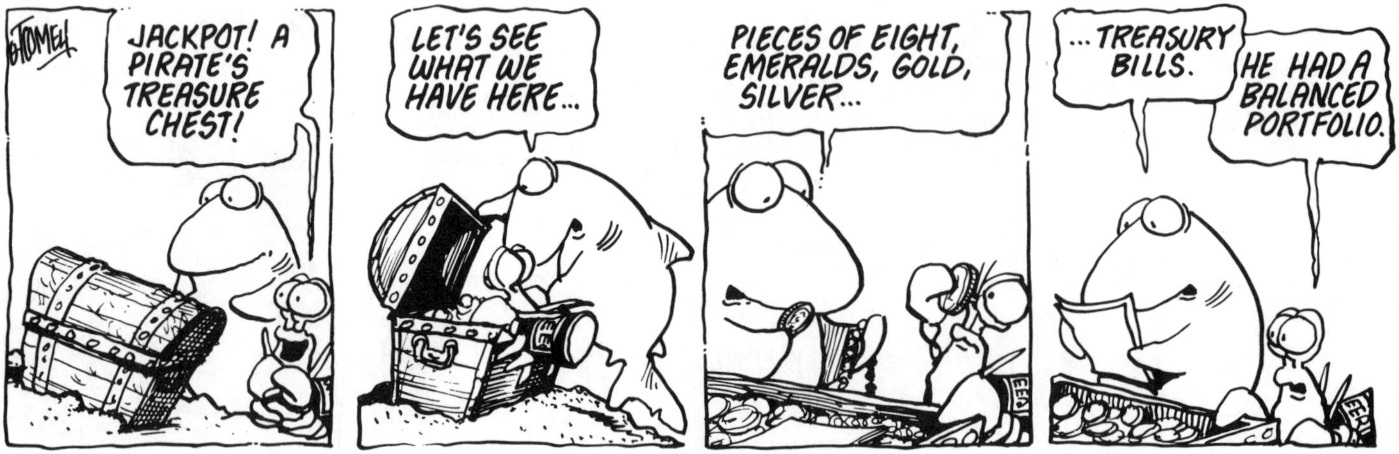
JACKPOT! A PIRATE'S TREASURE CHEST!
LET'S SEE WHAT WE HAVE HERE...
PIECES OF EIGHT, EMERALDS, GOLD, SILVER...
...TREASURY BILLS.
HE HAD A BALANCED PORTFOLIO.

Panel 1: LOOK AT YOU, YOU RIDICULOUS-LOOKING BOTTOM DWELLER!

Panel 2: YOU JUST SIT THERE ALL DAY TRYING TO BLEND IN. GET A LIFE!

Panel 3: (no dialogue)

Panel 4: I WASN'T TALKING TO YOU.

Panel 5: SHERMAN, IS IT OK IF I YANK ONE OF YOUR TEETH OUT? — HUH?

Panel 6: I JUST GOT THIS BOOK ON HOME DENTISTRY. — READING A BOOK DOESN'T MAKE YOU A DENTIST.

Panel 7: ACTUALLY, I JUST READ THE DUST JACKET. — YOU DIDN'T EVEN READ IT?

Panel 8: WHAT GOOD ARE BOOKS, ANYWAY? C'MON, OPEN UP. — STAY AWAY FROM ME!

Panel 9: ARE YOU TELLING ME SHARK'S TEETH CAN FETCH FIVE BUCKS APIECE? — THEY'RE A HOT ITEM IN GIFT SHOPS NOW.

Panel 10: AS YOUR DENTIST, I HUMBLY RECOMMEND WE YANK ABOUT SIX OR SEVEN.

Panel 11: YOU'RE GOING TO NEED THAT MUCH CASH ON HAND.

Panel 12: WHAT FOR? — TO PAY THE DENTAL BILL.

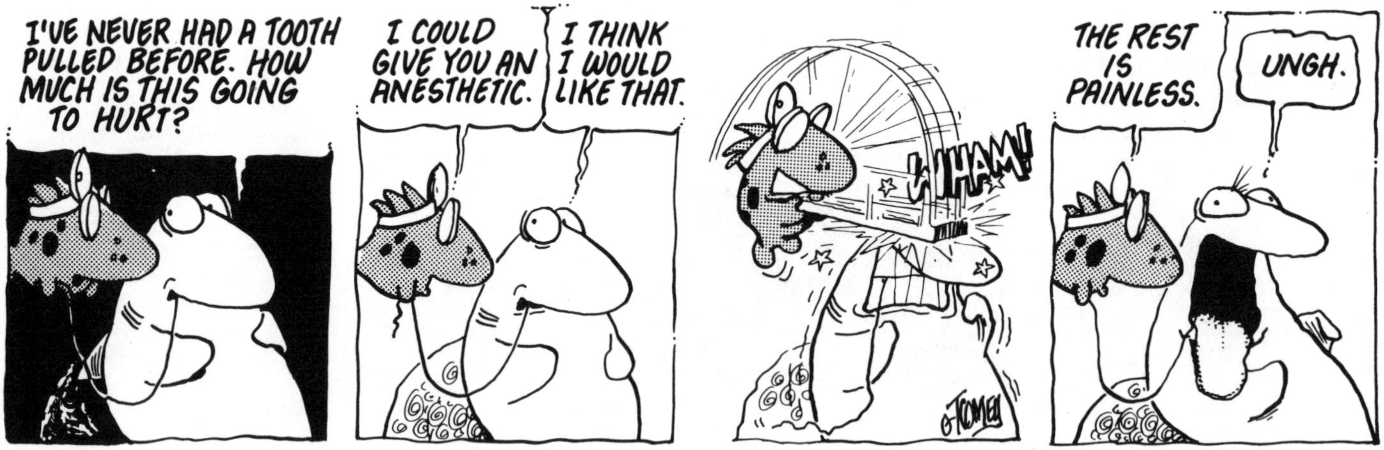
I'VE NEVER HAD A TOOTH PULLED BEFORE. HOW MUCH IS THIS GOING TO HURT?
I COULD GIVE YOU AN ANESTHETIC.
I THINK I WOULD LIKE THAT.
WHAM!
THE REST IS PAINLESS.
UNGH.

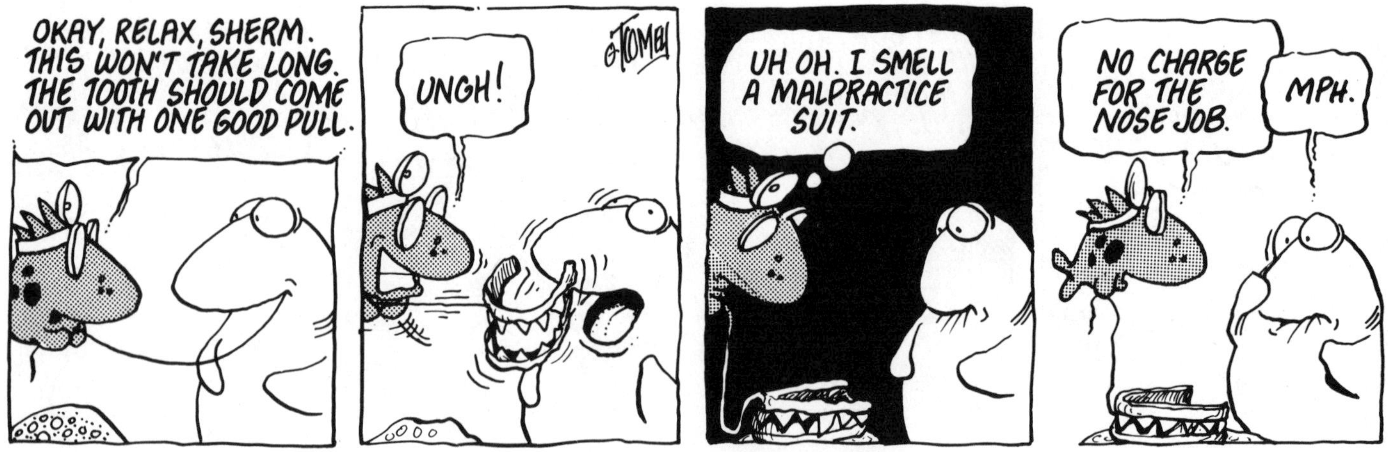
OKAY, RELAX, SHERM. THIS WON'T TAKE LONG. THE TOOTH SHOULD COME OUT WITH ONE GOOD PULL.
UNGH!
UH OH. I SMELL A MALPRACTICE SUIT.
NO CHARGE FOR THE NOSE JOB.
MPH.

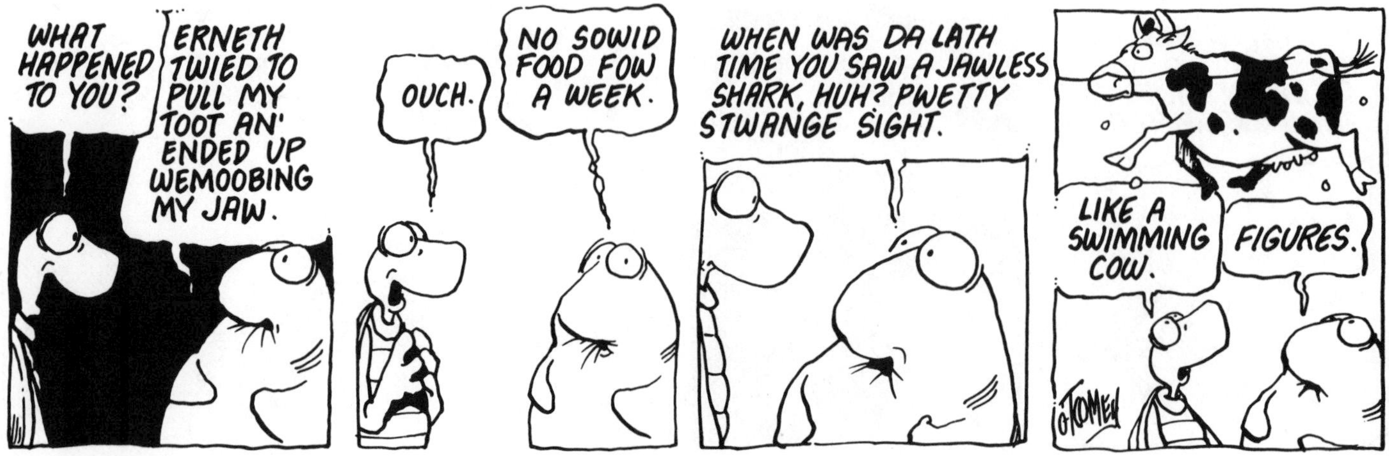
WHAT HAPPENED TO YOU?
ERNETH TWIED TO PULL MY TOOT AN' ENDED UP WEMOOBING MY JAW.
OUCH.
NO SOWID FOOD FOW A WEEK.
WHEN WAS DA LATH TIME YOU SAW A JAWLESS SHARK, HUH? PWETTY STWANGE SIGHT.
LIKE A SWIMMING COW.
FIGURES.

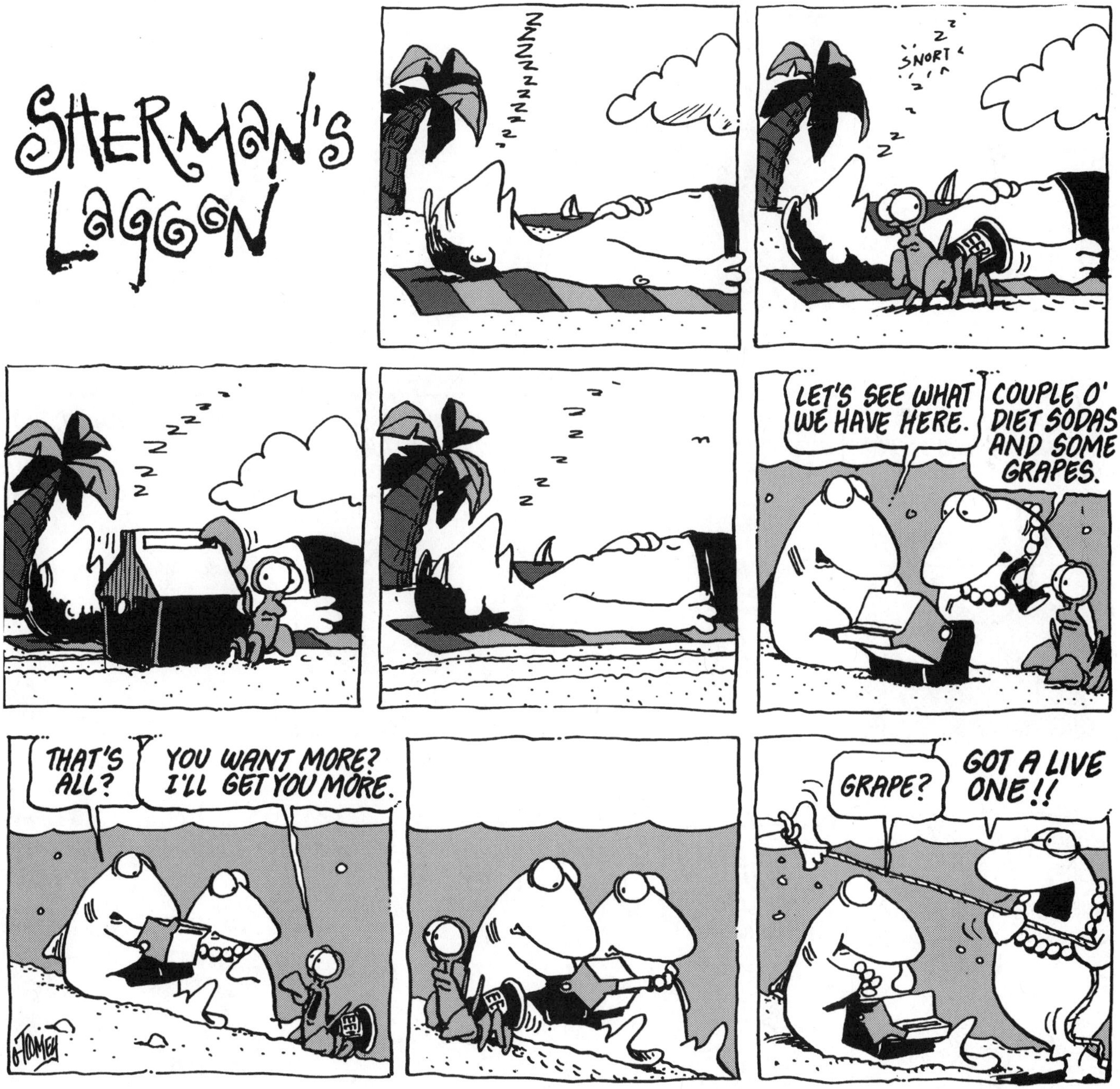
SHERMAN'S LAGOON
SNORT
LET'S SEE WHAT WE HAVE HERE.
COUPLE O' DIET SODAS AND SOME GRAPES.
THAT'S ALL?
YOU WANT MORE? I'LL GET YOU MORE.
GRAPE?
GOT A LIVE ONE!!
TOOMEY

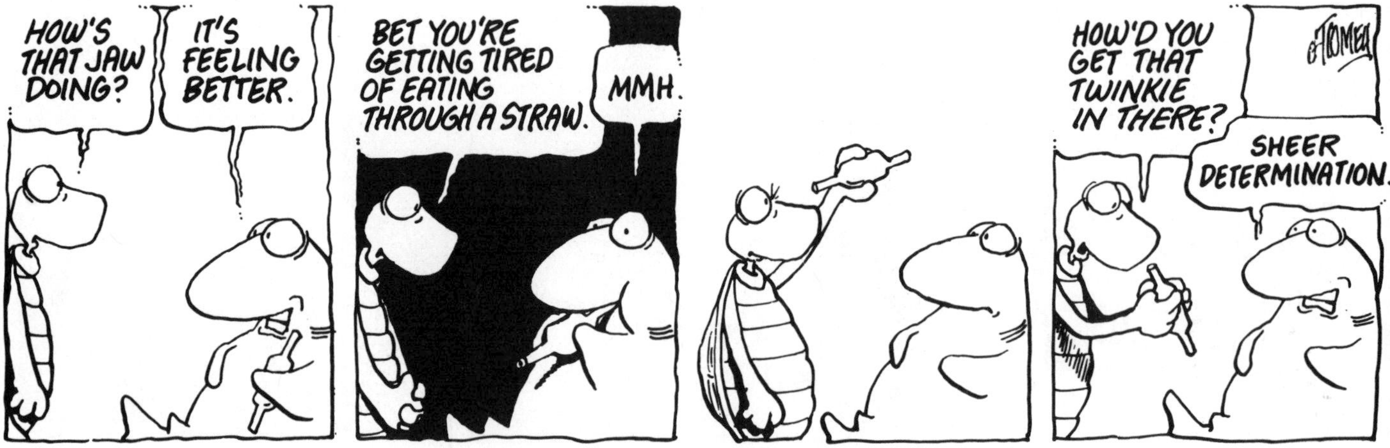
HOW'S THAT JAW DOING?
IT'S FEELING BETTER.
BET YOU'RE GETTING TIRED OF EATING THROUGH A STRAW.
MMH.
HOW'D YOU GET THAT TWINKIE IN THERE?
SHEER DETERMINATION.
O'TOOMEY

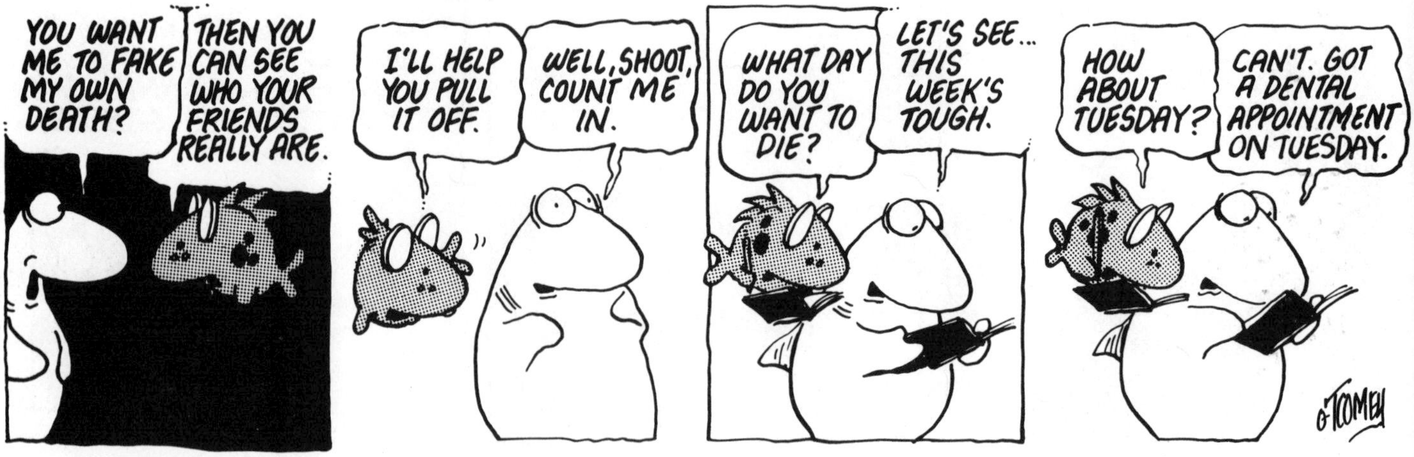
YOU WANT ME TO FAKE MY OWN DEATH?
THEN YOU CAN SEE WHO YOUR FRIENDS REALLY ARE.
I'LL HELP YOU PULL IT OFF.
WELL, SHOOT, COUNT ME IN.
WHAT DAY DO YOU WANT TO DIE?
LET'S SEE... THIS WEEK'S TOUGH.
HOW ABOUT TUESDAY?
CAN'T. GOT A DENTAL APPOINTMENT ON TUESDAY.
O'TOOMEY

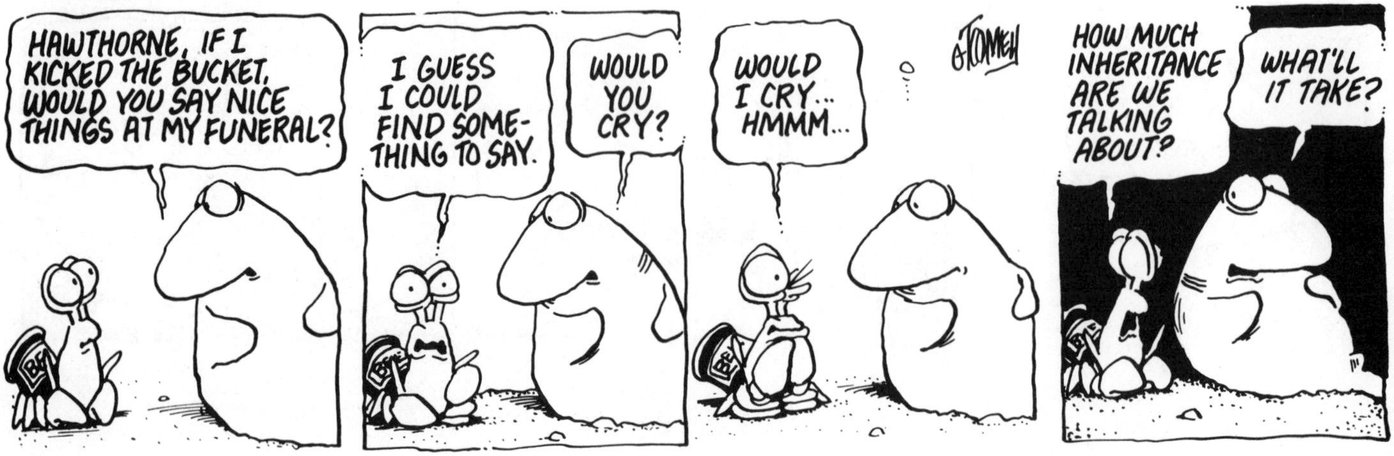
HAWTHORNE, IF I KICKED THE BUCKET, WOULD YOU SAY NICE THINGS AT MY FUNERAL?
I GUESS I COULD FIND SOMETHING TO SAY.
WOULD YOU CRY?
WOULD I CRY... HMMM...
O'TOOMEY
HOW MUCH INHERITANCE ARE WE TALKING ABOUT?
WHAT'LL IT TAKE?

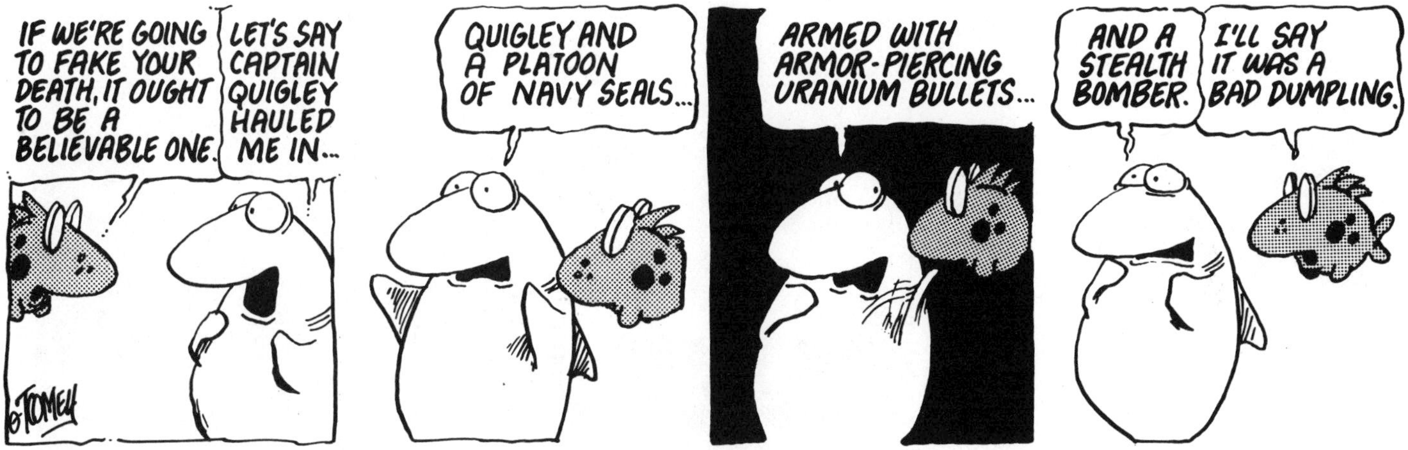
IF WE'RE GOING TO FAKE YOUR DEATH, IT OUGHT TO BE A BELIEVABLE ONE.
LET'S SAY CAPTAIN QUIGLEY HAULED ME IN...
QUIGLEY AND A PLATOON OF NAVY SEALS...
ARMED WITH ARMOR-PIERCING URANIUM BULLETS...
AND A STEALTH BOMBER.
I'LL SAY IT WAS A BAD DUMPLING.
O'TOOMEY

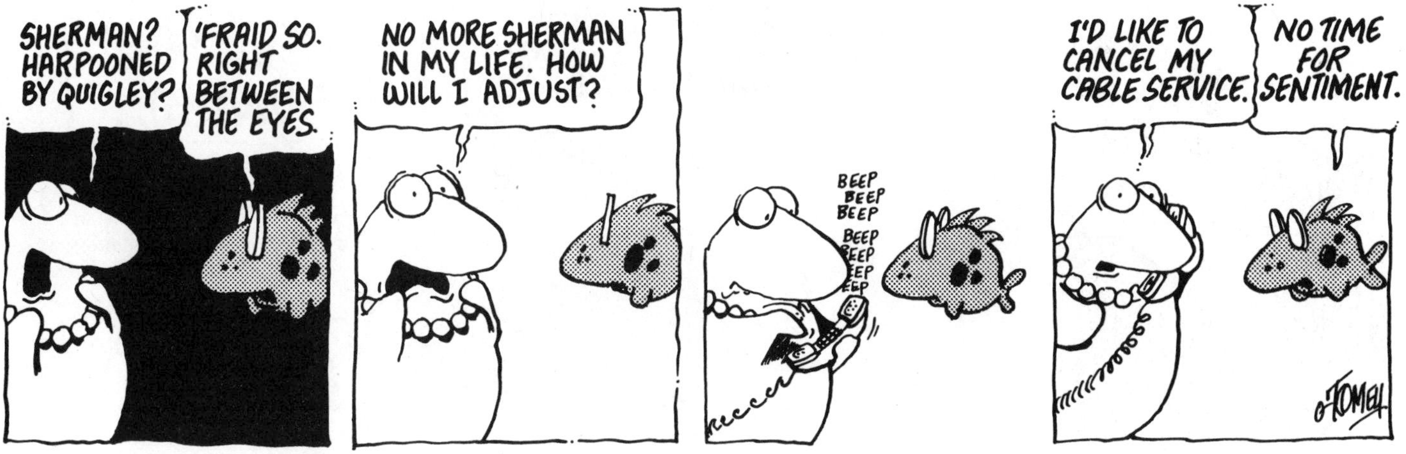
SHERMAN? HARPOONED BY QUIGLEY?
'FRAID SO. RIGHT BETWEEN THE EYES.
NO MORE SHERMAN IN MY LIFE. HOW WILL I ADJUST?
BEEP BEEP BEEP
BEEP BEEP EEP EEP
I'D LIKE TO CANCEL MY CABLE SERVICE.
NO TIME FOR SENTIMENT.
O'TOOMEY

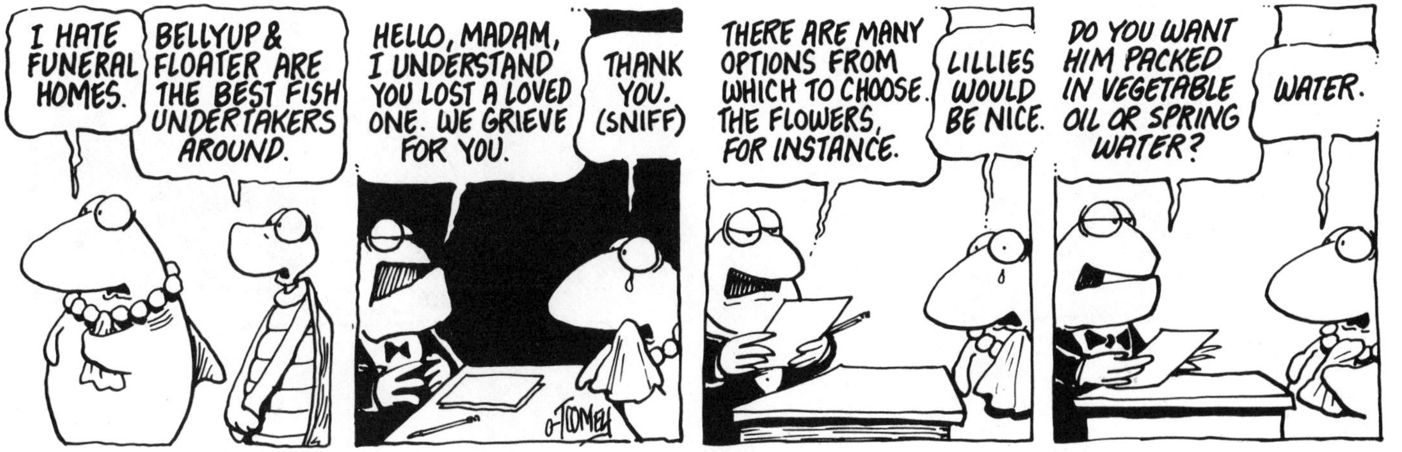
I HATE FUNERAL HOMES.
BELLYUP & FLOATER ARE THE BEST FISH UNDERTAKERS AROUND.
HELLO, MADAM, I UNDERSTAND YOU LOST A LOVED ONE. WE GRIEVE FOR YOU.
THANK YOU. (SNIFF)
O'TOOMEY
THERE ARE MANY OPTIONS FROM WHICH TO CHOOSE. THE FLOWERS, FOR INSTANCE.
LILLIES WOULD BE NICE.
DO YOU WANT HIM PACKED IN VEGETABLE OIL OR SPRING WATER?
WATER.

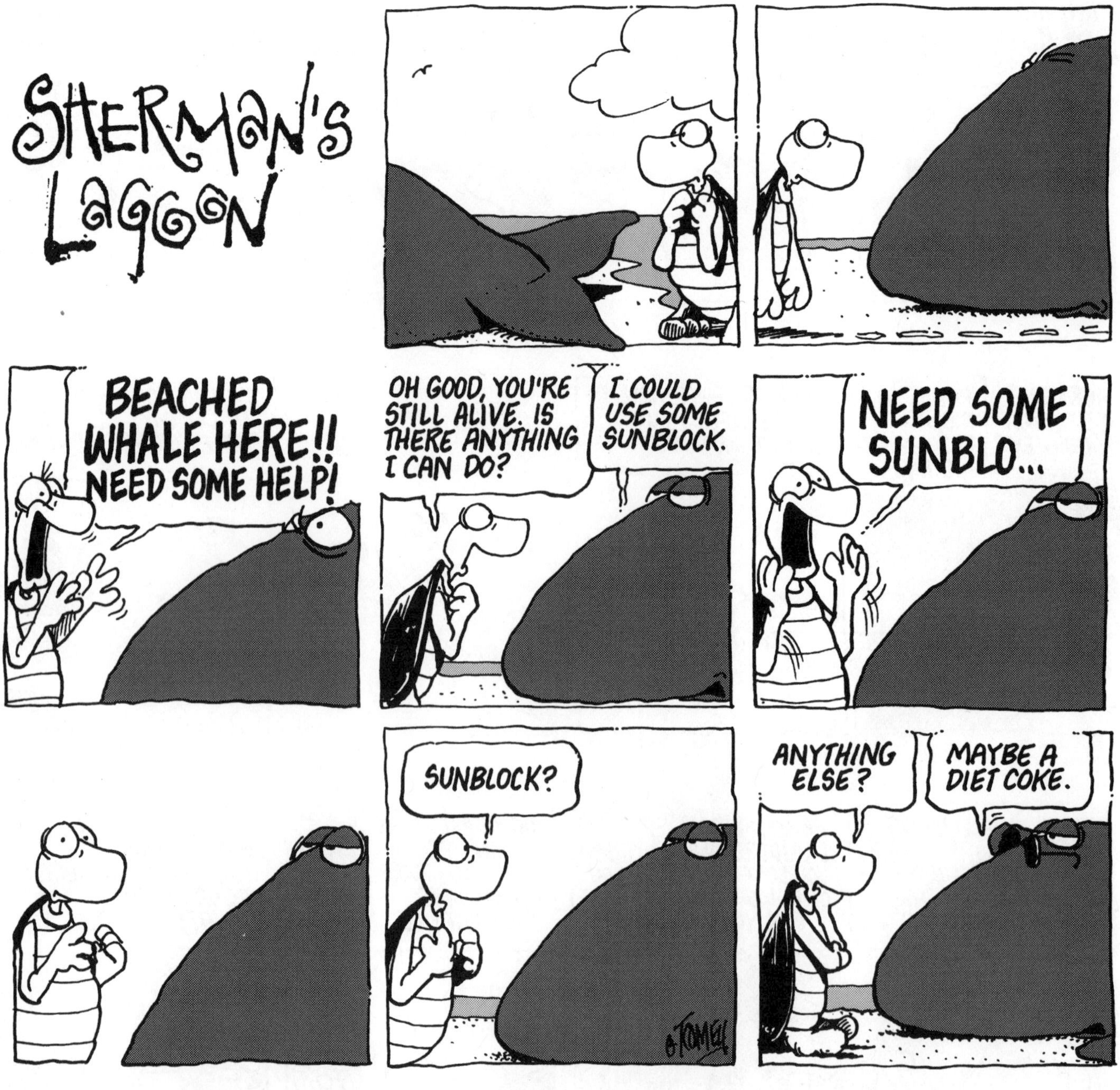
SHERMAN'S LAGOON
BEACHED WHALE HERE!! NEED SOME HELP!
OH GOOD, YOU'RE STILL ALIVE. IS THERE ANYTHING I CAN DO?
I COULD USE SOME SUNBLOCK.
NEED SOME SUNBLO...
SUNBLOCK?
ANYTHING ELSE?
MAYBE A DIET COKE.

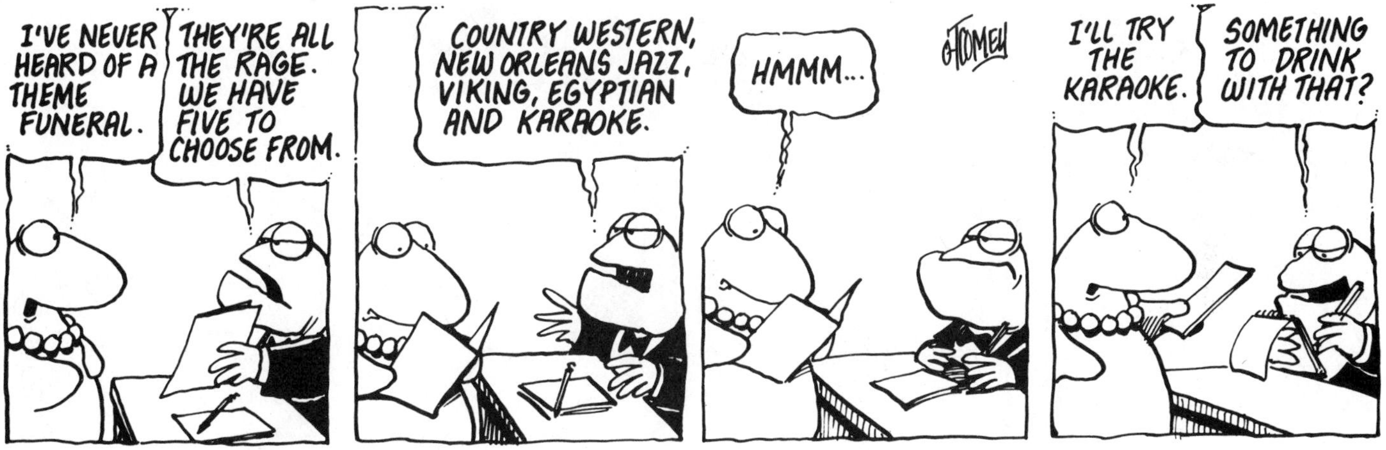
I'VE NEVER HEARD OF A THEME FUNERAL.
THEY'RE ALL THE RAGE. WE HAVE FIVE TO CHOOSE FROM.
COUNTRY WESTERN, NEW ORLEANS JAZZ, VIKING, EGYPTIAN AND KARAOKE.
HMMM...
I'LL TRY THE KARAOKE.
SOMETHING TO DRINK WITH THAT?

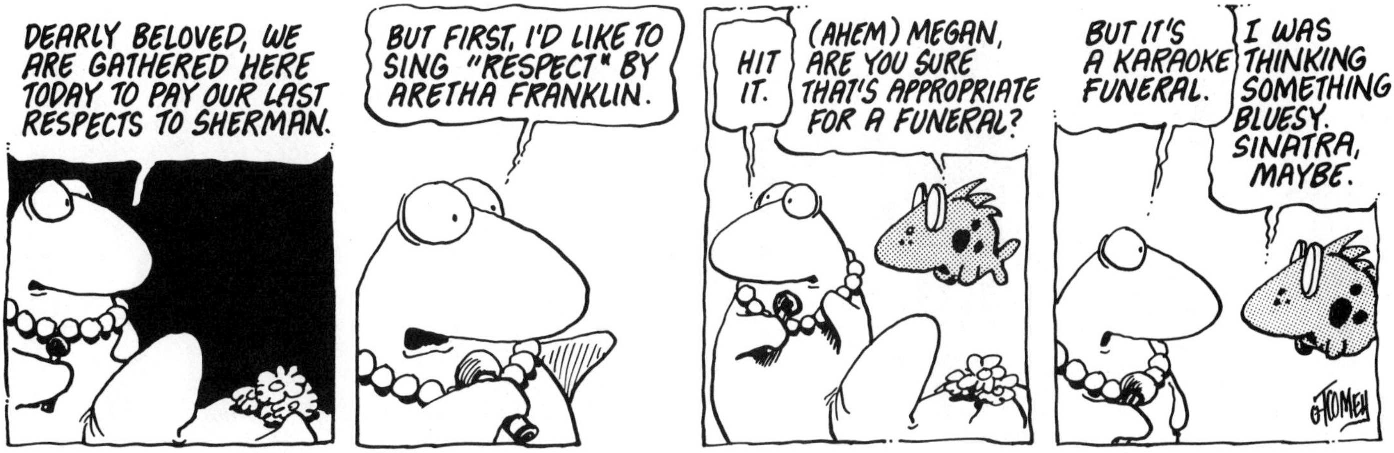
DEARLY BELOVED, WE ARE GATHERED HERE TODAY TO PAY OUR LAST RESPECTS TO SHERMAN.
BUT FIRST, I'D LIKE TO SING "RESPECT" BY ARETHA FRANKLIN.
HIT IT.
(AHEM) MEGAN, ARE YOU SURE THAT'S APPROPRIATE FOR A FUNERAL?
BUT IT'S A KARAOKE FUNERAL.
I WAS THINKING SOMETHING BLUESY. SINATRA, MAYBE.

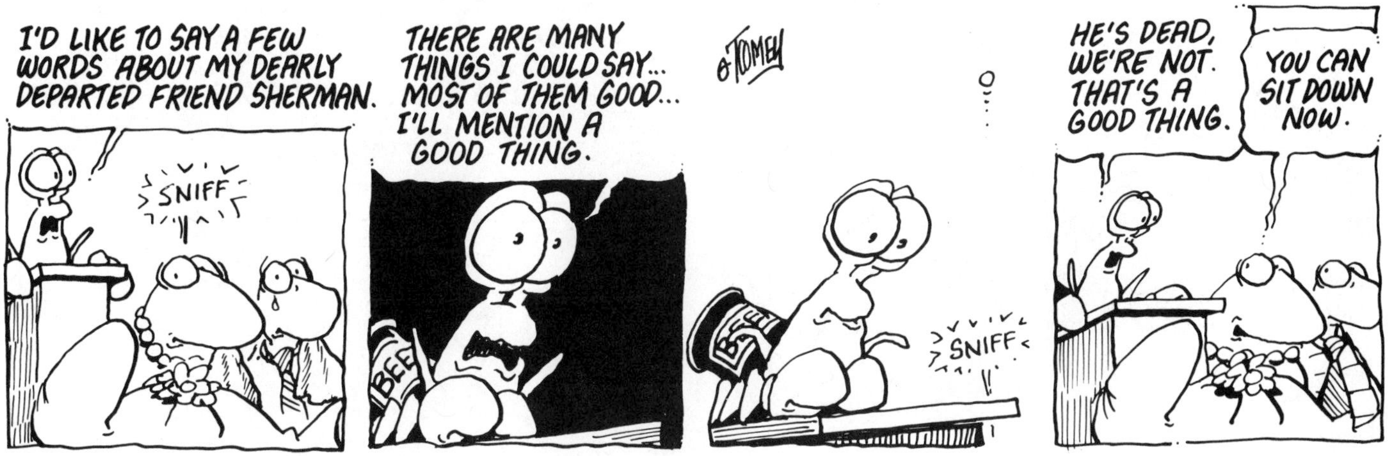
I'D LIKE TO SAY A FEW WORDS ABOUT MY DEARLY DEPARTED FRIEND SHERMAN.
SNIFF
THERE ARE MANY THINGS I COULD SAY... MOST OF THEM GOOD... I'LL MENTION A GOOD THING.
SNIFF
HE'S DEAD, WE'RE NOT. THAT'S A GOOD THING.
YOU CAN SIT DOWN NOW.

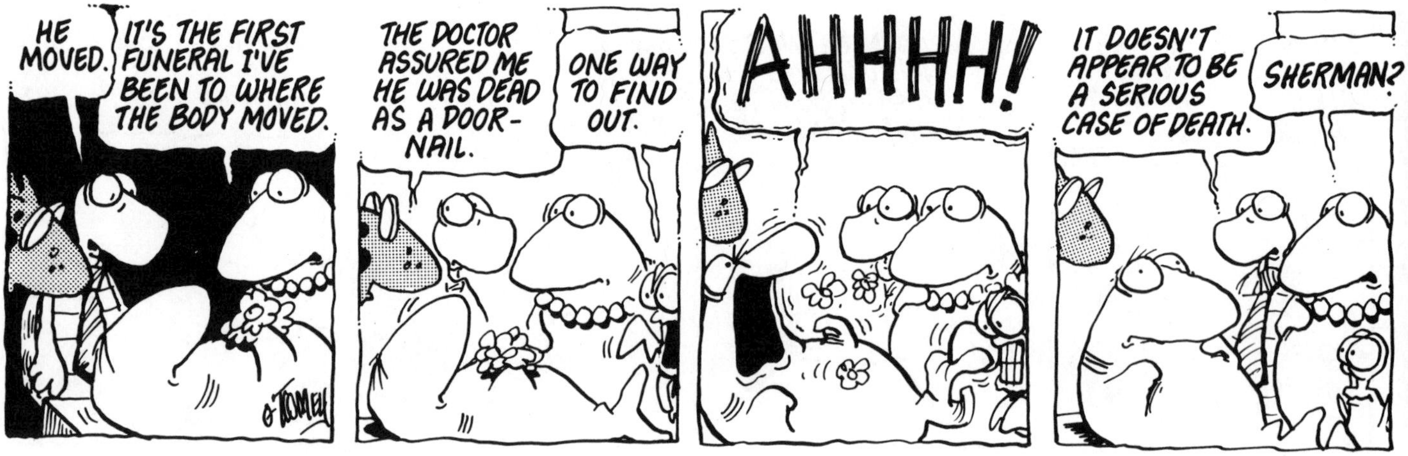
HE MOVED.
IT'S THE FIRST FUNERAL I'VE BEEN TO WHERE THE BODY MOVED.
THE DOCTOR ASSURED ME HE WAS DEAD AS A DOOR-NAIL.
ONE WAY TO FIND OUT.
AHHHH!
IT DOESN'T APPEAR TO BE A SERIOUS CASE OF DEATH.
SHERMAN?

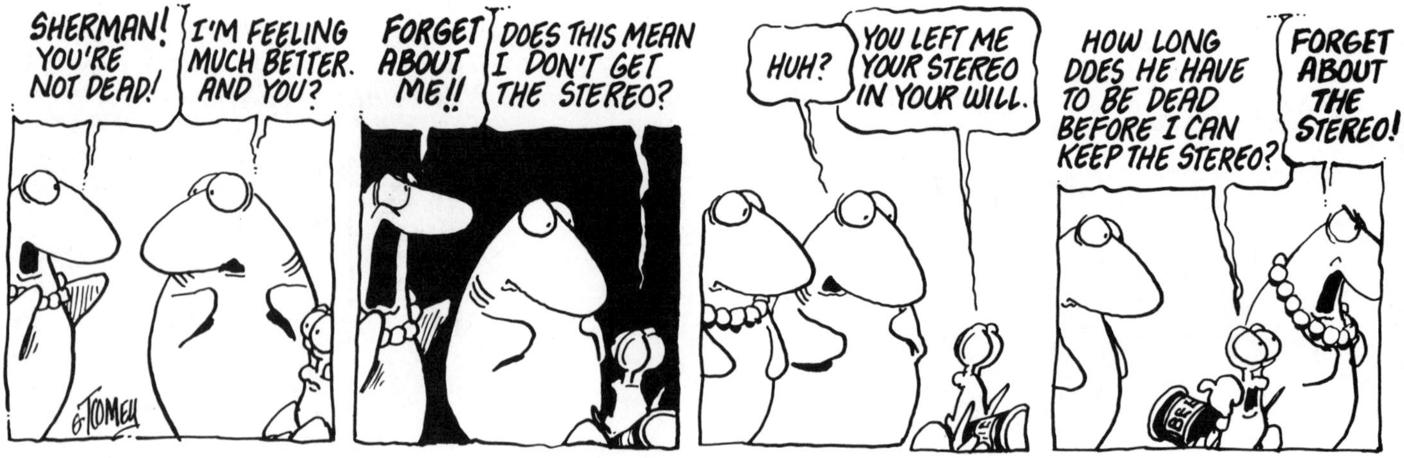
SHERMAN! YOU'RE NOT DEAD!
I'M FEELING MUCH BETTER. AND YOU?
FORGET ABOUT ME!!
DOES THIS MEAN I DON'T GET THE STEREO?
HUH?
YOU LEFT ME YOUR STEREO IN YOUR WILL.
HOW LONG DOES HE HAVE TO BE DEAD BEFORE I CAN KEEP THE STEREO?
FORGET ABOUT THE STEREO!

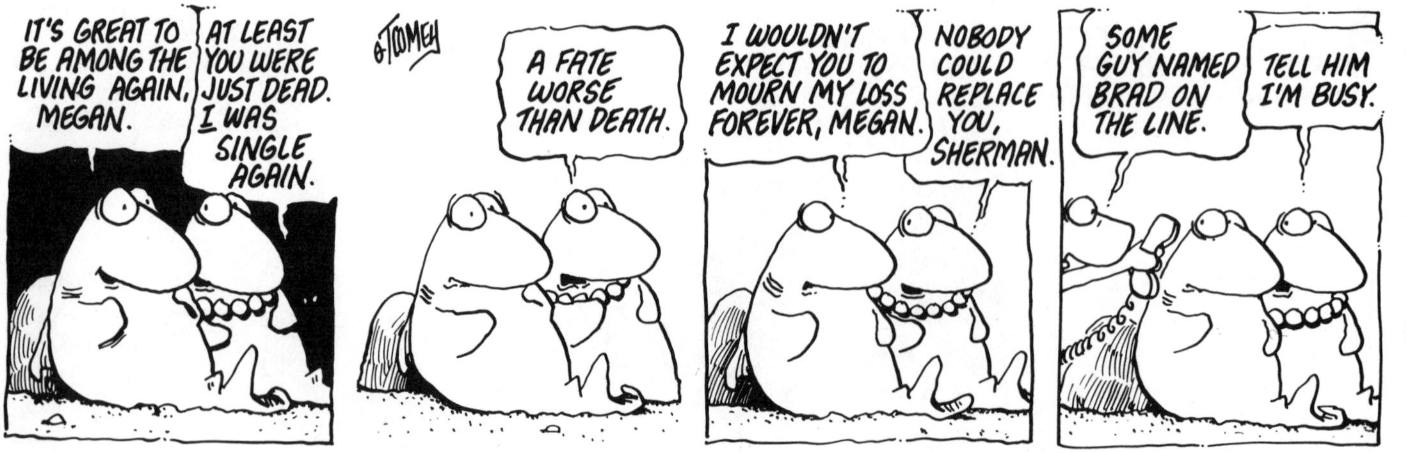
IT'S GREAT TO BE AMONG THE LIVING AGAIN, MEGAN.
AT LEAST YOU WERE JUST DEAD. I WAS SINGLE AGAIN.
A FATE WORSE THAN DEATH.
I WOULDN'T EXPECT YOU TO MOURN MY LOSS FOREVER, MEGAN.
NOBODY COULD REPLACE YOU, SHERMAN.
SOME GUY NAMED BRAD ON THE LINE.
TELL HIM I'M BUSY.

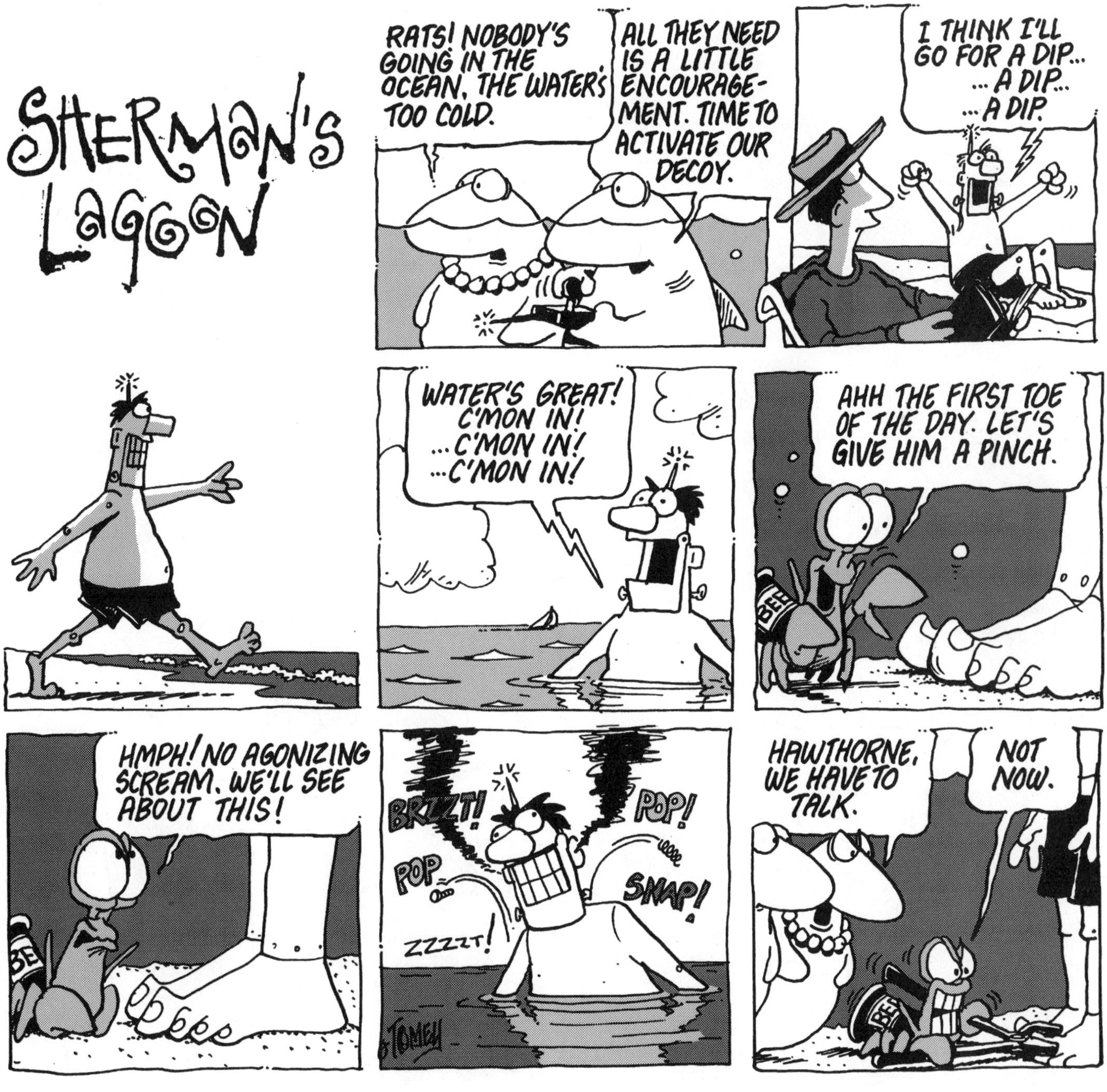
SHERMAN'S LAGOON
RATS! NOBODY'S GOING IN THE OCEAN. THE WATER'S TOO COLD.
ALL THEY NEED IS A LITTLE ENCOURAGEMENT. TIME TO ACTIVATE OUR DECOY.
I THINK I'LL GO FOR A DIP... ...A DIP... ...A DIP.
WATER'S GREAT! C'MON IN! ...C'MON IN! ...C'MON IN!
AHH THE FIRST TOE OF THE DAY. LET'S GIVE HIM A PINCH.
HMPH! NO AGONIZING SCREAM. WE'LL SEE ABOUT THIS!
BRZZT!
POP!
POP
SNAP!
ZZZZT!
HAWTHORNE, WE HAVE TO TALK.
NOT NOW.

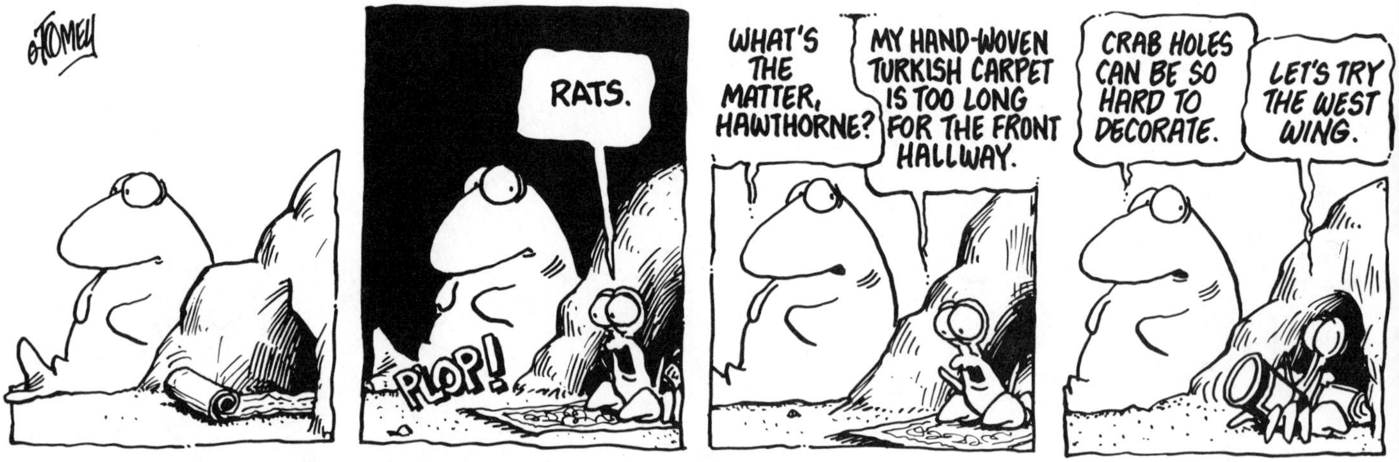

RATS.
PLOP!
WHAT'S THE MATTER, HAWTHORNE?
MY HAND-WOVEN TURKISH CARPET IS TOO LONG FOR THE FRONT HALLWAY.
CRAB HOLES CAN BE SO HARD TO DECORATE.
LET'S TRY THE WEST WING.

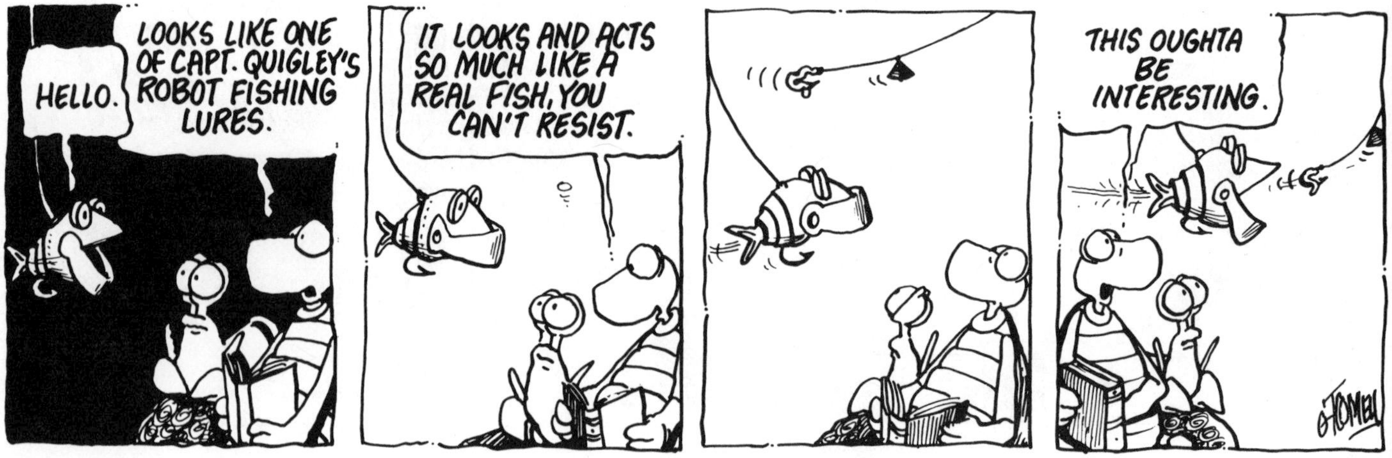

HELLO.
LOOKS LIKE ONE OF CAPT. QUIGLEY'S ROBOT FISHING LURES.
IT LOOKS AND ACTS SO MUCH LIKE A REAL FISH, YOU CAN'T RESIST.
THIS OUGHTA BE INTERESTING.

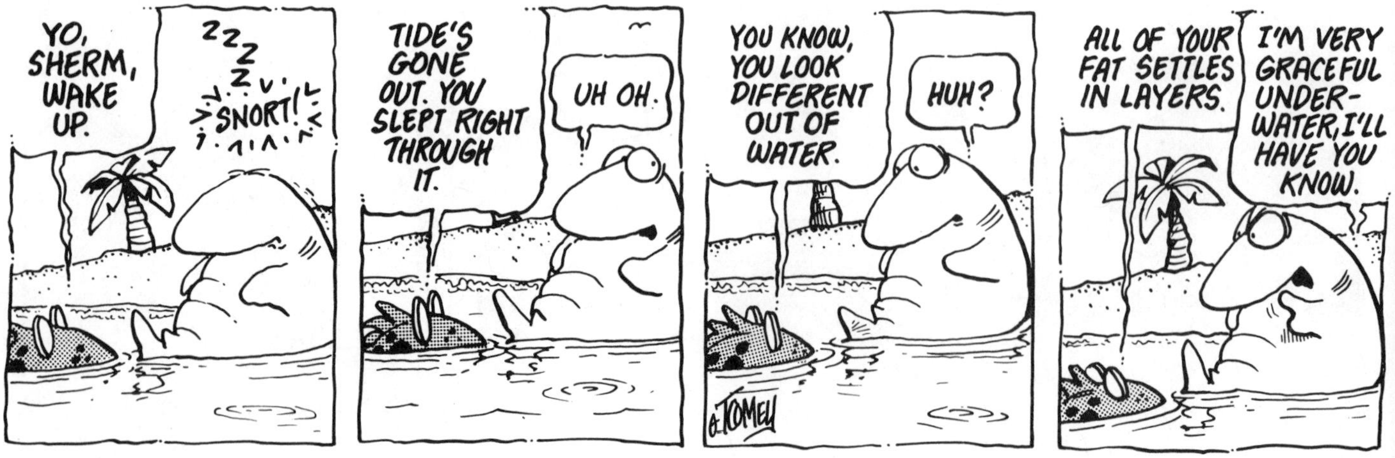

YO, SHERM, WAKE UP.
ZZZ
SNORT!
TIDE'S GONE OUT. YOU SLEPT RIGHT THROUGH IT.
UH OH.
YOU KNOW, YOU LOOK DIFFERENT OUT OF WATER.
HUH?
ALL OF YOUR FAT SETTLES IN LAYERS.
I'M VERY GRACEFUL UNDER-WATER, I'LL HAVE YOU KNOW.

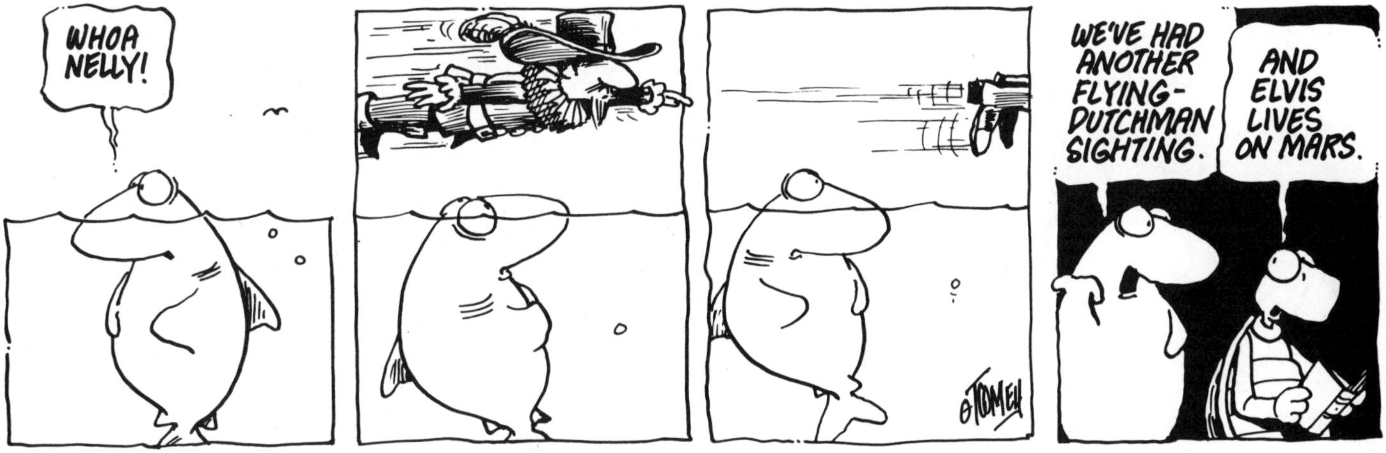
WHOA NELLY!
WE'VE HAD ANOTHER FLYING-DUTCHMAN SIGHTING.
AND ELVIS LIVES ON MARS.

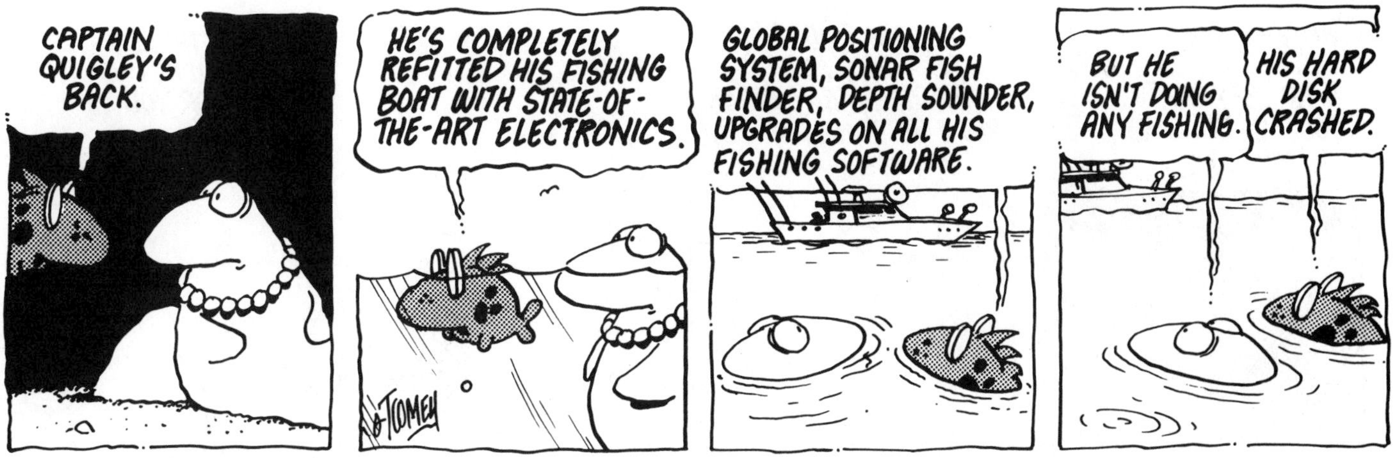
CAPTAIN QUIGLEY'S BACK.
HE'S COMPLETELY REFITTED HIS FISHING BOAT WITH STATE-OF-THE-ART ELECTRONICS.
GLOBAL POSITIONING SYSTEM, SONAR FISH FINDER, DEPTH SOUNDER, UPGRADES ON ALL HIS FISHING SOFTWARE.
BUT HE ISN'T DOING ANY FISHING.
HIS HARD DISK CRASHED.

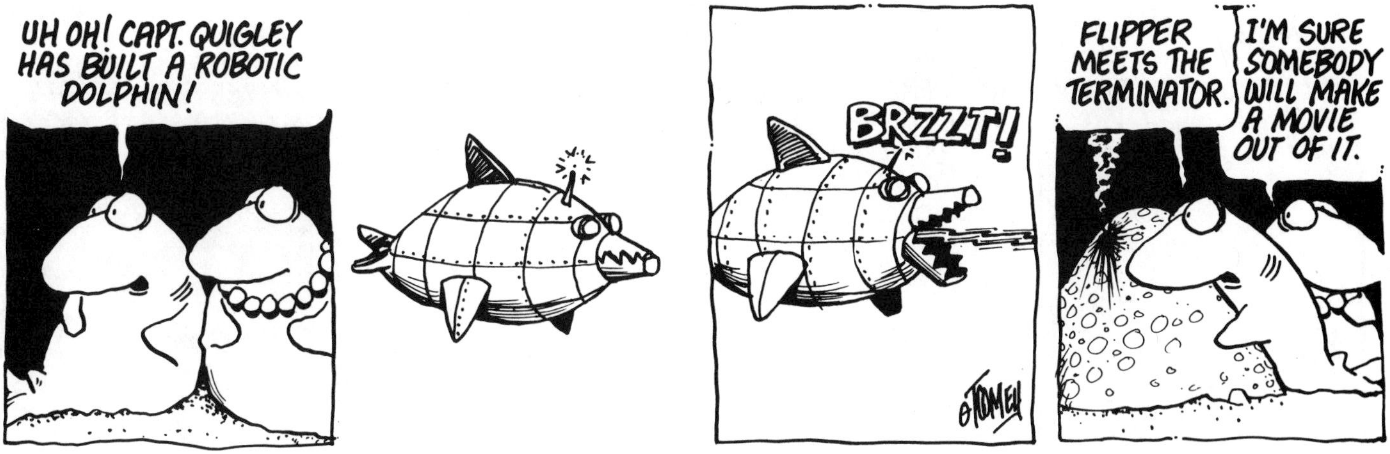
UH OH! CAPT. QUIGLEY HAS BUILT A ROBOTIC DOLPHIN!
BRZZZT!
FLIPPER MEETS THE TERMINATOR.
I'M SURE SOMEBODY WILL MAKE A MOVIE OUT OF IT.

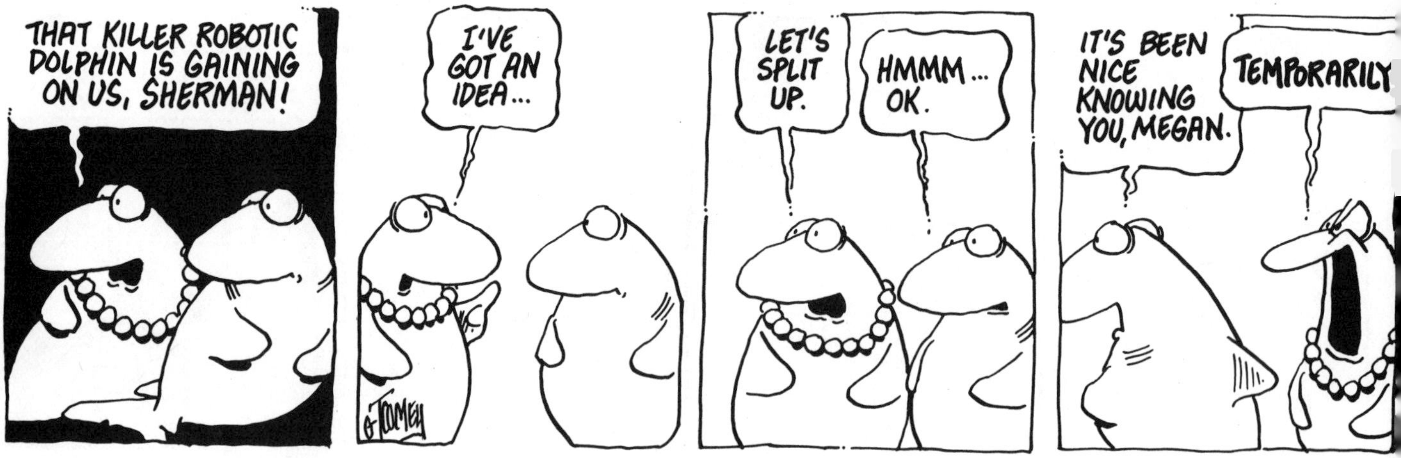
THAT KILLER ROBOTIC DOLPHIN IS GAINING ON US, SHERMAN!
I'VE GOT AN IDEA...
LET'S SPLIT UP.
HMMM... OK.
IT'S BEEN NICE KNOWING YOU, MEGAN.
TEMPORARILY

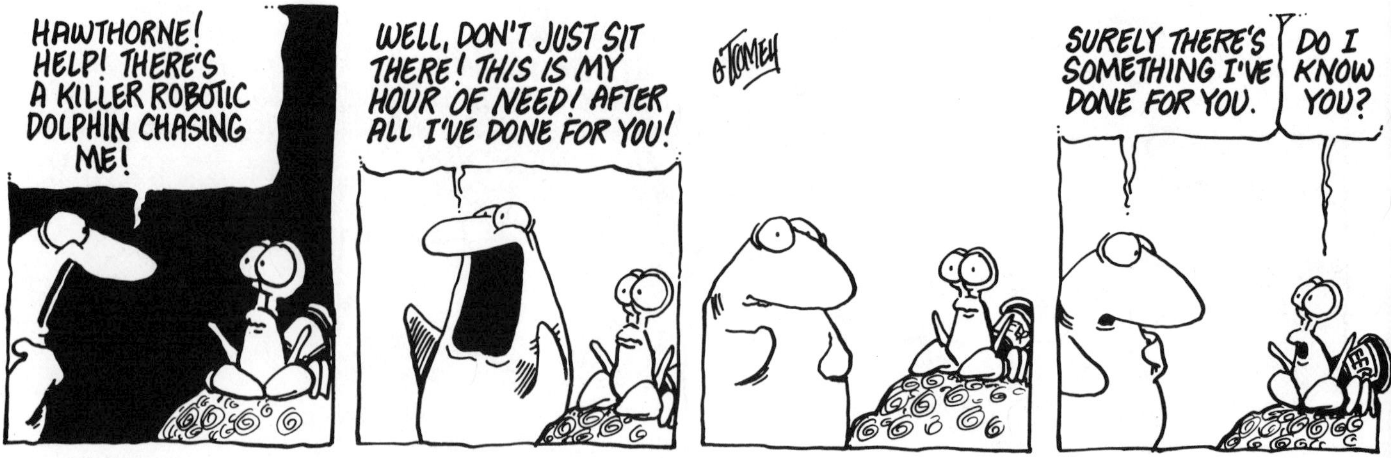
HAWTHORNE! HELP! THERE'S A KILLER ROBOTIC DOLPHIN CHASING ME!
WELL, DON'T JUST SIT THERE! THIS IS MY HOUR OF NEED! AFTER ALL I'VE DONE FOR YOU!
SURELY THERE'S SOMETHING I'VE DONE FOR YOU.
DO I KNOW YOU?

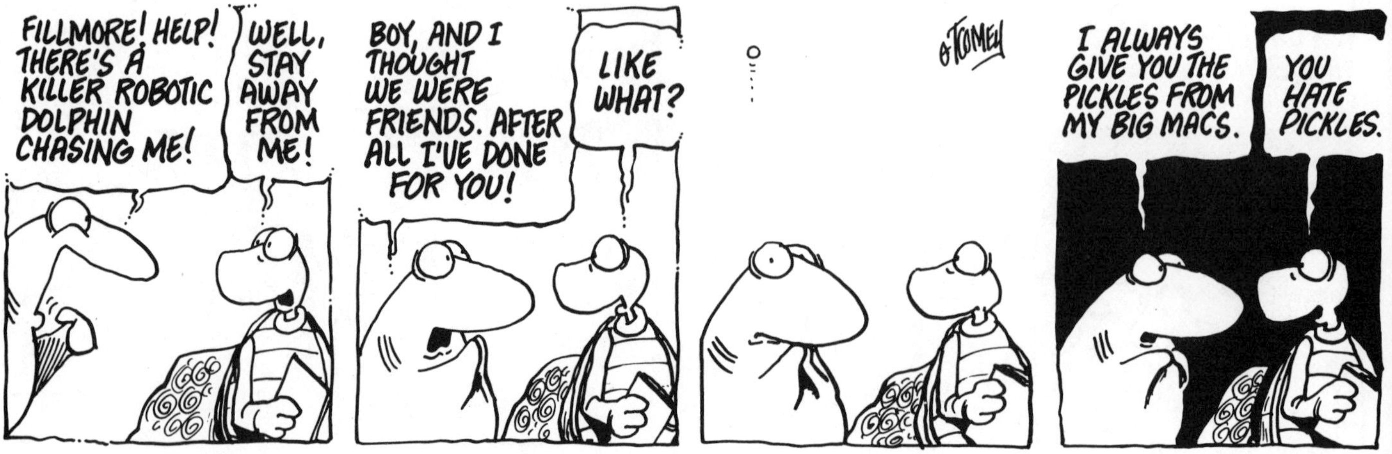
FILLMORE! HELP! THERE'S A KILLER ROBOTIC DOLPHIN CHASING ME!
WELL, STAY AWAY FROM ME!
BOY, AND I THOUGHT WE WERE FRIENDS. AFTER ALL I'VE DONE FOR YOU!
LIKE WHAT?
I ALWAYS GIVE YOU THE PICKLES FROM MY BIG MACS.
YOU HATE PICKLES.

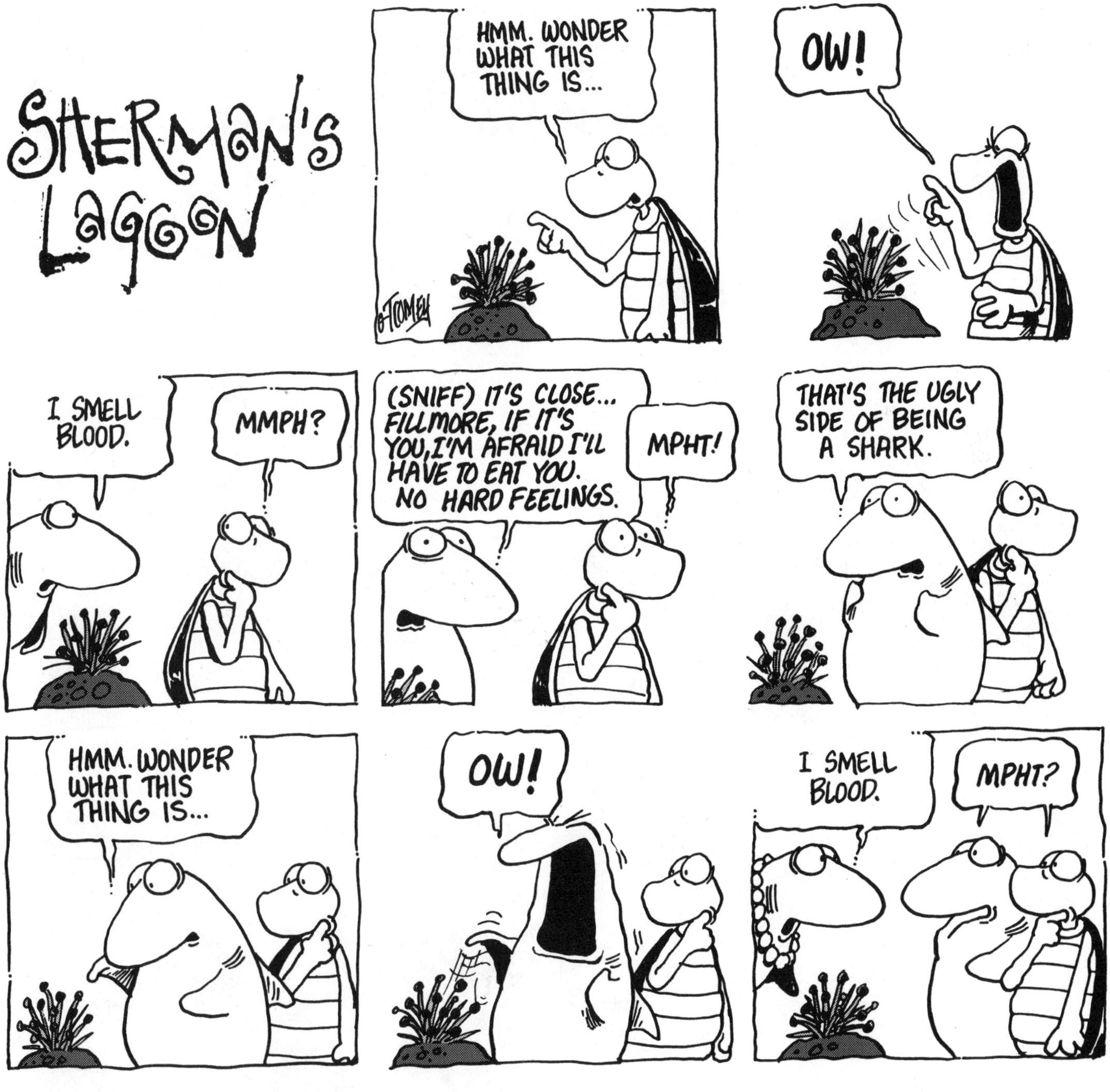
SHERMAN'S LAGOON
HMM. WONDER WHAT THIS THING IS...
OW!
I SMELL BLOOD.
MMPH?
(SNIFF) IT'S CLOSE... FILLMORE, IF IT'S YOU, I'M AFRAID I'LL HAVE TO EAT YOU. NO HARD FEELINGS.
MPHT!
THAT'S THE UGLY SIDE OF BEING A SHARK.
HMM. WONDER WHAT THIS THING IS...
OW!
I SMELL BLOOD.
MPHT?

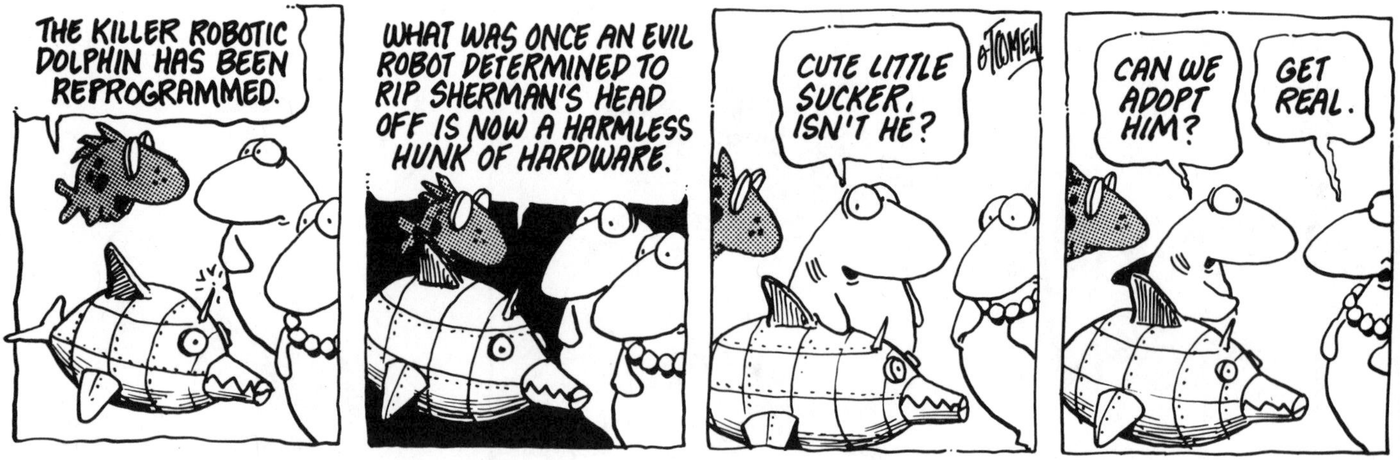
THE KILLER ROBOTIC DOLPHIN HAS BEEN REPROGRAMMED.
WHAT WAS ONCE AN EVIL ROBOT DETERMINED TO RIP SHERMAN'S HEAD OFF IS NOW A HARMLESS HUNK OF HARDWARE.
CUTE LITTLE SUCKER, ISN'T HE?
CAN WE ADOPT HIM?
GET REAL.

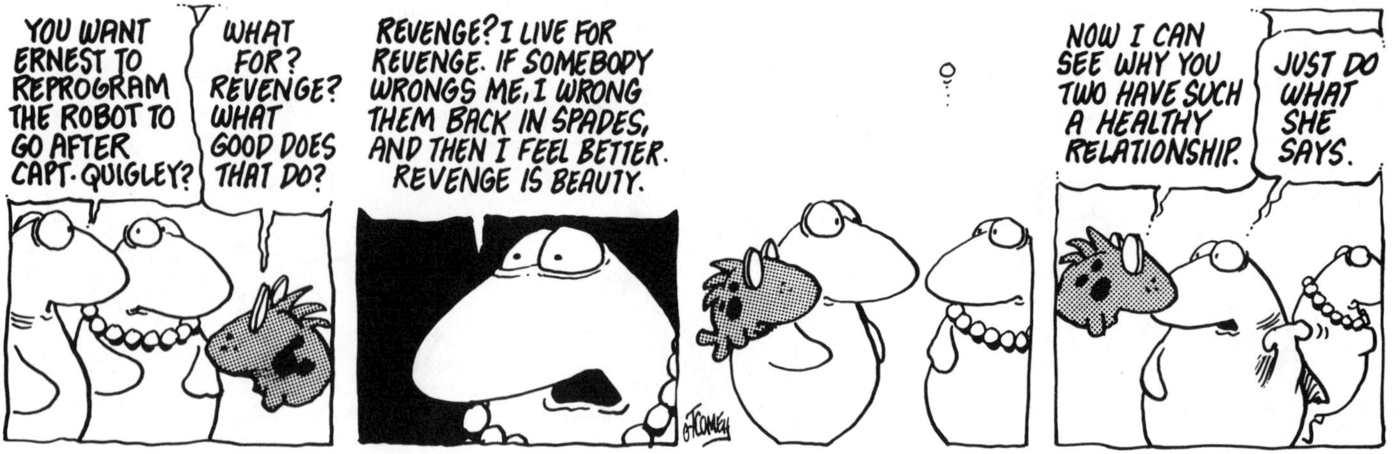
YOU WANT ERNEST TO REPROGRAM THE ROBOT TO GO AFTER CAPT. QUIGLEY?
WHAT FOR? REVENGE? WHAT GOOD DOES THAT DO?
REVENGE? I LIVE FOR REVENGE. IF SOMEBODY WRONGS ME, I WRONG THEM BACK IN SPADES, AND THEN I FEEL BETTER. REVENGE IS BEAUTY.
NOW I CAN SEE WHY YOU TWO HAVE SUCH A HEALTHY RELATIONSHIP.
JUST DO WHAT SHE SAYS.

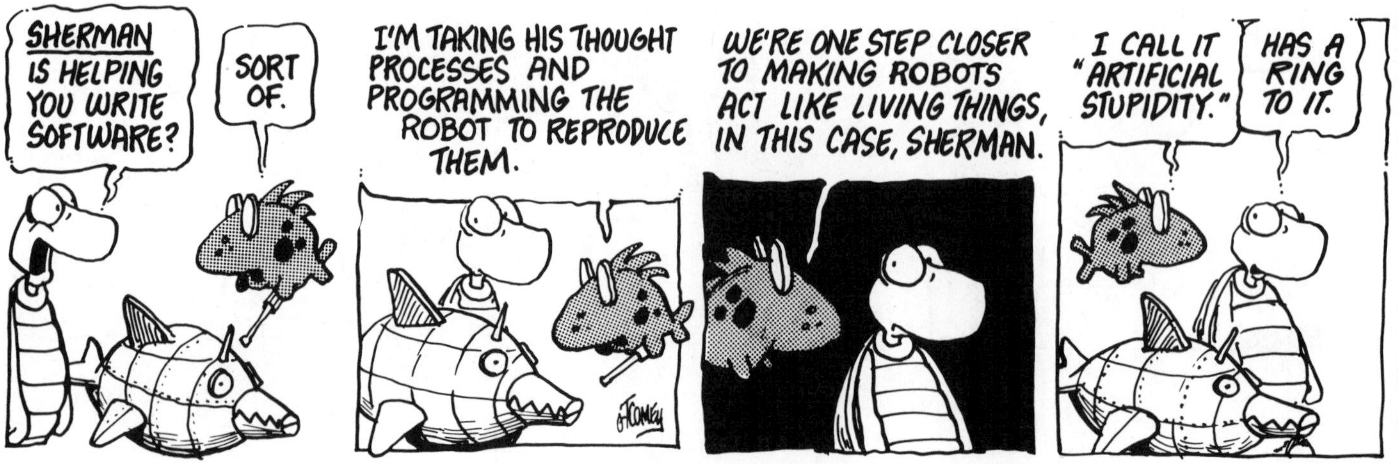
SHERMAN IS HELPING YOU WRITE SOFTWARE?
SORT OF.
I'M TAKING HIS THOUGHT PROCESSES AND PROGRAMMING THE ROBOT TO REPRODUCE THEM.
WE'RE ONE STEP CLOSER TO MAKING ROBOTS ACT LIKE LIVING THINGS, IN THIS CASE, SHERMAN.
I CALL IT "ARTIFICIAL STUPIDITY."
HAS A RING TO IT.

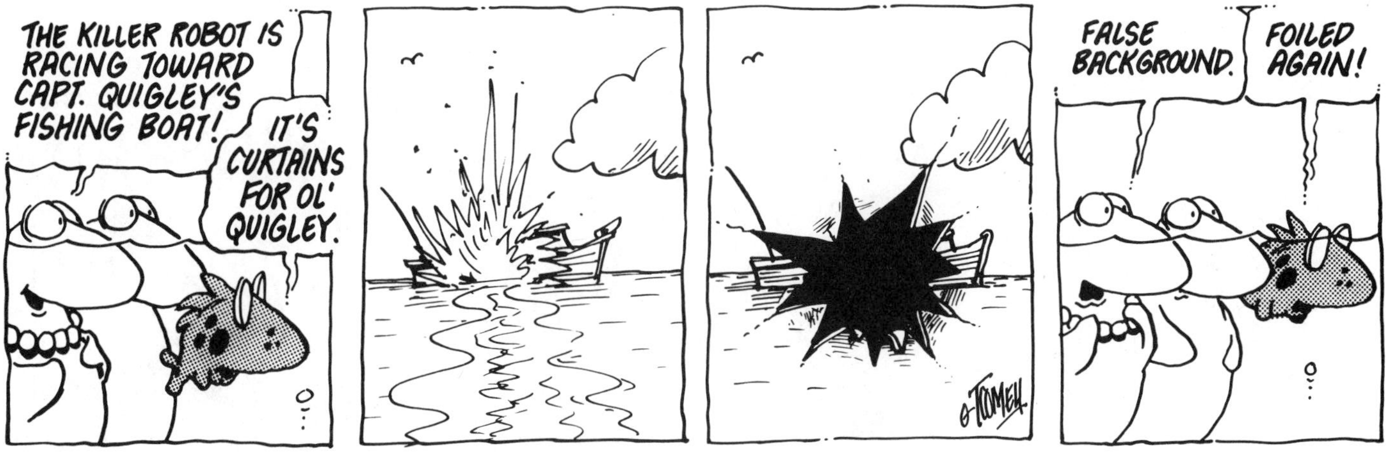
THE KILLER ROBOT IS RACING TOWARD CAPT. QUIGLEY'S FISHING BOAT!
IT'S CURTAINS FOR OL' QUIGLEY.
FALSE BACKGROUND.
FOILED AGAIN!

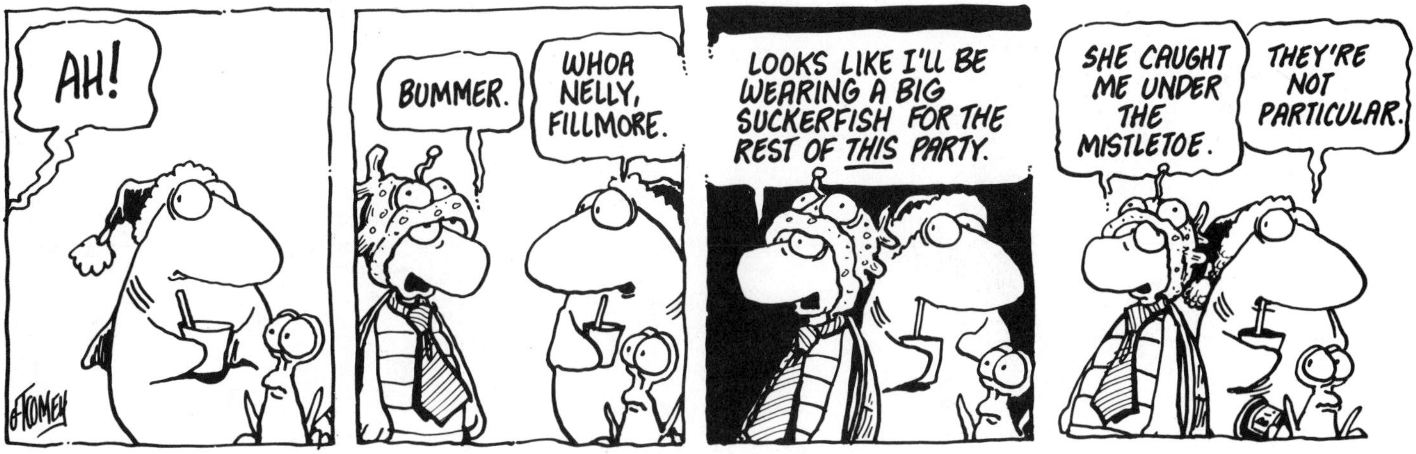
AH!
BUMMER.
WHOA NELLY, FILLMORE.
LOOKS LIKE I'LL BE WEARING A BIG SUCKERFISH FOR THE REST OF THIS PARTY.
SHE CAUGHT ME UNDER THE MISTLETOE.
THEY'RE NOT PARTICULAR.

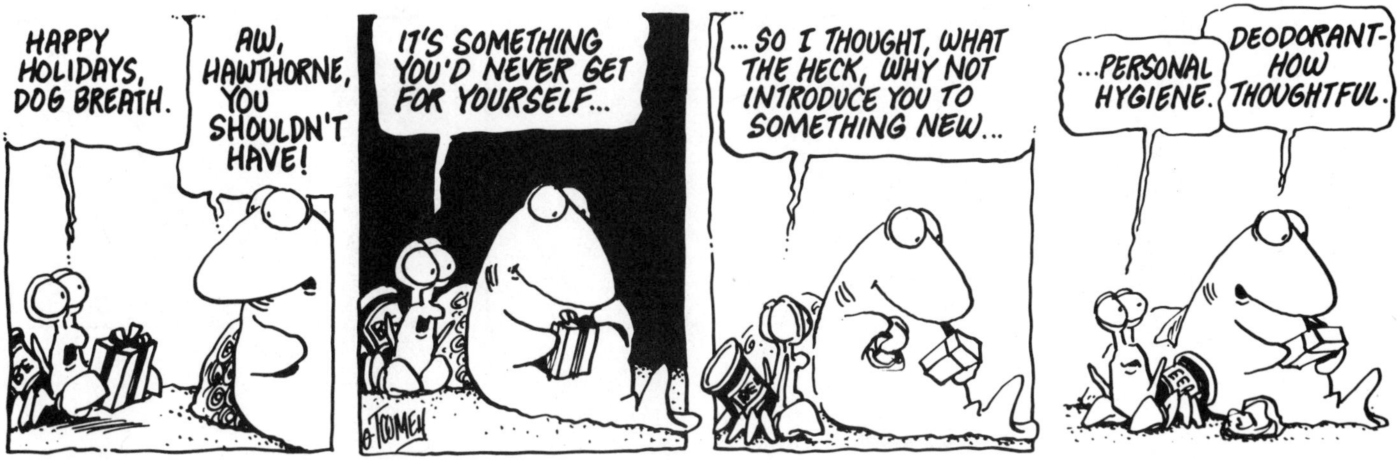
HAPPY HOLIDAYS, DOG BREATH.
AW, HAWTHORNE, YOU SHOULDN'T HAVE!
IT'S SOMETHING YOU'D NEVER GET FOR YOURSELF...
...SO I THOUGHT, WHAT THE HECK, WHY NOT INTRODUCE YOU TO SOMETHING NEW...
...PERSONAL HYGIENE.
DEODORANT- HOW THOUGHTFUL.

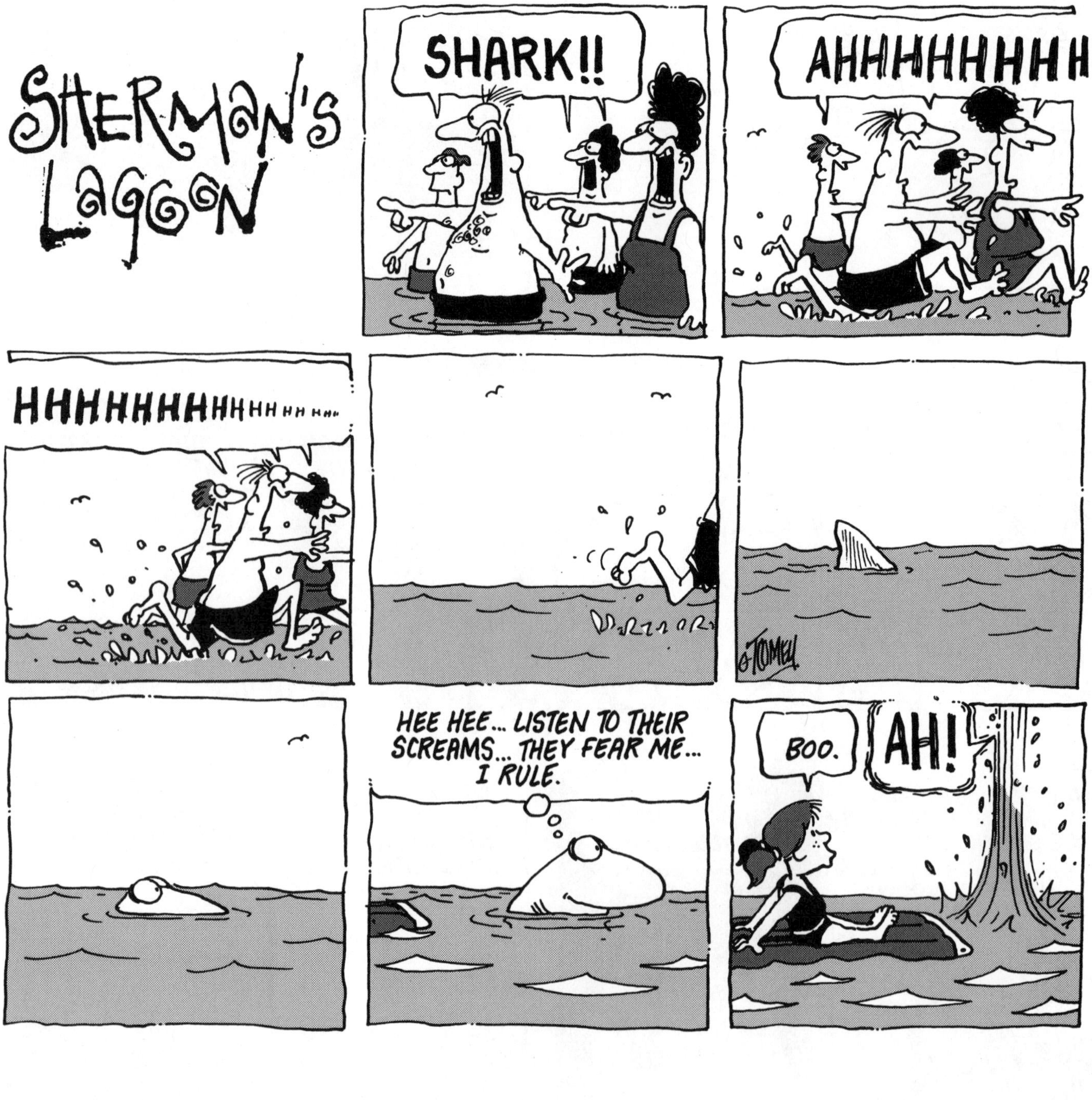
SHERMAN'S LAGOON
SHARK!!
AHHHHHHHHH
HHHHHHHHHHHHHH
HEE HEE... LISTEN TO THEIR SCREAMS... THEY FEAR ME... I RULE.
BOO.
AH!

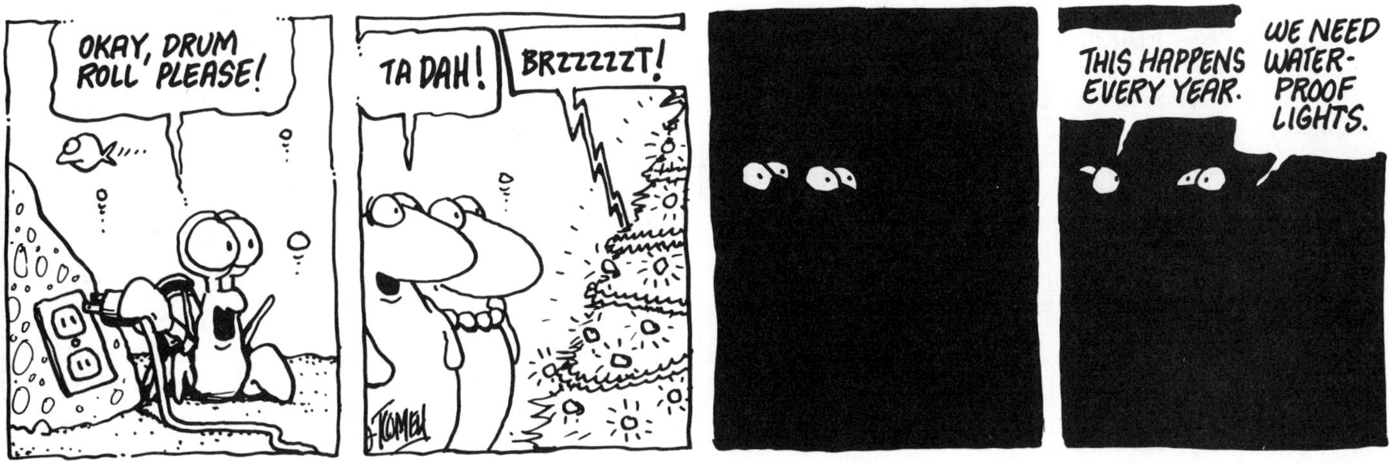
OKAY, DRUM ROLL PLEASE!
TA DAH!
BRZZZZZT!
THIS HAPPENS EVERY YEAR.
WE NEED WATER-PROOF LIGHTS.

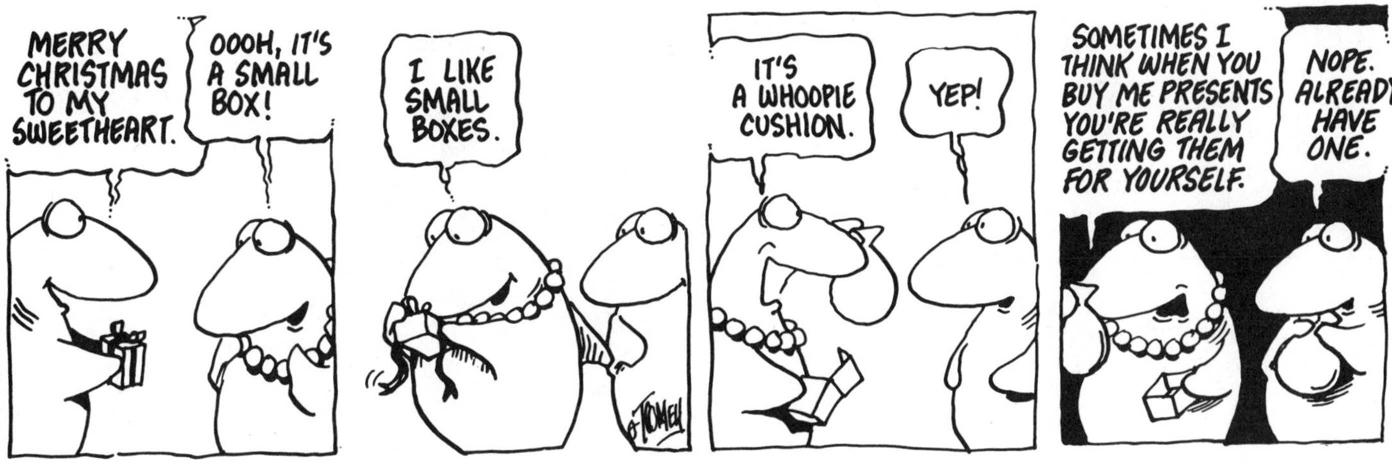
MERRY CHRISTMAS TO MY SWEETHEART.
OOOH, IT'S A SMALL BOX!
I LIKE SMALL BOXES.
IT'S A WHOOPIE CUSHION.
YEP!
SOMETIMES I THINK WHEN YOU BUY ME PRESENTS YOU'RE REALLY GETTING THEM FOR YOURSELF.
NOPE. ALREADY HAVE ONE.

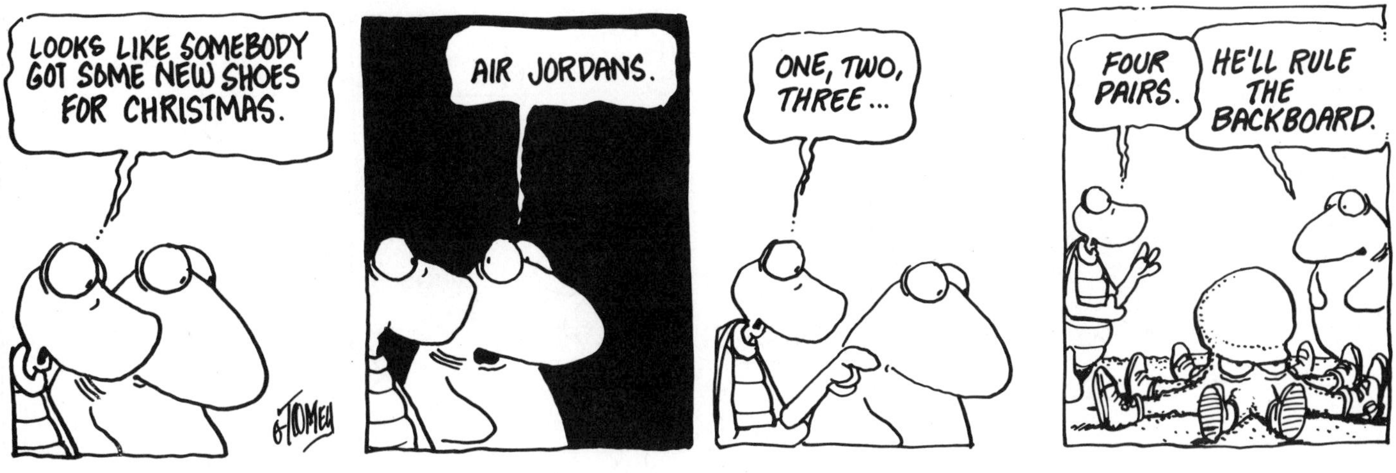
LOOKS LIKE SOMEBODY GOT SOME NEW SHOES FOR CHRISTMAS.
AIR JORDANS.
ONE, TWO, THREE...
FOUR PAIRS.
HE'LL RULE THE BACKBOARD.

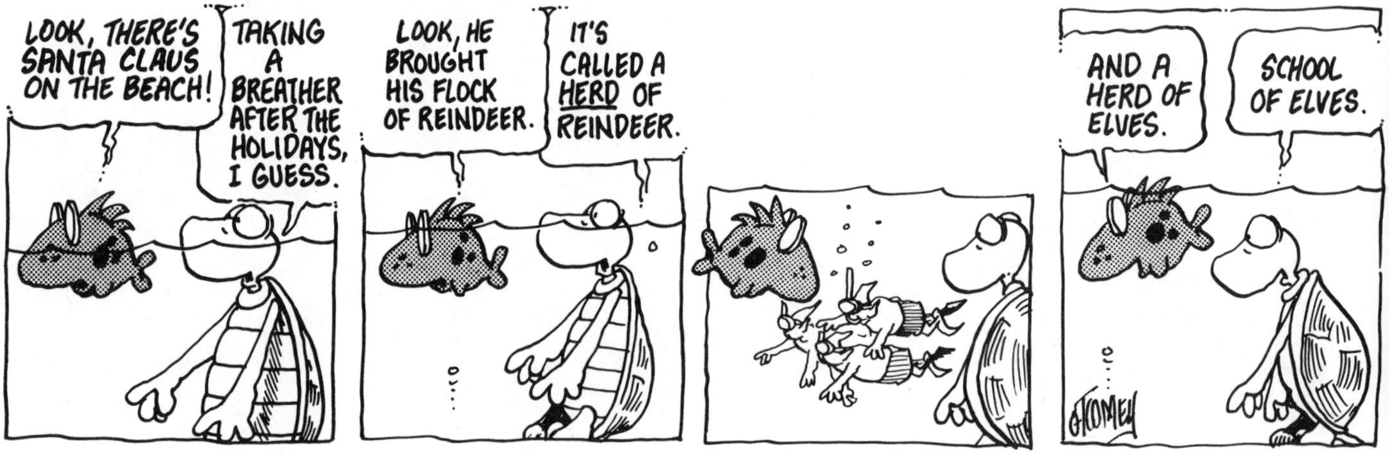
LOOK, THERE'S SANTA CLAUS ON THE BEACH!
TAKING A BREATHER AFTER THE HOLIDAYS, I GUESS.
LOOK, HE BROUGHT HIS FLOCK OF REINDEER.
IT'S CALLED A HERD OF REINDEER.
AND A HERD OF ELVES.
SCHOOL OF ELVES.

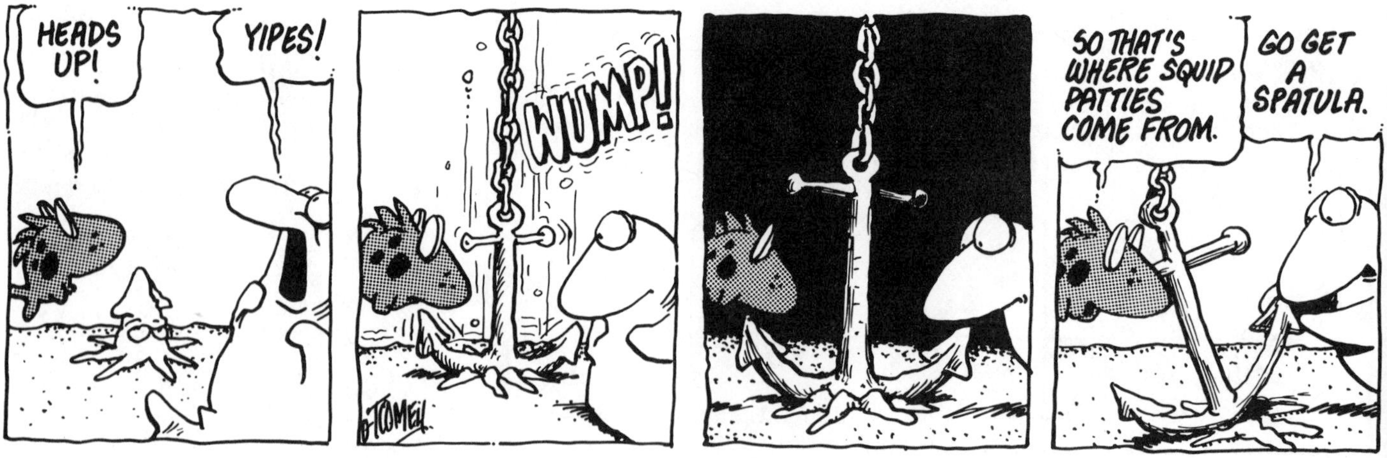
HEADS UP!
YIPES!
WUMP!
SO THAT'S WHERE SQUID PATTIES COME FROM.
GO GET A SPATULA.

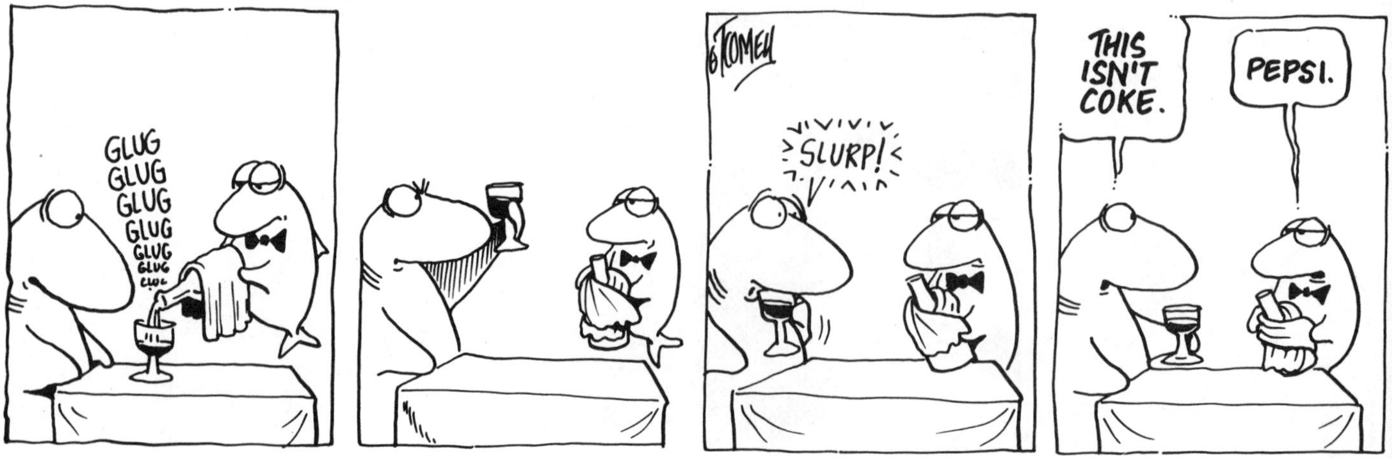
GLUG GLUG GLUG GLUG GLUG GLUG
SLURP!
THIS ISN'T COKE.
PEPSI.

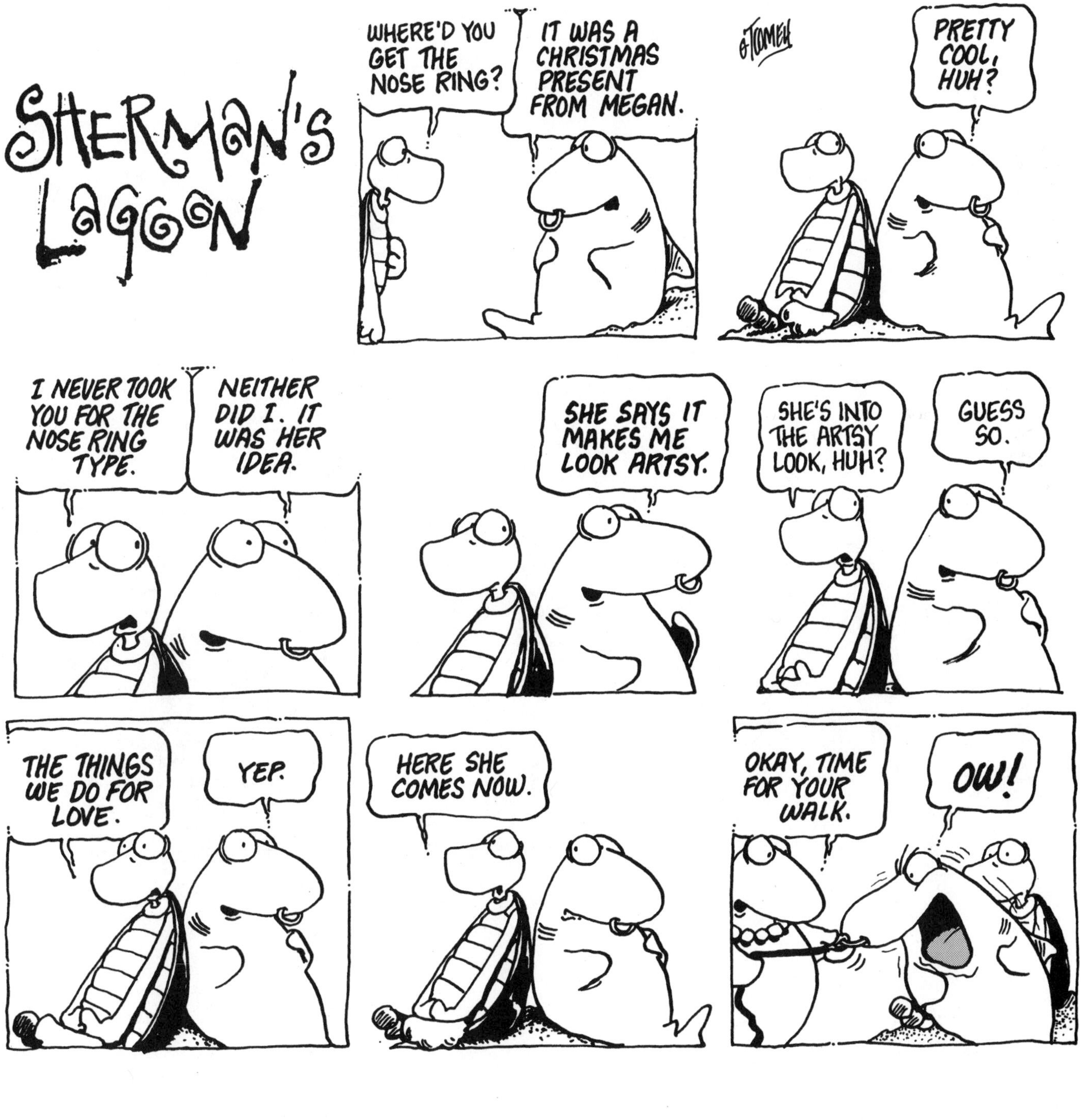
SHERMAN'S LAGOON
WHERE'D YOU GET THE NOSE RING?
IT WAS A CHRISTMAS PRESENT FROM MEGAN.
PRETTY COOL, HUH?
I NEVER TOOK YOU FOR THE NOSE RING TYPE.
NEITHER DID I. IT WAS HER IDEA.
SHE SAYS IT MAKES ME LOOK ARTSY.
SHE'S INTO THE ARTSY LOOK, HUH?
GUESS SO.
THE THINGS WE DO FOR LOVE.
YEP.
HERE SHE COMES NOW.
OKAY, TIME FOR YOUR WALK.
OW!

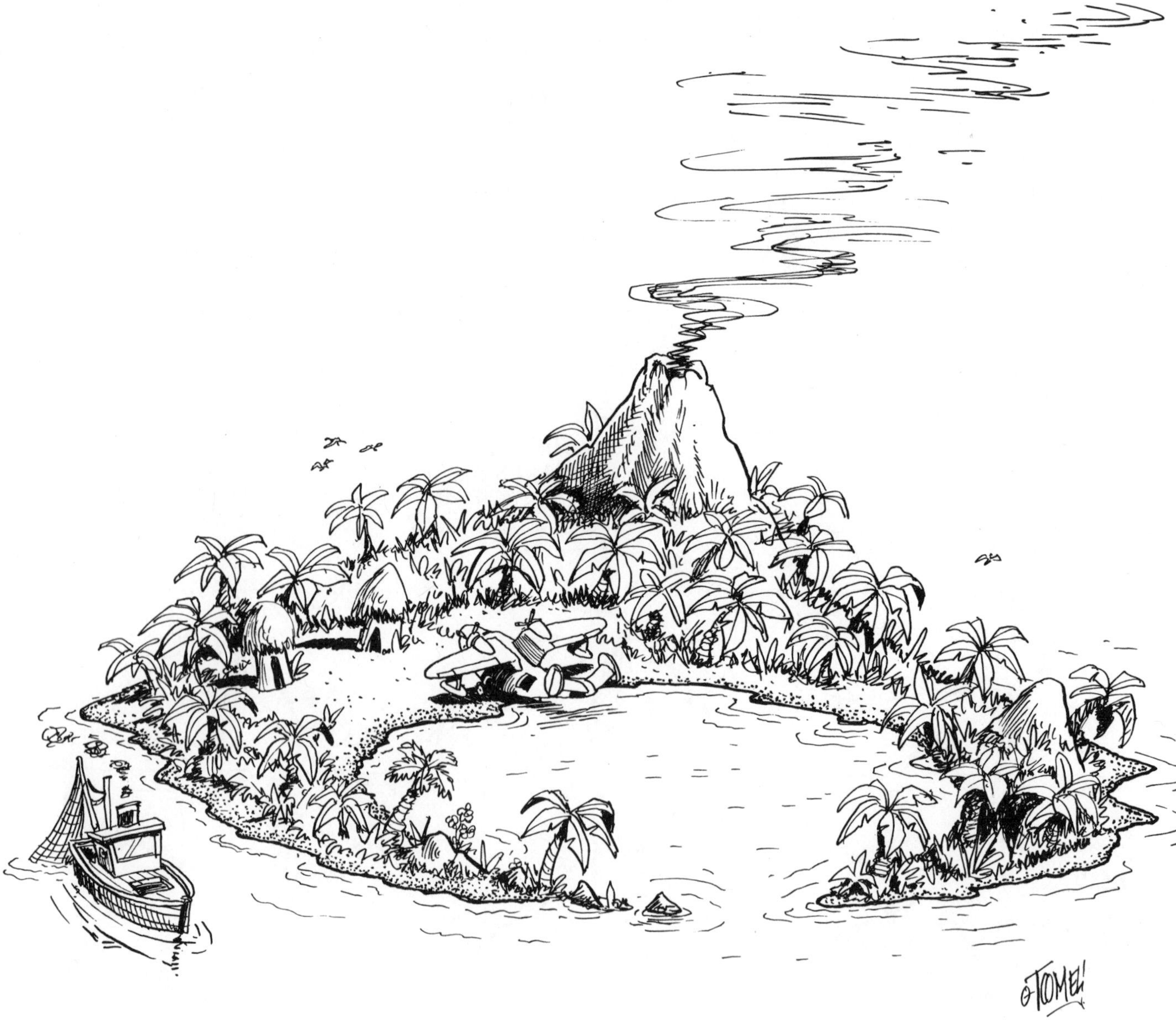